FATAL AFFAIRS

Kate Clarke

Non-Fiction
by the same Author

Murder At The Priory: The Mysterious Poisoning of Charles Bravo
(with Bernard Taylor) (Short-listed for the CWA's Gold Dagger Award)

Journal: Volume One (as Kate Paul)
(All subsequent volumes at the Mass Observation Archive
Special Collections/Sussex University Library)

Who Killed Simon Dale? & Other Murder Mysteries

Bad Companions: Six London Murderesses

In The Interests of Science: Adelaide Bartlett and the Pimlico Poisoning

*Deadly Service: Murderous Maids,
Devious Housekeepers and Butlers Who Kill*

Deadly Dilemmas

Copyright © 2016 Kate Clarke
FATAL AFFAIRS: A revised/combined version of *Fatal Affairs*
and *Lethal Alliance*, first published by Carrington Press

The right of Kate Clarke to be identified as the author
of this work has been asserted in accordance with
the Copyright, Designs & Patents Act 1988.

All rights reserved. No part of this book may be reprinted or reproduced
or utilised in any form or by any electronic, mechanical or other
means, now known or hereafter invented, including photocopying
and recording, or in any information storage or retrieval system,
without the prior permission in writing of the publishers.

ISBN: 978-1-911273-53-0 (softcover)
ISBN: 978-1-911273-02-8 (hardback)
ISBN: 978-1-911273-04-2 (ebook)

Published by Mango Books
www.mangobooks.co.uk
18 Soho Square, London W1D 3QL

FATAL AFFAIRS

Acknowledgements i
Introduction iii

❦

1
MARY BLANDY and CAPTAIN CRANSTOUN

75
ELIZABETH JEFFRIES and JOHN SWAN

104
KATHARINE NAIRN and PATRICK OGILVIE

154
SARAH GALE and JAMES GREENACRE

220
CHRISTIANA EDMUNDS and DR CHARLES BEARD

❦

Selected Bibliography and Resources 303
Index 307

Acknowledgements

My special thanks to the crime-writer Mark Ripper (M W Oldridge) for his support and unstinting assistance during the writing of this book. Also David Green for creating the index and for his expertise and invaluable contribution to the production of the book. I am grateful to Adam Wood for his sustained interest and encouragement during its preparation.

The following writers have also been generous with their encouragement: Martin Edwards, Douglas d'Enno, Mark Stevens and Richard and Molly Whittington-Egan. I am also grateful for the support of Anne Dewell, Sasha and Anil Mahendra, Andy Dixon, Dorothy Allam, Milly Eagle, Noelle Beales, Derek Addyman, Anne Brichto, Molly Huddlestone and Paula Chihaoua.

My thanks to the following for permissions regarding the reproduction of images: Chris Horlock for his photograph of Mr Maynard's Confectionary Shop, West Street, Brighton. The Bodleian Library and the curators of the John Johnson Collection.

The President and Fellows of Harvard College for permission to reproduce the drawings of Sarah Gale and James Greenacre in the pamphlet, *Authentic particulars of the life of James Greenacre and Sarah Gale; and their extraordinary trial for the wilful murder of Mrs. Hannah Brown*, held in the Harvard Law School Library.

The extensive research undertaken by William Roughhead when editing his *Trial of Mary Blandy*, published in 1914, and *Trial of Katharine Nairn*, in 1926, has proved invaluable.

Chapter headings quotes:
1, 2, 3, William Shakespeare; 4 & 5, Lord Alfred Tennyson.

Introduction

The partnerships that feature in this book are not in the same league as those fabled romantic liaisons celebrated in history; they have none of the dramatic splendour of Antony and Cleopatra or the heady, clandestine frisson of Heloise and Abelard or, indeed, even remotely mirror the plethora of fictional affairs of the heart dramatised in films, opera and the theatre. They bear no resemblance to the tragic and heart-breaking tales of Romeo and Juliet, Orpheus and Eurydice or Tristan and Isolde. Nor are they on a par with those more recent, sordid and notoriously murderous partnerships – Myra Hindley and Ian Brady, Fred and Rosemary West – or those callous renegades glamorised in films, Bonnie and Clyde.

By comparison, the people in this book were fairly unremarkable characters whose affairs were dramatic only in that they spiralled out of control and ended in murder. In this respect, such destructive relationships were just as dramatic as any portrayed in the arts. Yet these were lives that might have remained mundane and unrecorded had the protagonists not met and embarked on such fatal alliances the balance of which was often arbitrary and one-sided.

Although the nineteenth and early twentieth centuries have become synonymous with some of the great classic murder cases in which affairs of the heart were to play a central part in the drama – Florence Maybrick and Alfred Brierley, Florence Bravo and Dr James Manby Gully, Adelaide Bartlett and the Rev. George Dyson, Madeleine Smith and Émile L'Angelier - and, a little later, Edith Thompson and Frank Bywaters, Alma Rattenbury and George

Stoner - the eighteenth century also had its fair share of equally catastrophic affairs.

It is difficult, however, to understand why, in 1752, Mary Blandy found Captain William Henry Cranstoun so devastatingly attractive for contemporary descriptions of him were far from complimentary. He was, however, considered to be charming in company, a lively conversationalist and a master of flattery, which greatly appealed to the ladies of the day. Though already married, he paid court to Mary for several years - despite her father's disapproval - hoping to benefit from a reputed £10,000 dowry. She allowed herself to be drawn into systematically administering the poison that killed her father, was found guilty of parricide and suffered the shame and terror of being publicly hanged from a tree in the grounds of Oxford Castle.

In that same year, Elizabeth Jeffries, a victim of her wealthy uncle's abuse, enlisted the help of her lover, John Swan, to murder him before he had the chance to carry out his threat to write her out of his will. They were both convicted for the crime and died together on the gallows in Epping Forest. Swan was described as tall and good-looking but appears to have been a hard-drinking drifter, easily persuaded to kill by Elizabeth, a forceful and rebellious young woman who bore an understandable grudge and was bent on vengeance.

It was in 1765 that Katharine Nairn fell madly in love with Lieutenant Patrick Ogilvie, only three weeks after she had married his brother, Thomas. She seems to have been a reckless, somewhat whimsical young woman unable to take life too seriously even when she was on the run, having escaped from the notorious Tolbooth prison, in Edinburgh, and with a death sentence on her head.

We can only speculate on the expectations and preferences prevalent in the social mores of the eighteenth century and cannot, of course, fully appreciate the qualities and accomplishments that would have appealed to these women. Four of the women in this book were fortunate to have been born into financially secure families, yet they had few options other than marriage, whereby

Introduction

they exchanged dependence on the family for that of a husband. Those that were still unmarried by the age of thirty could expect to be labelled an 'old maid' and, more often than not, take on the role of carer for their elderly parents.

Both Mary Blandy and Katharine Nairn were completely in thrall to military men, a trend knowingly observed in the novels of Jane Austen; perhaps it was their spectacular scarlet uniforms, adorned with brass buttons and an abundance of gold braid, that made them so attractive and their dashing appearance did much to deflect from their licentious lifestyle and blatant mendacity.

In the case of Elizabeth Jeffries, however, the stature and good looks of her lover, John Swan, needed no such adornment. But the passions that fired all three relationships were ultimately destructive and ended in violent death, not only for their victims, but also for themselves.

Nor did the story of Sarah Gale and James Greenacre, in 1837, have any of the delights and romantic tensions of artistic interpretation. The drama of their affair was played out in the teeming, unhealthy courts and tenements of the malodorous and chaotic areas of the Metropolis – Camberwell, Tottenham Court Road, Woolwich and the Elephant and Castle. The main character in this sordid tale, James Greenacre, headed a cast of washer-women, maids-of-all-work, straw-hat makers, shoe-makers and anchor men – those men and women whose labours kept the city of London up and running.

Greenacre saw himself as an entrepreneur but was branded by the judge at his trial as a man who had acquired 'a revolting celebrity; an odious notoriety in the annals of cruelty and crime'. He, on the other hand, described himself as a property dealer, inventor of domestic appliances and herbal medicines – a man who was forever wheeling and dealing and hatching money-making schemes. Arrogant and self-centred, he was quite prepared to live with Sarah Gale and use her as a sexual partner and domestic drudge but he was not prepared to marry her for she had no money. In fact, while they were still living together he specifically advertised for a fourth wife with money, a scheme that had resulted in the involvement of Sarah in the murder of Hannah Brown, the woman he promised to marry on the erroneous assumption that she had money.

In thrall to Greenacre Sarah spent days scrubbing out the blood stains at the scene of the crime – the kitchen where her lover had dismembered the body of his victim with a kitchen knife before dumping the severed remains at various venues around London. Yet this oddly matched couple seemed genuinely attached to each other and after his arrest Greenacre repeatedly exonerated Sarah from any knowledge or blame for the murder of Hannah Brown. He also reminded his solicitor, just before stepping up to the gallows, to give his spectacles to Sarah Gale.

After their trial and sentencing at the Old Bailey, the writer of a contemporary pamphlet[1] witnessed the two prisoners descending the steps to the cells below and saw Sarah Gale 'kiss Greenacre with every mark of tenderness and affection.' It was also reported that she was distraught when she was refused permission to visit him in the condemned cell at Newgate. Although James Greenacre was hanged for killing Hannah Brown, Sarah, convicted of being an accessory to murder, was spared the gallows: instead, she was transported to New South Wales, only to die, according to a contemporary account, twenty-one years later, by falling from her horse and crashing into a tree – by which time she was a wealthy woman.

Christiana Edmunds's affair with Dr Charles Beard had all the hallmarks of an attachment that was one-sided and delusional. The setting was Brighton, 1871, a town that presented a glittering and glamorous public face and yet, as in all densely populated conurbations, it had its fair share of extreme poverty and criminal activity. The world of Christiana Edmunds however, was far removed from those for whom life was a constant struggle for survival. With little to occupy her mind other than the acquisition of the latest fashionable bonnets and indulging in a round of social visits she nurtured an intensely romantic attachment for a local, married physician, Dr Charles Beard. It seems that this passion was

---

1 *Life, Trial, Confession & Execution of James Greenacre, for the Edgware Road Murder, 1837.*

not reciprocated and the whole affair was in her mind – a fevered figment of her own desire and febrile imagination.

She subsequently caused the death, though not intentionally, of a four year old boy, Sidney Barker, who was on holiday with his family and had inadvertently eaten one of the chocolates Christiana had laced with poison. Having attempted to poison Dr Beard's wife, Emily, by the same means, she tried to divert suspicion by sending parcels of poisoned sweetmeats, fruit and cake to a number of prominent Brighton citizens.

Much to the disapproval of many who followed every dramatic detail of her subsequent trial for murder at the Old Bailey she was found guilty and sentenced to death. However, she was subsequently reprieved on the grounds of insanity and spent the remainder of her life as an inmate in the Broadmoor Hospital for the Criminally Insane, where she died in 1907, aged seventy-eight.

Mary Blandy and Captain William Cranstoun

*'But love is blind, and lovers cannot see
The pretty follies they themselves commit'*

To illustrate the veracity of Shakespeare's observation one need look no further than the case of Mary Blandy. By no means wanting in social standing and intelligence, the strength of Mary's emotional attachment to Captain William Henry Cranstoun led her to poison her father and, at the age of thirty-two, suffer the ultimate penalty – death by hanging in April, 1752. Though her paramour was equally to blame, he escaped the gallows but died, exiled and in extreme agony, that same year.

Who was this man who had the power to so blind Mary to his many faults and scandalous indiscretions that she was prepared to believe he would eventually marry her, despite the fact that he already had a wife and child in Scotland?

One might imagine that Captain Cranstoun cut a fine figure, a man of military bearing and a worthy recipient of Mary's devotion but, according to contemporary accounts, he was an ill-favoured, puny, pockmarked man with a squint, an ungainly gait and known to be chronically devious in his dealings.

According to a description in the *Newgate Calendar*, 'his person was diminutive, and he was so marked with the small-pox that his face was in seams, and he squinted very much; but he possessed that faculty of small-talk which is unfortunately too much esteemed by many of the fair sex'.

Mary's father, Francis Blandy, was a well-respected gentleman, an attorney by profession, who also served as the Town Clerk of Henley-on-Thames, in Oxfordshire. Her mother, Anne, was described as 'graceful in person, in mind elevated' and it was she who schooled her daughter, Mary, in her formative years. The family, who loved to entertain and were generous hosts, lived in a well-appointed property, Blandy House, in Hart Street, close to the River Thames at Henley Bridge.

Mary, also known as Molly, was educated and indulged, accustomed to having servants and enjoying a high standard of living. She was also, as an only child, much loved by her parents. It was said that her complexion had been marked by smallpox, the scourge of the eighteenth century, but that she had 'a good figure, luxuriant hair and dark, appealing eyes'. It was also said that 'her person had nothing in it remarkably engaging, but she was of a sprightly and affable disposition, of polite manners, engaging in conversation, and was much distinguished by her good sense'.[2]

Despite these qualities Mary was still unmarried at twenty-six and though she had entertained several suitors, nothing had come of these relationships. A clue may be found in a review of a book, *Remarkable Trials*,[3] in which the writer states that Mr Blandy '...from a foolish paternal weakness he encouraged the prevailing idea that she would have a fortune of £10,000 – an enormous exaggeration. She was sought after eagerly by recruiting officers and other military adventurers, who obtained access to the paternal domicile, and according to common report, flirted more than strict modesty allowed with some of the seductive sons of Mars'.

2 *Newgate Calendar.*
3 A review from The Dublin University Magazine in *Reynolds's Newspaper*, dated Sunday 18th July, 1869, 117 years later. Presumably this information had been gleaned from the many pamphlets published immediately after Mary's execution.

Another clue may be found in the following extract from a report in the *Newcastle Courant of* Friday, 16th August 1878:

> Mr Blandy, it appeared, had given it out always that he was a man of £10,000 fortune, in order to encourage wealthy suitors for his daughter's hand; but invariably declined to settle anything upon her at her marriage when a match was proposed. On this account, many matches were broken off, because Mr Blandy would advance no money with his daughter, but only promise to leave it her at his death.

In the summer of 1746, Mary and her parents were invited to dine at Paradise, the home of Lord Mark Kerr. It was here that Mary was to meet her nemesis, Lord Kerr's nephew, the Hon. William Henry Cranstoun,[4] presently engaged in army recruitment in the area. He was nearly forty years old and described as being 'remarkably ordinary, his stature is low, his face freckled and pitted with the smallpox, his eyes small and weak, his eyebrows sandy, and his shape no ways genteel; his legs are clumsy, and he is nothing in the least elegant in his manner.'

A year later, Mary and Captain Cranstoun met for a second time at Lord Mark Kerr's house in Henley. One can see why Mary Blandy was an attractive proposition for a man on the make, a very suitable match for a man short of funds and moral fibre, spurred on by the prospect of getting his hands on a fortune. He was determined to pursue her and at their second meeting Cranstoun set about seducing Mary. She must have been dismayed, however, when he admitted there was a lady, Anne Murray, in Scotland, with whom he had once co-habited, who was claiming, quite falsely, that they were legally married, which he strenuously denied. But Mary was desperate after so many delays and was not prepared to let any such inconvenience

---

4   He was a First-Lieutenant in Sir Andrew Agnew's Regiment of Marines but was given the courtesy title of Captain, a commission purchased by his family. He was the fifth son of William, Lord Cranstoun, and his wife, Lady Jane Kerr, a family with links to some of Scotland's aristocratic families.

curtail the courtship. Her father, too, was initially impressed by Cranstoun's aristocratic family connections and welcomed him as a guest in his house. Mrs Blandy was even more taken with her daughter's latest suitor, admiring him as a fashionable man of the world – a well-connected gallant in a fetching uniform, especially fond of wearing elaborately embroidered silk waistcoats – and she enjoyed the novelty of his company and was pleasantly entertained by the easy flow of his conversation.

One can imagine their shock when they were informed by Lord Mark Kerr that the Captain had, indeed, married Anne Murray, in Edinburgh in 1744, and a daughter had been born to them the following year. When challenged, Cranstoun maintained that as Anne Murray's family were Roman Catholics and, moreover, some of its members had been sympathetic to the Jacobite rebellion, it was decided to keep quiet about the marriage lest it should jeopardise the prospect of promotion in his military career. At first Anne had agreed to this deception but, perhaps when she became aware of her husband's pursuit of Mary Blandy, she applied to the Commissary Court of Scotland to decide whether her marriage was valid or not. Whilst the decision was still pending, Mr Blandy, anxious not to antagonise his daughter's suitor, ignored Lord Kerr's caution and welcomed Captain Cranstoun as a guest in his house for a period of six months. In addition, he must have been fully aware that, in 1748, when Cranstoun eventually left for London, he and Mary continued their affair with a fervent exchange of letters.

On 1st March, 1748, the Commissary Court in Edinburgh had declared that the marriage between Captain Cranstoun and Anne Murray was valid and he was ordered to pay maintenance of £50 a year for his wife and the child. Having been humiliated by her husband's refusal to acknowledge their marriage, which amounted to a scurrilous slur on her respectability, Anne subsequently sent a copy of the decree to Mary's father, a missive guaranteed to infuriate him and brand Cranstoun, once and for all, as completely unsuitable as a prospective son-in-law.

Meanwhile, whilst Captain Cranstoun was away on military duties in Southampton, Mary and her mother paid a visit to Mrs Pocock at Turville Court, near Henley. During their stay, Mrs Blandy became ill and, according to Mary's subsequent account, begged her to send for Captain Cranstoun. Once he had arrived, Mrs Blandy refused to take any medicine unless Cranstoun himself administered it. When she was sufficiently recovered, Francis Blandy, accompanied by both Mary and Cranstoun, took his wife back home to Henley. Cranstoun was persuaded by the ladies of the household to remain as a house guest for a further six months – until his regiment was disbanded at Southampton, at which time he was put on half-pay. By now, however, Mr Blandy, who was having grave doubts about Cranstoun's intentions towards his daughter and tiring of his presence in the house, was unable to mask his animosity and was sometimes very rude to him.

Early in 1749, Mary and her mother made the journey to London seeking medical advice for Mrs Blandy's recurrent health problems. They stayed in the home of Mrs Blandy's brother, Mr Henry Serjeant Stevens, at the Doctors' Commons. However, Mary had continued to correspond with Captain Cranstoun and, no doubt at Mrs Blandy's urging, he made daily visits to the house. Offended by Cranstoun's roguish reputation, Mr Stevens refused to have him in the house. The family friend, Mrs Pocock, resolved the problem by suggesting that Mary and her lover could meet at her house in St James's Square. Unfortunately, as Mrs Pocock and Captain Cranstoun were escorting Mary and her mother in a carriage to have dinner in St James's, Francis Blandy, also in town that day on business, saw them and embarked on an unpleasant verbal exchange before returning alone to Henley.

According to her subsequent account, Mary stated that it was during this visit to London that she and Captain Cranstoun were secretly married though no record of this has been found. Later accounts given by Mary, and also by Cranstoun, indicate that it was at

Mary's insistence that a 'marriage' had taken place as they had been intimate; this may have been, in Mary's eyes at least, a convenient interpretation of a marriage.

During the London visit, Mrs Blandy, it seems, had either overspent or the cost of her medical treatment had proved extortionate, for she had somehow accrued debts totalling forty pounds. As she professed to being too scared to tell her husband, Captain Cranstoun lent her the full amount before she and Mary returned to Henley.

Six months later, on Thursday, 28th September, 1749, Mrs Blandy became ill once more, this time seriously. Mr Benjamin Norton, a local apothecary, was sent for; so, too, was Mrs Blandy's other brother, the Rev. John Stevens, of Fawley, who happened to be playing bowls with a group of friends in the Bell, in Henley.[5] As her condition deteriorated, Dr Anthony Addington,[6] from Reading, was called to the house but Mrs Blandy died two days later, on 30th September. Mr Blandy remained at her bedside during her last hours and she begged him to accept their daughter's suitor, saying, 'Mary has set her heart upon Cranstoun; when I am gone, let no one set you against the match.'

A neighbour, Mrs Mounteney (Mary's godmother who was described as a possible wife for Francis Blandy should he decide to marry again), came to offer her condolences.

When Mary wrote to Captain Cranstoun to tell him of her mother's death and to beg him to come to see her he replied that he was unable to leave London as he feared a visit from the bailiffs. His financial shortfall was on account of his having to pay maintenance for his wife and daughter; he was also on half-pay after his regiment

---

5   Now renamed Old Bell, Henley. It has been established that it is the oldest building in the town, dating from 1325.

6   Dr Anthony Addington (1713-1790) physician. Treated William Pitt, the Elder, and in 1788, as a specialist in mental diseases, attended King George III. His son, Henry, Viscount Sidmouth, became Prime Minister (1801-1804) and, as Home Secretary in 1815, he turned down the appeal for a reprieve in the Eliza Fenning case; see author's book, *Bad Companions*.

had disbanded. This news prompted Mary to borrow forty pounds from Mrs Mounteney, fifteen of which she sent to the Captain to free him from his pressing financial predicament. This settled, he arrived in Henley and stayed for a number of weeks during which time Mr Blandy could barely conceal his contempt for his guest. Despite her father's disapproval, Mary and Cranstoun spent many hours walking in the grounds of Park Place, across the Thames, at Remenham - now known as Miss Blandy's Walk - no doubt anticipating a time when they could, at last, if not marry (as divorce from Anne Murray was not an option), at least go to Scotland and set up home together with the help of the Captain's mother, Lady Cranstoun.

It was during this period that Captain Cranstoun first told Mary that Mrs Morgan, a so-called wise woman[7] that he knew in Scotland, could prescribe 'love-powders' which, once ingested, could radically change a person's attitude towards another. He said he had taken some himself with the result that he had a change of heart after falling out with a friend. Maybe, he suggested, they could try one of these powders on Mr Blandy in the hope that his antipathy towards Cranstoun would change to one of acceptance, friendship even? Mary, however, said she had no faith in such philtres but before he could persuade her to at least try them he was forced to return to London to face the bailiffs once more; his greatest fear was that they would turn up in Henley demanding remuneration, which would have infuriated Mr Blandy still further. On this occasion, Mary gave him another fifteen pounds from Mrs Mounteney's loan.

On 1st of August, 1750, Captain Cranstoun was back in Henley but the relationship between him and Francis Blandy deteriorated still further, so much so that Mary was often in tears and her anxious and disgruntled father spent nearly every evening at the coffee house so as to avoid the company of the unwelcome guest in his house.

To convince Mary that the 'love-powders' were beneficial, not harmful, the crafty Cranstoun put or pretended to put, some of the

---

7   In an age when access to medical treatment was, unless one was wealthy, at best random and often dangerously basic, many resorted to the administrations and remedies of so-called wise women or quacks who advertised their often bizarre 'miracle cures' aimed at the sick and gullible.

powder in Mr Blandy's tea at breakfast one morning. When the old man subsequently appeared far less grumpy than usual and seemed to have suffered no ill effects after taking the tea, Mary was persuaded that the powders might provide an answer to the problem of her father's antipathy towards her lover.

In October, a year after the death of Mrs Blandy, Captain Cranstoun started complaining that he was unable to sleep at nights on account of strange music, the loud banging of doors, the sound of footsteps and unexplained rustling noises. These manifestations, he concluded, were signs emanating from the ghost of Mrs Blandy warning that a death would occur in the house. On one occasion, Cranstoun insisted that he had seen the spectre of Francis Blandy wandering about his room, dressed in his night-shirt. Mary colluded in this nonsense by telling the maids that she thought her father would be dead within the year.

Cranstoun's misdemeanours seemed to be manifold for, in addition to his marriage to Anne Murray - the validity of which he still disputed - he now confessed that, about a year before he and Mary had met, he had enjoyed a liaison with a Miss Capel, by whom he had a daughter. He managed to persuade Mary that this was of no consequence and keeping a mistress was by no means uncommon amongst men serving in the military. Mary accepted this, and though it was unfortunate, she was quite prepared to overlook the discretion as it had occurred before she and her lover had met. She even gave him money to support the child. However, Mary, formerly so trusting, now seemed to have had some sneaking suspicions regarding Cranstoun's amatory exploits for one day when the Captain was absent from the house, Mary unlocked his private chest and found a recently written letter from yet another lady with whom he was currently consorting.

An explosive scene ensued and Mary, understandably angry and upset, ordered him out of the house; but, after a couple of hours of the Captain on his knees begging forgiveness with much wringing of hands and floods of crocodile tears - at one point throwing himself face down on the bed and threatening to kill himself - she relented.

Not long after this, in November, 1750, Cranstoun was informed that his mother, Lady Cranstoun, was very ill. He seemed distressed that he was unable to afford to travel to Scotland to see her. Mary, gullible as ever, provided the means and at six o'clock the following morning, he boarded a post-chaise to Scotland. Mary bade farewell to her lover in floods of tears and Mr Blandy, no doubt glad to see the back of him, handed over a half-pint bottle of rum to sustain him on the journey.

Mary and the Captain continued to exchange letters, the content of which may be assumed for, early in 1751, Cranstoun informed Mary that he had acquired some Scotch pebbles (a fashionable decorative item at the time) which he would send to her along with some powder, purchased from the quack, Mrs Morgan, with which to clean them.

In June of that year, Francis Blandy's health began to deteriorate. He was sixty-two years old at the time and, although he had been fairly healthy, he had long suffered from episodes of gout and heartburn. He always had his tea served in a special dish and one morning the elderly maid, Susan Gunnell (formerly Mrs Blandy's personal maid), seeing that her master hadn't drunk the tea, took some herself; almost immediately she was violently sick and remained very unwell for several days. An old charwoman, Ann Emmet (always referred to as Dame) still employed occasionally by the family, also took some of her master's tea and was afterwards taken very ill. On hearing this, Mary seemed very concerned and yet, despite the old woman's illness after sampling the tea intended for Mr Blandy, she still professed to remain convinced that the 'love-powders' were harmless. Having mentioned the tricky problem of servants sampling the contaminated tea in one of her letters to Captain Cranstoun in Scotland he wrote back suggesting the following alternative:

> I am sorry there are such occasions to clean your pebbles; you must make use of the powder to them by putting it in anything of substance wherein it will not swim a-top of the water, of which I wrote to you in one of my last. I am afraid it will be too weak to take off their rust, or

at least it will not take too long a time.

Mary's manipulative lover went on to praise the beauty of Scotland and said that his mother, Lady Cranstoun, apparently now recovered, was furnishing an apartment in her house especially to accommodate Mary when she was free to join her son in Scotland.

During this period of separation, Mary and Captain Cranstoun exchanged numerous letters, often posted daily. A certain degree of subterfuge was thought necessary so Mary's letters were signed not MB, but MC, lest they should somehow be intercepted by Cranstoun's wife or any of her relatives.

The letters were posted for Mary by Robert Littleton, her father's clerk, and addressed to the Honourable[8] Mr William Henry Cranstoun, 'to be left at the Post-House, at Berwick.'

The following three, extremely incriminating, letters were found amongst Cranstoun's belongings after his death and subsequently published.[9] By this time, Mary had been tried, found guilty of murder and hanged. Had these letters been available to the prosecution at her trial their content could only have emphasised her guilt and endorsed the jury's verdict of guilty. They also make a mockery of her protestations of innocence, throughout her imprisonment and even on the gallows.

The first was written on 30th June, 1751:

> Dear Willy, - These, I hope, will find you in Health, as they leave me, but not in so much Perplexity: for I have endeavoured to do as directed by yours, with the Contents of your Presents, and they will not mix properly. The old woman that chars sometimes in the House, having drank a little Liquor in which I had put some is very bad: and I am conscious of the Affair being discovered, without you can put me into some better, and more proper Method of using them. When you write, let it be as mystically as you please, lest an Interception should

---

8 A misnomer if ever there was one. It would be difficult to find a gentleman less honourable than William Cranstoun.

9 A contemporary pamphlet entitled *Captain Cranstoun's Account of the Poisoning of the late Mr. Francis Blandy*. London. Printed for R. Richard, Holborn. March, 1753. The pamphlet included the three incriminating letters Mary had written to Captain Cranstoun which he said would be published after his death.

happen to your Letter, for I shall easily understand it.

When I think of the Affair in Hand, I am in great Distress of Mind, and endeavour to bear up under it as well as I can: but should be glad if you was near me, to help to support my fleeting Spirits: But why should I say so, or desire any such Thing, when I consider your cogent Reasons for being at a Distance: as it might, as soon as the Affair is completed, be the Occasion of a bad Consequence to us both. I have nothing more to add, but only desire you would not be long before you send me your Answer.

Yours affectionately, &c.

The second letter, dated 16th July, 1751, read as follows:

Dear Willy, - I received yours safe on the 11th Instant, and I am glad to hear you are well. I particularly understand what you mean, and I'll polish the Peebles as well as I can, for there shall not be wanting any Thing in my Power, to do the Business effectually. They begin to come brighter by the new Method I have taken: and as soon as I find the good Effects of the Scheme, you shall have intelligence with all convenient Speed.

Adieu, for this Time, my Spirits damping much: but pray God keep us in Health, till we have the Happiness of seeing each other.

Yours affectionately, &c.

The third letter, dated 1st August, 1751, two weeks before Francis Blandy died, read as follows:

Dear Willy, - I have been in great Anxiety of Mind since last Post-Day, by not hearing from you. Your letter of the 24th of last Month, I received safe Yesterday, and am somewhat enlivened in my Spirits by understanding that you are well.

I am going forward with all convenient Speed in the Business: and have not only a fatiguing Time of it, but am sometimes in the greatest Frights, there being constantly about me so many to be insensible of the Affair.

You may expect to hear again from me soon: and rest yourself assured, that tho' I suffer more Horrors of Mind than I do at this Time, which I think is impossible, I will pursue that, which is the only Method, I am sensible, left, of ever being happy together. I hope, by my next, to inform you that the Business is completed.

Yours affectionately, &c.

On Sunday, 4th August, Mary ordered the maid, Susan Gunnell, to make some water gruel[10] for her father. The following day, Mary told Susan that she had gone into the pantry and eaten some of the oatmeal at the bottom of the pan. Later that evening, when she took up Mr Blandy's mug of gruel, Susan saw her mistress stir the contents with a spoon and then rub the spoon between her fingers. Almost immediately after drinking some of the gruel, Mr Blandy was violently sick and suffered further bouts throughout the night.

The next morning, on Tuesday 6th August, a local apothecary, Mr Benjamin Norton, was sent for and when he asked what the old man might have eaten to cause such a fit of vomiting Mary mentioned some peas he'd eaten on the previous Saturday; she did not mention the gruel he had eaten the night before. The apothecary let some blood and prescribed some medication – commonly referred to as 'physic' - and promised to return the following day.

That same afternoon, Mary Blandy went into the kitchen to speak to the cook, Elizabeth Binfield, saying, 'Betty, if one thing should happen, will you go with me to Scotland?'[11]

'If I should go there,' replied the cook, cautiously, 'and not like it, it would be expensive travelling back again.'

That evening another helping of the gruel was warmed up and given to Mr Blandy with the result that he was violently sick once more.

---

10 Probably a thin, watery type of porridge made with oatmeal. Beef tea or broth was another favourite beverage for the sick.
11 If, at this stage, Mary really believed that the love powder she had put in her father's gruel would bring about a change of heart regarding her relationship with Captain Cranstoun, this remark to Betty might be interpreted as meaning should this happen she would be able to join Cranstoun in Scotland and would Betty like to accompany her as her maid. Alternatively, she was already anticipating the imminent death of her father.

Early the following morning, the cook, Betty Binfield, fetched the remaining gruel from her master's bedroom. The old charwoman, Ann Emmet, was in the kitchen at the time and Susan Gunnell told her she was welcome to eat the remains brought back to the kitchen. This she did and was violently sick; the effect of the gruel was so devastating that she was still unwell some months later, so much so that she was unable to give evidence at the subsequent trial and her daughter had to give evidence in her place.

At nine o'clock Susan Gunnell went upstairs to help Mary get dressed;[12] when she told her how ill Ann Emmet was, her mistress showed such concern for the old woman that she ordered some sack-whey and a thin mutton broth to be sent to help settle her stomach. Later that day she told Susan to warm up some more of the gruel for her father as he had taken some of his medicine and ought to take some nourishment with it. Susan offered to make some fresh gruel as the original batch, made four days before, was now stale but Mary thought this unnecessary as the maid was in the middle of ironing. She did, however, mention to Betty Binfield, the cook, that if someone as old as Susan should sample the gruel that was still in the pan it might make her extremely ill.

Although stomach upsets and sudden bouts of vomiting were common at the time, prior to the introduction of refrigeration and a better understanding of kitchen hygiene, the servants had grown suspicious of so much sickness plaguing various members of the household. The old maid, Susan, having decided to ignore her mistress's instructions and make a fresh pan of gruel, first inspected the remainder still in the pan. Both she and the cook, Betty Binfield, noticed that there was a gritty white sediment at the bottom. Despite this, Susan Gunnell was foolish enough to taste it and was violently sick once more. At this point the women wisely decided to lock the gruel pan containing the suspect deposit in a cupboard overnight.

12 Ladies of Mary's class wore such elaborate corsetry and layers of underclothes, topped with dresses adorned with rows of tiny buttons, bows and lace cuffs – the plaited hairstyles were equally intricate – that they needed the assistance of a maid to perfect the whole ensemble before presenting themselves to public view.

The following day, Thursday, 8th August, Susan took the pan and showed it to the Blandys' neighbour, Mrs Mounteney. She, in turn, showed it to Mr Norton, the local apothecary, for his opinion. He laid the sediment out on white paper to dry before making any judgement.

On Friday 9th August, Francis Blandy's brother-in-law, the Rev. John Stevens, arrived at the house, having been informed of Blandy's illness. Susan told him about the gruel and its distressing after effects. On reflection, he thought it would be wise to inform Mr Blandy of her suspicions. This Susan did the following morning, Saturday 10th August, in the presence of Stevens. She informed her master that it seemed likely that his daughter, Mary, had poisoned his gruel. Shocked by such terrible news, Mr Blandy wanted to know where she had acquired the poison to which Susan boldly suggested that Captain Cranstoun might have been the supplier.

'Oh, that villain!' the old man cried. 'I believe so too, for I remember he has talked learnedly of poisons. I always thought there was mischief in those cursed Scotch pebbles!'

Despite the shock of discovering his daughter's treachery, he dismissed the suggestion that he should take possession of all the letters that Cranstoun had sent to Mary, saying, 'I have never in all my life read a letter that came to my daughter from any person.'

He did, however, order the loyal maid, Susan Gunnell, to search for any of the lethal powder that remained in the house.

Though in great agony, Francis Blandy went downstairs that morning where he found Mary and his clerk, Robert Littleton, at breakfast. Mary passed her father his tea in his special dish. Whilst fixing her with a steadfast gaze, the old man took a sip.

'This tea has a bad taste,' he said.

Having said that two of his friends had previously been poisoned by something consumed at the coffee house, but that he had not been affected, he added that he thought it was now his turn to be poisoned. In disgust, he poured the tea into the cat's dish on the window sill.

Realising that her father was aware that he was being poisoned, Mary burst into tears and, 'trembling and confused', ran upstairs to her room. She immediately tried to cover her tracks by eliminating anything they might incriminate her and Captain Cranstoun. Gathering up all Cranstoun's letters and the remaining packet of poison she hurried down to the kitchen and, under the pretext of drying the ink on a letter she had just written to her uncle, threw the lot on the fire, stirring it with a stick before hurrying from the room. It seems likely that, their suspicions aroused, the servants were already watching her every move for, at that moment, the cook, Betty Binfield, lowered some more coal onto the pile of papers, hoping this would prevent them from being completely consumed in the flames. Unfortunately, the letters were burned but from the charred fragments the servants carefully removed a small paper packet containing some white powder on which was written in Cranstoun's hand:

'The powder to clean the pebbles with'

Susan Gunnell, who could not read but had been told by the other servants the wording on the packet, kept it in her apron pocket until Mr Norton called later that day. She gave him the packet and explained how she and Betty Binfield had rescued it from the fire. Mary was still extremely agitated and, as Mr Blandy's condition had deteriorated, she asked Mr Norton to send for Dr Anthony Addington, of Reading. The doctor subsequently arrived at the Blandys' house at midnight. He was sure his patient had been poisoned and, when he left on the morning of Sunday 11th August, he took from Mr Norton the packet of powder rescued from the kitchen fire and the dried sediment found in the pan of gruel. So sure was he that poison was to blame for Mr Blandy's sickness that, before taking his leave, he warned Mary that, if her father died, she would be blamed.

In desperation, Mary wrote a letter to Captain Cranstoun warning him that they were both, by association, under suspicion. Foolishly, in a panic and incapable of sensible thought, she asked her father's clerk, Robert Littleton, to post the letter to Cranstoun. She had used him for this purpose many times before and must have assumed he would remain discreet. Littleton, however, either from loyalty to his master or to distance himself from a charge of complicity, opened the letter. It read as follows:

> Dear Willy, - My father is so bad that I have only time to tell you that if you do not hear from me soon again, don't be frightened. I am better myself. Lest any accident should happen to your letters, take care what you write.
>
> My sincere compliments. I am ever yours.

Robert Littleton made a copy of the letter and then gave the original to Mr Norton who decided to read it to Mr Blandy. His reaction was, in the circumstances, quite extraordinary, for he simply said, 'Poor love-sick girl! What won't a girl do for a man she loves?'

At this point, Francis Blandy's brother, Mr Blandy of Kingston, who had come to the house to visit him, on hearing the misgivings expressed by other members of the household, decided to bar Mary from the sickroom. However, after a while, Mary's father seemed anxious to speak with his daughter and sent for her. During their conversation he let her know that not only had her letter to Captain Cranstoun been intercepted by Robert Littleton and read to him but that the maids had managed to retrieve the packet of white powder from the fire in the kitchen. Devastated, she admitted that she had put some powder in his gruel but insisted it was given to her 'for another intent'. Distraught, she knelt beside the bed and begged for her father's forgiveness. Turning over in his bed, Blandy cried:

> Oh, such a villain! To come to my house, eat and drink of the best my house could afford, and then to take away my life and ruin my daughter! Oh, my dear, thou must hate that man, must hate the ground he treads on, thou canst not help it!

To which, Mary replied: 'Sir, your tenderness towards me is like a sword piercing my heart – much worse than if you were ever so angry. I must down on my knees and beg you will not curse me.'

'I curse thee, my daughter!' her father retorted, 'how canst thou think I could curse thee? Nay, I bless thee, and hope that God will bless thee also and amend thy life. Do, my dear, go out of my room and say no more, lest thou shouldst say anything to thine prejudice.'

That was the last time she saw her father alive. He died at two o'clock on the afternoon of Wednesday, 14th August.

Dr Addington, meanwhile, had examined the little packet of powder and the sediment found at the bottom of the gruel pan as best he could and concluded that the powder was, in fact, white arsenic.[13]

Realising that Mr Blandy's death was probably the result of poisoning with criminal intent, he sent for Dr William Lewis, of Oxford. After reviewing the circumstances, the doctors ordered Mary to stay confined to her room under guard and her keys and papers were removed and 'all instruments wherewith she could hurt either herself or any other person'.

During the afternoon Mary offered the footman, Robert Harman, £500 if he would aid her escape but he refused. That evening, the cook, Elizabeth Binfield, was ordered to sit with Mary throughout the night as she was unable to sleep. Mary asked her,

> Betty, will you go away with me? If you will go the Lion or the Bell and hire a post-chaise, I will give you fifteen guineas when we get into it, and ten guineas more when we get to London.

When Betty learned that the proposed journey might eventually involve a sea voyage to some foreign land she declined on the grounds that she was a poor sailor. At this, Mary burst out laughing and said that she was only joking.

---

13 Dr Anthony Addington was the first doctor to give medical evidence for the prosecution in a murder trial although his tests for arsenic in the gruel sediment and the packet of white powder were basic. It was not until 1836 when the Marsh test was devised, followed by the more complex Reinsch test in 1841, that the presence of arsenic and other poisons in body tissue could be accurately measured. These tests were to prove invaluable in supplying forensic chemical analyses used in evidence in cases of death by poison.

Next morning, Thursday, 15th August, the post-mortem examination of the body of Francis Blandy was conducted within the Blandy home by Drs Anthony Addington, William Lewis and Edward Nicholas. Understandably, Mary, still confined to her room, was extremely agitated. The person consigned to make sure Mary didn't escape was an old suitor of hers and an erstwhile employee of Mr Blandy, Edward Herne, a church sexton and local parish clerk. However, he was called away on church business - digging a grave - and left Mary unattended, whether on purpose or not. Desperate to get out of the house and, as she explained later, 'to get some air' Mary, wearing just some undergarments – a bonnet, a loose chemise and an un-hooped petticoat – ran from the house and across the nearby Henley Bridge over the Thames, into Berkshire. Her agitated manner and inappropriate dress attracted a group of children in the street and before long a large crowd of local people who, having heard the news of Francis Blandy's death and rumours of poison, followed her, uttering oaths and making threatening gestures. Mrs Mary Davis, the landlady of the Angel, a small ale-house, took her in for her protection. Extremely agitated, Mary asked a gentleman, Mr Lane, who was there with his wife, what would become of her.

'Madam', he replied, 'you will be sent to Oxford Gaol; you will then be tried for your life. If you are innocent, you will be acquitted; if you are guilty you will suffer death.'[14]

On hearing this, Mary stamped her feet and retorted:

'Oh, that villain!' Then, after a brief pause, she added, 'But why do I blame him? I am more to blame myself, for I gave it, and I knew the consequence.'[15]

Mrs Lane, who was also present during this conversation, described Mary as being 'in a great fright'. Not surprisingly, the defence at the subsequent trial did not refer to this incriminating piece of evidence.

A sergeant, Mr Robert Stoke, was sent by the Mayor to prevent

---

14 In some accounts the word *'death'* is replaced by *'accordingly'*.
15 Questioned later at the trial, Mrs Lane was unsure whether Mary Blandy had said *'knew'* or *'know'* – a crucial difference in interpretation and in law.

Mary from leaving the ale-house but it fell to a family friend, Alderman Richard Fisher, who had also been sent for, to bring Mary back the short distance to the house in a closed carriage to escape the attentions of the mob.

That same afternoon the inquest into Francis Blandy's death was opened at the home of John Gale, in Henley, presided over by the Mayor and Coroner, Mr Richard Miles, before a jury of twelve men, one of whom was Alderman Richard Fisher. Many of the statements given by Drs Addington, Lewis and Nicholas, the apothecary, Mr Norton, the footman, Robert Harman, Edward Herne, the old maid, Susan Gunnell, the clerk, Robert Littleton, and the cook, Elizabeth Binfield, were extremely detrimental to Mary and a warrant was issued for her arrest on suspicion of murdering her father.[16]

After the inquest had closed, Alderman Richard Fisher went to speak to Mary at her home in the presence of her uncle. He asked to see Captain Cranstoun's letters but Mary replied, 'Dear Mr Fisher, I am afraid I have burnt some that would have brought him to justice.'

She then gave him a key and directed him to search a drawer in her bedroom but not one of Captain Cranstoun's letters was found. At this, Mary said, 'My honour to him [by shielding him from blame by burning the incriminating letters] will prove my ruin.'

At four o'clock on the morning of Friday 16th August, 1751, Mary Blandy, escorted by two constables, was taken to Oxford County Gaol in a coach and four. She was permitted to have a maid, Mrs Dean, (formerly in service with the Blandy family) to accompany her as well as taking canisters of her favourite blend of the finest teas and other personal possessions. Her greatest fear was that she

---

16 A full account of the inquest, including all the verbatim depositions of the witnesses, was published in several newspapers prior to the murder trial, drawing adverse comment from both prosecution and defence.

would be fettered. The party reached the gaol at Oxford Castle at eleven o'clock that morning but not for Mary a dark and dingy cell and the unpleasantly close proximity of the other prisoners – she and her maid were accommodated in comfortable rooms in the gaol keeper's house. A press report some months later stated that:

> At present she lives without shewing much Concern about her Circumstances... the greatest Concern she has shewn at any Time since her Commitment, was to hear, that upon collecting her Father's Effects by her Uncle, it did not appear that he was worth more than the 400*l*. When being inform'd that a Warrant was issued and sent into the North to apprehend her Lover, Mr. C---n, she with great earnestness said, "I pray God that they make take the villain, that he may suffer for it; for it is all owing to his Request and Advice." And being afterwards told, that he had escaped the Warrant, she shew'd Tokens of great Discontent. But whatever she might secretly suffer from Remorse and Disappointment, she appeared to be cheerful, and partook of every Amusement of which her Situation would admit, as drinking Tea twice a day, walking frequently in the Keeper's Gardens, and playing at Cards at Night...[17]

These privileges only lasted for a couple of months however, for on the 25th October, in response to a rumour that Mary was planning an escape, the Secretary of State ordered her to be fettered and thereafter she was forced to wear a heavy leg iron attached to her left ankle. The friction from this eventually made her leg swell so badly that it was decided to remove the red flannel cuff between her ankle and the iron ring to accommodate it and restore the circulation. As a further precaution, Mrs Dean was warned that if she attempted to help Mary to escape she would be imprisoned for life.

With no more leisurely walks in the grounds of the Castle to distract her, Mary had to resign herself to a long, anxious wait for the date of her trial to be set. During this time it was reported that 'she appeared thoughtful, attended Divine Service, and behaved in a manner more suitable to her Circumstances'.

Her prospects were, indeed, grim. She stood accused of the heinous crime of parricide, one that society condemned as especially

---

17 *Derby Mercury*, dated Friday, 6th December, 1751.

reprehensible even in an age accustomed to many forms of brutality.

By 8th November of that year, the *Derby Mercury* - and several other newspapers - had already published verbatim accounts of all the witness depositions given to the Coroner in evidence during the August inquest. These statements showed that Drs Addington and Lewis, the servants and Edward Herne, all knew about the 'love-powders' sent to Mary by Captain Cranstoun and, although she had freely admitted putting some of the powder in her father's tea and gruel, she said she thought it was harmless. The report also included some damaging comments made under oath by the cook, Betty Binfield and the clerk, Robert Littleton, who both testified that they often heard Mary Blandy curse her father, calling him 'a toothless old dog', a 'rogue and villain'. She had also said in the servants' hearing 'who would grudge to send an old father to hell for £10,000'. These revelations were followed by detailed accounts of the whole affair between Mary and Captain Cranstoun and the death of Francis Blandy. The *Derby Mercury*, dated 6th December, 1751, carried the headline:

> A Genuine Account of that most inhuman Murder committed by Miss MARY BLANDY, upon the Body of her Father, Mr. FRANCIS BLANDY, containing more extraordinary Particulars concerning that tragical Affair, than has yet been published in any of the News-Papers.

Several newspapers had also supplied their readers with detrimental reports of Mary Blandy's behaviour whilst in gaol. By the time of her trial, therefore, her part in her father's death was already common knowledge and a supposition of guilt had already formed in the minds of those who followed the story so avidly, including, of course, the jurors who would eventually pronounce judgement upon her.

The Trial

It was not until the 2nd March in the following year, 1752, that a Grand Jury announced a True Bill against Mary Blandy. Her trial, held at the Oxford Assizes, was conducted in the hall of the Divinity

School of the University as the usual venue, the Town Hall, was undergoing building works at the time. It was reported that 'the Concourse of People who came to hear the Trial was so great, that the Judges were obliged to wait an Hour at the Court Door before they could get entrance, and the Witnesses were so fatigued with coming to Court, that several of them were scarce kept from fainting'.[18]

The proceedings were opened on Tuesday, 3rd March, and a verdict was reached the same day, after a thirteen hour sitting. The trial judges were The Honourable Heneage Legge,[19] and Sir Sydney Stafford Smythe, both were barons of the King's Court of Exchequer.

Representing the Crown Prosecution were The Honourable Mr Henry Bathurst,[20] Mr Serjeant Hayward, The Honourable Mr Barrington, Mr Hayes, Mr Naires, the Town Clerk of Oxford, and Mr Ambler – an impressive list that bode ill for the prisoner.

Mary's defence counsel consisted of Mr Ford, Mr Morton and Mr Aston. The indictment against Mary read as follows:

> You stand indicted by the name of Mary Blandy, late of the parish of Henley-upon-Thames, in the county of Oxford, spinster, daughter of Francis Blandy, late of the same place, gentleman, deceased, for that you, not having the fear of God before your eyes, but being moved and seduced by the instigation of the devil, and of your malice aforethought, contriving and intending him the said Francis Blandy, your said late father, in his lifetime, to deprive of his life, and him feloniously kill and murder on the 10th day of November, in the twenty-third year of the reign of our sovereign lord George the Second, now King of Great Britain, and on divers days and times between the said 10th day of November and the 5th of August, in the twenty-fifth year of the reign of His said Majesty...did knowingly, wilfully, and feloniously, and of malice aforethought, mix and mingle certain deadly poison, to wit, white arsenic, in certain tea...

---

18 *Newcastle Courant* dated Saturday 14th March, 1752. Unless otherwise stated all quotes are from a pamphlet entitled, *The Tryal of Mary Blandy*, published 1752.

19 The Hon. Heneage Legge (1703-1759) second son of William, first Earl of Dartmouth.

20 Hon. Mr Henry Bathurst (1714-1794) Solicitor General to the Prince of Wales, 1745; Judge of the Court of Common Pleas, 1751; Lord Chancellor in 1771; became Earl Bathurst in 1775.

Put more simply, the jurors had been informed that Mary Blandy, the prisoner at the bar, was charged with being responsible for the wilful murder of her father, Francis Blandy, by administering to him white arsenic between 10th November, 1750 and 5th August, 1751, in his tea and again between 5th August and 14th August, 1751, in his gruel.

The *Newcastle Courant*[21] gave a description of Mary as she appeared in court that day:

> The prisoner appeared in a black sack [loose coat], plain linen, and a thin black shade; her behaviour during the trial was serene and composed..., (except when Mrs Mounteney stood at her left hand to be sworn on behalf of the King). A chair was ordered by the Court as soon as she came in, to sit down when she thought proper. The unhappy woman is about 35 years of age; and though not reckoned a beauty, her face is agreeable, and her hair, eyebrows, and eyes black. She is of middle stature, a genteel person, and polite behaviour, as her father, who was a gentleman of an exceeding good character, had bestowed upon her a very liberal education, to which her capacity was adequate.

Having listened to the charge against her, Mary pleaded 'Not Guilty'. After the jurors had been sworn in, Henry Bathurst assured the court that a warrant for the arrest of Captain Cranstoun had been issued. He proceeded to open the case for the prosecution by addressing the court in rhetoric that was both forceful and emotive:

> May it please your lordships and you gentlemen of the jury, I am counsel in this case for the King, in whose name and at whose expense this prosecution is carried on against the prisoner at the bar, in order to bring her to justice for a crime of so black a dye that I am not at all surprised at this vast concourse of people collected together to hear and to see the trial and catastrophe of so execrable an offender as she is supposed to be.
>
> For, gentlemen, the prisoner at the bar, Miss Mary Blandy, a gentlewoman by birth and education, stands indicted for no less crime than that of murder, and not only for murder, but for the murder of her own father, for the murder of a father passionately

---

21 *Newcastle Courant* dated Friday, 16th August, 1878

> fond of her, undertaken with the utmost deliberation, carried on with an unvaried continuation of intention, and at last accomplished by a frequent repetition of the baneful dose, administered with her own hands. A crime so shocking in its nature and so aggravated in all its circumstances as will (if she is proved to be guilty of it) justly render her infamous to the latest posterity, and make our children's children, when they read the horrid tale of this day, blush to think that such an inhuman creature ever had an existence.

He went on to outline the case in great detail, covering all the events leading up to the day of Francis Blandy's death. The court was told of Mary Blandy's disregard for her father's well-being; when she noticed that his teeth were falling out, 'she d-----n'd him for a toothless old Rogue, and wish'd him at hell'.

It was then the turn of Mr Serjeant Hayward, who, after praising Francis Blandy, with whom he had been acquainted, launched into a lengthy speech aimed at the University students present in court, warning that disobedience to one's parents can lead to dire consequences:

> But you, young Gentlemen of this University, I particularly beg your attention, earnestly beseeching you to guard against the first Approaches of and Temptations to Vice. See here the dreadful consequences of Disobedience to a Parent. Who could have thought that Miss Blandy, a young lady virtuously brought up, distinguished for her good behaviour and prudent conduct in life, till her unfortunate acquaintance with the wicked Cranstoun, should be ever brought to trial for her life, and that for the most desperate and bloodiest kind of murder, committed by her own hand, upon her own father? Had she listened to his admonitions this calamity never had befallen her.

With reference to Captain Cranstoun he reminded the jurors that,

> The author and contriver of this bloody affair is not present here. I sincerely wish that he was, because we should be able to convince him that such crimes as his cannot escape unpunished. The unhappy prisoner, ruined and undone by the treacherous flattery and pernicious advice of that abandoned, insidious, and execrable wretch, who found means of introducing himself into the father's family, and whilst there, by false pretences of love, gained the affection of his only daughter and child. Love! Did I call it? It deserves not the name;

if it was love of anything it was of the £10,000 supposed to be the young lady's fortune...

In order to bring this about Cranstoun sends presents of pebbles, and also a powder to clean them, and this powder, gentlemen, you will find is the dreadful poison that accomplished this abominable scheme.

After giving the court further details of the circumstances connected with the crime, Mr Hayward ended by saying:

Thus, gentlemen, have I endeavoured to lay before you some observations upon this transaction, and hope you will think them not unworthy of your consideration. I trust I have said nothing that relates to the fact that is not in my instructions; should it be otherwise, I assure you it was not with design. And whatever is not supported by legal evidence you will totally disregard... We shall now proceed to call our evidence.

The first witness to be called to give evidence on behalf of the prosecution was Dr Anthony Addington who testified that he had attended Francis Blandy during his last illness. He had been summoned to the house in Henley on the evening of Saturday, 10th August and found the patient in bed; he was told that Blandy had drunk some water gruel on the night of Monday, 5th August, after which he experienced grittiness in his mouth, very painful burning and prickling in his tongue, throat, stomach and bowels and suffered with fits of vomiting and purging.

Questioned further, the doctor told the court that after taking more gruel the following evening, 6th August, the violent symptoms returned and, in addition, his stomach had become swollen.

There followed further descriptions of the deceased's sufferings on the Saturday night when the doctor was in attendance and, suspecting that his patient had been poisoned, he questioned Mary as to whether her father had any enemies. She replied that he was 'at peace with all the world, and that all the world was at peace with him'. When asked if he could have taken poison, the old man said it was possible although his daughter disputed it.

As Mr Blandy seemed a little better the next day, Sunday, 11th

August, Dr Addington took his leave at eight o'clock having agreed to return the following day, at Mary Blandy's request. However, as he was leaving one of the maids handed him the paper packet retrieved from the fire on which there was an inscription which clearly read:

The powder to clean the pebbles with.

Inside, the doctor found a small amount of white powder which he thought likely to be arsenic. The apothecary, Mr Benjamin Norton, then produced some of the substance that had sunk to the bottom of the gruel pan and the doctor assumed that this, too, was white arsenic.

By the time Dr Addington returned the following day, Monday 12th August, Mr Blandy's condition had deteriorated still further. Realising that the old man was unlikely to survive and suspecting poison, the doctor sent for another physician, Dr William Lewis, from Oxford, who eventually arrived at about eight o'clock that evening. During the day Dr Addington asked Mr Blandy if he thought he had been poisoned and he agreed, saying that his teeth had been decaying rapidly over the previous few months. When asked who he suspected might have given him poison, he forced a smile but his eyes filled with tears as he said; 'A poor love-sick girl – I forgive her – I always thought there was mischief in those cursed Scotch pebbles.'

The condition of Francis Blandy was even worse the next morning, Tuesday, 13th August, and his suffering continued throughout the day and grew even more intense during the night. He died at two o'clock the following afternoon, Wednesday, 14th August.

Dr Addington told the court that he had no doubt in his mind that his patient had died from poisoning and tests on the powder samples had been made by himself, Mr Norton, the apothecary, and, independently, two other chemists, the conclusion being that the poison involved was white arsenic.

Questioned about the post-mortem examination he performed the next day, Dr Addington read out a detailed report of his findings after which Dr Lewis, who had also attended the post-mortem, was asked if he agreed with Dr Addington's report and his diagnosis of death by poison. To this, Dr Lewis replied: 'Absolutely.'

Dr Addington then gave an account of the tests he had applied to the sample of white powder and his reasons for concluding that it was white arsenic. He was then asked about Mary Blandy's demeanour after her father's death and told the court that, in his view, she did not appear overly upset and seemed more concerned about her own situation. She intimated to the doctor that she didn't want to do or say anything to incriminate Captain Cranstoun as she considered him to be her husband.

The next witness to be called was the apothecary, Benjamin Norton; he confirmed that he had examined the sediment in the gruel pan handed over to Mrs Mounteney by the maidservant, Susan Gunnell. He left it to dry on a piece of white paper in the care of Mrs Mounteney until the Sunday morning when it was given to Dr Addington as he was leaving so he could take it away and test it for arsenic.

When questioned, Mr Norton confirmed that Mary Blandy had often mentioned the strange noises, thumps, rustlings and music she'd heard in the house which, she believed, was an omen of a pending death in the family. She even said Mr Cranstoun, during his last visit, had seen an apparition of Francis Blandy.

Mr Norton told the court that he had initially prescribed some medication in an attempt to ease Mr Blandy's symptoms but Mary Blandy urged him to let her know if, at any stage, he thought her father was dangerously ill so that Dr Addington might be called. He had treated Francis Blandy for minor ailments over the years and, as far as he could see, Mary behaved with 'true affection and regard' during his last illness. However, when the apothecary was asked bluntly who he thought might have poisoned the old man, he replied: 'I had [a] suspicion it was Miss Blandy.'

Mrs Mary Mounteney was then brought into court to give evidence. It was reported that when her godmother entered the witness box Mary cried whereas she remained impassive throughout all the other testimonies. Mrs Mounteney confirmed that when Susan Gunnell gave her the gruel pan that contained the sediment she had sent for Mr Norton and after he had examined it and put it out to dry on some white paper, she had locked it away until it was handed over to Dr Addington to carry out tests. She also confirmed that Mary Blandy always appeared to behave as a dutiful daughter whenever she saw Francis Blandy and her together.

Next to be called was the elderly maidservant, Susan Gunnell, who was described in one report as 'wore down to a Skelliton' by the trauma of it all. She confirmed that she had made the water gruel for Mr Blandy on the Sunday before his death and it was left in the pantry. Although she hadn't seen her, Mary Blandy told her that about midday on the Monday she had gone into the pantry and sampled some of the oatmeal at the bottom of the pan of gruel. On the Monday evening Susan gave Mr Blandy a half-pint mug of the gruel; she witnessed Mary 'take the teaspoon that was in the mug and stir the water gruel, and after put her finger to the spoon, and then rub her fingers'.

During the evening of the following day, Susan was told by Robert Harman, the footman, to warm up some of the gruel; it was then given to Mr Blandy by his daughter and he drank about half a mug full. Shortly after this, Susan had carried the candle to light his way upstairs to his bedroom but he immediately started to vomit and called for a basin. However, when she went up to his room about six o'clock the next morning to give him his medicine he seemed a little better although he had been sick during the night.

That same day, Wednesday, Miss Blandy asked Susan to warm up some more gruel for her father as he had taken his medicine. 'You need not make fresh,' she said, 'as you are ironing.' The maid, however, decided to make a fresh pan of gruel as the old batch was so stale. Before cleaning out the pan she and Betty Binfield, the cook, took a closer look at the sediment at the bottom, which looked too white to be oatmeal. Susan tasted a bit and said it was gritty and it made her sick.

Convinced it contained poison, the servants locked the pan in a cupboard and the next morning took it to Mrs Mounteney's house where the apothecary, Mr Norton, also inspected it.

Susan then told the court how the old charwoman was in the kitchen and gladly accepted some of the leftover water gruel. Almost immediately she started to vomit and was in 'the necessary house'[22] for an hour and a half, suffering constant retching and purging. When informed of the old charwoman's sickness Mary Blandy said that she was glad she hadn't seen her suffering in this way as she was very fond of the 'dame' as she called her.

Asked how Mary Blandy behaved towards her father, Susan said that she was sometimes affectionate towards him but at other times she would refer to him as 'an old villain'; sometimes wishing him a long life whilst at other times wishing him dead – if this should happen, she explained, she would be free to go to Scotland and live with Lady Cranstoun. The old maid admitted that father and daughter often exchanged cross words but these were 'generally over trifles'. Having been barred from entering her father's bedroom on the Sunday night he sent for her and she pleaded with him, saying:

> Banish me, or send me to any remote part of the world; do what you please, so you forgive me; and as to Mr Cranstoun, I will never see him, speak to him, nor write to him more so long as I live, so you will forgive me.

To this, Mr Blandy had replied; 'I forgive thee, dear, and I hope God will forgive thee; but thee shouldst have considered better than to have attempted anything against thy father...'

Mary answered; 'Sir, as for your illness, I am entirely innocent.'

At this point, however, Susan, the loyal servant, protested, saying;

> Madam, I believe you must not say you are entirely innocent, for the powder that was taken out of the water gruel, and the paper of powder that was taken out of the fire, are now in the hands that they must be publicly produced.

The maid had made this remark in front of Mr Blandy and she also said that she had been made sick from tasting the tea in her master's dish six weeks before.

Mary had protested, saying: 'I have put no powder into tea. I have

---

22 The 'necessary house' or privy; a specially built outhouse that offered some privacy – an improvement on the open dung heap.

put powder into water gruel, and if you are injured I am entirely innocent for it was given me with another intent.'

When Mr Blandy asked by whom his daughter had acquired the powder, Susan Gunnell suggested Captain Cranstoun might have been the supplier. Hearing this, Mr Blandy turned over in the bed and said to his daughter:

> Oh, such a villain! Come to my house, ate of the best, and drank of the best that my house could afford, to take away my life and ruin my daughter.

There followed evidence already given at the Coroner's inquest by Robert Harman, Mr and Mrs Lane, Mr Fisher and Robert Littleton, who repeated his assertion that he had often heard Mary curse her father and call him 'a rogue and villain' and 'a toothless old dog'.

Defence counsels were not at this time permitted to make speeches in court in defence of their clients but the accused were allowed to address the jury. It was reported that Mary defended herself with 'intelligence and zeal' as demonstrated by the speech she made in court that day.

> My lords, it is morally impossible for me to lay down the hardships I have received – I have been aspersed in my character. In the first place, it has been said that I have spoken ill of my father, that I have cursed him, and wished him to hell, which is extremely false. Sometimes little family affairs have happened, and he did not speak to me so kind as I could wish. I own I am passionate, my lords, and in those passions some hasty expressions might have dropped; but great care has been taken to recollect every word I have spoken at different times, and to apply them to such particular purposes as my enemies knew would do me the greatest injury.

> These are hardships, my lords, extreme hardships, such as you yourselves must allow to be so. It is said, too, my lords, that I endeavoured to make my escape. Your lordships will judge from the difficulties I laboured under. I had lost my father – I was accused of being his murderer – I was not permitted to go near him – I was forsaken by my friends – affronted by the mob – insulted by my servants. Although I begged to have the liberty to listen at the door where he died I was not allowed it. My keys were taken from me, my

shoes buckles and garters, too[23] – to prevent me from making away with myself, as though I was the most abandoned creature.

What could I do, my lords? I verily believe I must have been out of my senses. When I heard my father was dead, and the door open, I ran out of the house and over the bridge, and had nothing on but a half-sack and petticoat without a hoop – my petticoats hanging about me. Was this a condition, my lords, to make my escape in? A good woman beyond the bridge seeing me in this distress desired me to walk in till the mob was dispersed. The town sergeant was there. I begged he would take me under his protection to have me home. The woman said it was not proper; the mob was very great, and that I had better stay a little. When I came home they said I used the constable ill. I was locked up for fifteen hours, with only an old servant of the family to attend me. I was not allowed a maid for the common decencies of my sex. I was sent to gaol, and was in hopes there, at least, this usage would have ended. But was told it was reported I was frequently drunk; that I attempted to make my escape; that I never attended the chapel. A more abstemious woman, my lords, I believe does not live.

Upon a report of my making my escape the gentleman who was High Sheriff last year came and told me, by order of the highest powers, he must put an iron on me. I submitted, as I always do to the higher powers. Some time after he came again, and said he must put a heavier one upon me, which I have worn, my lords, till I came thither. I asked the Sheriff why I was so ironed. He said he did it by the command of some noble peer on his hearing that I intended to escape. I told him I never had such a thought, and I would bear it with the other cruel usage I had received on my character.

The Rev. Mr Swinton, the worthy clergyman who attended me in prison, can testify that I was a regular at the chapel whenever I was well. Sometimes I really was not able to come out, and then he attended me in my room. They likewise have published papers and depositions which ought not to have been published in order to represent me as the most abandoned of my sex and to prejudice the

23 A report in the *Newcastle Courant*, dated Saturday 14th March, 1752, added the following: '...nor was I permitted to have a Knife to cut my Victuals, insinuating that I might be wicked enough to destroy myself.' It also included, 'The next day after my Father's Death, I was told his body was to be open'd, and being ill with Confinement in my Room, and not being able to bear the Shock of being in the House during the Operation, I took a Walk over Henley Bridge to take the Air...'

world against me.

I submit myself to your lordships and to the worthy jury. I can assure your lordships, as I am to answer it before the grand tribunal, where I must appear, I am as innocent as the child unborn of the death of my father. I would not endeavour to save my life at the expense of truth. I really thought the powder an innocent, inoffensive thing, and I gave it to procure his love. It has been mentioned, I should say I was ruined. My lords, when I young woman loses her character is not that her ruin? Why, then, should this expression be construed in so wide a sense? Is it not ruining my character to have such a thing laid to my charge? And whatever may be the event of this trial I am ruined most effectually.

Mary's counsel had only managed to find a few witnesses to testify in her defence.

Anne James, a woman who 'used to wash for Mr Blandy', was the first in the witness box and, in an attempt to discredit the evidence of the cook, Betty Binfield, she recalled that about three months before Mr Blandy became ill, Mary and Betty had a quarrel and the latter was either fired or decided to leave.

'I have heard her curse Miss Blandy, and damn her as a bitch, and said she would not stay,' she added. 'Since this affair happened [the alleged murder] I heard her say, "Damn her for a black [i.e. black-hearted] bitch. I shall be glad to see her go up the ladder and swing."'

According to the witness, the cook was always gossiping about her mistress in the kitchen and when she cursed her in this way, several servants - Mary Banks, Nurse Edwards, Mary Seymour, and possibly the footman, Robert Harman - were also present.

Elizabeth Binfield then entered the witness box and denied ever saying the words attributed to her by the previous witness. She did admit, though, that she and her mistress had a 'little quarrel' after which she had threatened to leave. She told the court that she had often heard Mary Blandy say, 'Who would grudge to send an old man to hell for £10,000'. A number of times she had also heard her say she wished her father was dead and in hell.

The third witness to be questioned was Mary Banks who testified that Elizabeth Binfield *did* say the words repeated by Anne James. She was also able to inform the court that this conversation was on the day Mr Blandy's body 'was opened' – the post-mortem examination.

Edward Herne, a sexton of the parish, was called next. He had once worked for Mr Blandy for several years and was at one time considered as a possible suitor for Mary's hand. He told the court that although he'd left the Blandys' service twelve years previously, he was still a regular visitor to the house, sometimes calling up to four times a week. Mary Blandy, he insisted, had always behaved towards Mr Blandy in the manner expected of an affectionate and dutiful daughter. When he visited the house on 12th August, two days before the old man died, Mary was unable to speak for several minutes owing to 'the greatness of her grief'.

Furthermore, he testified, he had never heard Mary 'swear an oath or speak a disrespectful word of her father'.

He confirmed that Mary had told him that in August, 1750, she had seen Captain Cranstoun stir some powder into her father's dish of morning tea.

Edward Herne then told the court that he had visited Mary in Oxford Gaol and he was there when a rumour reached her that Captain Cranstoun, who had been on the run after Mary's arrest, had been captured. According to Herne, she said:

> I hope in God it is true, that he may be brought to justice as well as I, and that he may suffer the punishment due to his crime, as she should do for hers.

At this, Mary prompted her counsel to ask Herne to confirm that she had also told him she was quite innocent of the crime she was charged with and when she put the powder in her father's tea she did not intend to harm him.

Thomas Cawley, who had known the Blandy family for twenty years, also spoke well of Mary, saying that her behaviour towards her father was always dutiful.

Another family friend of some standing, Thomas Staverton, told the court that the relationship between father and daughter seemed to be a happy one. He had noticed that Francis Blandy's health had declined for some weeks before his death but could not comment on the state of his teeth. He did tell the court, however, that Mr Blandy was 'a good-looking man'.

Mrs Mary Davis, the landlady of the Angel ale-house at Henley Bridge, recalled the prisoner's foray across the bridge on the day of the post-mortem and the subsequent inquest. A large hostile crowd was following her though she was walking 'softly' and not running as though trying to escape. Seeing Mary's agitated state and inappropriate dress she asked her what was wrong and where she was going. To this, Mary replied that she needed to take some air and get out of the house as they were going to 'open her father'.[24]

Robert Stoke, a sergeant, was at the Angel that day and told the court that, as a result of the inquest, he had been ordered by the Coroner to detain her. He agreed that Mary didn't appear to be trying to escape; on the contrary, she seemed relieved that he had come to detain her. The witness then confirmed that he was present during the conversation between Mary Blandy and Mr and Mrs Lane in the ale-house that day but, as it was detrimental to her defence, he was not asked to repeat the conversation.

For a reason that is not entirely clear, a member of her defence counsel, Mr Ford, then rose to object to the 'printing and publishing the examination of witnesses before her trial – and very scandalous reports have been spread concerning her behaviour ever since her imprisonment'. He requested that the clergyman, the Rev. John Swinton, who had been a daily visitor to Miss Blandy during her imprisonment, should be called to give a favourable account of her behaviour in gaol.

This request was denied but the court was reminded to disregard anything that had been reported in the newspapers.

This brought Mr Bathurst, for the prosecution, to his feet to remind the court that Mary Blandy had sometimes admitted her

---

24 As in this instance, it was common practice to carry out a post-mortem examination in the deceased person's home. Mary's distress and urgent desire to get out of the house was, therefore, quite understandable.

crime whilst at others insisted that, although she had put the deadly powder into her father's tea and gruel, she did not know it would harm him.

On the contrary, she maintained that she put the powder into his beverages to make him love her and allow her to find happiness with Captain Cranstoun. Yet by all accounts, he argued, Francis Blandy was an extremely loving father so why did she need to administer a 'love powder'?

At this point, Mary, through her counsel, reminded the jury that she did not need to make her father fond of her – this he already was – but to make him fond of Captain Cranstoun.

Mr Bathurst went on to question why, having seen the effect of the poison in the gruel she'd given her father on the Monday and the Tuesday, did Mary insist on giving him more the following day? In addition, her attempt to burn the remaining powder was surely the act of a guilty person?

Lastly, Mr Bathurst agreed that the scandalous reports of witness statements, which had been given at the inquest concerning Mary's behaviour since her arrest, were 'a gross offence against public justice'.

Then, addressing the jurors, he said:

> But you, gentlemen, are men of sense, and upon your oaths; you will therefore totally disregard whatever you have heard out of this place. You are sworn to give a true verdict between the king and the prisoner at the bar, according to the evidence now laid before you. It is upon that we (who appear for the public) rest our cause. If, upon that evidence, she appears to be innocent, in God's name let her be acquitted; but if, upon that evidence, she appears to be guilty, I am sure you will do justice to the public, and acquit your consciences.

It now fell to the Judge, Mr Baron Legge, to deliver his summing-up speech to the jury. He began by reminding the court of the indictment against the prisoner:

> Gentlemen of the jury, Mary Blandy, the prisoner at the bar, stands indicted before you for the murder of Francis Blandy, her late father, by mixing poison in tea and water gruel, which she prepared for him, to which she pleaded she is not guilty.

He proceeded to reiterate the need for the jurors to disregard the publications concerning the case published before the trial:[25]

> In the first place, gentlemen, I would take notice to you a very improper and very scandalous behaviour towards the prisoner by certain people who have taken upon themselves very unjustifiably to publish in print what they call depositions taken before the coroner....
>
> I hope you have not seen them; but if you have, I must tell you, as you are men of sense and probity, that you must divest yourselves of every prejudice that can arise from thence and attend merely to the evidence that has now been given before you in Court, which I shall endeavour to repeat to you exactly as I am able after so great an examination.

The judge, with scrupulous care, then outlined all the evidence given that day starting with a lengthy catalogue of the many unpleasant and divers symptoms suffered by Mr Blandy during his final illness as described by Dr Addington and Dr Lewis – not only the fits of vomiting and purging accompanied by violent abdominal pain but also the swollen tongue and throat, the pricking sensation of the skin, bloodshot eyes, rotting teeth, yellowed complexion and difficulty in breathing. He followed this with a resume of the findings of the post-mortem, including the condition of the viscera which led to Dr Addington's conclusion that arsenic had been the cause of the old man's death.

Baron Legge then reminded the jurors of the sequence of events that led to arsenic being detected in the residue in the gruel pan which was passed by the servants to Mrs Mounteney and then to Benjamin Norton, the apothecary, who ascertained, to the best of his knowledge, that it was white arsenic. The illness of the old charwoman, Ann Emmet, after eating some of the contaminated gruel, presented symptoms that were mirrored by those of Mr Blandy.

There followed the judge's description of those who had witnessed

---

25 These were blatantly and unequivocally pre-empting a verdict of guilty on Mary – ignoring the concept of her being, in the eyes of the law, innocent until proven guilty - a breach of impartiality and an affront to fairness that would not be tolerated today.

the distressing deathbed scenes between Mary and her father – her plea for forgiveness in which she claimed that although she admitted that she had put poison in his tea and in his water gruel, she was innocent of wishing him harm; she believed that the powder, given to her by Cranstoun, would make her father more kindly disposed to the lovers. The jury heard again Mr Blandy's remarkably lenient response and willingness to forgive his daughter and lay full blame for his illness on Mr Cranstoun.

The judge then drew the jury's attention to the crucial subject of the Scottish pebbles sent to Mary with the packets of white powder with which to clean them. He reminded them of the letter Mary had written to Captain Cranstoun which was opened by Robert Littleton and then read to Mr Norton and Mr Blandy himself. Incredibly, Mr Blandy had responded with a heartfelt: 'Poor love-sick girl! What won't a girl do for the man she loves?'

The events of Thursday, 15th August, the day of the post-mortem and inquest on the body of Francis Blandy were recalled; Mary running from the house and across Henley Bridge only to be followed by an angry mob and then rescued by Mrs Davis, at the Angel alehouse; from there taken back to the house by Mr Richard Fisher - who was a member of the coroner's jury sitting later that day - and handed over to a constable. On his return from the inquest, Mr Fisher told Mary bluntly that unless she could produce any incriminating letters from Cranstoun, her position was bleak. To this she replied that she had burned most of his letters and that her protection of him would prove her ruin.

After referring to the witnesses called to speak in Mary Blandy's defence the judge addressed the jury:

> This, gentlemen, is the substance of the evidence on both sides, as nearly as I can recollect it. I have not wilfully omitted or misstated any part of it; but if I have, I hope the gentlemen who are of counsel of either side will be so kind as to set me right.
>
> A very tragical story it is, gentlemen, that you have heard, and upon which you are now to form your judgement and give your verdict. The crime with which the prisoner stands charged is of the most

heinous nature and blackest dye, attended with considerations that shock human nature, being not only murder, but parricide – the murder of her own father...

In all cases of murder it is of necessity that there should be malice aforethought, which is the essence of and constitutes the offence...

Poison in particular is in its nature so secret, and withal so deliberate, that whenever it is knowingly given, and death ensues, the so putting to death can be no other than wilful and malicious. In the present case, which is to be made out by circumstances, great part of the evidence must rest upon presumption, in which the law makes a distinction. A slight or probable presumption only has little or no weight, but a violent presumption amounts in law to full proof, that is, where circumstances speak so strongly that to suppose the contrary would be absurd. I mention this to you that you may fix your attention on the several circumstances that have been laid before you, and consider whether you can collect from them such a presumption as the law calls a violent presumption, and from which you must conclude the prisoner is guilty...

I cannot now go through the evidence again, but you will consider the whole together, and from thence determine what you think it amounts to. Thus far is undeniably true, and agreed on all sides, that Mr Blandy died by poison, and that poison was administered to him by his daughter, the prisoner at the bar. What you are to try is reduced to this single question – whether the prisoner, at the time she gave it to her father, knew that it was poison, and what effect it would have?

If you believe that she knew it was poison, the other part, viz., that she knew the effect, is consequential, and you must find her guilty. On the other hand, if you are satisfied, from her general character, by what has been said by the evidence on her part, and from what she has said herself, that she did not know it was poison, nor had any malicious intention against her father, you ought to acquit her. But if you think she knowingly gave poison to her father, you can do no other than find her guilty.

The members of the jury remained in the courtroom and, after talking amongst themselves for about five minutes, indicated that they had reached a verdict. The Clerk of Arraigns, having asked Mary to confirm her name by holding up her hand, addressed the jury:

Gentlemen of the jury, look upon the prisoner. How say you, is Mary Blandy guilty of the felony and murder whereof she stands indicted or not guilty?

The foreman of the jury replied; 'Guilty'.

After it was ascertained that Mary had no goods, chattels, lands or tenements,[26] the court crier announced:

> Oyez! My lords the King's justices do strictly charge and command all manner of persons to keep silence whilst sentence of death is passing on the prisoner at the bar, upon pain of imprisonment.

Turning to Mary in the dock the judge said this:

> Mary Blandy, you have been indicted for the murder of your father, and for your trial have put yourself upon God and your country. That country has found you guilty.
>
> You are convicted of a crime so dreadful, so horrid in itself, that human natures shudders at it – the wilful murder of your own father! A father by all accounts the most fond, the most tender, the most indulgent that ever lived. That father with his dying breath forgave you. May your heavenly Father do so too!
>
> It is hard to conceive that anything could induce you to perpetrate an act so shocking, so impossible to reconcile to nature or reason. One should have thought your own sense, your education, and even the natural softness of your sex, might have secured you from an attempt so barbarous and so wicked.
>
> What views you had, or what was your intention, is best known to yourself. With God and your conscience be it. At this bar we can judge only from appearances and from the evidence produced to us. But do not deceive yourself; remember you are very shortly to appear before a much more awful tribunal, where no subterfuge can avail, no art, no disguise can screen you from the Searcher of all hearts...
>
> Let me advise you to make the best and wisest use of the little time you are likely to continue in this world. Apply to the throne of grace, and endeavour to make your peace with that Power whose justice

---

26 Though it was later reported that Mr Gillingham Cooper received, as lord of the manor of Henley, the forfeiture of two fields belonging to Miss Blandy. By strange coincidence, he also received a malt-house belonging to Elizabeth Jeffries – see letters between Mary Blandy and Elizabeth Jeffries and an extract from one of Horace Walpole's letters.

and mercy are both infinite.

Nothing now remains but to pronounce the sentence of the law upon you, which is –

That you are to be carried to the place of execution and there hanged by the neck until you are dead; and may God of His infinite mercy receive your soul.

At this, Mary spoke up with a request of the judge:

My lord, as your lordship has been so good to show so much candour and impartiality in the course of my trial, I have one favour more to beg, which is, that your lordship would please to allow me a little time till I can settle my affairs, and make my peace with God.

'To be sure, you shall have a proper time allowed you,' replied the judge.[27]

Once the court had been dismissed Mary was transported back to the keeper's house at Oxford Gaol. It was reported that the keeper and his family were very upset over the death sentence imposed on Mary – though they must have known this would be the penalty for parricide as so many comparatively minor offences carried the death sentence on conviction.[28] Mary, however, despite the sentence and thirteen hours of gruelling court procedure, seemed calm and ordered mutton chops and apple pie for her supper and, during the six weeks she remained there until her execution, she was treated very well.

In fact, Mary was fortunate in this respect for in June of that year, 1752, the Murder Act of 1751, became law, stipulating that all those found guilty of murder were to be hanged within two days of conviction and during that time fed only bread and water.

---

27   The judge would have had to apply to the Secretary of State for an extension of time between sentence and execution, a request that would have been presented before the King and Privy Council at a 'Hanging Cabinet'.
28   There were more than 200 offences that carried the death sentence; murder, treason, arson, burglary, highway robbery, sodomy, forgery, coining and stealing or killing sheep or horses, etc. but after The Judgement of Death Act of 1823 the death sentence ceased to be mandatory, except for murder and treason, and many convicts were transported to the Colonies, mainly in Australia, instead.

Furthermore, the body after execution was to be sent to anatomists for dissection.[29]

Mary was attended daily by the Rev. John Swinton, the prison chaplain, no doubt eager to persuade her to make a full confession and thereby save her soul from eternal hellfire. She also corresponded with another clergyman, thought to be the Rev. William Stockwood, Rector of Henley, who was anxious to do the same. In an unsigned letter, dated 7th March, 1752, he accused Captain Cranstoun of being an 'infidel' and then launched into a written form of a sermon of some length in which he informs Mary that 'death has no stings to wound innocence. Guilt alone clothes him with terrors (to the guilty wretch he is terrible indeed!). And at the resurrection, and at the last day, you will joyfully behold Jesus Christ your Saviour, join in the triumphant multitudes of the blessed, and follow them into the everlasting mansions of glory.'

In her reply two days later, Mary admitted that she had put the powders into her father's beverages, but insisted that she had been duped into being 'the fatal instrument' and did not know they would cause him harm. Echoing the clergyman's pious verbosity she proclaims her innocence and pleads for sympathy and understanding. At the end of her reply she asks of the clergyman; 'Pray comfort Ned Hearne, and tell him I have the same Friendship for him as ever.'

Clearly under the influence of priestly administrations and, perhaps, some of the sentimental ballads she had read, Mary also composed a long and whimsical ode entitled, *A Poetical Epistle from Miss Blandy to Capt. Cranstoun, a little before her Execution*. It begins:

> Where'er you roam, whatever ills you know,
> Attend the Tale of my Superior Woe.
> If yet your Breath against Remorse is steel'd,
> Nor Murder's Self can teach it how to yield,
> My piteous Story may try to move,
> A Tear will fall for our disastrous Love.

29 This helped to prevent an unseemly scramble by friends and relatives of the hanged to grab the bodies, often to sell on to anatomists eager to acquire cadavers for research and teaching purposes.

A little further, it bewails her fate in the following words:

> No Mercy here! – Behold o'erwhelming Shame;
> Death ignominious, and a Blacken'd Name!
> Reproach now rears her ever-dreary Head,
> And Human Law now bids its Victims bleed.
> But Still, my Breath, let Perturbation cease;
> Sweet Innocence is mine, and her's in Peace!
>
> For You! – What Tortures must your Bosom know,
> Condemn'd to roam a Vagabond below;
> Mark'd out by Vengeance, for the Guilt that's past,
> To bear a Murderer's Anguish to the last;
> Farewell!! – If Justice yet shall strike you here,
> O drop me a penitential Tear:
> Let Truth then sway;- and, with your latest Breath,
> Confirm me guiltless of a Father's Death.
> Farewell! – to you may Penitence be given,
> And wing your fervent Prayers to pitying Heaven.
>
> For me! – One Pang shall bid my Sorrows cease,
> And raise my Soul to the Abodes of Peace,
> Array'd in Innocence, I yield my Breath;
> Conduct me, Angels! Thro' the Vale of Death.

The newspapers were quick to print accounts of the case during the time Mary was imprisoned in the Castle awaiting execution. One pamphlet carrying a report of the trial sold 3,000 copies in ten hours. Perhaps to counteract some of the more scurrilous publications, Mary wrote her own account which was published four days after her execution, under the title: *Miss Mary Blandy's Own Account of the Affair between her and Mr Cranstoun*.[30] It was described by the writer, Horace Bleakley, as 'the most famous apologia in criminal literature', it began:

> My acquaintance with Mr. Cranstoun, who was lieutenant of a regiment of marines, commenced at Lord Kerr's, in one of the summer months, as I at present apprehend, of the year 1746. At first we entertained of each other only sentiments of friendship, I

---

30 *Miss Mary Blandy's Own Account of the Affair between her and Mr Cranstoun* Printed by A. Miller, The Strand, April 10th 1752. (price 1s 6d)

> being on the point of marrying another gentleman; which, for some prudential reasons, was soon put off, and at last came to nothing. Some months after our first interview, Mr Cranstoun left Henley; and, about the following summer, returned to his uncle, Lord Mark Kerr, who lived at a house he had hired in that town, called Paradise. After his arrival at Henley, our friendship continued for some time...

Mary continues with an account of the growing affection between her and Cranstoun which culminated in his marriage proposal at which point he confessed to being involved with another woman (Anne Murray) though he denied that he was, in fact, married to her. During a conversation with Mrs Blandy about his desire to marry her daughter, Mary insists that Captain Cranstoun was told that the rumoured £10,000 dowry was an exaggeration but that he had gallantly replied, 'If Mr. Blandy will give me his daughter, I shall not trouble him about that.'

The fact that Cranstoun was always short of money and over the years had amassed a catalogue of debts and downright fraud, Mary's suggestion that he didn't care about her fortune, seems, at best, naïve.

In this, Mary seems determined to emphasise that Cranstoun's love for her was not influenced by the prospect of a considerable dowry. She also 'recalls' a conversation with her father in which he endorses the affair and gives her permission to correspond with Cranstoun until his marriage is proved to be illegal and they are free to marry.

> Tho' I did not see Mr. Cranstoun for several months, our correspondence still continued; letters passing and repassing between us almost every post.

Describing the period when Cranstoun was a guest in the Blandy household for six months, Mary admitted that there were disagreements and harsh words yet writes that her father '....thought Mr.Cranstoun a most agreeable man' and when Cranstoun returned to stay with them at Henley for the second time, he was received by Mr Blandy 'with great tenderness' and on another occasion agreed that the lovers 'were very well matched.'

Further into Mary's account she maintains that Captain Cranstoun suggested a secret marriage while they and Mrs Blandy were staying in London, meeting at Mrs Pocock's house in St James's Square. She refused to enter into a secret marriage in case the law court in Scotland declared his marriage to Anne Murray legal. Yet she had given Dr Addington the impression that she considered herself married to Cranstoun.

The account recalls Cranstoun generously lending Mrs Blandy forty pounds - probably borrowed - to settle her debts before relating her illness and death in 1749. There came a description of Mr Blandy reading a letter of condolence sent by Captain Cranstoun -'the tears ran down his cheeks, and he cried out, 'How tenderly does he write!' after which Mr Blandy said she must write to Cranstoun 'in order to ease the poor soul as much as I could; and let him know that he was as welcome to my father's house, whenever he would be pleased to come, as he was before.'

After Mary had sent Cranstoun the money to pay the bailiffs in London he returned to Henley and 'stayed some weeks with my father, who received him with great marks of affection and esteem.'

Yet, it appears, that it was during this visit in August, 1750, that Mr Blandy appeared 'much out of humour' and Cranstoun suggested trying Mrs Morgan's 'love powders' to make him more amenable to his guest. At this time Mary had lent Cranstoun more money to return to London to pay his creditors and so prevent the bailiffs arriving at the Blandy home in Henley.

It was at this point in the story Mary said that Mr Blandy, having spent his evenings in the coffee-house (probably to avoid Cranstoun or to allow the lovers some privacy), would return to the house in a foul mood during which times he was often harsh to his daughter and extremely rude to Mr Cranstoun.

Cranstoun thought this was the opportune time to put some of the 'love-powder' in the old man's tea though Mary maintained that she never did believe they would work. She then recounts Cranstoun telling her about one of his other mistresses, Miss Capel, with whom he had a daughter. Affecting a semblance of shame and repentance,

Cranstoun begged for Mary's forgiveness which she gave him; she was clearly beginning to doubt her lover, however, for on an occasion when he was out of the house she searched his belongings and found a letter from 'a woman he kept'.

After a prolonged period of pleading in which he 'threw himself on the bed, crying out, 'I am ruined, I am ruined. Oh, Molly, you never loved me!' Mary, of course, forgave him and then gave him the money to make the journey to Scotland to see his sick mother. She describes the heart-rending departure scene as Cranstoun set off in a post-chaise armed with love and a bottle of rum to sustain him.

Mary's account continues with descriptions of the ghostly music and apparitions that both she and Cranstoun had perceived after her mother's death. She records her anger that the old maid, Susan Gunnell, denied ever hearing these strange phenomena, saying, 'You see and hear, Madam, with Mr. Cranstoun's eyes and ears.'

This had made Mary very angry which might explain why Susan, fearful that her mistress would sack her before repaying the money she had borrowed, had, a little later, apologised to her mistress and declared that she, too, had heard the strange noises. In other words, she - and Betty Binfield - decided to humour her. That night, after Mr Blandy had retired for the night, Mary and Susan went to Mr Cranstoun's room at midnight to listen for ghostly noises. Susan fell asleep at three o'clock but later said that she was awakened by the sound of footsteps and thumps and strange spectral manifestations which the gullible Mary believed to be connected to her dead mother – and a possible premonition of another death in the family – her father's.

Back in Scotland, Cranstoun wrote to Mary urging her to address her letters, not to his home, but to the post office at Berwick, disguise her handwriting to be more masculine and to sign the letters M.C. not M.B. in case they were intercepted by any of Anne Murray's family as they were jealous of their affair. She then said that Lady Cranstoun, considering her as wedded to her son, wrote to her as Mary Cranstoun.

Mary said that her father's temper did not improve and he berated her for turning down marriage proposals from other men who were, at least, in a position to marry her. It was in May, 1751, that Captain Cranstoun first suggested he send some Scotch pebbles and a love-powder referred to as powder to clean the pebbles. Throughout the lengthy description of her father's illness and death Mary insists that she was innocent of intent to murder but had been 'made the fatal instrument of his death - and that by listening to the man I loved above all others, and even better than life itself. I had depended upon his, as I imagined, superior honour, but found myself deceived and deluded by him.'

She admitted that the servants seemed set against her, harbouring 'vindictive sentiments' towards her.

The account ends with the words:

> May God forgive me my follies, and my enemies theirs! May he likewise take my poor soul into his protection, and receive me to mercy, through the merits of my Mediator and Redeemer, Jesus Christ, who died to save sinners! Amen. The foregoing narrative, which I most earnestly desire may be published, was partly dictated and partly wrote by me, whilst under sentence of death, and is strictly agreeable to truth in every particular.
>
> MARY BLANDY Witness my hand.
>
> Signed by Miss Mary Blandy, in the Castle at Oxford, April 4, 1752, in presence of two clergymen, members of the University of Oxford.

Mary also exchanged letters with young Elizabeth Jeffries who was under arrest in Chelmsford Gaol for aiding and abetting the murder of her wealthy uncle, Joseph Jeffries, by her lover, John Swan. They were both eventually tried and found guilty; their harrowing story is told in the following chapter. The letters between Mary Blandy and Elizabeth Jeffries, written from prison, were published in a pamphlet shortly after both women had been hanged. This extraordinary correspondence was first instigated by Mary Blandy, who wrote the following letter whilst they were both awaiting trial:

> Oxford, Jan.7, 1752.
>
> Madam,
>
> Tho' I have not the Pleasure personally to know you, yet as our

Circumstances are somewhat similar, I could not resist the strong inclination I have to correspond, console, and sympathise with one whose Case is so much like my own, and who I hope is as innocent. We are both accused (and the ill-natured are too apt to believe it) of destroying the only Persons in the World we ought in Nature, Duty and Gratitude to have preserved; You, an Uncle who, I hear, had taken you even in Infancy under his Care, cherished, and carefully brought you up, and at last adopted you as it were, and design'd you Heir of all: I am no less thought guilty of serving the same Manner one of the best of Fathers, to whom I was as dear as the Apple of his Eye; of which I had such a Sense, that I can't so much as accuse myself of a single Thought to his Prejudice. But however conscious we may be of our own Innocence, the World, who are apt to believe that worst, will not see it in the same Light.

We are prejudged, and without hearing condemned, and all we can say in our own Defence is unheeded or disregarded. But whatever Light they see it in, we, that know our own Hearts and Innocence, ought to bear it up with a Firmness unknown to Guilt.

This, dear Miss, I have taken the Freedom of communicating to you, that, if you chuse it, we may correspond, and mutually comfort and support one another; being, with the greatest Respect, Mary Blandy

Elizabeth Jeffries's reply was as follows:

Chelmsford, Jan.13, 1752

Madam,

I Receiv'd your's of the seventh Instant, and cannot but with as much Joy, as my unhappy Circumstances are capable of, embrace the Offer you so kindly make, and which is likely to turn out so much to my Advantage. 'Tis true, as you observe, our Cases are very much alike, and it is no less so that we are equally odious to the prejudiced World (and indeed, were the Crimes laid to our Charge true, very justly.)

What remains therefore for us, but, as we know our own Innocence, to comfort and support one another to the utmost of our Power, in which, dear Miss, I have greatly the Advantage from your superior Abilities and Education. However, what is in my Power shall not be wanting, which I hope you will be so good to accept of; and this I can assure you, that if what comes from me cannot boast of a knowing Head, yet I hope I may and ever shall lay Claim to a sincere and honest Heart. I am, Madam,

Your devoted Friend and Servant,
E.JEFFRIES.

Five days later, Mary Blandy sent the following letter to Miss Jeffries:

Oxford, Jan.18, 1752

Dear Miss,

When I did myself the Pleasure to write to you, desiring a Correspondence between us, I expected Comfort instead of Compliments, which I take to be not very Suitable to our Situation. For as our Cases are so much alike, as we are alike persecuted and insulted, traduced and blackened in the most shocking Manner, it would I thought be some Alleviation to our Sufferings to unbosom ourselves to one another without Ceremony or Compliment, which seldom speak the Language of the Heart.

I would, therefore, intreat you, dear Miss, to give me an Account by your own Hand (for common Reports and common News-Papers I have little Regard for) of the whole Affair, how the Catastrophe happened, why and upon what Grounds you should be suspected, be taken in Custody, and persecuted with that Violence and Rancour hardly to be match'd, as if there had been a settled Design to destroy you right or wrong.

This, dear Miss, as it will be a Relief to yourself to relate it, so it will be a Satisfaction to me to have it from so authentick a Hand: And I in Return will give you a Detail of my whole Affair, in the same artless Dress and Simplicity, which are or ought to be inseparable from Truth and Sincerity. Permit me, dear Miss, to be

Your most sincere Friend and humble servant,
MARY BLANDY

Elizabeth Jeffries replies with a detailed account of the murder of her uncle:

Chelmsford, Jan. 21, 1752

Dear Miss,

In order to satisfy you and myself (for I never till now experienced what it was to have a Friend to unburthen one's Mind to) and to give a clearer Light to the Affair, I must begin with some Account of my late dear Uncle, whose partial, and I am afraid fatal Favour to me is the Source of all my Misfortunes. He was a plain honest Man, a Butcher by Trade, diligent, frugal, and in the Beginning of his Life very Parsimonious; he had acquired a very handsome Fortune, and for some Time had left off Business, and lived retired at Walthamstow.

It was his Misfortune to have no Education, for he could neither write nor read, and as he took me an Infant, was too negligent to me in those Acquirements, for poor Man, as he did not know the Value of them in himself, he did not know the loss of them in another.

However, his Indulgence to me made up for everything else, and I did not regret the Want of what I never knew the Value of. This my Uncle's Indulgence, as I said above, was naturally look'd upon with an evil Eye, by those who were equally near to him in Blood, who thought themselves altogether as deserving of his Favour, and who I have Reason to believe did me all the ill Offices with him in their Power, but in vain; for tho' he had not Learning, he had good Sense, and could see through all their little Art and Envy, which only served to rivet more and more in his Esteem, insomuch that (as you was rightly informed) except a few inconsiderable Legacies, he left me all he had.

Now I leave you and all the World to judge what Inducements I could have to commit a Crime so shocking in itself, and so horrid in its Circumstances, on a Person to me so good, so generous, and so inflexible in my Interest. But I have already exceeded the Bounds of a Letter, and must refer the rest to another Opportunity. I am, dear Miss, your's, etc.

E. JEFFRIES.

Elizabeth continues her version of the murder of her uncle in the following letter:

Chelmsford, Jan. 22, 1752

Dear Miss,

I Come now to relate the horrid Catastrophe, the very Remembrance of which chills my Blood, and enervates my whole Frame. You must know then, that on the third of July last, about Two o'clock in the Morning, I was alarmed by the Noise of a Pistol going off, and soon after with the dying Groans of a Person not far distant from where I lay.

Strangely surprised, I ran into my Uncle's Room, and saw him (Oh, shocking!) horribly butcher'd and welting in his Blood. Unknowing what I did, it seems I ran into the Street almost naked, and gave the Alarm. But observe the Malice of my Enemies; what they could not effect by their Insinuations with my Uncle, hath been so successful with the Publick as to blacken me, and make them believe I was the Perpetrator of that cruel Murder, resolving to have my Fortune even at the Expence of innocent Blood: But all that could be alledged against me was so trifling, that the Justices, before whom I was examined, permitted me to attend my Uncle's Funeral, and soon after to administer to his Will. I am much affected with the Sufferings of a poor faithful Servant, whom, when they found they could not corrupt nor involve him in their Guilt, they were determined to involve in my Sufferings, for he is sent to the same Jail, and loaded with the same Infamy.

But God, who is the Protector of the Innocent, will I hope in his own Time extricate us out of all our Troubles, and cover our Enemies with Shame and Confusion. I am, dear Miss, with that greatest Sincerity,

Your's, etc. E. JEFFRIES

This tale received great sympathy from Mary Blandy, who responded in soothing terms:

Oxford, Jan. 25, 1752

Dear Miss,

Your two Letters are affecting to the last degree, in your plain and honest Narrative. What Injustice and Distress have you gone through! But if Guilt had been added, you must certainly have sunk under it. Nothing but Innocence could have supported you. O Innocence, thou heavenly Gem, thou Jewel above all Price, what this World and all it affords in comparison to thee? Without thee, Pomp, Titles, and the most affluent Fortune are tasteless, troublesome, and indeed intolerable.

Dear Miss, I heartily share with you in all your Sufferings (and for a while have forgot my own) and shall long till it please God to work our Deliverance, to be nearly and intimately acquainted with you, for I shall think all my Sufferings overpaid in the Friendship and Affection of a Person so oppress'd and injured, and so little deserving it.

I shall now endeavour to acquit myself of my Promise and give you in my Turn an Account of my Affair, which, with all the Parts and Acquirements you are pleased to compliment me with, will be neither so interesting nor affecting as yours.

You are to know then, Dear Miss, I was the only Child of my Parents, my Father was an Attorney of good Character and great Practice, and my Mother, one of the best of Women, who both by Example and Precept shew'd me the Road to Virtue and Happiness. My Father, though a very honest worthy Man, was not over and above equal in his Temper, and withal parsimonious, which we, who knew not his Circumstances, but believed them to be better than indeed they were, thought somewhat blameable: However, he spared no Pains or Expence in my Education and Improvements, and if I was not flatter'd, I made no inconsiderable Progress; nor did he fail to indulge me in the Innocent Amusements that my Youth and Fortune might require: I might add, for I firmly believe it, that for my Sake and Interest only he affected to be thought richer than he was. This naturally procured me Suitors of some Eminence, whom I submitted to entertain rather out of Duty than Inclination. My Father's Scheme I believe was, that a suitable Person might be found, fond enough, knowing I was an only Child, to have me without any Conditions, but when he perceived a Gentleman not so inclined, he always found some Pretence or other to break off the Match, not being willing to expose his Circumstances; and I, whose Heart was never over and above engaged, easily bore the Disappointment.

At last Fate and my evil Genious brought Mr. Cranston to Henley: But I must abruptly break off, for Company is coming in, with whom I am downright oppress'd, some out of Impertinence, some through Curiosity, some with propensed Malice to insult me, but alas how few out of Friendship to advise and assist me! I am, Dear Miss,

Your's, M.BLANDY

Mary continues to inform Elizabeth of events following her fateful meeting with Captain Cranstoun in the following letter:

Oxford, Jan. 27, 1752

Dear Miss,

In my last I just mention'd Mr Cranston; he was an Officer in the Marines, is a younger Brother of a noble and honourable Family in

Scotland, and allied to some of the first Families in England. He was soon introduced to our House, and I soon distinguish'd by him, to the Mortification, Envy, and implacable Resentment of several Persons both in Town and Country. This naturally flatter'd my Pride, and I am afraid I did not bear my Triumph with that Moderation I ought, and which I know will never be forgiven, and I doubt not has done me no little Disservice in my unhappy Affair.

But what was begun out of Pride and Vanity, by Degrees got admission to my Heart. Mr Cranston, tho' he had nothing extraordinary in his Person, had a certain Ease and Dignity in his Address, and a most insinuating Tongue as ever Man had.

I confess my Weakness, he too easily gain'd my Heart, nor were my Parents averse to it, till they heard of a prior Marriage, which stagger'd them, and almost overwhelmed me, add to which, a Character given of him not very advantageous by his great Uncle, Lord Mark Kerr, a Man of great Honour and Dignity. From that Time he was not received with that Cordiality he used to be, some of my Mother's Friends in particular, could never endure him afterwards; but nothing discouraged him, he either was, or pretended to be so much in Love, that he bore all their Coldness and Insults with a Resolution not to be shaken.

About this Time I lost my dear Mother, my Prop and Stay, and he a warm Friend, who never so much as varied in her Esteem for him. Thus left to myself, strongly solicited by him, and not altogether discouraged by my Father, I too easily admitted his Excuses and Asseverations about his pretended Marriage.

But here follows what I even blush to remember. I told you my Father was not always equal in his Treatment of him, sometimes cold, sometimes cordial, now he would admit him, then he would forbid him his House. He told me a long story of the Virtue of certain Powders, that would keep him steady in his Interest (than which I wished for nothing more) and prevail'd with me, even against my Judgement and Inclination, to administer them, which ended in the fatal Catastrophe.

O Miss, who can express the Agonies and Horrors I was in, at seeing the Consequence of them; and to think I was so much as the innocent Cause of the Death of a most dear and indulgent Father, is what I don't know how to bear, and shall never get over.

You and all the World I know must blame my Credulity; but, O Miss! If ever you was in Love, you must know how easy it is for the Person beloved to decoy us into the Belief of what they please, even against our own Judgement and Understanding! [It may be noted that Mary no longer indulged in whimsical accounts of ghostly music and apparitions foretelling the death of her father as she had done with the gullible Mr Swinton].

Dear Miss, administer me what Comfort you can, for all my Stock of Philosophy and Resolution sinks under me. O how I envy your Happiness, who tho' a younger Woman, and consequently easier imposed upon, having nothing of this to upbraid yourself for, but when this severe Trial is over, must shine out with a fresh Lustre to the utter Confusion of your Enemies; whilst I, let it issue how it will, must languish under a Melancholy never to be got over! O Miss, let me have your Prayers, and believe me

Ever Your's,
M. BLANDY

The self-deluding charade of innocence continues in Elizabeth Jeffries's reply from Chelmsford Gaol on 30th January, 1752:

Dear Miss,

Your two last Letters have affected me to a Degree not to be express'd, and the more so, as I see you are afflicted out of Measure, and almost beyond Consolation. But, my dear Miss, I must impeach you of Partiality to your own Disadvantage, and out of all Reason, and am positive you are severer to yourself than any body will, or any Jury can. Are you the first worthy Person that has been deluded and decoy'd by a worthless Man? No sure, nor will be the last. 'Tis true, I have neither your Capacity nor Experience, yet I have both heard and read of Persons of greater Abilities than either of us pretend to, who have been more grossly abused and imposed on than has yet appear'd in your Case. My dear Miss, I must conjure you to summon up all the Resolution and Philosophy, and what is more, your Innocence, which must acquit you to God and your own Conscience, if so, who or what have you to fear, or be so afflicted at? Lay aside this Gloominess, which is and ought only to be the Companion of Guilt; but you may, and I hope will enjoy many happy Days.

I am pleasing myself, when all is over, at the Happiness I shall enjoy in the Company and Conversation of a Person I have so great a Value for, and whom such odd Accidents have endear'd to one another. Dear Miss, if you would keep me in Spirits, keep up your own, for by a strange Sort of Sympathy I feel when you are cast down I can't keep up.

One of my Council was with me the other Day, who in discoursing of your Affair (in which I could not help expressing a more than common Concern) assured me, that as far as he yet could see, there was nothing either of us had to fear. Courage then, Madam; it would be no little Triumph to our Enemies to see us sink under their unjust Persecution, and which they would not fail to improve to our disadvantage, nay construe to be the Effect of downright Guilt. I shall be quite unhappy till I hear from you, which I beg may be as soon as possible; till you do, I am and can't be otherwise then

Yours Afflicted Friend, E.Jeffries

Mary Blandy gratefully replied and proposed a delightful plan for their future together when their freedom had been secured:

Oxford, Feb.3, 1752

Dear Miss,

Your last was a Cordial to my drooping Spirits, and like Balm to a desperate Wound. O how seasonable is Comfort, when administer'd by a friendly, a tender, and able Hand! I am ashamed of the Weakness I betrayed in my last; Your friendly Advice has had such an Effect as to reinstate my former Resolution and Composure, for, as you have justly observed, if we can acquit ourselves to God and our own Conscience, who, or what else have we to fear?

You will laugh when I tell you I have been planning out a Scheme for our future living together, when this Storm is over, being firmly persuaded we shall never part, for as our similar Misfortunes have brought us together, our Friendship will not suffer us to separate. I have a delightful Spot in my Eye, far from any Road or Bustle, which if you approve of, we will bid adieu to the World, and retire to, where with a well chosen Library, and a few select Friends, we may wear away an easy, innocent and agreeable Life here, and with less Interruption prepare for a better hereafter. I shall be quite unhappy, if you approve not to my Plan, for I have set my Heart on it and you, and sure I have good Reason for both. Till I hear from you I shall be

Your Impatient Friend, M.Blandy

Elizabeth Jeffries seemed keen on the idea of a retreat:

> Chelmsford, Feb. 6, 1752
>
> Dear Miss,
>
> How comes it to happen we think so alike? Sure one Spirit actuates us both. The very Retreat you writ of, I was wishing for and longing to enjoy. Young as I am, I have seen enough of the World, to despise it and all its Vanities, and shall think myself bless'd, doubly bless'd, in having such a Friend, Guardian, and Companion, for the Conduct of my future Life, and shall wholly resign myself to you (for I cannot be in better Hands) and leave every thing to your Direction.
>
> As to the Spot, I fancy you will not wish it to be near Henley, and I should not chuse it to be near Walthamstow; all other places are alike to me: And as to the Collection of Books, my poor Uncle, as he knew nothing of them himself, did not take the Care I could wish to recommend them to me; so that you will have a double Task, both to chuse the Books, and direct my Reading.
>
> Why did you touch on this dear, this desirable Retreat? You have thereby raised an Impatience I was an utter Stranger to before. I perpetually figure to myself our little Seat and Garden, our Evening and Morning Walks, our silent and entertaining Books, our useful and friendly Conservation: Thus Life will glide away with Ease and Innocence.
>
> I am, dear Miss, your's, etc. E.Jeffries

This rather pathetic fantasy continues in Mary Blandy's reply on 10th February, 1752:

> Dear Miss,
>
> You have such a lively Fancy, that if one gives you but a Hint, your imagination outstrips the Wind. I had hardly any Hopes of your Consent, or at least was in some Fear lest you should not approve my Scheme, when on the contrary, to my excessive Joy, you are in Raptures. Well, since you desire it, I shall take upon me to order every thing for our Retreat, for I think I may say without Vanity, I have some Taste in the Choice of Houses and Gardens as well as Books, assuring you, that as you would not chuse Walthamstow, so I never more can like Henley, no, the very Name is odious to me.
>
> The Place I have in View is an obscure but pleasant Village; the House

is at one End, small, but convenient, the Gardens not large, but rather useful than elegant, at the Bottom of which runs a little Brook, clear as Chrystal, in which you see Trout and other Natives of the watry Element glide and wantonly play, on the other side is a delightful Meadow, which yields a beautiful and extensive Prospect. I propose to have but one Servant and a Gardener, and I have a young Lady that will be very fond to make one among us; she is a Person of very great Worth, and though her Misfortunes are not so conspicuous as ours, yet she has undeservedly had her Share, which hereafter you will know more at large.

In this sweet Retreat, and with this Company, what Pleasures do I propose, being fully determined neither to visit nor be visited; for after what has happened to us, we can never expect to be on an equal footing with the rest of the World, and I believe neither of us would chuse to be insulted by it.

My Trial comes on the 3d of March, when I expect (nay, without bad Practices, it can't be otherwise} to be clear'd, after which, the Lady I spoke of and myself will come down to Chelmsford, and take you along with us, never I hope during Life to part. Your poor Servant and Fellow Sufferer must be taken Care of; If he is a Gardener, he might make one in our little Family, if not, I must interest myself in some Provision for him, for his Integrity and undeserved Sufferings. I continue, dear Miss,

Your's, sincerely, M.Blandy

The desperate notion of a fantasy retreat remains the topic of the following letter from Elizabeth, dated 15th February, 1752:

Dear Miss,

I am quite ravish'd at the Description you give of our little Retreat, as well as the Expectation of that Lady's Company you speak of. I shall call it my Paradise, and I am persuaded we shall all make use of our best Endeavours to render it so to each of us. As to visiting or being visited, I must agree with your Sentiment, tho' there are some few of my Relations I would except out of the general Exclusion, but that we shall settle at meeting.

You speak of your Trial with as much Coolness as if you had nothing at stake; but, my dear Miss, though I never doubted your Innocence, I can't help my Fear, for who can tell what a Prejudiced World, or a bias'd Jury may do? We see nothing more frequent than Persons confessing to Crimes that others had suffer'd for before. I do not say this to discourage you, only beg you would not be too secure. I hope you have a good Council, for which I conjure you to spare no Cost, and if you are short of Cash to command from me what you want. I can't say I find my Trial approach with the same Indifference you do your's, for I have a strange Despondence, and Foreboding, which I can neither account for, nor get clear of, but I have spared no cost for good Council both for myself and poor Swann, and each of them still give me good Hopes. O how impatient I am, until I hear there's a happy Conclusion made of your Affair, being, dear Miss,

Your's, affectionately, E. Jeffries

On 4th March, the day after Mary Blandy's trial, she wrote to Elizabeth Jeffries:

Dear Miss,

It is now all over, the Jury having been pleased to bring me in guilty. I can't but say my Trial was fair and candid, and if any have stretch'd in their Evidence I heartily forgive them, and I pray God may do so too. I have the Pleasure to tell you, that though I could be well content to live, yet I have no Fear at all to die. Innocence of Intention is what I shall maintain to the last Moment of my Life, and God, who knows my Heart, is my Witness. So I bless God I am in perfect Peace with all the World, even with that poor Wretch who has brought all this upon himself and me.

I pray God may forgive him, and open his Eye to Repentance in this World, before eternal Perdition overtake him in the next.

And now, dear Miss, I beg you would not grieve; I shall, I hope, be eternally happy soon, beyond the Reach of Malice, Envy, or Persecution.

I heartily thank you for all your Favours, particularly for the Offer of Cash you was pleased to make me; but I had no Occasion, my own little Fortune was more than sufficient for what I wanted, and if it had not, some of my Relations were generous enough to offer me their Assistance.

The Lady I wrote to you about will be down with you at your Trial, which I pray God may turn out to your Honour and Safety, and I should take it exceeding kind to see you both at Oxford before I die. So wishing you all Happiness in this World, as well as that to come, I am, dear Miss,

Your's, M. BLANDY

Two days later, Elizabeth Jeffries sent the following letter from Chelmsford Gaol:

Dear Miss,

My Uncle's sad Catastrophe did not shock me more than the News of your Affair, and the more so as I made myself sure you would be clear'd. Would to God I had died before the News had reached me. In vain you bid me not to grieve, it's not in my power to prevent it. O! had I that accursed Wretch that has been the Cause of all this, I could tear him in ten thousand Pieces. Why do you tell me of Life and Happiness, when the only Person I thought worth while to live for, is torn from me for ever. Pardon my Distraction, for I have vented Execrations against Judges, Jury, Evidence, Audience and all; why did they not rescue you from so unjust a Sentence? Ought they not to have hazarded their own Lives to save an innocent Person's, Dastards as they are! The only Comfort I am capable of is, that the royal Mercy will interpose, for were your Case properly represented to his Majesty, I am persuaded he would never so much as hesitate. O dear Miss, I am

Your distracted, inconsolable Friend, E. Jeffries

On 9th March, Mary wrote again to Elizabeth from Oxford Gaol:

Dear Miss,

For my Sake, for your own Sake, for your own Preservation, be more composed. As your Trial comes so soon, it's fitting you should have your Judgment cool and clear, and all perhaps little enough for your own Safety; for I have learnt by fatal Experience, that Innocence is not always sufficient Security: Besides, this Raving may, nay, must hurt yourself, but can neither serve your Friend, nor answer any End.

If this will make you easy, be assured I am so, never more so in my Life. It's true, there is Interest making for the royal Mercy, but whether it succeeds or not I am perfectly resigned, God's Will be done. I am more concerned and anxious about your Affair than my own, and I would again beg of you to behave with that Composure,

Calmness and Dignity, that is worthy of Innocence and a good Cause. Thus wishing and praying for a happy Issue, I am, while I live,

Your's, etc. M. Blandy

Elizabeth Jeffries's trial and conviction had taken place on 11th March at Chelmsford Assizes. Her next letter to Mary Blandy, dated 13th March, 1752, contained an astonishing confession that must have come as a terrible shock to Mary.

Madam,

How can I approach you whom I have abused, deceived, and imposed on, having all along represented myself as an innocent Person, when in my Conscience I knew I was the most horrid Hypocrite and Monster of Cruelty that ever existed. But now the Mask is torn off, and I am cast, justly cast for my Life, and condemned to die a shameful and ignominious Death. But Oh! What is that to what I feel! Hell and all its Horrors are let loose upon me, ten thousand Furies tear me to Pieces, and not a Ray. Not a Glimpse of Comfort can I have.

Wherever I look around me all is dark and horrible; Despair, eternal Despair and Perdition is my Portion. To be the sole Cause of drawing and involving poor unhappy Swann in the same Destruction, to insinuate, safely insinuate it was a Conspiracy and Contrivance of my innocent Relations to have me cut off, for the Sake of my Fortune, all or any of these Things is too much to bear. If you can forgive, pity, and pray for me, do' for I myself can hope for no Favour from either God or Man.

The Wretched and Miserable, E. Jeffries

Mary Blandy replied to this distressing letter on 16th March, 1752:

Dear Miss,

Your Letter gave me more Concern than your Doom, or indeed my own. But why these Agonies, why this Despair?

Your Crime is very great, but are not the Mercies and Merits of a blessed Saviour sufficient for the greatest of Sinners. Call in to your Assistance some pious and worthy Divine, who will give you his Prayers and proper Directions for Repentance, which (when sincere) is never rejected by a merciful God.

Your deceiving of me was a small Crime, it was deceiving yourself; for no Retreat, tho' ever so pleasant, no Diversions, no Company, no not Heaven itself, could have made you happy, with those Crimes unrepented of in your Breast. I heartily wish (and shall be a Suitor for you at the Throne of Mercy) that God may give you his Grace, and grant you Repentance and eternal Happiness.

M. BLANDY

Elizabeth Jeffries's reply, dated 19th March, 1752, was the last letter to pass between the two women:

Dear Madam,

You are all Goodness, so easy to forgive the vilest and most wretched Creature that ever lived, who had so grossly imposed on you. Whether God will forgive me I know not, but this I know, that I can never forgive myself. I took your Advice, and am assisted by two worthy Divines, who spare no Pains nor Prayers in my Behalf. How they will succeed with a justly incensed God, is much to be doubted, but I have reap'd this great Benefit and Advantage by their pious Labours, that I have more Composure, more Contrition (but still more Dejection of Spirit) than I thought I was capable of. I will now lay open my whole Soul to you (if possible to atone for my late Imposition) My Uncle, tho' a rich Man, was vulgar in his Manners, and brutal in his Passions, had no Religion nor Morals, and took great Pains to debauch mine, in which I blush to tell you he was too successful: Thus brought up, thus principled, what was not such a Wretch capable of doing, when threaten'd with Beggary and Want, as was my Case?

I say this not to excuse myself, or extenuate my Guilt; no, this is impossible, but I wish it may be a Warning to Parents or Guardians how they principle those under their Care, lest like my Uncle they reap the Fruit of their own Wickedness.

Now, dear Miss, as your Time is too precious for me to break in upon or interrupt, and myself have too great a Work before me to be diverted from, I bid you a last and eternal Adieu.

E. JEFFRIES

When one of the worthy 'lady visitors' who were drawn to make sanctimonious prison visits expressed surprise that Mary should correspond with Miss Jeffries, Mary remarked: 'I can't bear these over virtuous women. I believe that if ever the devil picks a bone it will be one of theirs.'

The Execution

The execution of Mary Blandy followed nine days after the hanging of Elizabeth Jeffries. It had originally been planned for Saturday 4th April, 1752, but as this date fell within Holy Week, it was thought 'improper and unprecedate' for it to go ahead. It was, therefore, postponed until Monday 6th April. The following account of the execution is from *A Genuine and Impartial Account of the Life of Miss M. Blandy*, published on April 9th, 1752, just three days later.

> She was attended daily by the Rev. Mr Swinton, before whom, there is no doubt, she behaved properly...

There followed reference to the ghostly music and strange phenomena that Mary professed to experiencing – fanciful stuff that the writer inferred Swinton also believed in most wholeheartedly.

> Some days before her execution, she said that she intended to speak at the tree, if she had spirits when she came there, but that she was afraid the sudden shock of seeing the gallows might be too much for her to withstand, and that her spirits might fail her, unless she had an opportunity of seeing it beforehand, which she did, as the reader will find hereafter.

> We are now arrived at the verge of this unfortunate's life; the day before her execution she receiv'd the Holy Sacrament of the Lord's Supper, and sign'd and deliver'd the following paper, in order to convince the world how much she had been imposed on and seduc'd.

> 'I, Mary Blandy, do declare, that I die in a full persuasion of the truth and excellency of the Christian religion, and a sincere, though unworthy, member of the Church of England. I do likewise hope for a pardon and remission of my sins, by the mercy of God, through the merits and mediation of Jesus Christ, my most blessed Lord and Saviour. I do also further declare, that I did not know or believe that the powder, to which the death of my dear father has been ascribed, had any noxious or poisonous quality lodged in it; and that I had no intention to hurt, and much less to destroy him, by giving him that

powder;[31] All this is true, as I hope for eternal salvation, and mercy from Almighty God, in whose most awful and immediate presence I must soon appear. I die in perfect peace and charity with all mankind, and do from the bottom of my soul forgive all my enemies, and particularly those who have in any manner contributed so, or been instrumental in bringing me to the ignominious death I am soon to suffer. This is my last declaration, as to the points therein contained; and I do most earnestly desire, that they may be published after my decease.

Witness my hand, MARY BLANDY

The pamphlet commented once more on the ghostly music Mary professed to have heard before describing the scene at her execution:

As a report had been universally spread that she would be executed on the Friday before, a very great concourse of people were got together upon the Castle Green, to be spectators to the execution. Miss went up several times into the room facing the Green, where she could view the great crowd of people about it; which she did with all the calmness and unconcern imaginable; and only said that she would not balk their expectations, tho' her execution might be deferred a day or two longer.

About ten o'clock on Sunday night, being informed that the Sheriff was come to town, she sent a message to him, to request that she might not be disturbed till eight in the morning, and that as soon after as he pleased she would be ready for the great task she had to undergo. Accordingly, about half an hour after eight, the Sheriff, with her attorney, and the Rev. Mr Swinton, went to the Gaol, and after half an hour's private prayers with the clergyman, she came down into the Gaol yard, where the Sheriff's men were, and held two guineas in her hands for the executioner, which she took with her to the fatal tree.

The night before her execution, she spent the chief of her time in prayers. She went to bed about the usual hour, and had a little rest in the fore part of the night, but was at prayers in bed between three and four o'clock; after ending of which, she got up and dress'd herself;

---

31 Mary was still able to protest her innocence on the brink of death as the three incriminating letters she had written to Captain Cranstoun were yet to be revealed.

and some time after this, went up into the upper rooms of the house to look at the gallows, which is opposite the door of the gaol, and made by laying a poll across upon the arms of two trees, when she observed that it was very high. She went out of the Castle about nine o'clock, attended by the Rev. Mr Swinton, dress'd in a black crape sack, with her arms and hands ty'd with black paduasoy ribbons, and her whole dress extremely neat; her countenance was solemn, and her behaviour well suited to her deplorable circumstances; but she bored up under her misfortunes with amazing fortitude.

When she came to the gallows Mr Swinton read several select prayers suitable for the occasion and then asked if she had anything to say to the populace? to which she answered, yes. She then begged the prayers of all the spectators, and declared herself guilty of administering the powder to her father, but without knowing that it had the least poisonous quality in it, or intending to do him any injury, as she hoped to meet with mercy at that great Tribunal before whom she should shortly appear...

As she ascended the ladder, after she had got up about five steps, she said, 'Gentlemen, do not hang me high, for the sake of decency.' And then being desired to step up a little higher, she did two stops, and then turning herself about, she trembled, and said, 'I am afraid I shall fall'.

After this, the halter was put about her neck, and she pulled down her handkerchief over her face, without shedding one tear all the time. In this manner she prayed a little while upon the ladder, then gave the signal, by holding out a little book which she had in her hands.

There was not a large concourse of people at the execution, but the most thinking part of them were so affected with her behaviour and deplorable circumstances, that they were in tears.

After hanging about half an hour the Sheriff gave orders for her being cut down. Thus far the utmost decorum was observed, but for want of some proper person to take care of her body, this melancholy scene became still more shocking to human nature. There was neither coffin to put her body in, nor hearse to carry it away; nor was it taken back to the Castle, which was only a few yards, but upon being cut down was carried through the crowd upon the shoulders of one of the Sheriff's men in the most beastly manner, with her legs exposed very indecently for several hundred yards, and then deposited in the Sheriff's man's house, 'till about half an hour past five o'clock, when the body was put in a hearse, and carried to Henley, where she was interred about one o'clock the next morning in the church [in the chancel, the oldest part of the church] between her father and mother, where was assembled the greatest concourse of people ever known upon such an occasion.[32] The funeral service was performed by the same clergyman as wrote the letter, dated the 7th of March to whom, among seven guineas which she left for seven rings [of the church bell] she bequeathed one of them.

A report on Mary's execution published in the *Newcastle Courant*, on Friday 16th August, 1878, stated that Mary had 'offered five guineas, without success, for a female executioner...'

It also reported that when 'she went out of the gaol she gave the sheriff's men a guinea for drink, and took two guineas with her for the executioner. Her behaviour at the gallows was becoming a person in her unhappy circumstances and drew not only great compassion, but tears from the spectators.

When she got up about five steps of the ladder, she said, "Gentlemen, I beg you will not hang me high, for the sake of decency" and being desired to go a little higher, she did two steps more, and then, turning herself on the ladder, had a little trembling, and said, "I am afraid I shall fall."

After she had turned herself upon the ladder, Swinton asked her if she had anything to say to the public.

Mary then declared for the last time that she was innocent of the death of her father (and strongly denied the rumour that she had caused the death of her mother as well). The report continues:

> ...and then desiring all present to pray for her, she pulled a white handkerchief, which was tied around her head for that purpose, over her eyes, which not being low enough, a person standing by stepp'd up the ladder and pulled it further down; then giving the signal, by

[32] The same report stated that the plate on the coffin was inscribed simply with M. Blandy, 1752. According to a report in *Reynolds's Newspaper*, dated Sunday, 18th July, 1869, Mary told the crowd that she forgave those who had turned against her and added; 'Good people, take warning by me to be on your guard against the sallies of any irregular passion, and pray for me that I may be accepted at the throne of grace.'

holding out a little book which she had in her hand, she was turned off.

The church of St Mary the Virgin and its curtilage, having undergone several changes since 1752, there is now no trace of the grave.

But what of Captain Cranstoun in the aftermath of the trial and execution of Mary, his partner in crime?

According to contemporary pamphlets, newspaper reports and the letter from Dunkirk read to the court at the beginning of the murder trial, when Mary was arrested and taken to Oxford Gaol, Cranstoun, with a warrant issued for his arrest, lay low for several months, either in Scotland or the North of England. On the 18th March, after Mary had been found guilty of parricide and sentenced to death, Cranstoun, under the name of Dunbar, (the maiden name of Mrs Ross, a relative who was also on the run from creditors in England) with the help of his influential family and friends, boarded a ship to Boulogne (some accounts said Calais) arriving on 27th March. As eleven days after Mary's conviction the War Office ordered the Paymaster General to strike Captain Cranstoun's name from the Half Pay list, he had to borrow the money, which he did not repay, to make his escape. He remained in France incognito, afraid that some of his wife's relatives who were serving in the army there would, no doubt, given the chance, have taken their revenge. He was funded in part by his brother, Lord Cranstoun, but still managed to cheat and lie to obtain fancy goods and avoid detection by both his creditors and the English law.

He stayed in Boulogne until mid-July when, with his companions, he travelled to Paris on foot. According to a pamphlet published in 1753,[33] whilst the friends were on the road they openly discussed the Captain's various amorous affairs and his relationship with

---

33 *The Genuine Lives of Captain Cranstoun and Miss Mary Blandy.* Printed for M. Cooper, Paternoster Row and C. Sympson, Chancery Lane, 1753. Price 1s.

Mary Blandy in particular. He admitted that when he first went to Henley he was told by other gentlemen in the area that it was well-known that Miss Blandy was in line to inherit a fortune and he was determined to acquire it by whatever means necessary - even the removal of her disapproving father. He also admitted that he had initially put a small amount of poison in Mr Blandy's tea to fool Mary into believing that it was merely a 'love-powder' and could do no harm. Later, however, seeing the effect of the contaminated gruel on two of her servants, she knew this to be false and was, thereafter, completely complicit in the plan to kill her father.

Cranstoun also boasted to his friends how Mary was pathetically trusting and gullible, giving him money whenever he needed it, even borrowing the £90 savings from old Susan Gunnell, which she was unable to pay back. On another occasion, on the death of the Prince of Wales, her father had given her twenty guineas to buy mourning clothes; she spent just £5 and sent the remainder to him in Scotland.

He even recalled persuading Mary to forgive him when he admitted he had a child with a Miss Capel and bragged still further about his ability to pacify Mary when she found the letter from his current mistress. From this account it seemed that Cranstoun was proud, not only of his treachery with regards to the women he seduced, but also about his various nefarious financial dealings.

Following the trip to Paris, Cranstoun travelled to Furnes, in Flanders, where he lived in a house known by the Sign of the Burgundy Cross. Whilst there, he was afflicted by a terrible illness during which, according to a subsequent report in *The London Magazine*, February, 1753, he suffered excruciating pain in every limb and joint and his stomach swelled to such a degree that 'it was thought by the physician and apothecary that attended him, that he would have burst, and by the great agonies he expired in, he was thought to be raving mad'.

He died in agony, aged forty-six, on 2nd of December, 1752. It was said that he felt he was cursed 'for injuring the character of so good a wife [Anne]'. Shortly before his death he was received into the Roman Catholic Church and was afforded a 'pompous' funeral.

'He was buried in great solemnity, the corporation [city dignitaries] attending the funeral, and a grand mass was said over the corpse in the cathedral church, which was fine illuminated, and in which he was buried.'

After his death, Captain Cranstoun's Will and other papers, including Mary's letters, were sent to his brother, Lord Cranstoun, in Scotland, and his fancy clothes and other belongings were sold to pay off some of his debts. His wife and daughter, then living in Hexham, received £75 a year, the interest on a legacy of £1,500 from his father in recompense for 'the Troubles and Vexations he had occasioned her'. He also felt that Mary Blandy had put too much blame on him for the death of her father; he referred to 'particulars' - probably the three incriminating letters he had received from Mary - which would only be known after his death.

The character of Mary Blandy is more difficult to fathom. She isn't as easily defined as the love-lorn eccentric, Christiana Edmunds, or the 'unfortunate' Sarah Gale (who also feature in this book). The incriminating letters sent to Captain Cranstoun clearly show that the murder of her father was planned by Mary and her lover and carried out with determination to rid themselves of any resistance to their relationship. It was the volatile desperation of the affair with Cranstoun that deteriorated into a toxic alliance that ended in death. Had she not become so obsessed with Captain Cranstoun she might well have accepted the fact that she would remain a spinster and, after her mother's death, automatically fall into the role of nurse and companion to her aging father. Was this convenient scenario already in Francis Blandy's mind, selfishly hoping to keep her to himself to comfort him in his dotage?

Yet Mary had other ideas and was fast losing patience with her father's procrastination and parsimony Her anger and resentment towards her father was understandable for every time she came close to marriage, he put a stop to it by reneging on his promise to provide her with a large inheritance. Though Francis Blandy was considered by some to be a commendable character it is evident that he could also be devious, boastful and stingy, vastly overestimating his worth and not a man of his word whilst presenting a benevolent image to his cronies.

He may also have been a martinet in the home, bullying Mrs Blandy over finances - she was afraid to admit to him that she owed money and even mentioned his ill-use of her on her deathbed. Mary also commented upon his cantankerous nature and bouts of vindictive verbal abuse. Yet articles in the newspapers reporting on the case depicted him as 'a gentleman of the strictest honour, a most tender Husband, an indulgent Father, and a Sincere friend.' but it was often the case that gentlemen of a certain status in society were usually described in these sycophantic, glowing terms whereas lesser mortals - usually the poor – were often described in derogatory terms, banded together as miscreants or 'ne'er do wells'. The press loved to lace its prose with sanctimonious religious dogma, with its emphasis on sin, repentance and the horrors of hellfire – punitive rhetoric guaranteed to fan the flames of outrage and disgust in its readers. By depicting Francis Blandy as a paragon of fatherly devotion, it allowed the reading public full rein to be suitably shocked by Mary's most terrible and unforgivable crime - parricide.

Indeed, there were no lengthy debates in the newspapers as to her guilt or innocence as there would be in the case of Eliza Fenning.[34] Nor were petitions set up and an appeal for a reprieve lodged with the Home Secretary. In fact, there were even spurious suggestions that she had also poisoned both her mother and the family friend, Mrs Pocock, which seems most unlikely as both women were in favour of Mary's relationship with the Captain.

As for William Henry Cranstoun, the other deadly player in this

---

34 In 1815, Eliza Fenning, a young cook/maid, was executed for attempting to poison members of the Turner family for whom she worked in Chancery Lane. She proclaimed her innocence to the end and there followed a plethora of newspapers articles and letters from the public debating her guilt or innocence. Petitions and appeals for a reprieve were rejected. A detailed study of the case can be found in the author's book, *Bad Companions*.

drama - how can one begin to fathom the fatal attraction that Mary Blandy felt for him, a passion so strong that she seems to have lost all reason?

It may be true that for some women a man in uniform can turn their heads and in the 18th century members of the militia were certainly dressed to impress - the brightly coloured, lavishly braided coats and fancy waistcoats, embroidered in silk, were fashioned to accentuate the broad shoulders and narrow waists of the wearer. Moreover, the tight fitting breeches were cut to expose a shapely calf considered to be an attractive attribute. Yet this manner of dress was commonplace at the time and therefore in no way as exotic as it might appear to a modern woman – no more or less attractive than the khaki uniform worn by the military of today. The mode of dress for women with money or status was equally elaborate and flamboyant as illustrated by the contemporary drawings of Mary Blandy in gaol, wearing a sumptuous dress even though her left leg was adorned with a heavy leg iron which, incidentally, is now on public display at Oxford Castle.

Yet the contemporary descriptions of Cranstoun as puny, with small squinty eyes, a 'seamed' face and an ungainly gait were far from flattering. The presence of the pockmarks on his face would have been shared by many in the eighteenth century who were lucky enough to have survived the ravages of smallpox, including Mary Blandy; blemishes such as these would not have been remarkable or necessarily repugnant. Indeed, in the modern world some highly successful entertainers have enjoyed matinee idol status despite having complexions that clearly showed the ravages of acne suffered in their youth. One would have thought, however, that the evident flaws in Captain Cranstoun's character would have been much more difficult to ignore. Yet Mary was so besotted with him that, as reported in the *Newcastle Courant*, in 1878:

> He, notwithstanding his professions of love for her, had an illegitimate child, and was obliged to maintain it. Yet such was the violence of her passion that though she knew it to be true, it did not in the least damp the fire of her love, for she contributed all in her power to

its maintenance, as she did for the support of him who proved the greatest villain upon earth.

To finance her lover, Mary even had the gall to borrow - and not pay back - the life savings of the old maidservant, Susan Gunnell. It was clear from their testimony in court that Mary was not popular with the servants and blamed her downfall on the gossip and rumours they had spread about her after her father's death. They were probably the source of the rumours about her drinking habits, use of foul language and un-ladylike behaviour referred to by the judges at her trial and also by Mary herself in the account she wrote while imprisoned at Oxford Castle gaol. Did they find Mary haughty and spoiled? In its article on the coroner's inquest, the *Derby Mercury*, dated 6th December, informed its readers that:

> About Eight o'Clock that Night, Miss called for supper; and they not to put too much Confidence in their Mistress, since he might think it her Interest to poison them all. 'Servants not carrying it up so soon as she expected, she d----n'd them, and behaved very confidently, and in such a manner, that they were frightened, and could hardly be prevailed upon to go to her. It seems Dr Addington had given Caution not to put too much Confidence in their Mistress, since he might think it her Interest to poison them all.

As a family the Blandys did, however, retain their servants into old age - the ancient retainers, Susan Gunnell and Ann Emmet, for instance - although this may have been from convenience rather than sentiment. It is perhaps significant that both these old women seemed accustomed to partake of any food and drink left over which might indicate that their own rations were meagre by comparison with those enjoyed by the family.

Mary and Captain Cranstoun indulged in a remarkable degree of personal contact for a courting couple in 1750 - perhaps not approved of by the gossiping maids. Her parents, it must be said, were extremely lenient, allowing such freedom while Cranstoun was a guest in their home. In view of such intimacy, it could be that, in Mary's mind at least, she was married, though not legally.[35] Nor was

---

35 An article in *The London Magazine* stated that 'he and Miss Blandy were

she averse to being entertained by various gentlemen. In an extract from *Reynolds's Newspaper* it said that 'she was eagerly sought after by recruiting officers and other military adventurers who obtained access to the paternal domicile and, according to common report, flirted more than strict modesty allowed...'

Indeed, Captain Cranstoun was often in her bedroom till the early hours (supposedly listening for ghostly noises while the maid was fast asleep) and, on one occasion flinging himself on the bed pleading for forgiveness from Mary when she found out about one of his other women. They also enjoyed many un-chaperoned country walks in Henley and it was apparently deemed acceptable for the two lovers to meet in Mrs Pocock's house in St James's Square when in London, which far exceeded the licence usually given to courting couples in the eighteenth century.

Clearly, Cranstoun was an expert in the art of seduction and his sexual prowess may well have been remarkable in order to sustain such a passionate attachment of some six years, with no real probability of matrimony.

Finally, the promise of a £10,000 dowry that Cranstoun believed had been settled on Mary may well have been an incentive at the start of the relationship; however, when the Commissary of Scotland decreed that Anne Murray was his legal wife, he must have known that, as long as she remained alive, there was no way he could have married Mary Blandy legitimately and thereby receive the £10,000. One wonders why, if financial gain had been his prime incentive, he didn't abandon Mary, as he had done with some of his other mistresses. Could it be that, with Mary's connivance - she being so tired and resentful of her father's lies and mealy-mouthed stinginess – Cranstoun had, from the start, decided to seduce Mary into killing her father, as the only way they could, at least, be together and enjoy her inheritance.

Perhaps Mary, too, was of a mercenary nature? If the money was not important to her she could easily have gone to Scotland with

privately married before the death of her mother, which was near two years before Mr Blandy was poisoned.'

Cranstoun and lived with him and his mother, Lady Cranstoun, who seemed favourable to the idea.

Was it Mary who was holding out for her father's money, reluctant to make the break from him and thereby so enraging him that he would cut her off without a penny? The report in the *Derby Mercury* referred to the scene in Oxford Gaol when Mary was awaiting trial in which she was angry that her father's assets were far less than he had led everyone to believe and, furthermore, his estate had passed to her uncle. Throughout her life, as an only child, she had been indulged by her doting parents, waited on by servants and had become accustomed to a high standard of living. She may, therefore, have been loath to give it all up - far better to claim both prizes - her lover, Captain Cranstoun, and her father's supposed fortune? The plot to poison Mr Blandy hatched between the two lovers provided a solution – Mary would inherit his money and be free to join Cranstoun as his common-law wife without restriction or condemnation. What is extraordinary is that someone of Mary Blandy's intelligence should imagine that she could poison her father and get away with it, especially under the prying eyes of the servants.

We cannot know whether the tears shed by Mary during her father's final days - especially when the old man forgave her for poisoning him - were genuine or not, but ultimately, her love for Cranstoun was greater than that for her father.

Mary showed courage at the gallows though we cannot know whether, by this time, she had grown to hate Cranstoun for his cowardice in leaving the country and allowing the woman he professed to have loved so dearly to bear the terrible punishment for their crime alone. If she had at last realised his callow perfidy what a pity she never knew that he died in agony and in exile within eight months of her own ignominious death.

On Monday, 20th April, 1752, just two weeks after Mary's execution, the pamphlet entitled, *Miss Mary Blandy's Own Account of*

the Affair between her and Captain Cranstoun, was widely advertised in the press; 'published at her dying Request' Price 1s.6d. The advertisement ended with a note: 'The original account may be seen with A.Miller, London, the publisher.'

Horace Walpole mentioned the cases of Mary Blandy and Elizabeth Jeffries in several letters to friends. On 28th August, 1752, he sent a letter to George Montague, in which he wrote:

> I have since been with Mr Conway at Park Place, where I saw the individual Mr Cooper, a banker [died 1768, aged eighty] and lord of the manor of Henley, who had those two extraordinary forfeitures from the executions of the Misses Blandy and Jefferies, two fields from the former, and a malthouse from the latter. I had scarce credited the story, and was pleased to hear it confirmed by the very person...

Over the years the case of Mary Blandy has been studied in numerous books and articles, one of which, published in *Reynolds's Newspaper*, some 117 years later, on Sunday, 18th July, 1869, retold the whole story from beginning to end.

Again, 126 years after the event, the *Newcastle Courant*, of Friday, 16th August, 1878, recalled the case in some detail, including a description of Mary in court, which must have come from a contemporary witness account.

Another account, originally published in the *Cornhill Magazine*, and reprinted in the *Shields Daily Gazette*, on 29th May, 1882, bore the heading, *An Eighteenth Century Tragedy*. It ended with the following paragraph describing her execution:

> ...in spite of her moving conduct, however, the "prejudices she had to struggle with had taken too deep a root in some men's minds" to allow of her getting a pardon [which was not possible as murder carried a mandatory death sentence]. And so, 5,000 people saw poor Miss Blandy mount the ladder in a black bombazine, short sack, and petticoat, on an April morning at Oxford, and many, "particularly several gentlemen of the University" were observed to shed tears. She left a declaration of innocence which, in spite of its solemnity, must have been a lie...

An article in the *Evening Telegraph*, dated 2nd April, 1922, erroneously informed its readers that Mary Blandy in court was

> ...robed in white, and bearing an immense nosegay, captivating a whole Court by her sweet and innocent face, for five days [in fact, only one day] she listened while her life hung in the balance. Eventually, after a savage summing up by the senior Judge, she was sentenced to death. She spent her last hours preparing a robe of death, and went to the scaffold clad in black silk bombazine, whilst in her hand she carried an immense prayer-book.

And so it seems that writers and their readers have retained their interest in the case of Miss Mary Blandy, not only in books and articles but also in theatre enactments and radio plays in the years since her death. Inevitably, of course, there have been rumours of ghostly sightings connected with her - the usual manifestations, laced with the romanticism of folklore - distressed damsels in flowing white frocks and suchlike.

As early as 4th August, 1753, in a letter that Horace Walpole had sent to John Chute, he writes - possibly with his tongue firmly in his cheek - of strange goings-on in the now empty Blandy House, in Hart Street:

> The town of Henley has been extremely disturbed with an engagement between the ghosts of Miss Blandy and her father, which continued so violent, that some bold, persons, to prevent further bloodshed, broke in, and found it was two jackasses which had got into the kitchen.

Not surprisingly, considering the enduring interest in the case of Mary Blandy, there have been many other reports of hauntings at Blandy House, at Oxford Castle and both the Bell and the Angel public houses, none of which, of course, have been substantiated with audio recordings or photographic evidence. There is even a website with the heading 'Mary Blandy is Innocent'.

Elizabeth Jeffries and John Swan

'We that are true lovers run into strange capers'

We are familiar with some aspects of Elizabeth Jeffries's life through reading the letters she wrote to Mary Blandy while they were both waiting to be executed. She barely refers to her life before she murdered her uncle, Mr Joseph Jeffries (sometimes given as Jeffryes or Jeffriess) although, in her last letter to Mary, dated 19th March, 1752, nine days before her execution, she was quite specific about the reason behind the hatred that drove her to kill him.

From accounts in the *Newgate Calendar* and various contemporary newspaper reports it appears that Elizabeth was born in July 1727, in Bridgnorth, Shropshire, of 'very honest Parents'. Her father was a boat-builder, and 'she had many relatives in Bewdley, Worcestershire'.

When she about five years old she was adopted by her childless uncle, Mr Joseph Jeffries, who lived in Walthamstow. He was a wealthy man and, having made his fortune as a butcher in London, he was able to provide his young niece with a comfortable home and an education at a local boarding school for girls. In addition, he made out his will in her favour by which she stood to inherit a substantial legacy.

It was alleged that Joseph Jeffries abused his young niece from the age of fifteen, though whether the abuse was physical, mental or sexual was not made absolutely clear until *after* the subsequent trial. Shortly before her execution Elizabeth said that he had 'ill used' her though this may have referred to discipline she considered excessively harsh. It was only in her final letter to Mary Blandy that she admitted there had been sexual abuse, a claim later collaborated by a letter from someone who knew the family and had contacted the press.

If these allegations were true it is little wonder that, as she reached adolescence, she became so resentful and rebellious that her uncle threatened to change his will if her behaviour did not improve. She later admitted that her resentment against her uncle festered to the extent that for two years she had contemplated murdering him. She eventually hatched a plan that would involve the help of John Swan, one of her uncle's servants. He was about twenty-seven years old, born in rural Cambridgeshire, where his father was a brick-maker. Described as tall and very good-looking, for a while Swan followed in the same trade; he married at twenty and had a daughter although his wife had died about five years before the murder.

It was rumoured that Elizabeth and John Swan were lovers or, as it was also suggested, she cajoled him into carrying out the murder with the promise of sexual favours, though the former seems more likely. Between them they decided to shoot Joseph Jeffries and make it look like a botched burglary, one that had escalated into murder. To this end they hid some silver and other valuables in a sack and threw it into one of the ponds near the house. Once Jeffries was dead, the plan was to raise the alarm and report a break-in some hours later.

They managed to persuade another of Mr Jeffries's servants - a casual labourer of low intelligence called Thomas Matthews, who had only been working for him for four days - to join in the plan by offering him one hundred pounds. Such a sum represented a veritable fortune to a casual worker like Matthews, who lived from hand to mouth, and he agreed to help them, but only 'in an honest way'. Confronted with this unforeseen moralistic response John Swan joined in the negotiations with an offer of £700 with the result that Matthews was successfully drawn into the murder plot. Swan gave him half a guinea to buy a brace of pistols. The plan was to meet in the pantry of the Jeffries's house at ten o'clock on the evening of Tuesday 3rd July, 1751. Arriving at the house as planned and finding the latch on the garden door open, Matthews hid behind a tub in the pantry and Swan subsequently brought him some cold boiled beef. As an itinerant worker he was probably on the road for much of the time and was grateful for some food.

According to the *Newgate Calendar* account, about midnight John Swan said to him: 'Now it is time to knock the old miser, my master, on the head.'

At this point, however, Matthews lost his nerve and refused to join in the killing, saying, 'I cannot find it in my heart to do it'. Elizabeth was furious and cursed him, saying, 'You may be damned for a villain, for not performing your promise!'

Accepting the set-back, John Swan made Matthews promise not to speak of the murderous plot 'unless it was to save his own life'.

Thomas Matthews said later that as he was leaving the house that night he heard a gun shot before hurrying off in the direction of Enfield Chase, anxious to clear some distance between him and the scene of the crime as quickly as possible.

When the supposed robbery and murder was investigated it became clear that there hadn't been any forced entry into the house and it was an 'inside job'. Elizabeth and Swan were arrested and when questioned, implicated Matthews, but as he could not be found, they were released - only to be re-arrested when Matthews was found some four months later.

On 1st November, 1751, the *Derby Mercury*, reported:

> We hear that the Person sworn to be a material Witness for the Prosecution against Miss Jeffries and John Swan and upon whose Account of whose Absence their Trial was put off at the last Essex Assizes, was apprehended in London on Thursday last, upon the warrant of the Worshipful Justice Altham, a worthy Magistrate for

the County of Essex, and after a very strict Examination, was by the said Gentleman committed to Barking Gaol; And altho' several persons deposed before the said Gentleman, that they heard the said Person say that he knew who murdered the said Mr. Jeffries, better than those that were in Chelmsford Gaol, yet he denies ever having said such Words, and insists, if he did say them, he was either drunk or mad.

After Thomas Matthews had been questioned and made his statement he was taken into custody and both Elizabeth Jeffries and John Swan were taken to Chelmsford Gaol to await their trial for murder. As Matthews's attempt to abscond had delayed the trial it had to be re-scheduled for the next Lent Assizes, due in the spring of 1752, with the result that Elizabeth Jeffries and John Swan had to remain in Chelmsford Gaol for a further eight months.

The Trial

The trial was opened on Wednesday 12th March, 1752, in Chelmsford, Essex, before two High Court Judges - Hon. Sir Martin Wright and Sir Michael Foster. The prosecution counsel consisted of Mr Harvey, Mr Bertie, Mr Hatsell, Mr Cox, Mr Gascoyne and Mr Lacy. Mr Robinson and Mr Knowler were representing the accused. John Swan was charged with Petty Treason 'for the cruel and wicked murder of his late master' and Elizabeth Jeffries was charged with 'aiding, helping, assisting, comforting and maintaining the said John Swan to commit the murder'.[36]

Before any witnesses were called the circumstances of the murder of Joseph Jeffries were summarised for the all-male jury and members of the court. He was depicted as a self-made and kindly man who had indulged Elizabeth, his niece, providing her with a home and a very comfortable lifestyle. He was also portrayed as a fair master to

---

36 The same charge was made against Sarah Gale – see chapter 4 – for aiding and betting the murder of Hannah Brown by her partner, James Greenacre, in 1837. The 'doctrine of common purpose' was applied to Edith Thompson, in 1922, who was hanged even though it was her lover, Frank Bywaters, who actually stabbed her husband to death.

his servants, rhetoric that was contrived to make the couple's killing of Joseph Jeffries particularly barbarous and unforgivable. It was a crime that was inconsistent with 'all the Notions of Justice and common Humanity.'[37]

As to the relationship between the two defendants in the dock it was remarked that 'the Manner of Life that passed between him [John Swan] and Miss. Jeffries was by no means honourable.' The court heard that 'they did often converse together in a very improper Manner' [criminal conversation was a euphemism for sexual intercourse outside marriage] and indulged in the excessive consumption of alcohol.

The prosecution then produced several witnesses, most of whom were close neighbours of the murdered man. The first to be called was Mr Edward Buckle who told the court that he lived about thirty yards from Mr Jeffries's house and in the early hours of 4th July, he was awoken by the sound of Elizabeth Jeffries repeatedly crying out, 'Oh! They have killed him, I fear!' She was outside a neighbour's house wearing just a shift, 'without shoe or stocking'. She rejected Mr Buckle's suggestion that she put on some clothes, saying, 'Don't mind me, see after my uncle.'[38]

When Mr Buckle reached Mr Jeffries's house it was John Swan who unbolted the door from the inside; he was wearing just a shirt and said: 'Go up and see my master, whom I fear some cruel rogues have killed.'

Entering the bedroom, Mr Buckle found Joseph Jeffries lying on his right side with three wounds to the left side of his head. To ascertain whether he was conscious he urged him to squeeze his hand if he could not speak. Elizabeth, still seemingly very agitated, asked Mr Buckle to go and notify the authorities about the atrocity so that the murderers might be apprehended. She also thought that if he made known which items had been stolen from the house there might be

---

37 From *The Genuine trial of John Swan and Miss Elizabeth Jeffreys* published in Dublin, 1752.
38 Unless otherwise stated all quotes are from a contemporary pamphlet: *The Only True and Authentic Trial of John Swan and Miss Elizabeth Jeffries, for the MURDER of her Uncle, Mr. Joseph Jeffries, of Walthamstow, in Essex.*

a chance of recovering them. She suggested he took another man with him, possibly insinuating that the 'cruel rogues' were still in the area. It was estimated that a silver cup, a tankard and fifteen pewter plates were missing.

Another neighbour, Mrs Mary Adams, stated that she had heard the sound of a pistol shot at about half past two that morning but the alarm was not raised by Elizabeth until about three quarters of an hour later. She went into the house and saw the body of Joseph Jeffries but couldn't stay long as she was heavily pregnant at the time. As she helped Elizabeth put on her shoes she drew attention to her injured ankle, which she said was caused by jumping from her bedroom window when she thought the house was on fire.

At this point in the proceedings, Thomas Matthews, the third person involved in the murder of Joseph Jeffries, was called to give evidence. Described in the press as a 'poor simple fellow', he explained that he had first met Joseph Jeffries and John Swan in Epping Forest. As a casual labourer who walked from place to place looking for odd jobs, he agreed to work for Mr Jeffries for nine days in exchange for food and a roof over his head. Elizabeth Jeffries, John Swan, a maid and a young child were also living in the house at the time. When he left, Mr Jeffries gave him a shilling. After leaving, he managed to find a few days' work at the home of a Mr Hughes, in Wood Street, Walthamstow.

Asked to tell the court how he became involved in the plot to murder Joseph Jeffries, Matthews explained that while he was working for him, he was told to go upstairs to clean a chest of drawers and some chairs. Elizabeth followed him and asked what he would do for a hundred pounds; he replied that he would be willing to do anything 'in an honest way'. She then sent him down to the garden where John Swan took him into an outhouse and offered him seven hundred pounds if he would 'knock the old miser on the head'. Elizabeth joined them and said that she could not 'have a moment's peace while that miser was living' and she would make sure the money was paid if he, Matthews, did as they asked.

Although he had no further conversation with Elizabeth about the murderous proposition, John Swan had taken him drinking in the Duke's Head, in Wood Street, Walthamstow, and then, a couple of days later, he gave him half a guinea 'to buy a case of pistols, on purpose to shoot Mr Jeffries as he came back from Chelsea along with one Mr Gallant'.

According to some accounts Matthews handed over the pistols although others stated that he spent the money drinking in the Green Man, in Walthamstow. Keen to get him back, John Swan gave chase, overtaking him on the road. After cursing Matthews, he took him to the Green Man and Bell, in Whitechapel. Swan was at that time 'almost drunk' and ordered half a pint of wine after which they stayed there drinking beer until eleven o'clock that night. Then Swan suddenly got up and challenged a man to a fight for a guinea. Matthews, also drunk, stripped off, eager to join in the punch-up but the lining of Swan's coat, thrown over a chair, was scorched by the fire. When the coat was picked up two pistols were discovered in the pockets, which suggests that Matthews did, in fact, purchase the pistols and hand them over to Swan. There were also three earrings which Swan said he was going to pawn for Elizabeth. The landlord, Mr John Gall, alerted the authorities and the two men were taken by the Watch - a man authorised to sort out drunken disputes and minor crimes in the neighbourhood - and put into the Cage, a single cell lock-up, for the night.

The following morning they were brought before the magistrate, Sir Samuel Gower, and after he had questioned the two men he sent them to Bridewell[39] where they remained for twenty-four hours. With both men in gaol and fearing that the planned murder was no longer possible, Elizabeth Jeffries hired a coach in Walthamstow and arrived in London to plead on their behalf; she explained that she had given the earrings to Swan to pawn and the pistols belonged to a gentleman who had undertaken a long journey and they were on their way to be cleaned. Both men were released without charge. Elizabeth gave Thomas Matthews a shilling and he immediately went back to the pub. She brought with her a man called Thomas Smith,

---

39 Bridewell Hospital and Prison, Clerkenwell.

whose presence was not fully explained but he seems to have been acting as an intermediary between John Swan and Joseph Jeffries so that, despite the latter's displeasure at the intimacy between his niece and Swan, some sort of compromise might be reached.

Thomas Matthews continued to relate various drinking sessions and drunken arguments between himself and John Swan - clearly Swan was keeping a close watch on Matthews in case he disappeared again before the murder was done. The crucial meeting between the three conspirators came about one afternoon a week before the murder, near Walthamstow Church, when the plan to kill Joseph Jeffries was finalised - he, Matthews, was to come to the house on the night of 3rd July, at ten o'clock. The garden door would be left open. However, when Matthews arrived he waited for some two hours outside the garden gate thinking it was locked but, in fact, it was only on the latch. He went into the pantry and hid behind a tub until Swan brought him some cold beef. At about midnight both Swan and Elizabeth came down to speak to him. Elizabeth said, 'Now's the time to knock your master on the head.' When he said he didn't have the heart to do it, Elizabeth cursed him and Swan threatened to 'blow his brains out'. The other two, intent on carrying out the murder with or without Matthews, made him swear 'on a book' that he would never speak of the matter unless his life was in danger. Elizabeth and Swan went upstairs and, half an hour later, Matthews heard a pistol shot. Hurrying from the house he made his way to London after which he went down to Kent where he 'stayed all the harvesting'.

Thomas Matthews then informed the court that John Swan had told him that Joseph Jeffries had to be killed because Elizabeth was pregnant and if he found out they would both be banished from the house.[40] Not surprisingly, Swan chose not to mention the fact of

---

40 There was no evidence that this was true. Indeed, if it had been she would have given birth during the eight months she was incarcerated in Chelmsford Gaol awaiting trial - or at least appeared in the dock heavily pregnant, which was not the case. At the end of a murder trial proof of pregnancy deferred execution of the mother until after the birth of the child. A number of women facing a death sentence claimed to be pregnant - Charlotte Harris, Christiana Edmunds, Sarah Malcolm, Kate Webster and others - hoping to escape the gallows and perhaps ultimately succeed in obtaining a pardon.

Mr Jeffries's will by which Elizabeth stood to inherit his fortune on his death.

When challenged by the defence counsel it became abundantly clear that Thomas Matthews was an habitual liar, a drunk and a totally unreliable witness.

A surgeon, Dr Thomas Forbes, testified that between three and four o'clock on the morning of the murder John Swan had arrived at his house on horseback urging him to accompany him back to the house.[41] When he arrived and examined Mr Jeffries he found a bullet wound to the left side of his head and a four inch deep cut to the right ear. There was a sharp pointed knife on the floor but he noted that Swan was wearing a clean shirt with no traces of blood on it.

Next called to give evidence was the maid, Sarah Arnold, who told the court that she had lived in the house for four years and John Swan had been a live-in servant for about two years. On the day of the murder Mr Jeffries had been entertaining guests - his apothecary, Mr Clifton, and his wife and his daughter-in-law, Mrs Martin, and her two children. They had gone out for afternoon tea at the Royal Oak after which Mrs Martin and the children returned to the house for supper. Swan, already slightly drunk, had been waiting at table and, no doubt, desperate for the guests to leave but as they were still there at midnight Elizabeth had to persuade her uncle to see his guests on their way and go to bed. He instructed the maid to lock all the doors and then went up to his room. The maid did as she was told and then followed Elizabeth upstairs. Elizabeth, she said, slept in a room 'divided from her uncle's by a very thin partition, which had a hole in it, and Swan lay on the same floor'.

Sarah had not heard a pistol shot but was woken by the noise made by Elizabeth who was standing in the yard below. Told by Swan that thieves had broken in, she went to her master's bedroom and found him 'lying on his back, his legs drawn up, and rattling in his throat, and putting her hand on his wounds, she found the blood quite

---

41 In the nineteenth century surgeons, as opposed to physicians, were unqualified medical practitioners not far removed from Barber-Surgeons. However, for the sake of clarity, all general medical practitioners will be referred to as Dr throughout the book.

congealed'. Her master's knife, which had been left on the bench by the garden door, was by the bedside but was not bloodstained. There were some defence wounds to his left hand. She and Swan both remarked on the fact that one of Joseph Jeffries's pistols that used to hang over the fireplace in the kitchen was missing and there were fragments of bullets on the kitchen floor.

Asked about the relationship between her master and his niece, Sarah said that he was not pleased with the intimacy between Elizabeth and John Swan and often threatened to change his will if her behaviour did not improve. The will was always kept in a small metal box by his bedside but, on the morning of the murder, it was missing.

The next witness was Joseph Jeffries's barber, Mr Anthony Gallant, who said that he had a meeting with Elizabeth about a week before the murder in which she had asked him to take her uncle on a trip to Bucket's Hill and get him drunk, promising to reimburse him for any money he spent. She told him she would soon have money and offered him two or three guineas to get her uncle drunk and keep him out all night as when he was in that state 'he did not use to enquire after her'.

When he called at the house a couple of days after the murder Elizabeth 'threw herself into a chair, crying out, 'Oh! I shall die a worser death than my uncle!"

A surgeon, Dr James Thornton, was next to be brought into the witness box and described how a man-servant had fetched him at about three o'clock on the morning of the murder. He said that Joseph Jeffries had lost a great deal of blood, mainly from the knife wound by his right ear which had severed a small artery. He estimated that this injury had been inflicted at least an hour before. When he had asked Elizabeth why she hadn't alerted the neighbours straight away she explained that she had been asleep and dreaming that the house was on fire. When she woke up she heard 'four fellows run down stairs, cursing and swearing, saying, "Now we have done all the mischief we can, let us set the house on fire." Frightened, she had leapt out of bed and jumped from her bedroom window to the yard below.

Mr William Scowley, a coach driver, came next and described driving Elizabeth Jeffries from Walthamstow to Whitechapel where she persuaded the magistrate, Sir Samuel Gower, to release John Swan and Thomas Matthews from custody after their arrest for drunkenness and possession of the earrings and pistols. On the way back Elizabeth, Swan and Smith travelled inside the coach, while Matthews had to walk behind. Both men were made to get out of the coach about a hundred yards from Mr Jeffries's house which may have indicated that both men, especially John Swan, were not welcome in the house.

Mr John Gall, the landlord of the Green Man and Bell, in Whitechapel, described the evening Swan and Matthews - who he referred to as 'a ragged Rascal' - were drinking there and a fight was about to start when Swan's coat got burned and the pistols were discovered in the pockets. He then related Elizabeth Jeffries's intercession on behalf of the two men, insisting that the earrings belonged to her and the pistols were being cleaned for a gentleman who had been on a long journey.

Mr John Mills informed the court that about six o'clock on the day of the murder Swan came to his house on the Stratford coach and called for a gill of rum. He mentioned the murder at Walthamstow and said that 'the niece' had jumped from the bedroom, three storeys up. Three hours later, when the coach stopped for the horses to drink, Swan 'seemed very much in liquor, quite stupid, and did not stir or speak all the time the coach staid'.

When questioned, Mr Jeffery Mead - it was not made clear whether he was a constable on duty or simply another neighbour trying to help - said he went to the house that morning and checked to see if there were any signs of a break-in but found none. He asked Swan to fetch two men and some rakes so they could search the ponds. A sack was dredged up containing some pewter and brass. When Elizabeth Jeffries was apprehended she told him she had given Mrs Martin, her uncle's daughter-in-law, bank notes worth £500 and a bond worth £500 - and, as she climbed into the coach she 'put her hand into her bosom and pulled out a £100 Bank Note' and gave it to Mrs Martin to be divided between her children.

Mrs Elizabeth Gallant, who was also at the house after the murder, swore that she had heard Elizabeth Jeffries order Mrs Buckle to fetch a box of papers - referring to the will - from her uncle's bedroom, put it in her own bedroom and lock the door.

Mr Richard Clarke testified that about three months before the murder Swan had asked him if he was a good shot; if so he could get him £50 and a horse, an offer that he declined.

The landlord of The Green Man, in Walthamstow, said he and Mr Tipping, an apothecary, went to Joseph Jeffries's house when they heard about the attack. He said to Mr Jeffries, who was still alive, 'If you think you know who did the murder hold up your hand, with that he held up his left hand; he was dabbing his wounds with his handkerchief, but as soon as this was mentioned of holding up his hand, he dropt his handkerchief and held up his hand.'

That ended the case for the prosecution and it must have been evident to members of the jury that, in fact, any evidence against the two accused was purely circumstantial.

The prisoner's defence counsel then addressed the prisoners in the dock: 'You have heard what has been charged against you, now is your time to make your defence.'

To this, John Swan replied, 'I leave it to my council [sic]'.

Asked if she had any witnesses to call in her defence, Elizabeth answered: 'I conclude most of them are perjured. I will leave my cause to be pleaded by my counsel.'

Called as a defence witness, Mrs Elizabeth Diaper, a neighbour of Mr Jeffries, had this to say:

> I live a few yards from Mr Jeffries's house and was alarmed by Miss Jeffries that morning. I jumped out of bed and went to my chamber window. There I saw her in her shift, at her chamber window, between two and three o'clock; she said, 'Diaper! Diaper! Do for God's sake come! There are rogues in the house, and they are going to set the house on fire.' I took my gown and endeavoured to put it on, she still repeated her calls of Fire and thieves! I snapped her and said, I am coming as fast as I can; the maid was sitting on the garret window, with her right thigh on the window-board and her hand on her thigh, saying there were thieves in the house. I raised the street and when I came to the gate there I saw Mrs Buckle at the door...

Elizabeth was calling out, 'Where is my uncle? Oh, for God's sake, my uncle and Joe Martin. John Swan open'd the door, and came out directly.'

Having said this, the witness fell into a faint and was obliged to be carried from the court.

Her husband, John Diaper, took her place in the witness box and estimated the window of Elizabeth's bedroom was about ten or eleven feet above ground but a coving above the door, which was directly below the window, would reduce the drop by three or four feet. Whilst skirting the house looking for the intruders Mr Diaper said that in a field close to the house the night dew was still thick on the ground but there were no footprints leading towards or away from the house - yet he noticed that his own footmarks were clearly visible. He and Mr Joseph Baker had searched the house from top to bottom by candle light but found nothing. He told the court that both Elizabeth and Swan seemed very frightened and both were wearing garments that were devoid of blood stains but had clearly been slept in.

At this point, Elizabeth Jeffries fainted and suffered convulsive fits for a further forty minutes while Mr Diaper gave his evidence. He said he had seen bloodstains on the staircase – a bloodied imprint of a right hand. Questioned about the relationship between Joseph Jeffries and his niece, the witness said that 'they have always lived in a loving, amicable way. I have many times seen her cry when he has been sick, fearing he should not get up again. He treated her with a great deal of affection and civility. My wife has sat up with him in his illness by Miss's desire.'

When cross-examined by the prosecution the witness's testimony was somewhat discredited when John Diaper admitted that he owed Joseph Jeffries three years' rent and had been threatened with eviction. His support of Elizabeth, possibly his future landlady, if she was proven innocent, was therefore open to question.

Having recovered from her fainting fit, his wife, Elizabeth Diaper, was recalled and described going into Joseph Jeffries's bedroom where the maid told her that her master's throat had been cut from ear to ear. Mrs Diaper sent her to bring down the small child who was also living in the house and she handed him over to the care of Mrs Martin.[42]

She stated that in her opinion the distress shown by Elizabeth Jeffries was genuine. She had known her for fourteen years and she had 'endeavoured to oblige him [her uncle] in all respects whatsoever'.

She also testified that had John Swan wished to kill his master he could have done it at any time.

> I have seen them come home together when Mr Jeffries was drunk, at two, three or four in the morning, they had use to come over the Common, and Swan by the side of his horse to hold him by the lappet of the coat, and he has led him home on foot, when he had been dead drunk, many a time.

She also informed the court that she wasn't surprised that Elizabeth had managed to get out of her bedroom window without hurting herself because she'd done it many times before 'with her cloaths on to pick jessamine'.

Another neighbour, Mr William Davies, was also questioned about the morning of the murder. As with previous witnesses, he hadn't seen any blood on the clothes of either Elizabeth or John Swan.

> I went up stairs, there I saw Mr Jeffries lying on his bed; I helped them, and lay behind him for some time; he blowed his nose with a handkerchief and wiped it. As I was coming downstairs I saw some blood upon the banister; there was the mark of three fingers and a thumb, done by a right hand; and two or three drops of blood on the stairs.

Elizabeth Jeffries had asked him and the others gathered about to search the house and the grounds; she said she would pay us for our trouble. When asked if Miss Jeffries had seemed frightened or upset he said: 'She appeared to be in middlingish spirits; a little matter affrighted.'

42 Mrs Martin was described as Joseph Jeffries's daughter-in-law so she must have been married to a son of his late wife as he had no children of his own. The child, Joe Martin, was probably one of Mrs Martin's children, and the grandchild specifically favoured by Jeffries as mentioned in the letter.

He confirmed that when they searched the pond with rakes they dredged up '16 pewter plates, 2 pewter dishes, a copper pot, 2 brass candlesticks, a silver tankard, and a silver two-handle cup'.

Mrs Buckle was called to give evidence and testified that Elizabeth and her uncle 'seemed to live always agreeable together. Miss was always very loving to her uncle, and always very tender of him, when he was ill; they lived quite loving and well together, for what I saw'.

Next came another neighbour, Catherine Griffiths; she told the court that Elizabeth had helped to hoist her uncle upright in his bed and she had then knelt on the floor and said, 'Dear Uncle, if you can speak, speak to me.' She told him to raise his hand if he knew who she was and he squeezed her hand.

Called to give evidence, Mr Clifton, Mr Jeffries's apothecary, said he had dined with him the night before his murder. Early next morning, when John Swan had ridden over to his house to tell him about the murder, Mr Clifton told him to go and fetch Dr Forbes, the surgeon at Woodford, and bring him back. When he got to Mr Jeffries's house he found another surgeon (Dr Thornton) already there; they were soon joined by Dr Forbes, who was certain that nothing could be done to save the victim but suggested some warm white-wine whey was squirted down his throat with a syringe as he was unable to swallow. Concerned, Elizabeth had suggested sending for a third doctor, saying she would pay for any assistance necessary to save her uncle's life.

Whilst saying that he thought Elizabeth's distress was genuine Mr Clifton admitted that she often sought ways to get her uncle out of the house so she could entertain company or sneak out to meet friends she'd made at boarding school. He admitted that on several occasions he had agreed to persuade her uncle to go for a long walk with him simply to get him out of the house so the coast was clear for her and her friends.[43] Mr Clifton concurred with the previous witness, testifying that John Swan could have killed his master

---

43 During the trial three other witnesses – Frances Casbolt, William Fellows and Nathaniel Ladyard – also admitted that they had helped Elizabeth by taking her uncle away from the house on various drinking sprees so she could entertain her friends.

on any number of occasions as they staggered home across the Common, late at night and very drunk. 'His horse once went into a pond,' he told the court, 'and he fell off his neck, and Swan saved him and on this account Mr Jeffries had always a great regard for him.'

Asked how Elizabeth and her uncle got along together he had this to say:

> She always behaved like a tender child would to a parent. I know there have been a little uneasiness in the family, Miss having a desire to see a friend at home or abroad, when he would not consent to it; for he would not permit her to have any company.

The witness also suggested that anyone shooting the pistol might have been injured themselves as the pistol 'shivered so much'. This would probably have resulted in the victim's blood being sprayed on the perpetrators yet witnesses had confirmed that neither of the accused had exhibited any blood stains on their clothing. However, it would not have been lost on those listening in court, that the accused could have changed their clothing and destroyed evidence of their guilt in the three quarters of an hour between the attack and the raising of the alarm.

Cross-examined by the prosecution, Mr Clifton denied that he had received money from Elizabeth Jeffries - except, he insisted, for services rendered. She had also paid £20 as part of a debt of £22 she had owed to his son-in-law.

The apothecary's wife, Mrs Anne Clifton, described seeing Elizabeth at the house at four that morning, crying. Mrs Martin, Joseph Jeffries's daughter-in-law, was also there and was dreadfully upset, saying that she had lost 'the best friend she had in the world'. She also told Mrs Clifton that, on the day he was murdered, Mr Jeffries had intended to change his will in favour of her and her family.

Mrs Clifton told the court that Elizabeth and her uncle 'lived in friendship; I believe I have heard of little quarrels, such as happen in all families'.

The large sums of money Elizabeth had given Mrs Martin as she mounted the coach after her arrest were not mentioned but may well have had some bearing on the witness's testimony. It was not explained why Mrs Martin was not called to give evidence, either for the prosecution or the defence even though - or perhaps because - she stood to inherit her father-in-law's wealth if Elizabeth Jeffries was found guilty and executed.

After Sir Samuel Gower had described his questioning of Thomas Matthews after his arrest for drunken brawling, his clerk, Mr James Warriner, told the court that Matthews had lied outrageously during the first few examinations - giving a false name and insisting that he was in Virginia, USA, at the time of the murder - but eventually he confessed to having been promised £700 by the two accused if he had participated in the murder of Joseph Jeffries. Mr Warriner had taken down his confession and Matthews, who could not read or write, signed it with his mark.

Following this, the Judge proceeded to sum up all the evidence for and against the prisoners in the dock. Admitting that the evidence was purely circumstantial, he said that 'it appeared to him as strong and convincing'. At the end of the Judge's summing-up the jurors retired to consider their verdict. They returned to court within an hour and pronounced both prisoners guilty as charged. The trial had lasted from six o'clock in the morning until one o'clock the next day. Elizabeth Jeffries and John Swan were taken back to Chelmsford Gaol until the end of the Lent Assizes, when sentences for all those tried in the sessions would be announced. As their case was one of murder they could have been in no doubt that they would receive a death sentence.

According to one press report Elizabeth 'sat very sullen, and seemed but little affected until the Jury brought in their Verdict and then she began to weep' whilst another account said that she fainted. 'When she spoke, it was with an air of Undauntedness. John Swan appeared from the Beginning to the End of his Trial wholely [sic] unconcerned, and seemed perfectly undaunted without the least sign of Remorse.'

It was reported that the two met only twice after their conviction and each time resorted to accusing each other of the crime.

The following letter - unfortunately the author's signature is indecipherable - was sent from Chelmsford and published in *The Only True and Authentic Trial of John Swan and Miss Elizabeth Jeffreys...* 14th March, 1752, two days after the murder trial:

Sir,

As I sent you before the remarkable Trial of Miss Jeffries, taken in Short-hand by a Person I employed for that Purpose, so now I send you some Account of her Behaviour at the Trial, and her Confession since, and likewise of her vile Companion, John Swan.

As I imagined the Court would be exstreamly crouded [sic] I took care to be there as soon as the Doors were opened. On the first Appearance of the Prisoners the whole Assembly seemed greatly agitated, though with very different Emotions; some expressing their Horror of the Guilt by Reproaches on the Criminals, while the more humane and tender-hearted spared the Persons of the Guilty, and pitied them, at the same time that they shewed an utter Abhorrence of their cruel and unnatural Crime.

The miserable young Lady seemed to engross the Attention of the whole Assembly; and indeed it was impossible to see her without being moved, though she herself shewed very little Emotion, till the Jury brought in their Verdict. But as most People believed her, From the strong Circumstances, to be guilty, she was undoubtedly considered as already doomed to Death.; in this Situation, a young Creature in the Pride of Life, with no contemptible Person, born, or rather adopted to a happy Affluence, excited the strongest Sensation of Compassion by the dreadful Comparison of what would soon be deplorable, the just Reward of her Crime.

She is about twenty-six Years old, has a blooming Complexion, and a pretty good Shape, but a little inclined to Fat. One could read no Malevolence in her Countenance, nor indeed much Sensibility; none of that which is inspired by Dignity of Thought, and conscious Innocence, instead of which a kind of stupid Inattention sat on her Features, till a Woman, who was under great Obligations to her Bounty, was seized in the Middle of a Speech in her Favour, with a fainting Fit, and carried out of the Court senseless, then she herself, probably struck with the Glare of every Eye turned upon her, fell into a deep and long Swoon, out of which she was with much Difficulty recovered. Her dress was a genteel Half-Mourning and a Shade.

She was, during her Trial, permitted to sit, a Distinction paid to her Sex and Station. Her Accomplice was but little minded: though he is a really good-looking Fellow, and perhaps much more an Object of Pity than Miss Jeffries, since it appears it was in Compliance with her Solicitations, which she had made use of for two Years, that he engaged in the Murder.

She was, all the Time of her being in Prison, from her Commitment to her Trial, buoy'd up with an Assurance of being acquitted, which in some measure accounts for that strange Unconcernedness, which she appeared in at the Beginning of her Trial.

Since her being remanded back to Prison, her Conscience, stung with the sense of her Guilt, has made her confess, that what was sworn against her by the Witnesses, especially Matthews, was true, excepting only the Circumstance of his being in the House at the Time when the Pistol went off; that she and Swan had concerted Matthews in such a manner between them, as to appear as though but just risen from their Beds, when they alarmed the Neighbours; that she did not get out of the Window, making only the alarm there, but was let out of the Street-door by Swan, who bolted it after her, and unfastened it again, when the Neighbours came; that before they committed the Murder, they packed up some Pewter and Plate in a Sack, and threw it into a neighbouring Pond, on purpose that it might be found again, in order to corroborate the Story of the Murder being done by Thieves.

Swan is quite enraged at Miss Jeffries's confessing the Fact, and refuses to see her; he says that Matthews, and not himself, did the Murder; but I fancy, before his Execution, he will own that he was the Perpetrator of it.'

A contemporary pamphlet entitled *The Trial and Execution & Elizabeth Jeffreys*[44] offered a few more details from Elizabeth's confession. It transpired that on the night of the murder, Elizabeth and Swan waited until the maid was asleep before creeping into her uncle's bedroom and taking a silver tankard, a silver cup and some spoons from the chest of drawers; downstairs, they gathered up some pewter and brass items taken from the shelves in the

---

44 From *Curiosities of Street Literature*, compiled by Charles Hindley (London 1871).

kitchen, put everything in a sack and threw it into the pond. This done, they both drank a large dram of brandy and made their way to their respective bedrooms. Elizabeth undressed and got into bed and waited for Swan to let her know when her uncle was dead. At this point, she was to sound the alarm and alert the neighbours. However, perhaps from the effects of the brandy, she fell asleep and woke to hear the sound of someone gasping for breath. She opened her window and cried out for help. She did not climb out of the window as she had previously claimed, but ran downstairs in her shift and without shoes for Swan to let her out of the front door. She ran to the house of her closest neighbour, Mrs Diaper. Swan locked the door after her and when the neighbours had gathered outside the house, he came out, dressed only in a shirt, as though he had just been woken by the noise.

Elizabeth also admitted that they had cut the bell rope in Joseph Jeffries's room which was connected to the maid's room so he couldn't call for help.

The Execution

As we have seen in the previous chapter, Elizabeth Jeffries started corresponding with Mary Blandy during the time she was waiting to stand trial – between 7th January and 19th March, 1752. The letters ceased only after she had confessed to the murder of her uncle, shortly before her execution, eight days before Mary, too, died on the gallows.

According to an announcement in the *Derby Mercury*:

> ...a few days before she died, she was, by Order of the High Sheriff, removed from Prison into a private Apartment in the Gaoler's House, in order to be taken care of, but whether she has made any Discovery [confession] of that horrid Affair is at present kept a Secret.[45]

The *Derby Mercury* also informed its readers:

> The Evening before her Execution, Miss Jeffries desired her Coffin

---

45 The article adds that on the death of Elizabeth Jeffries, 'a fortune of £6000 devolves to her Brother, who is now at sea'.

might be brought into her Room, in the Gaol, which she got into with her Cloaths on, to see if it fitted her, and she found fault that it was too big for her over the Shoulder Part; after which she put into it a plain Cap, with a white Ribbon to tie it with, a Callico shift, a Pair of white Cotton Stockings, and a Pair of black Sleeve Buttons; and then putting on the Lid of the Coffin, she laid upon it almost the whole Night. The Coffin was cover'd with Black, with a black Plate, black Handles and Nails, and lined and quilted with white Satin; all of which was her own particular Desire.

The following account of the horrendous twenty-three mile journey which took nine hours from Chelmsford Gaol to Epping Forest for execution also appeared under the heading:

> LONDON, March 31. A particular ACCOUNT of the Execution of Miss Jeffries and John Swan, in Epping-forest, near Walthamstow, on Saturday last, for the barbarous Murder of Mr. Joseph Jeffries.
>
> About Five o'Clock on Saturday Morning last John Swan and Miss Jeffries were brought out of Chelmsford Gaol. Swan was put into the Sledge[46] with a heavy Pair of Irons on his Legs, and Hand-cuffs on his Hands; the Irons on his Legs were chained to each Side of the Sledge, and he had a Halter round his shoulders. Miss Jeffries swooned away when her Hand-cuffs were put on, and she was brought down in four Mens Arms, quite insensible, and put into the Cart, where the Executioner put a Halter round her Neck, and fastened her to the Back of the Cart, where she remained insensible for about a Mile, and then recovered pretty well, as she said, considering her condition. She desired, as she came on the Road, a religious Book to read in, and accordingly Nelson's Practice of True Devotion was borrowed for her at a Publick-House.
>
> About eight Miles from Chelmsford she fell in a strong Fit, in which she continued near half an Hour, and notwithstanding her being tied, there were three Persons to hold her.
>
> At Brentwood Swan drank a Glass of Wine and Water; Miss did not

46   As he had been convicted of Petty Treason – killing his master – it was a mandatory part of his punishment to be transported to the place of execution on a sledge usually pulled behind the horse-drawn cart carrying the condemned to the gallows. The *Caledonian Mercury* included a few other details: 'Swan went first in a Sledge or Hurdle, drawn by six Horses, and Miss Jeffries followed in a Cart, accompanied by Mrs. Brown, her Nurse, who attended her during her Confinement [imprisonment].'

take any Thing all the Way, tho' often ask'd, but a little Water with some Hartshorn Drops.⁴⁷

Nothing remarkable happened till their Arrival on Epping-forest, about Two o'Clock in the Afternoon. The Cart stopt a little before it came to the Gibbet, when Mr. Bateman, a Justice of the Peace at Walthamstow [he was also a juror at the murder trial] and another Gentleman, came to her; and Mr. Bateman asked her, if she truly and sincerely repented of her Crime, and whether she acknowledged the Justice of her Sentence? To which she answered, that she hoped she had sincerely repented and she acknowledged the Justice of her Sentence, and forgave all the World, as she hoped to be forgiven; adding that none but God and herself knew all the ill Usage she had met with, which induced her to do what she did.

When they came up to the Gibbet, which was erected for the Execution, about a hundred yards beyond the Obelisk, on Epping-forest, there was a large Ring made by the Constables that attended the Procession from Chelmsford⁴⁸; and the Sledge being drawn in first, and the Cart afterwards, the Cart was drawn under the Gibbet, and Swan taken out of the Sledge, when coming up to the tail of the Cart, he shook hands with Miss Jeffries before he got into it.

The Mourning Coach that brought Mr. Griffith [the Rev. Mr Griffith, prison chaplain], Mrs. Martin, and Mr. M'Coon, (hired by the latter, who used to transact the Affairs of the late Mr. Jeffries and to whom we hear Miss Jeffries gave most of her Effects before her Conviction) not coming up to the Gibbet, nor the Clergyman so soon as was expected, Swan said, 'What! Must I die like a Dog, and no Prayers said for me!'

Presently after Mr. Griffith and Mr. M'Coon came up to the Cart,

---

47   The *Caledonian Mercury*: 'When they [the prisoners] came to Brentwood they were ordered to stop a little while for the Sheriff and his Attendance to refresh, but had nothing given to them; and then proceeded towards Walthamstow, amidst an innumerable Multitude of Spectators, who lined the Road from Chelmsford...'
48   The procession would have included a posse of Sheriffs, on horseback and in full regalia, javelin men and constables – there to prevent any precipitous lynching or a last minute dash for freedom. The whole spectacle would have been witnessed by people gathered en route – some twenty miles - jeering, cheering and throwing stones, rotten fruit, etc. at the condemned, those on the sledge particularly prey to missiles and dirt flung up from the horses hooves on the dusty, rutted tracks.

where Mr. M'Coon shook hands with Miss, and she was remarkably eager in reaching out her Head to take the parting Kiss from him, which she did. After this, Mr. Griffith prayed with them about half an Hour, and then asked them repeatedly if they repented all their Sins, especially that for which they were going to suffer; They answered that they sincerely repented, and hoped for Salvation, etc. Then Mr. Griffith asked Swan if he had any Thing to add to his former Confession; or whether he had any Thing to discover [reveal] for the Good of the Publick; when Swan replied, that Matthews was a very great Villain; that he was the Person who cut one Galley's Eyes out, and would have stole a horse from Sir William Maynard, if he had not prevented him. Mr. Griffith told him, that those Expressions favoured of Uncharitableness, and admonished him to forgive him, and if he had done any Wrong to him; to which Swan replied that he forgave him with all his Heart.

Miss Jeffries, on being ask'd, said she had nothing more to say. The Executioner then put on her a sort of Hood, made like a Purse, prepared on Purpose in Chelmsford Gaol, which drew together with Strings, and tied behind; when this was put on her Head, she swooned away, and did not recover before she was turned off. She was put upon a Chair in the Cart, to put a Halter about her Neck; [she was only 5ft 1in tall] but Swan being very tall, the Halter was put round his Neck as he stood in the Cart. When they were both fixed in their Halters, Mr. Griffith, in a short Prayer, recommended their Souls into the Hands of Almighty God, and then the Cart drew away.

After they were turned off, Mr. Griffith declared, That John Swan had solemnly declared to him, that he alone murdered his Master, by shooting him with a Pistol loaded with Pieces of Bullets; that there was no Stab given; and that the several Wounds were given by the Pieces of the Bullets, and by the Splinters of the Pistol that burst when it was fired off; and that Matthews was not at the House for five Days before the Murder was committed; all which Mr. Griffith said was what had desired might not be mentioned till he was dead.

There was never, perhaps, so great a Number of People assembled of both Horse and Foot, upon any Occasion whatever; All the way from Chelmsford to the Gibbet, the Road was covered; the Hedges and the Trees by the Road Side, were filled with Spectators, as were the Windows all along the Road. The Ropes that hung them were so long, that though the Gallows was near twenty Feet high, yet their Feet were within four Feet of the Ground, which deprived great Numbers of the Sight.

There were some Thousands of People assembled in Wood-street, in Walthamstow, occasioned by the lucrative View of some Persons, who had hired Houses, and built Scaffolds to let out to Persons that came to be Spectators of the Execution; and to draw People together, they had, at their own Expence, erected a Gallows, facing where Mr. Jeffries lived, and without any Order from the Sheriff to do so. The original Order for the Execution was, that the Gibbet should be erected on Epping-forest, about a hundred Yards from the Obelisk; that they were to be executed; and Swan was afterwards to be hung in Chains on the same Gibbet. But while they were under the Gibbet, at Prayers, a new Order came to the Under-Sheriff, from Mr Justice Wright, directing that the Body of Swan should not be hung in Chains there, it being in full view of some Gentlemen's Houses on the Forest; but left it to the Gentlemen of Walthamstow to fix a proper Spot to erect the Gibbet on; whereupon it was agreed that Buckets-Hill, near the Bald-fac'd Stag, was a proper Place, not only in Point of Situation but being a Place where Mr. Jeffries often resorted, and from whence Swan used to fetch him.

When their Bodies were cut down, Miss Jeffrye's was put into her Coffin, and conveyed in a Hearse to an Undertaker's in the Borough of Southwark, from whence it was privately interred on Sunday Night, in St Saviour's Church. The Body of Swan was put into his Irons and hung up Yesterday. Notwithstanding the prodigious Multitude of People at this Execution, we do not find that any one received the least Hurt.

Miss Jeffries was dressed in a Black Bombazine Gown, with a Capuchin on,[49] the Hood pulled over her Head, without Ruffles, or Hat, and leaned her Head against Mrs. Brown, her Nurse, who sat in a chair in the Cart almost all the Way; Swan wore his Hat flapped, that no Person could see his Face till he came to the Gallows. When they were both Haltered, Swan pulled out of his Pocket seven or eight shillings, Part of which he gave to a poor Man who attended him, and the Remainder he gave to Jack Ketch [the executioner][50]; and Miss Jeffries having made a Sign,

49 Capuchin: a fashionable hooded cape or cloak, similar in shape to those worn by Capuchin monks.
50 John 'Jack' Ketch: a notoriously brutal executioner between 1663 and 1686. Subsequent hangmen were sometimes referred to as 'Jack Ketch'; it was also used as a euphemism for death.

for she could not speak, for Mrs. Brown to take her Capuchin, and her Hood being pulled over her Face, they were both turned off together, Miss Jeffries's Head hanging against Swan's Breast. As soon as they were turned off, Jack Ketch seized on the Capuchin, but the Sheriff, observing Miss Jeffries's Intention, by her Motion, for Mrs. Brown to have it, he ordered it to be given to her.

Both had confessed their guilt before they died and exonerated Thomas Matthews, saying that he had already left the house before the fatal shot was fired. It was noted that, although they had been intimate and partners in crime, Elizabeth and John Swan did not 'speak, touch or look at one another during the whole time they were in the cart' waiting to be 'turned off'.

Had Elizabeth Jeffries modified her behaviour and allowed her uncle to die of natural causes she would have inherited most of his wealth. In July, 1751, soon after the murder, the will he had written on 13th October, 1746, was proved. He had bequeathed most of his considerable estate to Elizabeth consisting of money, property, all his household goods and also his diamond ring and his late wife's gold watch. To his nephew and namesake, Joseph, son of his brother, Francis Jeffries, he left £500 to be paid when he reached the age of thirty. He left fifty pounds to the eldest son - not named - of his late brother, Thomas Jeffries, and the sum of twenty pounds to his sister, Elizabeth Harding, and a further ten pounds to each of her children. All that remained was to be left to Elizabeth Jeffries; he also nominated her as the sole executive of his will.

We can only guess at the strength of the hatred Elizabeth harboured for her uncle. It had been obliquely rumoured that he had 'ill-used' her - corroborated in her last letter to Mary Blandy - but the full horror of her situation came to light when the following letter was sent from Walthamstow to the pamphleteer on 13th March, 1752, the day after the murder trial:[51]

51 *The Only True and Authentic Trial of John Swan and Miss Elizabeth Jeffreys, etc* (London, 1752).

Sir,

As I imagine any Particulars relating to Miss Jeffries will be acceptable to you, I shall now tell you what I know of her. Her father, who is an honest, industrious Man, is still living, and has two Sons besides this unfortunate Daughter; one of them proving a little wild, was, about a year and a half ago, sent to sea, and is not yet returned Home.

Mr. Jeffries, her Uncle, having no Children, took Bett [Elizabeth] under his Care when she was very young and no more than between four and five years old, which was before he left off his Business of a Butcher in London. He sent her to a Boarding-school here, and had her brought up in what he thought a genteel Manner.

She seemed naturally active, cunning and artful; and as he had made her hope that he would leave her all he was worth, she found it her Interest to please him, and therefore rendered herself as agreeable to him as possible. He had another Niece, who came to live with him; but Miss. Bett had Art to obtain such an influence over her Uncle as to have her employed in all the laborious offices of a Servant; And this occasioned her going away.

When she was grown up (if we may believe what is here asserted by almost everybody, tho' I wish it could be proved to be untrue) that her Uncle, after all he pretended Kindness, had the Villainy to debauch her, and to continue in an incestuous Intercourse with her for several Years, and has had two Children by her, one of them a fine Boy, and said to be still living.

Her Uncle indulged her in every Extravagance and with respect to her, acted rather the Part of a passionate Lover than of a covetous Uncle. She then kept the Keys of the Closets, Cellar, etc. Thus stripped of the Restraints of Virtue, and left entirely to her own Conduct, she set no bounds to her Extravagance; and she admitted some of mean Rank to partake with her in the Plenty of her Uncle's House, she gained the Character of a free-hearted, good-natured Lady.

It is said that she was often guilty of irregular excess in the use of Spirituous Liquor; and her Uncle, while fond of her, would give no Credit to any Thing told him to her Disadvantage. He abridged her Allowance; and, as she knew not how to contract her Expences [sic] she was drove to great Straits to procure Money to support them. These Difficulties, it is supposed, first put the diabolical Design of murdering her Uncle in her Head, as she knew she was appointed his Executrix, and would, by his Death, be put in Possession of an ample Fortune; but what perhaps hastened the Execution of the Fact was the fear of entirely losing his Favour, and by that Means of being excluded from his Fortune at his Death; which was highly probable would have been the Case as he was lately grown excessively fond of a little Boy, who was the Grandchild of his deceased Wife.[52] It is also reported that her Uncle often advised her to keep Company with the reputable of the Neighbourhood, but she slighted his admonishments under the Pretence of thinking herself above Tradesmen, tho', as companions of her voluptuous Excesses, she generally chose those of the meanest Rank; but Vice is every Way inconsistent.

I almost forgot to tell you that she appeared at her Trial in a flowered Half-Mourning Petalair.[53]

I am, Sir, Yours, etc.

P.S. While the Coroner's Jury were sitting on the Body of the late Mr. Jeffries, Miss. Bett came to Town and administered. From the Time of her Imprisonment to her Trial, she lived in a very extravagant manner; as if by this Conduct she endeavoured to exclude all Reflection and to alleviate the Unhappiness of her Condition, and the Misfortune of Confinement, by all the Gratifications in her Power. She endeavoured to make away with every thing, and it is said, actually wrote a Letter to Sir. William Maynard, Lord of the Manor, to persuade him to hold a court here, to empower her to sell her Uncle's Estate in this Place; but she had the mortification to receive a positive Refusal.

It is clear from this letter that it was common knowledge amongst the neighbours that there had been a long-standing incestuous relationship between Elizabeth and her uncle. From an early age he had groomed, corrupted and violated her and considered her a chattel, belonging only to him. Her subsequent intimacy with the young, tall and good-looking servant, John Swan, must have infuriated him. He also did his utmost to stop her entertaining friends - to rub salt in the wound they were eating and drinking at his expense for Elizabeth had the keys to the cellar - and indulging in sexual activities that he considered his sole prerogative. So

---

52 Most probably the child referred to as Joe Martin, a favourite of his step-grandfather, Joseph Jeffries.
53 A mis-spelling of the word petenair – a waist length jacket.

desperate was she to have a life of her own, away from the cloying, claustrophobic confines of the house, that she regularly persuaded neighbours to take her uncle away to London on prolonged drinking sprees, leaving the coast clear for her to indulge herself with her chosen companions. At least when he had been drinking to excess - he was often brought home slumped over his horse's neck with John Swan hanging on to him by his coat lapels - and even falling into the pond on one occasion, too drunk to hang onto the horse - at least on those occasions Elizabeth was more likely to be left unmolested - as she said, when he was drunk 'he did not use to enquire after her'.

It would be difficult to feel any sympathy for Joseph Jeffries, a butcher by trade, all too familiar with the cruel and bloody carnage of 18th century slaughter houses and therefore not perhaps the most sensitive of souls. In her last letter to Mary Blandy, dated 19th March, Elizabeth describes her uncle in this way:

> My Uncle, tho' a rich Man, was vulgar in his Manners, and Brutal in his Passions, had no Religion nor Morals, and took great Pains to debauch mine, in which I blush to tell you he was too successful.

He was a dissolute drunk and licentious seducer of his own niece and, no doubt, he regularly spied on her through the hole in the thin partition between their bedrooms. Little wonder that Elizabeth's behaviour deteriorated into alcoholic excess and rampant promiscuity in the wake of her uncle's disgusting attentions. It may be that she was so groomed that she was willing to be coerced into sexual activity with him in exchange for the luxuries of life until, that is, younger and more attractive partners presented themselves. She may even have been so corrupted that she thought such behaviour was normal and acceptable within a family. Yet she must have dreaded that her suffering was all for nothing, knowing that her uncle might carry out his threat to disinherit her and leave all his money to his little grandchild, Joe Martin, already singled out for special treatment.

With some knowledge of the sort of life Elizabeth had been living prior to the murder the pathetic dreams of a safe and beautiful haven she imagined in her letters to Mary Blandy appear even more poignant. Since an early age she had been deprived of peace and safety in the only home she knew, prey to the lustful and grossly inappropriate attentions of her uncle. In her letters she imagines this wonderful place of happiness in the company of Mary Blandy - though she likes to imagine there would be a place for 'poor unhappy Swann' who she admits to having coerced into carrying out the murder, to make them a garden which would enhance the idyll and complete her happiness; she pictures 'an obscure and pleasant Village; the House at one End, small, but convenient, the Gardens not large, but rather useful than elegant, at the Bottom of which runs a Brook, clear as Crystal, in which you see Trout and other Natives of the watry Element glide and wantonly play, on the other side is a delightful Meadow, which yields a beautiful and extensive Prospect'.

In another letter she refers to 'our little Seat and Garden, our Evening and Morning walks, our silent and entertaining Books, our useful and friendly Conversation; Thus Life will glide away with Ease and Innocence.'

Sadly, it was all a hollow dream for Elizabeth was to hang nine days later, in death her head resting on John Swan's chest. Her only solace during her remaining days on earth had been Mary Blandy, another woman who had murdered a family member for approval and monetary gain, and the affinity between the two, even as they waited to be executed, spoke volumes about the damage done to them by the very persons that should have loved and protected them.

Katharine Nairn
and
Lieutenant Patrick Ogilvie

'Love to faults is always blind, always is to joy inclined. Lawless, winged, and unconfined, and breaks all chains from every mind'

Whereas, in the case of Mary Blandy, her partner in crime, Captain Cranstoun, escaped the gallows leaving Mary to die hanging from a tree in the grounds of Oxford Castle, the reverse was true in the third case in this trio of fatally amorous females. Katharine Ogilvie, née Nairn, the lively and attractive daughter of the late Sir Thomas Nairn, of Dunsinnan, was nineteen when she married Thomas Ogilvie on 30th January, 1765 and went to live in his modest farmhouse at Eastmiln, in the county of Forfar, about sixteen miles north of Dundee. The partnership did not bode well for the groom was forty years old, lived with his mother and was, moreover, in poor health. The final ingredient in this potential recipe for disaster was the arrival of Thomas's younger brother, Patrick Ogilvie, a fiddle-playing lieutenant in the 89th Regiment of the Foot, returning from service in the East Indies. The mutual attraction between the young bride and her brother-in-law was immediate and within three weeks they had embarked on an affair, cavorting together in her bedchamber in full view of other members of the household and making no attempt to disguise their passionate attachment from either Katharine's husband or the servants.

It seems that, initially at least, Thomas Ogilvie chose to turn a blind eye to the affair for at the end of February he went away to Dunsinnan for three or four nights leaving his bride and his brother together. However, on 1st March, someone else joined the household, someone who made it her business to watch the couple and note every instance of impropriety. This proverbial 'fly in the ointment' was a woman in her thirties called Anne Clark and the pivotal part she was to play in the subsequent sequence of events will become clear as the story unfolds. Her motives for employing such guile and malevolence will be suggested at a later stage. Suffice it to say that Anne Clark was a cousin in the Ogilvie family - her aunt was Isobel McKenzie, the widowed mother of the three Ogilvie brothers, who was living at Eastmiln. In contemporary accounts she was sometimes referred to as Lady Eastmiln but for the sake of clarity in this narrative she will be called old Mrs Ogilvie. Anne Clark had, at one time, co-habited with Alexander, the youngest of the three Ogilvies. She was described as 'a woman of the most infamous character, and who, for a course of years, had lived as a common servant-maid, in one of the most notorious stews or lewd houses in Edinburgh, and other houses of bad fame, till at length she took up residence with the said Alexander Ogilvie'.[54]

However, shortly before his elder brother, Thomas, had married Katharine Nairn (it was not uncommon for women to retain their maiden names) Alexander married Anne Rattray, described as 'a woman of the lowest rank, the daughter of a common porter in Edinburgh, which gave great offence to his two brothers'.[55] It may be assumed that their mother, old Mrs Ogilvie, also strongly disapproved of the match and so it was that Anne Clark was dispatched ostensibly to live at Eastmiln in the hope that she might bring about some sort of reconciliation between members of the Ogilvie family. When this plan failed, whether under instructions from Alexander or on

---

54 *Trial of Katharine Nairn* – Notable British Trials series: edited by William Roughead in 1926.
55 Ibid. All quotes are from this title unless otherwise stated.

her own volition, she took note of the behaviour of Katharine and Patrick Ogilvie and reported back to Thomas. She made sure he was fully aware of the shockingly licentious behaviour of his bride and his brother but at first his reaction to being so blatantly cuckolded remained benign. However, persuaded by Anne Clark to attempt to separate the lovers, after a heated argument between the brothers on 23rd March, concerning a legacy from their late father, Thomas ordered him from the house; thereafter, for the two weeks before Thomas's death he was obliged to stay with various friends who lived within a short distance from Eastmiln.

The passion between Patrick and Katharine was not easily extinguished, however, and the affair continued behind Thomas's back; the lovers exchanged letters that were left under a stone in the grounds – and they even had the temerity to continue to enjoy romantic trysts in various outhouses and the surrounding fields.

Clearly still lacking in any justifiable jealousy or resentment towards the pair, Thomas Ogilvie wrote to Patrick promising to bequeath a large part of his estate to both of them and, moreover, he begged Patrick to return to the house, saying, 'My wife cannot be happy without you'.

By this time, however, echoing the case of Mary Blandy and her Scottish captain, Katharine had already asked Patrick to send her some white arsenic[56] and foolishly told Anne Clark that she intended to poison her husband and that her lover, Patrick, had promised to obtain the arsenic for her. Having returned from military service abroad it was said that he was 'shattered and broken' and accustomed to taking laudanum, some of which he kept in his army chest which Andrew Stewart - a shopkeeper who was married to Patrick's sister, Martha - would collect from Dundee. He could also, he said, acquire some arsenic. Armed with this vital piece of information, Anne, the resident spy in the house, wasted no time in warning Thomas Ogilvie (who was already suffering from recurrent

---

56 In 1886, Adelaide Bartlett persuaded her lover, the Rev. George Dyson, to obtain the chloroform that killed her husband, Edwin – he had also encouraged his wife's affair with the young preacher. See the author's book on the case, *In the Interests of Science; Adelaide Bartlett and the Pimlico Poisoning*.

stomach problems) not to eat or drink anything sent to him by his wife unless she was prepared to taste it first.

Patrick was as good as his word. As the laudanum in his army chest amounted to so little he needed to acquire some more. At the end of May he met with some friends, Lieutenant George Campbell and Patrick Dickson, at Colin Smith's establishment at Brechin where Dr James Carnegie was dining. Patrick asked if he could supply some laudanum as he suffered from gripes - also some arsenic to 'destroy some dogs that spoiled the game.'[57] The next day he went again to Smith's to dine and Carnegie privately supplied him with a small glass phial of laudanum and between half an ounce and an ounce of arsenic for which he charged the Lieutenant one shilling. It was customary to take 'receipts'[58] from 'low people' but, he said later in evidence, as Lieutenant Ogilvie was known to him and 'a gentleman,' this was not required. He said that he sold him white arsenic and he 'wrapt it up in the form of a penny-worth of snuff, under three paper covers'.

That same night, Anne Clark said that Katharine told her that she was very unhappy with her husband and that 'she wished him dead or, if that could not be, she wished herself dead'. She had earlier in the day sent a letter by the maid, Elizabeth Sturrock, to Lieutenant Ogilvie, who was staying with Andrew Stewart suggesting that the Lieutenant should give the drugs to Andrew Stewart to deliver to Katharine in person, as she thought it unwise to entrust them to the maid.

In anticipation of his arrival later that day, Katharine and Anne Clark had gone out, hoping to meet him on the road to Eastmiln but missed him as he had decided to come by another route. When they returned to the house, Andrew Stewart was sitting with old Mrs Ogilvie but straightaway followed Katharine up to her bedroom.

---

57 Christiana Edmunds, in the Brighton poison case of 1871, used the destruction of a dog as reason for purchasing strychnine.
58 A precursor of The Sale of Arsenic Regulation Act of 1851 which stipulated that any sale of poison should be entered in a book or register; the entry to include the type and amount of poison sold, the purchaser's name, address and signature, also the signature of a person known to the purchaser.

Taking the phial of laudanum and the package of arsenic, she locked them in the drawer of a small cupboard before rejoining the rest of the family downstairs.

During supper that evening, Thomas seemed perfectly well although he did mention that earlier that day, when he was out visiting his tenant farmers, he had 'swarfed or fainted on the hill' and for that reason he wasn't drinking ale. He was given a dram of whiskey instead and 'thereafter seemed hearty and in good spirits'.

Breakfast the next morning was earlier than usual as Andrew Stewart wanted to make an early start. Both he and the maid, Elizabeth, had seen Katharine in the kitchen, mixing the tea with milk and sugar, and saw her carrying the bowl upstairs to her husband who was still in bed. A little later Thomas had gone out on farm business without having any breakfast but returned about an hour and half later, feeling very unwell. He was helped upstairs by the maid and put to bed, by which time he was vomiting profusely. When told of this by one of the maids, Anne Clark ran upstairs and when she returned she was crying, saying Thomas had 'had a bad breakfast', insinuating that the tea Katharine had given him was to blame. By this time, Thomas was vomiting and purging violently and begging for cold water saying he was 'burning up and all wrong inside'.

Andrew Stewart suggested they call a doctor but Katharine didn't agree, saying that her husband would soon feel better. When he persisted she said that she feared Anne Clark's spurious suspicions would give her a bad name. Stewart assured her that Dr Meik, a surgeon from Alyth, was a 'discreet person'. After supper that evening, Andrew Stewart, old Mrs Ogilvie and Anne Clark were discussing the drugs sent by the Lieutenant which were locked away in the chest in the guest bedroom. They toyed with the idea of taking the keys from Katharine's pocket or, alternatively, breaking open the drawer but old Mrs Ogilvie, who admitted she heard and saw very little that went on in the house, thought this was inappropriate.

The suffering of Thomas Ogilvie that day and his death later that night will be described in the words of those called to give evidence at the subsequent trial.

While Patrick was making arrangements for the funeral, the ubiquitous Anne Clark took it upon herself to inform her ex-paramour, Alexander Ogilvie, of his brother's death and, moreover, she also suggested that Thomas had been poisoned. Alexander's reaction was to arrive at Eastmiln a few days later accompanied by the Under-Sheriff of the county and two surgeons. By this time, however, six days had passed since Thomas Ogilvie's death and it was decided not to carry out a post-mortem examination: according to the *Newgate Calendar* 'as it was now the middle of June, and the weather intensely hot, this was opposed by the surgeons, lest some noisome effluvia should arise from the body'. Witnesses at the subsequent trial stated that it was Alexander who had persuaded the surgeons not to operate.

On 10th June, Anne Clark was ordered from the house and four days later Katharine and Patrick were arrested and charged on two counts – incest and murder. They were first taken to the prison in Forfar and a week later, on 21st June, transferred to the notoriously grim Tolbooth prison in Edinburgh to await trial. They were closely guarded during the journey - part of which was via Queensferry - and forbidden to speak to one another. According to an account published in 1833, a crowd, having already heard of the scandalous charges, had gathered to see the prisoners:

> On her arrival at Leith, in an open boat, whose whole bearing betrayed so much levity, or was so different from what was expected, that the mob raised a general cry of indignation, and were on the point of stoning her, when she was with some difficulty rescued from their hands by the public authorities.[59]

Whilst the two accused were housed in the Tolbooth the prosecution team was kept busy compiling an initial list of sixty-four witnesses. They were also anxious to find Anne Clark who had made

---

59 From *Minor Antiquities of Edinburgh*: Robert Chambers, 1833.

herself scarce since leaving Eastmiln after Thomas Ogilvie's death. Notices were issued to try to locate her and on the evening before the trial of Katharine and Patrick was due to begin she delivered the following letter to the Lord-Advocate:

> Lord Advocat.
>
> Upon my coming to town, I am informed that you have been searching for me. It would never bread in my breast to kept out of the way had it not been for terror of imprisonment; but houping you will be more favourable to me I shall weat upon you tomorrow morning at eight o'clock.
>
> Sunday evening, eight of the clock.[60] Anne Clark.

As a result of her finally presenting herself as a prosecution witness she and two of Thomas Ogilvie's maid servants, Anne Sampson and Elizabeth Sturrock, were confined within the Castle prior to their appearance in court.

The Trial

On 20th July, Katharine and Patrick were indicted for two capital offences - the murder of Thomas Ogilvie and for the crime of incest.[61] They were then given the names of the jurors and a list of the witnesses to be called upon to give evidence after which the Court was adjourned. The trial opened on Monday, 5th August, but before the questioning of the witnesses could begin, the defence counsel, Mr Alexander Lockhart, immediately protested that Anne Clark should not be incarcerated with the two maid servants lest, as a hostile witness, she tried to influence their evidence and thereby prejudice the accused. His request that Anne Clark should be housed separately was granted and she was moved to another room but only for one night before being allowed to rejoin the maids. By way

---

60 This letter was found by William Roughead in the Justiciary Office, in Edinburgh and published in his book on the case in 1926.

61 Incest, at the time a capital offence, was defined as 'carnal knowledge of a man and the wife of his brother-german (his full brother, sharing both father and mother).

of explanation, Lord George Beauclerk, commander of the garrison, considered it would be safer to keep her in the original room, which was more secure, and thereby prevent her escape at all costs.

The trial of Katharine Nairn and Patrick Ogilvie was resumed at eight o'clock on the morning of Monday, 12th August, and continued without intermission until three o'clock on the Wednesday morning. The proceedings were presided over by the Lord Justice-Clerk, Sir Gilbert Elliot, assisted by five other judges. It is unfortunate and extremely frustrating for any chronicler of this case that, as the proceedings in court had to be taken down in longhand, it was only the evidence that was recorded in this way - the questions put to the witnesses by both the prosecution and the defence lawyers were not included.

After the court had been familiarised with the events leading to the crimes for which the prisoners had been charged, the first witness for the prosecution was called. He was a neighbouring farmer, forty-two year old David Rattray, who declared that it was common knowledge that Katharine Nairn and Patrick Ogilvie were having an affair and he had seen them walking in the area arm-in-arm and he had also seen them kissing.

This evidence was endorsed by the next witness, forty-seven year old John Lamar; he, too, was aware of the 'incestuous' relationship of the two accused and had 'seen them walking arm-in-arm, and their arms about each other's neck', even in the company of Anne Clark and Thomas Ogilvie.[62] As he lived just across the river from the house at Eastmiln he had a clear view of the comings and goings and had seen Alexander Ogilvie (he called him Dr Alexander but he was still a medical student in Edinburgh) and Anne Clark there but only saw Katharine Nairn after her marriage to Thomas Ogilvie.

More evidence of the reckless and inappropriate behaviour of the lovers was given by twenty-six year old carpenter, John Gilloch. Two weeks after the marriage of Katharine and Thomas he was asked to go to Eastmiln and repair some brass-work and fit locks on a drawer

---

[62] All quotes from the trial are from William Roughead's edited, *Trial of Katharine Nairn*, 1926.

in the room where Patrick Ogilvie was in bed. Katharine came into the room, saying, 'What? Are you not up yet?' She then sat on a small cabinet by the side of the bed and 'they eat some sweet bread together, which had been got at the market'.

The witness had also noticed that Katharine had her hand 'about the bed-clothes, just upon Lieutenant Ogilvie's breast, at which time she said to him; 'You are not poor [unwell, sickly] but pretty fat' although the carpenter wasn't sure whether 'her hand was below the bed-clothes, or above'. There was more to scandalise those in court that day many of whom would have been of a strict religious persuasion. The witness stated that when Katharine was leaving the room 'Lieutenant Ogilvie kicked up the bed-clothes with his feet and threw them upon his body, upon which Mrs Ogilvie said, "Ah! You daft dog!" So exposed was he that the witness 'saw so much of the said Lieutenant Ogilvie's body, that he, the deponent, could judge whether he was a man or a woman'.

After breakfast that morning, Katharine came back upstairs and gave the witness a dram of whiskey and also gave some to Patrick, who was now dressed. In the week before Thomas Ogilvie's death, John Gilloch was again called to the house to carry out some minor maintenance work; one of the maid servants, Elizabeth Sturrock, said that Lieutenant Ogilvie was due to come to the house that day and she wanted to prevent a fractious meeting between him and his brother, Thomas. Later that evening he saw both Katharine and Anne Clark walking back towards the house at Eastmiln and it was assumed that they had met with Lieutenant Ogilvie some distance from the house.

The next witness was twenty-seven year old Katharine Campbell, a former servant of Thomas Ogilvie, who admitted that she had been dismissed by Katharine Nairn for theft and, through ill-will and malice, had sworn revenge. This naturally raised objections from Mr Alexander Lockhart. Firstly, he declared that, in view of the malice born by the maid towards the defendants, her evidence should be discounted. Furthermore, on a legal technicality, her name had not been on the list of witnesses; the reason given was that as she had moved away from Eastmiln to the north, crossing two seas – probably referring to some remote offshore island - she had been difficult to locate. These objections were dismissed by the Lords Justice-Clerk and Commissioners of Justiciary and, as the maid's command of the English language was limited – she spoke Earse (an early Scottish variant of Irish) - two interpreters, James Frazer and Robert Gray, had to be brought into court to translate the witness's evidence into standard English, which would be more accessible to all members of the court.

In evidence Katharine Campbell said that she had been employed for ten weeks as a washer-woman at the Ogilvie house in Eastmiln. She had witnessed the scandalous behaviour of the accused and had seen Lieutenant Ogilvie 'frequently kissing Mrs Ogilvie' and 'showing a great fondness for her'. When she had remarked that he was too affectionate towards his sister-in-law, the Lieutenant had replied that 'his brother had desired him to be fond of her, to keep her chearful in the beginning'.[63]

During the time Thomas Ogilvie was away from home on the visit to Dunsinnan for three or four days shortly after the marriage, the maid had made up beds for her mistress and the Lieutenant in separate rooms but the following morning she noticed that the latter's bed had not been slept in. Katharine's bed, however, was 'much tossed and tumbled'. She added, for good measure, that the sounds coming from the bedroom that night were like those of 'a man and woman in bed together'. As the maid was accustomed to sleeping in the kitchen and the ceiling was not plastered, she was able to hear 'every small noise' from the bedrooms upstairs that night and she professed to being 'terrified', so much so that she could not sleep. She admitted that, as far as she knew, that was the only time that the Lieutenant's bed had not been slept in. It was during this time, when Thomas Ogilvie was away from the house, that Anne Clark had arrived.

The maid told the court that she did not receive any wages during

---

63 The fact that a laundry maid felt entitled to make such a remark – even in a teasing manner – says much about the lax level of decorum in the household at Eastmiln.

the time she worked at Eastmiln - only given a pair of shoes - and when she protested she was told by Katharine, in the presence of Thomas, Anne Clark and Patrick Ogilvie, that she was lucky not to be charged with theft. After she had left Eastmiln she told Katharine's mother, Lady Nairn, about her daughter's immoral behaviour.

No doubt it was with curiosity and anticipation that those present in the court that day scrutinised the next witness for the prosecution to take the oath - Anne Clark. Mr Henry Dundas, for the defence, rose to object, saying that she was 'a person of an infamous character, being held and reputed to be a notorious liar and dissembler, a disturber of the peace of families, and sower of dissension, and also a common whore and prostitute'. She had, he informed the court, lived for three and a half years in a 'noted bawdy-house within the city of Edinburgh, as a common prostitute, notwithstanding that at the same time the said house was frequently visited by the constables as a house of bad fame, and that frequent disturbances happened therein, to the great offence and scandal of the neighbourhood'.

He also suggested that, in collusion with Alexander Ogilvie, she had spread 'scandalous and malicious aspersions' about the prisoners and had caused trouble between the late Thomas Ogilvie and his young wife. She had also, he said, 'threatened repeatedly to do all she could to bereave them of their lives'.

The response from Sir David Dalrymple, for the prosecution, demanded these objections be dismissed. The character of a witness bore no relevance to their evidence, he said, and if persons deemed of low moral character were exempt or prevented from giving evidence, many crimes would go unchallenged. As to the charge of spreading malicious rumours, if these rumours were subsequently proved to be based on the truth, they could not be categorised as lies.

Once again, the objections raised by the defence were dismissed by the Lords Justice-Clerk and Commissioners of Justiciary and the trial continued with the testimony of Anne Clark. Taking her place in the witness box she recalled, no doubt with some relish, that on Sunday, 19th May, she, Patrick and Katharine were talking together in a downstairs room while the rest of the household were at church. After a while, Katharine and Patrick had left Anne and went upstairs to the guest bedroom where Patrick slept, which was immediately above the parlour. Keen to spy on the lovers, the witness said that she had crept up the stairs and listened through the thin partition between the alcove bed and the stair wall. She was not disappointed; the noises she heard left her in no doubt that the couple were making love - in her words - 'abusing their bodies together...lying carnally together'. In the pre-trial statements of the two maids, Elizabeth Sturrock and Anne Sampson, they said that the bed was creaking 'like an old ferry boat'.

Eager to find more to gossip about Anne entered the room and saw Patrick standing by the side of the bed in which Katharine lay, buttoning up his breeches. She also noticed that his shirt was hanging out and Katharine was wearing a red and white calico nightdress. The same thing happened, said the witness, on the Monday, Tuesday and Wednesday of that week. Unable to resist, she told Thomas Ogilvie, and his mother what she had seen. His mother, who it was said, had always favoured Patrick, thought Katharine was to blame, being the cause of 'ill-blood and high words between the two brothers'. On the Thursday, after more angry scenes, Thomas had ordered his brother from the house.

Anne Clark went on to testify that Katharine was greatly distressed by Patrick's dismissal and threw herself on the Lieutenant's bed 'and there fell a-tearing and crying; and when her husband came to the room, she ordered him to go out of it'. In response, Thomas had remonstrated with her, telling her that her conduct was 'improper, and that she would ruin her reputation...'

Questioned further, Anne Clark said that, even prior to that Sunday session, she had seen Katharine and Patrick 'kissing one another, and him having his hand down her breast'. She had also heard heated arguments between Katharine and Thomas during which he had said that he wanted to leave the house and Katharine had seemed pleased with the solution. In late March, the witness, Thomas, Katharine and Patrick returned from a family visit to Glenkilry in 'very bad humour'. Katharine 'expressed her dissatisfaction with her husband, and said, if she had a dose [of poison] she would give it to him'. This sentiment was repeated to Anne Clark on a number of occasions and Katharine said she could get poison from Mr Robertson, a merchant in Perth, or Mrs Eagle, who kept a feed shop in Edinburgh - she would say she wanted to kill rats.

Of course, Anne Clark, guaranteed a rapt audience in court, hanging on her every word, she portrayed herself as a mediator between husband and wife (as Jane Cox had done in the Charles Bravo case) the voice of reason, trying to persuade Katharine against any such course of action. She did not succeed, however, for Katharine told her that the Lieutenant would get the poison for her. Two days before Thomas Ogilvie's death, Katharine had received a letter from Patrick, brought to her by a maid, Elizabeth Sturrock, telling her that he had managed to get the poison but, as he didn't trust the maid, it would be delivered to her the following day by his brother-in-law, Andrew Stewart. Hearing this, of course, Anne Clark insisted she had done her best to persuade Katharine to change her mind, saying that it 'would be bringing disgrace upon the family she was come of, and upon that into which she was married'. Katharine's mind was made up, however - she explained that 'she did not love her husband, and never could love him'.

Anne Clark even told the court that Katharine had expressed a wish that, if Thomas died, she, Anne, could live very happily with her and the Lieutenant. On the day before Thomas's death Katharine had become impatient for the arrival of Andrew Stewart who was to bring the drugs from Patrick. She and Anne Clark went out in the hope of meeting him on the road before he reached the house; however, he had come by a different route and when they got back to the house they found him sitting with old Mrs Ogilvie. Katharine and Andrew Stewart went upstairs for about half an hour, after which, Stewart came back downstairs alone. Waylaid by Anne Clark, she managed to get him to admit that he had brought Katharine some drugs, sent by the Lieutenant.

Katharine and Andrew Stewart then left the house and Anne Clark wasted no time in telling old Mrs Ogilvie that their visitor had brought drugs for Katharine and that the latter intended to poison her son, Thomas. She suggested that she should warn her son but the old lady thought this was improper; besides which, she knew Katharine would be able to persuade her husband that she needed the laudanum for her own use. The only solution, she thought, would be to simply warn Thomas not to eat or drink anything brought to him by his wife.

Anne Clark then hurried to find Thomas; he was at Kirton, in the home of one of his tenants, Fergus Ferguson, who kept a public house. Katharine and Andrew Stewart were also there but when the party left, they both hurried on ahead - 'like a shot from a pistol'. Bringing up the rear, Anne Clark warned Thomas Ogilvie to leave home for his own safety. He replied that he knew he was in danger from his wife but he couldn't leave the house and estate as he was committed to working the farm; he would, however, refuse anything that his wife offered him in the way of food or drink. That evening, after Thomas and Katharine had gone upstairs for the night, old Mrs Ogilvie, in the company of Anne Clark and Andrew Stewart, said she had also warned her son that his life was in danger. Stewart had seen Katharine put the drugs in a drawer in the Lieutenant's bedroom; it was suggested that they get a tradesman to prise open the drawer to check on the contents.

Earlier in the day, Thomas and Katharine had a bitter quarrel when he refused to pay for some cambric to make ruffles for Lieutenant Ogilvie. Thomas was so angry he went out to spend the whole day with his tenant farmers without having breakfast. When he returned that evening he said he was feeling unwell and went to bed without any supper - though this evidence differed from that of other witnesses. Questioned on Thomas Ogilvie's usual state of health, Anne Clark told the court that he had never been ill or suffered from either purging or vomiting.

The following morning, Katharine made tea earlier than usual and when Anne Clark went into the breakfast room she heard Katharine saying that her husband and the maid 'were well off that morning, for they had got the first of the tea'. After drinking his tea Thomas went out to attend to the farm but after a while he was back at the house and was put to bed as he was clearly unwell. Not long after this, Katharine came downstairs and told them that her husband 'was taken very ill'. The servants said he was suffering from 'purging and vomiting'. Old Mrs Ogilvie told Katharine to go up and see her husband, which she did, only to return in a short time, crying and saying that her husband was dying. After she went back upstairs with the maid, Elizabeth Sturrock, to sit with her husband, old Mrs Ogilvie asked Anne Clark to go as well 'to keep him from these two women'. Ever the martyr, she told the court that she stayed by Thomas's bed from mid-day until he died, between eleven and twelve o'clock that night.

During that time he drank large quantities of cold water and some small ale. His brother-in-law, Andrew Stewart, persuaded him to forgo the ale after which Anne Clark mixed some sugar in a glass of wine and he drank that instead. Besides the constant vomiting, Thomas complained of 'a burning in his heart and pains in the brawns of his legs' and asked Anne Clark to bind them up, which she did - but not with Katharine's silk stockings as Thomas refused to allow her to use them. He had great trouble breathing and 'he tried to open the windows to give him breath'. He was in great distress and constantly moving his head and limbs and, as the day wore on, he was unable to speak clearly as his tongue had become swollen. Shortly before he died he had a severe fit of vomiting, after which he fell back against the witness, who had been sitting beside him on the bed, supporting his body, and died.

Several friends had arrived at the house that day to enquire after Thomas. Asked about these visits Anne Clark said that she heard Thomas talking to James Millam, one of the farmhands, saying that 'it was either strong poison, or rank poison that was killing him'. She also heard old Mrs Ogilvie deriding her son for taking anything from his wife even though they had warned him not to. According to the witness, Thomas replied, 'It's too late now, mother, but she forced it on me.'

There seems to have been some confusion as to when a surgeon was sent for during the day that Thomas lay dying. It appears that Andrew Stewart did eventually fetch a surgeon, Dr Meik, from Alyth. Katharine had sent the miller, James Millam, to ride on horseback to Lieutenant Ogilvie and tell him of his brother's death. Patrick arrived at Eastmiln at about six o'clock the following morning and when Anne Clark confronted him about sending the poison he seemed concerned and confused but insisted that he didn't think Katharine 'had so barbarous a heart as to give it'.

Questioned further, Anne Clark said that she couldn't remember whether Thomas Ogilvie had gone out to see his workers as usual that morning although other witnesses confirmed that he did. Asked about Katharine's state of health, Anne Clark said that she had recently been 'blooded' and had been taking salts as she had not been sleeping well.

Questioned about the sleeping arrangements in Eastmiln, it became clear that the house was little more than a two-up, two down dwelling with a hallway between and the rooms were quite small. Anne Clark told the court that she had slept with old Mrs Ogilvie in the parlour but the two maids, Katharine Campbell and Elizabeth Sturrock, had to sleep in the kitchen. As space was so restricted, the third maid, Anne Sampson, had to sleep in an outhouse. In answer to further questioning, Anne Clark told the court that for the four days between Thomas Ogilvie's death and her dismissal, Katharine had been obliged to share her bed with her instead of the lusty Lieutenant but she had expressed her distaste by removing Anne's pillows!

On 10th June, clearly determined to free herself from Anne's malign presence, Katharine had given her notice to leave. After the Lieutenant and Katharine had been arrested and taken to the prison at Forfar, Anne Clark went back to Eastmiln for a few nights. At this time, Alexander Ogilvie 'had a roup of the cattle at Eastmiln'

- sold the cattle by auction. This was done with Patrick's permission as he was now the laird of Eastmiln after Thomas's death. When Katharine was arrested Alexander asked her if he should take care of her keys to which she replied that she didn't care who took care of them. Alexander then locked all the rooms in the house, put them in a drawer in the laigh room; [possibly the light room where oil lamps and candles were kept] which he then locked and took the key with him.

With this statement, Anne Clark was permitted to leave the witness box; her testimony had taken eight hours without a break although she was given some bread and wine during the proceedings.[64] It was reported after the trial that the adverse statements about the character of Anne Clark had been completely unfounded and that she had dodged the authorities prior to the trial hoping to avoid giving evidence *against* the accused.

Next to be questioned was one of the Ogilvies' maid servants, twenty-three year old Elizabeth Sturrock. She reiterated much of Anne Clark's evidence telling the court how she had noticed the amorous attachment between Katharine and Lieutenant Ogilvie; she had seen them kissing and hugging each other in the house and whenever Thomas Ogilvie was away they would go upstairs to the master bedroom, above the kitchen, and lie in bed together. She had seen the Lieutenant looking out of the window in his nightgown. Often, as she sat in the kitchen below the bedchamber, at her spinning wheel, she could hear every noise from above. She had also heard her master, Thomas Ogilvie and Katharine arguing about her behaviour, and on one occasion, her mistress had reprimanded her for eavesdropping.

Elizabeth repeated Anne Clark's evidence, saying that when Lieutenant Ogilvie was ordered to leave the house, Katharine was distraught and cried a great deal and that same evening she gave Elizabeth a letter to deliver to her lover who was staying at Little

---

64 Having sat for the eight hour duration of Anne Clark's testimony one of the judges, Alexander Boswell, 'brought on a suppression of urine, which, though removed, left him very much weakened'. *Scotland and Scotsmen in the Eighteenth Century.*

Forther, about three miles from Eastmiln. He told her to assure Katharine that he was well and that she should 'keep up a good heart'.

On another occasion, Katharine gave Elizabeth a letter to give to the Lieutenant, who had by then moved to Glenkilry; he, in turn, gave her a letter to take back to Katharine. On the day before her husband's death, she sent another letter to the Lieutenant, who had then moved on to Alyth. Once again, the maid was given a letter of reply with orders to deliver it to Katharine along with a bundle of linen. This last letter from Patrick Ogilvie was larger and thicker than the previous ones but she didn't think there was anything inside other than paper.

Contrary to other accounts, the maid repeated Anne Clark's assertion that Thomas Ogilvie had always, up until the time of his death, been in good health. On the day he was taken ill she was also confined to her bed in the kitchen with sickness. Katharine had come into the kitchen that morning and said that she had given her husband his tea and asked her, in 'a low voice, or a whisper', to say that she had also had some tea that morning, which, she said, she had not. It was shortly after drinking his tea that Thomas Ogilvie became ill with the onset of purging and vomiting; he refused breakfast but rallied sufficiently to venture out on the farm. When he returned a little later Elizabeth helped him up the stairs and into bed. Very soon after this he became worse and 'fell to vomiting and purging, and complained of every part of his body, saying that his heart was broken or riven, and he tossed very much'.

Old Mrs Ogilvie and Andrew Stewart went upstairs to sit with him and he called for quantities of cold water. He also said to them that 'he had been poisoned, and that woman had done it.' Those present assumed that he was referring to his wife and although his mother reproved him he insisted that 'it was very true, and his death lay at her door.' At one point during that dreadful day as Thomas lay dying, Anne Clark ordered the maid to go downstairs and fetch Katharine but she refused, saying she 'did not like to see dying people'. At lunch time, however, she did deign to accompany the preceptor from the church when he went up to say prayers at the sick-bed. She did not encourage visits from family and friends, however, saying she didn't want them to disturb Thomas in his suffering.

According to the maid, Katharine didn't seem unduly upset or show any 'great marks of grief upon her husband's death'. However, when Alexander Ogilvie arrived at the house some days later and refused to speak to her, she 'fell a crying, and wringing her hands, throwing herself back upon the bed'. The maid also told the court that Alexander had stopped the burial and sent for Dr Ogilvie of Forfar, and Drs Ramsay and Meik, 'to inspect the dead body of his brother'.

When Patrick arrived the day after Thomas Ogilvie's death Katharine asked to speak to him in the stables but they only talked in private for three or four minutes. When she heard later that the Sheriff of Forfar was due to arrive at the house to question everyone she again asked Elizabeth to say that she had seen her mixing the bowl of tea that morning and, moreover, that the maid had also drunk some of it without harmful effects. Her mistress went further, promising to take the maid with her when she moved away and 'if she had a halfpenny she would have the half of it.' Katharine had spoken to her in this way several times and in the presence of Lieutenant Ogilvie.

Questioned about the sleeping arrangements for the servants in Eastmiln, Elizabeth said that, before Katharine married into the family, she, Elizabeth, used to sleep in the parlour with old Mrs Ogilvie – until that is, Anne Clark joined the household. After that, Anne had slept with the old lady and Elizabeth was told to sleep in the kitchen with another maid, Katharine Campbell. A third maidservant, Anne Sampson, slept in an outhouse. Asked how many people came to see Thomas Ogilvie as he lay dying, the maid gave the names of George Spalding, of Glenkilry, William and Anne Froster, James Millam and David Walton.

Reference was made to the fact that, whilst awaiting trial, Elizabeth and the other maids, Anne Sampson and Katharine Campbell, had been housed in the same cell as Anne Clark. After the prisoners' defence counsel had objected, Anne Clark had been moved to another room 'where she remained a day and a night' before being returned to share accommodation with the three maidservants as before but 'they had some, tho' not much, conversation upon the subject of the trial' and they all decided it was their duty to tell the truth.

Elizabeth, when questioned about the bowl of tea given to Thomas Ogilvie on the morning he died, said that the following day she had seen 'something greasy in the bottom of it and intending to try if there was any thing poisonous in the grease, she put some broath into the bowl and gave it to the dog, who eat it up, but was nothing the worse for it.' However, Anne Sampson had often told Elizabeth that she had filled the same bowl with water and offered it to Thomas Ogilvie but he had 'refused to drink out of it, damning the bowl and saying he had already got his death out of it'.

Before leaving the witness box, the maid assured the court that her master had never before been 'troubled with vomitings, purgings or cholicks before the day on which he died; and that she never knew him indisposed, except for slight colds'.

Anne Sampson, who was 19 years old, was next to give her evidence which bore a marked resemblance to that already given by Anne Clark and Elizabeth Sturrock. It was clear that the maids had thoroughly enjoyed spying on their mistress and the Lieutenant and took every opportunity to listen on the stairs whenever the lovers were in bed together. They also listened to the frequently heated arguments between Thomas Ogilvie and Katharine. The maid stated that she had seen Katharine mixing sugar and milk into the bowl of tea that fateful morning - old Mrs Ogilvie and Anne Clark were also present. After stoking up the fire in the kitchen she had followed Katharine upstairs to the closet between the two bedrooms as she wanted some beef out of the beef-stand, but her mistress had got annoyed with her 'always wanting something'. She had seen Katharine stirring the bowl of tea in the closet but did not see her put anything into it. But she had seen a servant lad, Alexander Lindsay, standing at the top of the stairs, near the closet door, when her mistress was in there mixing the tea.

Asked to relate the events of that morning, the maid confirmed that Thomas Ogilvie had got up between nine and ten o'clock and went first to the stables to see his horses being fed. He then went to Shilling Hill to talk to some of his tenants. When he returned he was vomiting and clearly unwell and Elizabeth Sturrock helped him upstairs, followed by Katharine. The witness was asked to bring up some clean water for her master to drink; she used the same bowl from which he had drunk his tea earlier that day. When he refused to drink from that bowl she took it back downstairs and filled a tea-kettle with water instead. Repeating the previous testimony of Elizabeth Sturrock, the maid said that when she brought the bowl back to the kitchen she saw something greasy at the bottom; she had then put some broth in the bowl and gave it to the dog.

Although her mistress had frequently gone upstairs to see her husband during that morning, later in the day, as his condition worsened, she stayed downstairs. About mid-day Katharine had sent the maid two miles away to clip some sheep and she didn't return to the house until about nine o'clock that night. That being the case, the prisoners' defence counsel asked how she could testify that her mistress didn't go upstairs to sit with her husband during that afternoon if she was not there. She replied that the other servants had told her so.

Next to be questioned was Andrew Stewart, a thirty year old merchant in Alyth, married to Martha, sister to the Ogilvie brothers. He stated that he didn't know that the maid, Elizabeth Sturrock, had brought a letter from Katharine to Lieutenant Ogilvie when she called at his house to buy provisions - or that she had carried a reply with her when she returned to Eastmiln. However, a few days later, the Lieutenant gave him a small glass phial containing liquid which he said was laudanum and a small paper packet that he said contained salts. He was ordered to deliver these privately into Katharine Nairn's hands only. He had not seen the packet made up nor did he open it to examine the contents; it was sealed with wax and a wafer and attached to the packet were instructions for the use of laudanum.

He took the drugs to Eastmiln as arranged and sat talking to old Mrs Ogilvie until Katharine and Anne Clark returned to the house. The witness and Katharine then went upstairs and he gave her the packages which she immediately put away in a drawer. When they went back downstairs, Anne Clark cornered him and pressed him to tell her what he had brought from Lieutenant Ogilvie and once he had told her she said she was afraid that Katharine might poison her husband.

Following this, Anne Clark, in the presence of the witness and old Mrs Ogilvie, warned Thomas not to eat or drink anything prepared for him by his wife. During supper that evening Thomas seemed perfectly well but he did say that he had 'swarfed' or fainted on the hill that morning and for that reason he was not drinking ale. He was given a dram of whiskey instead and 'thereafter seemed hearty and in good spirits'.

Andrew Stewart confirmed that breakfast the next morning was earlier than usual as he had planned to leave the house early. He had seen Katharine mixing the tea with milk and sugar and saw her going upstairs carrying the bowl to her husband who was still in bed. Having left the house, Thomas returned about an hour and half later and they were told by the maids that he had been taken ill. Hearing this, Anne Clark ran upstairs and when she returned she was crying, saying Thomas had 'got a bad breakfast'. Stewart had then run upstairs and found Thomas violently vomiting and purging and begging for water, saying 'he was all wrong within' and burning up inside. Stewart suggested a doctor be called but Katharine didn't agree, saying that her husband would get better. When Stewart again tried to persuade her to seek medical assistance she still refused, saying that Anne Clark's suspicions would give her a bad name. At this, Stewart assured her that Dr Meik, a surgeon from Alyth, was 'a discreet person'.

Asked about Thomas Ogilvie's general state of health Andrew Stewart told the court that he had never known him to suffer from vomiting and purging before - his wife, however, (Martha Ogilvie) had remarked that 'he had the appearance of a tender [frail] man and that he would not be a long liver'. At one time, Thomas had told the witness that he was thinking about contacting Dr John Ogilvie (no relation) as he had been unwell with 'a cough and sore breast'.

Andrew Stewart then recalled that when the youngest brother, Alexander Ogilvie, arrived at the house after Thomas's death, he, the witness, had suggested to Lieutenant Ogilvie that he should 'make his escape; if guilty'. To this, the Lieutenant had replied that 'God and his own conscience knew that he was innocent'.

The court also learned that Katharine had been unwell for some time and had been 'blooded' the day before her husband's death and, as she had been taking laudanum and salts for her condition, it could be said that she had a legitimate reason for asking the Lieutenant to get some drugs for her.

After Andrew Stewart had left the witness box his place was taken by Dr James Carnegie, a surgeon from Brechin. He testified that at the end of May that year he met with the Lieutenant Ogilvie, Lieutenant George Campbell and Patrick Dickson at Colin Smith's establishment where he was dining. Lieutenant Ogilvie said he wanted to buy some laudanum as he suffered from gripes - also some arsenic to 'destroy some dogs that spoiled the game.' The next day he went again to Smith's to dine and privately supplied the Lieutenant with a small glass phial of laudanum and between half an ounce and an ounce of arsenic - normally sold to kill rats - for which he charged one shilling. He confirmed that as Lieutenant Ogilvie was known to him and 'a gentleman' a receipt was not required. He said that he had supplied white arsenic which he 'wrapt up in the form of a pennyworth of snuff, under three paper covers'.

Brought before the court, Lieutenant George Campbell, a member of the same regiment as Patrick Ogilvie, said that he had known the prisoner for five years; he confirmed that the purchase of the drugs was carried out between the Lieutenant and James Carnegie, in private.

Next to be questioned was a sixty year old merchant, Patrick Dickson, who had also dined with Lieutenant Ogilvie and Lieutenant

Campbell at Smith's when the drug deal was negotiated. Prior to the trial he had visited Lieutenant Ogilvie in prison and, during their conversation, Patrick had seemed concerned to learn that Dr James Carnegie had admitted to selling him arsenic.

Dr Peter Meik, a twenty-seven year old surgeon, was then sworn and told the court that when he eventually arrived at Eastmiln, Thomas Ogilvie had been dead for two hours. He found Katharine sitting by the bedside and 'she appeared to be in great grief and concern for her husband's death' but asked him to 'conceal from the world' the cause of his death. The Lieutenant also seemed to be very upset.

Nearly a week later, Dr Meik was called by Alexander Ogilvie to inspect the body. He noticed that the nails and parts of the chest were discoloured and that 'his tongue swelled beyond the natural size, and cleaving to the roof of his mouth'. Dr Meik was unable to say with any certainty whether these symptoms were caused by arsenic poisoning but was led to believe this might be so by Andrew Stewart's comments and Katharine's request to conceal the cause of death. Although he and another surgeon, Dr Gilbert Ramsay, were quite prepared to perform a post-mortem operation Alexander had refused to give permission unless Dr John Ogilvie [no relation] was present. However, as both he and Dr Ramsay were unable to wait for the arrival of the physician, the opening of the body was abandoned.

Dr Gilbert Ramsay, a thirty-eight year old surgeon, was of the opinion that death had been caused by arsenic – the violent vomiting and purging were typical symptoms - not an attack of colic as this would not have presented the symptoms such as a greatly swollen tongue and discolouration of other parts of the body. He confirmed that he and Dr Meik were quite prepared to perform a post-mortem examination but were prevented from doing so by Alexander Ogilvie who insisted that Dr Ogilvie should be present. However, even if the post-mortem had been carried out he doubted whether any evidence of poison would have been found as the body would have been in a state of advanced putrefaction.

Next in the witness box was a forty-eight year old physician, Dr

John Ogilvie, named by the previous witness. It was at the request of the Sheriff-substitute that he arrived at Eastmiln on 12th June to inspect the body of Thomas Ogilvie, which had been laid in a coffin in one of the outhouses. He reiterated the previous witness's observations about the state of parts of the body which were 'black and livid'. He was quite willing to open the body for inspection but the other two doctors had already left that morning. He, too, believed that little could have been discovered as the body was, by this stage, already badly putrefied.

When asked for his opinion on the cause of death, another surgeon, fifty year old, Dr Robert Smith, from Edinburgh, described a case where he had attended a woman who had died from arsenical poisoning; he confirmed that she had exhibited similar symptoms to those presented by Thomas Ogilvie. However, questioned by the defence, he agreed that a severe attack of 'bilious colick' could also produce similar symptoms.

Evidence was also given by the seventy year old, George Campbell, Sheriff-substitute of Forfar. He told the court that on 1st July he had gone to Eastmiln to search for any papers or letters belonging to the prisoners that could be used in evidence against them. His clerk, John Ure, then confirmed that besides the three letters which Katharine had written to Thomas Ogilvie before their marriage, the court would be shown the two separate declarations made by Katharine Nairn and Patrick Ogilvie while they were in prison at Forfar; they were dated 14th June, 1765, signed and witnessed by George Campbell and himself. The first declaration made by Katharine and signed Ketty Ogilvie was read to the court, part of which was as follows:

> ....that Andrew Stewart beside the letter brought her two doses of salts and a small phial glass with a little laudanum, and the letter was but a quarter of a sheet of paper, containing mostly directions about the salts, and how much of the laudanum to take...

The statement emphasises that Katharine only took some of the salts and laudanum to help her sleep in the days *after* her husband's death. She stated that Thomas had been feeling unwell for some time...

>....and that morning he complained of shortness of breath, and that thro' the night he had been distressed with it, she therefore gave him his tea in bed; and that when the rest of the family were at their tea, she filled up a bowlful for her husband, which with a bit of hard bisket from Dundee, she carried straight from the low room, where they were at breakfast, upstairs to her husband's room and gave him; and that she took the bisket out of a basket standing on a by-table in the room, aside the family then sitting at breakfast. But that she did not go into any closet with the tea, before giving it to her husband. That she never heard from her husband, nor any person else, that he blamed the tea for his illness. That Elizabeth Sturrock got so much of the tea Mr. Ogilvie left, as he did not drink it out, and also got another bowl of tea after, both which she gave her, out of her own hands. And this she declares to be truth.

The following day, 15th June, again from the prison and before the Sheriff-substitute, Katharine was re-examined and declared that the Lieutenant had said that he already had the salts and laudanum in his army chest that he had brought back from the East Indies and she had asked him to let her have some as 'she had much need thereof' as she was feeling unwell and unable to sleep properly.

In the first declaration made by Lieutenant Patrick Ogilvie from the prison at Forfar, on 14th June, he stated that after he returned from the East Indies in January of that year he had stayed at Eastmiln but, after 'surmises and reports' were spread about him and Katharine – which he said were false – he left his brother's house and since leaving 'he had no fix'd residence, but has been going about seeing his friends and old acquaintances'.

He admitted giving Andrew Stewart a glass phial containing laudanum and a small package of salts plus a note with instructions 'folded close by the glass'. He had asked Andrew Stewart to deliver the drugs to Katharine in person – as they were for her use only – but he had not asked him to do this in secret. He had been prescribed the salts and laudanum on account of his ill-health whilst serving abroad and for use on the journey home.

In his second declaration made the following day, 15th June,

Lieutenant Ogilvie explained that he had raised the glass phial to the light to show Andrew Stewart how much laudanum it contained. Katharine had returned the phial to the Lieutenant after his brother's death and it still contained about the same quantity of laudanum. The phial had since been sealed and lodged in the Sheriff's office. The Lieutenant denied acquiring any laudanum or arsenic from Dr James Carnegie.

There followed the reading of two papers recording the examination of Katharine Nairn and Patrick Ogilvie after their removal to the Tolbooth, in Edinburgh. The first, dated 22nd June, 1765, recorded the interrogation of Lieutenant Patrick Ogilvie in the presence of Mr James Balfour, Sheriff-substitute of Edinburgh. He was asked whether he had sent salts and other medicines to Katharine at Eastmiln; also, whether he had been accustomed to taking laudanum and salts on the same day, to which he answered 'that he was not'. However, he refused to answer any other questions about his use of laudanum. He also refused to explain the nature of the rift between him and his brother, Thomas, nor would he comment on the content of any of the letters Katharine had sent him. He also refused to answer any questions about his brother's illness and death or explain in which bedroom he had slept whilst staying at Eastmiln.

Questioned as to whether he had received any verbal messages or letters from Katharine during his imprisonment, he again refused to answer. He also chose not to answer when asked if he had acquired poison from James Carnegie but when asked about Katharine's marriage to his brother, Thomas, he said that he was present at the ceremony and had not known the bride before that day.

Patrick had clearly been advised by his defence team not to answer any questions and when asked why he was being so uncooperative he replied that he 'did not think it necessary to give any reasons'.

The court was then read the details of the examination of Katharine Nairn which took place in prison on 24th June, 1765, in the presence of Mr James Balfour. After her previous two declarations were read to her she had been asked the following questions – in which drawer had she put the drugs and the letter delivered by Andrew Stewart? Why did she ask Lieutenant Ogilvie to get drugs for her? Was she ill and if so, what was her ailment? Did she sleep with her husband on the night before his death? Did he ask her to get his tea the following morning and did she carry it up to him without stopping on the way? Did he show any unwillingness to drink the tea and did she give any that remained in the bowl to another person? Why did she oppose the idea to send for a surgeon when her husband became ill? Where did she sleep between the time of her husband's death and her arrest and imprisonment? Where was Lieutenant Ogilvie sleeping during this time?

As Patrick Ogilvie had done, Katharine refused to answer any of the questions and, moreover, she refused to sign the document.

Next to be questioned was James M'Kenzie, a forty year old session-clerk, who said he could not positively identify the handwriting in the letters Katharine had written to Thomas Ogilvie before their marriage but it was similar to a letter Alexander Ogilvie had shown him when they were both at Eastmiln, after the death of Thomas Ogilvie. Alexander had evidently considered it to be damning evidence for he told him to send the letter to the prison at Forfar as 'it might be evidence against Mrs Ogilvie'.

Also brought into court was one of Thomas Ogilvie's workers, thirty-six year old James Millam, who said that he had visited his landlord about two o'clock on the afternoon of his death and when he asked him what was the matter, he had replied, 'I am gone, James, with no less than rank poison!'

A neighbouring landowner, thirty year old, George Spalding, of Glenkilry, who was married to Bethia, Katharine's elder sister, was called next to give evidence. He was familiar with Katharine's handwriting and thought the letters produced were written by her although he did admit that he had seen her write 'sometimes better, and sometimes worse, according as her pen was'.

The last witness for the prosecution was the twenty-one year old servant, Alexander Lindsay. He had arrived for work at Eastmiln about six o'clock on the morning of his master's death and about nine o'clock he had seen Katharine Nairn standing in the closet at the top of the stairs, between the east and west bedrooms. He was on his way up to the garret to fetch a wheel when Katharine warned him not to walk across the floor above in case, by doing so, he dislodged flakes of dust and plaster from the ceiling into the closet below. When he reached the garret he saw the maidservant, Anne Sampson, standing at the top of the stairs close to the closet.

This evidence was the last to be given by the prosecution after which the list of the witnesses for the defence was given.

The prosecution team had brought forward twenty-four witnesses from an original list of one hundred and eight persons to testify against the prisoners but only ten were placed in the witness box in defence of the accused. Although old Mrs Ogilvie's name was on the original list prepared by Alexander Lockhart's defence team both Katharine and Patrick refused to have her called to give evidence on their behalf. Another person who did not attend was Andrew Stewart's wife, Martha, who, it was noted, couldn't ride and a hired chaise would have been required to get her from Alyth to Edinburgh for the trial.

The first to be called was thirty year old, George Spalding, of Glenkilry, who had also testified for the prosecution. He told the court that, contrary to the evidence of previous witnesses, Thomas Ogilvie's health was extremely poor and before his marriage he wore an unusually long 'stripped woollen night-cape' over his chest when he was out in the fields, presumably serving as some protection against the wind and rain. He had suffered with heart colic, pains in his stomach and a cough. Six years before he had suffered from 'an ulcerous fever' after which he had never fully recovered his health. Spalding had contacted Katharine's mother, Lady Nairn, on 13th February - two weeks after Katharine married Thomas Ogilvie - expressing his concern over the groom's health and suggesting the need for some financial provision for Katharine to be made should his life not be a long one.

The farm worker, James Millam, was recalled and confirmed that the day after Thomas Ogilvie had ordered his brother, Patrick, from his house he told the witness to take a letter - the one in which he asked him to come back to Eastmiln. Millam said that, although he had heard rumours about the 'indecent familiarities' between Katharine and the Lieutenant, he had never seen any evidence of it. He also told of an occasion, only four days before Thomas's death, when his master came to his house, complaining that he was cold, feeling ill and refusing to eat anything; saying he 'was fading as fast as dew off the grass'. When cross-examined later in the proceedings, however, Millam said that he had never heard his master complain of ill health before his marriage to Katharine Nairn, only afterwards. On the night before he died, he said, Thomas came again to his house, saying that he felt no better.

On the day after Thomas died, Millam had seen Lieutenant Ogilvie and his mother sitting on a bed, deeply upset - in fact, the Lieutenant was 'gushing out of tears' and 'could not be pacified'. Katharine was in another room. Before his death, Thomas had confided in the witness, insisting that Anne Clark was the cause of discord in the household. He had even borrowed a ten shilling note from the witness to pay for her journey away from Eastmiln. She left on 10th June, four days after Thomas's death.

Describing the day of his master's death, James Millam said that he was sent for about mid-day and found only Anne Clark sitting with Thomas but when he subsequently returned on several occasions there were other friends gathered around the bedside. Before leaving the witness box Millam confirmed that, while the two accused were in the prison at Forfar, the cattle at Eastmiln were sold off by Alexander Ogilvie, the sale being authorised by Patrick Ogilvie.

Jean Wallace, a thirty year old servant who had worked at Eastmiln but was now working for George Spalding, at Glenkilry, confirmed that Thomas Ogilvie had suffered from an ulcer some years before and while he was confined to bed she had frequently sat up with him.

A farm worker, Thomas Jack, testified that about ten o'clock on the morning that Thomas died, he had told him that he had been out the day before 'visiting some of his tenants biggings [outbuildings] and that he was very bad that day and had been obliged to rest himself three times'.

The next witness, thirty-five year old Elisabeth Ferguson, also saw Thomas Ogilvie on the day before he died and he told her that 'he was not very well' and had been feeling the same for some time. In evidence, twenty-two year old farm worker, John Paterson, also said that he and his sister, Margaret, had seen Thomas Ogilvie on the day before he died and were told that he was sick and that 'his bowels were all sore; and that he had not been so ill for six years. Then he lay down and took a sleep upon the ground.'

Confirmation of Thomas's state of health was also given by sixty year old, Margaret Reid, who saw him on the day before he died. He had told her that he was feeling unwell and had decided to get 'Dr Ogilvie to give him something to do him good'.

All the witnesses made a point of confirming that on the day before his death Thomas had been out *walking* the hills, not on horseback, as was his custom.

Dr James Scott, a physician from Edinburgh, was called to inform the court of some experiments he had conducted on arsenic. He said that the common form of arsenic sold to the public does not dissolve in warm water but sinks to the bottom. However, cross-examined by the prosecution, he admitted that if arsenic was put into a bowl of tea and vigorously stirred then the suspension would last long enough to kill a person drinking it - the suspension would last even longer if honey were put in the tea. Apparently, although the family at Eastmiln invariably used honey at breakfast, it appears that none was available on that particular morning.

The last witness called was George Campbell, the Sheriff-substitute, examined by the prosecutor. He told the court that after Thomas Ogilvie's death he went to the house at Eastmiln searching for any incriminating evidence. Not having any keys he broke into a cabinet belonging to the deceased. In one of the drawers he found 'some brownish white powder, wrapped up in two or three parcels.' He took these to James Carnegie, the surgeon who had provided the arsenic for the Lieutenant, but he couldn't confirm whether the powder was arsenic or not. George Campbell then said that, in the opinion of Dr Cullen, a physician in Edinburgh and a surgeon, James Russell, the powder he found was, in fact, saltpetre.

This evidence ended the interrogation of witnesses which had lasted for 33 hours for the prosecution and only 3 hours for the defence. This was followed by closing speeches of which, regrettably, no record has come to light. Suffice it to say that they would have been lengthy and heavily laden with stirring rhetoric for by the time they had been delivered it was two o'clock on the morning of the 14th August. Before the rush to the door the following announcement was made to the court:

> The Lords Commissioners of Justiciary ordain the Assize instantly to inclose in this place, and return their verdict at four o'clock this afternoon, being the fourteenth day of August current, and appoint the haill fifteen Assizers [the jurors] then to be present, and the pannels [the accused prisoners] in the mean time to be carried back to prison; and continue the diet to that time.

When the jurors returned to the court at four o'clock that afternoon they were ready to deliver their verdict - it was not unanimous but had been reached by a majority decision. They found Katharine Nairn and Lieutenant Ogilvie guilty on both counts – incest and murder.

Alexander Lockhart immediately rose to object, requesting that sentencing should be deferred on account of certain informalities in the way the trial had been conducted. This engendered a debate that lasted for a further four hours until, by eight o'clock in the evening, with all the court officials no doubt desperate for release after such a mammoth sitting, he was ordered to prepare his objections in a document to be presented to the court by eleven o'clock the next morning, Thursday, 15th August.

Despite a tense and arduous four day trial - during which he had transcribed all the evidence given in longhand - Lockhart gallantly produced his document as requested. His objections were quite justifiable and exposed the trial of Katharine Nairn and Patrick Ogilvie as a travesty of the law. He complained that while witnesses were giving evidence members of the jury had left the courtroom, eating and freely drinking alcoholic beverages in another room and conversing with prosecution witnesses and counsel – even the statutory quorum of judges was depleted every so often, at one time leaving only one judge presiding.

Lockhart also returned to the anomaly that, even before the trial, prosecution witnesses Anne Clark and the three maids - Elizabeth Sturrock, Katharine Campbell and Anne Sampson - were housed in the same room, despite Lockhart's attempt to have Anne Clark, clearly a hostile witness, accommodated separately. Little wonder that the testimony they gave in court was exactly the same for they were all reading from the same script, one that they were allowed many hours to rehearse, synchronise and perfect.

It was to no avail. Lockhart's objections were again dismissed and the verdict of guilty on both counts remained. It was at this point that he played his trump card, announcing that Katharine was pregnant and, as the law dictated that a pregnant woman could not be executed until after she had given birth - thus not killing an innocent embryo - her sentence must be deferred. It was agreed that a panel of midwives - Agnes Hill, Margaret Petrie, Grizel M'Queen, Mary Richardson and Mary Sheills - should be appointed to examine Katharine to determine whether she was, indeed, pregnant.

After this had been ordered, Patrick Ogilvie was sentenced 'to be hanged by the common hangman upon a gibbet in the Grassmarket, on Wednesday, 25th September, and his body thereafter delivered to Dr. Alexander Monro, Professor of Anatomy in the University of Edinburgh, and be by him publicly dissected and anatomised'.

The following day, 16th August, the five midwives appointed to examine Katharine delivered their verdict - that they could not be sure whether she was pregnant or not with the result that the Court decided to delay sentencing until mid day on the third Monday of November, until which time she should remain incarcerated in the Tolbooth. On account of her status and state of health she was probably housed in a private apartment whereas Lieutenant Ogilvie may well have been served with far less commodious accommodation.

Whilst awaiting his fate, Patrick seemed content to play his violin for long periods though he did put it aside to entertain a certain Miss Margaret Dow.

> This Margt. Dow drew up [had sexual relations with] with Peter [Scots equivalent of Patrick] the lieutenant after he was under sentence of Death, & in order that the keeper of the prison might admit her in to him, he told the keeper that she was one Miss. Ogilvie, a cousin of his come from London. The first of their Correspondence began from her frequenting a house opposite to that part of the prison where he was confined, where they used gesters and signs, and then by Letters.[65]

While Patrick was playing his fiddle and cavorting with the young lady, an English barrister, Mr M'Carty, joined the voices of dissent, ruffling the feathers of the Scottish law lords by vehemently challenging the proceedings in the trial and questioning the guilty verdict. His arguments were widely published in the press, including the *Edinburgh Weekly Journal*, the *Edinburgh Courant*, the *Caledonian Mercury* and the *Scots Magazine*:

'I am of the opinion,' he wrote, 'that if the crimes charged are considered severally, and the evidence produced to support one crime is taken singly without the assistance of the other, no jury in England would have found the prisoner [the Lieutenant] guilty.'

Furthermore, he protested, most of the evidence of incest, had come from 'the conjectures of women of very indifferent character and malicious dispositions'.

Nor, he suggested, was there any proof that Thomas Ogilvie had died

---

65 A note added to details of the marriage of Alexander Ogilvie and Anne Rattray, 13th January 1765, found by William Roughead.

of poison. It could be that he had succumbed to his well-documented chronic stomach trouble - whether poison was present in his body could have been determined by a post-mortem examination which the doctors, Peter Meik and Gilbert Ramsay, were willing to perform had Alexander Ogilvie allowed it - the very person who was not only in collusion with the hostile prosecution witness, Anne Clark, but also stood to gain from the death of his brother, Thomas, and the execution of Patrick.

> The great rule of evidence is to have the best proof the nature of the case can admit. That certainly has not been produced in this case. It was not opposed by the prisoners, but it was opposed by the man who wishes their destruction. The incest is supposed to be certain, because the husband is supposed to have been poisoned; and on the other hand, the man is believed to be poisoned, because there is a supposed proof of incest. Under these circumstances, it is difficult to find any means to prove the innocence of the prisoners...

Mr M'Carty suggests that an appeal against the guilty verdict and sentence of death should be presented to the House of Lords:

> It is not a common practice, I confess; but yet it has been done. I see neither reason nor law why the proceedings of the Court of Justiciary might not fall under the review of the supreme court, as well as those of the Court of Session.

Such criticism of Scottish law so incensed the Lords Commissioners of Justiciary that the publishers of the newspapers that had dared to print Mr M'Carty's damning assessment of the trial were brought to court. However, having argued that they hadn't published M'Carty's comments until *after* the trial and, 'having expressed due penitence for their transgression,' the publishers were dismissed with a rebuke.

The trial proceedings, the reliability of the evidence and the conflicting declarations made by the prisoners were reviewed and debated at great length in the press and in letters between court officials, judges and lawyers but the point was made that there was no denying the fact that Katharine Nairn had openly expressed her intention to poison her husband and also that Lieutenant Ogilvie had, despite his denials, purchased arsenic from James Carnegie in a covert manner.

Predictably, there were a number of petitions for clemency on behalf of Lieutenant Ogilvie presented to the Lord Advocate, the Solicitor General, the Lord Justice-Clerk and the Duke of Grafton, Secretary of State, who acted as an intermediary between the petitioner and King George III, the only person who could call for clemency and sanction a reprieve. As a result there were a total of four successive reprieves or stays of execution, the first for fourteen days and the last three for seven days each.

Asked to report on the points of law raised in Lieutenant Ogilvie's appeal, the Solicitor General, Mr James Montgomery, wrote to the Duke of Grafton in which he focussed on the appellant's purchase of arsenic and expressed the view that the jury had reached a correct verdict and as he had 'no doubt of their Guilt I cannot Consider any of them as proper Objects of the Royal Mercy'. He emphasised, however, that both the accused were either innocent or guilty of both crimes - murder and incest. Were Katharine, after the delivery of her child, to successfully appeal against the death sentence the question would surely be raised as to why Patrick Ogilvie had been executed when both prisoners had been together tried, convicted and sentenced to death for the same crimes. Death or clemency should apply to both.

The Lord Justice-Clerk also wrote to the Duke of Grafton on 27th September, in which he offered his appraisal of the case:

> I am humbly of the opinion, My Lord, that the Petitioner and the unhappy Lady had as fair a trial as ever I saw in that Court. The Lord Advocate did his duty in the Prosecution with the greatest Candour and Temper. Several Preliminary Points of Law were stated by the Council of the Defenders, but were all unanimously over-ruled by the Court, who were so far from being prejudiced against the Prisoners that I dare say (for the Honour of this Countrey and of Human Nature itself) they wished that the Pannels [the accused] might be found Innocent – at least I can say so much for myself. Our Juries here consist of fifteen persons, and the Plurality of Voices condemn or acquit. I never saw, I think, a better Jury impannelled in that Court;

they were all Gentleman of Distinction and Candour. Tho' the verdict bears that it was by the Plurality of Voices, yet there was but one or at most two, as I heard, who dissented.

The opinion of the Lord Advocate, Thomas Miller, was summed up in his letter to the Duke of Grafton, dated 23rd October:

> ....all I can say is that the Jury consisted of Fifteen Gentlemen of the highest Rank and Character I ever saw upon any Trial in that Court. The whole Judges were present, and neither at that time nor since have I heard it suggested that any of the Judges entertained the least doubt of the Justice of the Verdict. As to myself, I attended the Trial from the beginning to the end in my office as the Publick Prosecutor, and the Evidence appeared to me entirely satisfactory, and no circumstance whatever appeared in the whole course of the Trial which did then, or do now, induce me to think that the Jury has in over strong measure delivered their Verdict...
>
> Now it is exceedingly remarkable that in this Case the material part of the Evidence arises from the Prisoners themselves. The falsehood of their Declarations before the Sheriff, before they were put upon their guard by their Council to answer no questions; the clear Evidence of Lieutenant Ogilvie's having bought the Arsenick upon a false pretence; his denial of his having bought it, and when discovered, his not attempting to give an account how he disposed of it; the previous resolution and threatenings of Mrs Ogilvie to take away the life of her Husband, proved by the Depositions of Miss Clark and of Andrew Stewart, the Brother-in-Law of the Prisoners, and a most reluctant witness, so far as regard to his oath would permit him; her obstinate opposition to Andrew Stewart's advice and entreaty to call a Surgeon when her Husband was dying; her injunction to Andrew [sic] Meik, Surgeon, who arrived soon after her Husband's death; the Confederacy of both the Prisoners in contriving a false story for their Defence, recently after the Crime was committed; and endeavouring to Corrupt Elizabeth Sturrock to swear to that false story – these are all Circumstances of real Evidence, arising from the Prisoners themselves, which, joined to the other proofs do, in my humble apprehension, put their guilt out of all question.

The Lord Advocate finishes by offering a somewhat petulant swipe at the well-publicised opinion of Mr M'Carty:

I do not know what character that Gentleman bears in the Law of England; but I am sure no Scottish counsel would have put his name to such an opinion.

Ultimately, Lieutenant Ogilvie's luck had run out and all avenues for a fifth reprieve were removed. On 7th November, the Duke of Grafton wrote a letter to the Lord Advocate advising him that the King had, after careful consideration of all the material relevant to the case, finally rejected the appeal and no further reprieves would be given.

On the day before his execution Lieutenant Ogilvie wrote his 'dying speech' which was published in pamphlet form soon after his death:

> I, Lieutenant Patrick Ogilvy, considering myself upon the brink of this mortal life into eternity; and as I have but few hours to live, would chuse [sic] to employ them in the way that would most conduce to my eternal happiness; And though my years be few, and my sins many; yet I hope, through God's grace, and the interposition of my blessed Redeemer, that the gates of heaven will not be shut upon me, in whatever view I as a criminal may be looked on by the generality of mankind; and I hope those who best knew me, will do me justice when I am gone.
>
> As to the crimes I am accused of, the trial itself will show the propensity of the witnesses, where civility and possibly folly, are explained into actual guilt; and which possibly had the greater effect in making them believed; and of both crimes for which I am now doomed to suffer, I declare my innocence; and that no persuasion could ever have made me condescend to them. I freely forgive every person concerned in this melancholy affair; and wherein any of them have been faulty to me, I pray God to forgive them.

After thanking all those who had petitioned on his behalf and Captain James Robb, the keeper and other warders of the prison at the Tolbooth for 'their great kindness', he ends by saying:

> I desire to die in Peace with all Men, even my greatest Enemies, begging Forgiveness to them, as I hope for it from that God in whose presence I am soon to appear; hoping for the Pardon of my Sins, and Entrance into Eternal Bliss, through the Merits and Intercession of my Redeemer, to whom I recommend my Spirit; Come, Sweet Jesus, come quickly, and receive it.

The next morning, Wednesday 13th November, 1765, Patrick, having cast aside Miss Dow and his violin, was brought from his cell in the Tolbooth and escorted by armed City Guards and 'the magistrates with their white staves' to the place of execution - the Grassmarket, a cattle market in the shadow of Edinburgh Castle. The armed guards were employed to prevent attack and possibly death by members of the surging crowds, bellowing for the prisoner's blood. As members of Patrick's old regiment were stationed in Edinburgh Castle at the time they were confined to barracks until after the execution in case any of them attempted a rescue.

The following description of the execution appeared in the *Scots Magazine*, in October, 1765:

> A very moving incident happened at his execution. After he was turned over, the noose of the rope slipped, and he fell to the ground. He was immediately taken up, and dragged up the ladder by the assistance of the city-servants, he making what resistance he could; and then the executioner, having again put the rope about his neck, turned him over a second time, and he continued hanging until dead. He behaved with decency and resignation. His dying speech was immediately published but there is not the least mention of his unhappy partner.[66]

It was rumoured at the time that some of the prisoner's friends had bribed the hangman to loosen the rope in the mistaken belief that once an attempt to hang a person had failed, it could not be tried again. The added horror of the bungled hanging must have delighted the raucous crowds that assembled to watch the hideous spectacle, especially those - with many fashionable women amongst their number - who had paid good money to reserve seats from windows overlooking the Grassmarket. It was reported in documents unearthed by William Roughead that, soon after the execution, Dr Alexander Monro gave a public lecture during which he dissected the body of Lieutenant Ogilvie 'after which it was soldered up & carried off to be buried'.

---

66 The 'Dying Speech' of Lieutenant Patrick Ogilvie was printed as a broadside in 1765 (Signet Library).

On Monday, 18th November, 1765, Katharine was back in court for the verdict of the midwives; they testified that she was 'near six months advanced in her pregnancy' and the court agreed to delay the sentencing until mid-March. In the meantime, the midwives were to make regular visits to Katharine in the Tolbooth until the birth.

Three days later Katharine petitioned the court for a person in authority to be appointed to manage her late husband's estate at Eastmiln and guard the interests of his unborn child. As heir-presumptive, Alexander was questioned but he stated that his life had become 'very uncomfortable' and he felt unable to remain in Scotland; it was his intention to leave the country - when he could afford it. Although he agreed to the appointment of someone to guard the unborn infant's inheritance he couldn't resist adding; 'It is at least rendered very doubtful if that child was procreate of the deceased Thomas Ogilvy of Eastmiln' - an assertion impossible to prove, of course, prior to the development of DNA profiling in paternity disputes and criminal investigations.

On 27th February, the following year, Katharine gave birth to a daughter in prison and on Monday, 10th March she was due to appear in court once more, this time to be sentenced to death. As she was too ill to attend she was required to make her court appearance the following Monday, 17th March. However, the judges, in view of Katharine's health, went to the Tolbooth to issue the sentence but they were in for a shock. The prison keeper, Captain James Robb, informed them that she had escaped at seven o'clock in the evening of the previous Saturday – leaving her newborn child behind - and a warrant for her capture had been issued on Sunday, 16th March. The following day the magistrates offered a reward of one hundred guineas for anyone who managed to apprehend her and a similar notice was issued by Government officials:

> There is reason to suspect the said Katharine Nairn went off on Saturday night in a post-chaise for England by the way of Berwick,

and had on when she went away an officer's habit and a hat slouched in the cocks, with a cockade in it. She is about twenty-two years of age, middle-sized, and strong made; has a high nose, black eyebrows, and of a pale complexion.

That Katharine Ogilvie...made her escape out of prison on Saturday, the 15th instant, about seven o'clock in the evening; that the escape was not discovered or made known to the Magistrates till the next day between one and two in the afternoon, when a search was immediately made through the city, and a messenger despatched to endeavour to trace, and if possible overtake her on the London road; but all the intelligence he could get was that a young gentleman, very thin and sickly, muffed up in a great coat, and attended by a servant had passed through Haddington on Saturday at midnight, and pushed on with four horses, day and night, from stage to stage, towards London.[67]

Naturally, such a daring escape became the subject of fevered conjecture and it was suggested that Katharine's uncle, the advocate Mr William Nairn (later Lord Dunsinnan, a Senator of the College of Justice) helped in her daring bid for freedom. The prison keeper, Captain James Robb, of course, also came under suspicion. In March, the *Gentleman's Magazine* reported that whilst in the Tolbooth she was awarded certain privileges and her escape was well planned:

> She was indulged on account of her weakness with a quiet and privacy which the nature of her illness required. She desired, however, that her room door might be left open for the benefit of the air, and being left alone for the night, she took occasion to dress herself in man's apparel, and walking out into the court and mixing with the strangers that were going out, passed unnoticed by the keepers. She seems to have been well seconded, for certain information was received at Mr Fielding's office that she was in Dover on the Wednesday following, in the dress of an officer, endeavouring to procure a passage to France,

---

67 On 23rd March, a week after Katharine's escape from prison, her daughter died, having lived for less than a month. It was recorded that her death was caused by being '*overlaid*'. This may have meant that she was smothered or succumbed to disease, which was rife in the prison. Most prisoners, some as young as 12, were kept in cramped and appallingly filthy conditions whilst those able to pay could be housed in a separate room and even have the use of a bed.

which probably she has since obtained.

Further speculation appeared in the *Gentleman's Magazine* in April:

> Mrs Ogilvy not having an opportunity to get off to France, returned from Dover to London, took a hackney coach to Billingsgate, got on board a Gravesend boat with a gentleman to accompany her, agreed with a tilt boat there to take them over to France for eight guineas and a guinea a day for waiting for them four days in order to bring them back; which tilt boat landed them at Calais, but is since returned without them.

In William Roughead's book on the case he expresses the view that the real story behind Katharine's dramatic escape lay elsewhere. He refers to an account given by Sir Daniel Wilson, 'on the authority of Charles Kirkpatrick Sharpe' in his book, *Memorials of Edinburgh*, in which he suggests that one of the midwives in attendance on Katharine during her confinement was instrumental in the daring escape. In the years following the event, Mrs Mary Sheills, widow of a wigmaker in Edinburgh, made no secret of the part that she and others had played. Mrs Sheills had, during the time she was supervising Katharine's confinement, been suffering from severe toothache and was accustomed to arriving and leaving the prison with her head completely muffled up 'in divers wrappings'. Once the prison guards became used to her familiar figure coming and going she exchanged her clothes with Katharine that Saturday evening allowing her to make her escape, groaning as with toothache for good effect, and passing through the gates of the prison without the guards suspecting that the figure scuttling past them was any other than the midwife, Mary Sheills, going about her duties.

Once free, Katharine, agitated and confused, made the mistake of knocking on the door of Lord Alva's house in James's Court, believing it to be the home of the family lawyer, Mr Smyth. The foot-boy who answered the door recognised Katharine and raised the alarm but she ran to the home of her uncle, the advocate William Nairn, in Parliament Close, where she hid in the cellar. It was here that she put on the officer's uniform and left in a post-chaise for Dover, in the company of William Nairn's clerk, James Bremner. William Roughead quotes an account of the journey:

> Notwithstanding her very critical situation, Mr Bremner was in momentary dread all the way of a discovery, in consequence of her extreme frivolity of behaviour, as she was continually putting her head out of the window and laughing immoderately.[68]

According to a letter from Calais, published in the *Public Advertiser*, on 20th June, 1766, once she reached France Katharine soon found a temporary protector, an Irish officer in the French service, to whom she pretended to be married while they were staying at the Silver Lion, in Calais;

> But he having when in liquor quarrelled with Mons. La Bouillie, the Governor's son, whom he wounded in a duel on the Ramparts, she and her gallant were obliged to decamp in haste; but being pursued, were taken and brought back to Calais, and committed to prison; but were soon released, though not until after the officer (a second lieutenant) was degraded. He has since left her, and she has no means of subsistence than the charitable contributions of her fellow countrymen.

There were many rumours concerning Katharine's whereabouts after her escape. One conjecture was that she married a French gentleman, had a large family and died at a good age. In other accounts she was married to a Dutch gentleman or alternatively, she fled to America where she married and had many children. It was also widely reported that she had entered a convent in Lille, near the French-Belgian border, and was still there a decade later though it seems doubtful whether she, still in her early twenties and having had more than one amorous liaison, would have settled for the convent life - even with a charge of murder and incest over her head.

Despite William Roughead's extensive enquiries at the National Archives in Paris and other official records in Lille he was unable to verify this as most of the convent records were destroyed during the French Revolution. However, during his researches in the Signet

---

68 From *A Series of Original Portraits and Caricature Etchings*. John Kay, Edinburgh 1842.

Library, in Edinburgh, he found a note in the copy of the trial that had belonged to the antiquary, James Maidment, which seemed to give some credence to Katharine's sojourn in a convent:

> The above statement is correct. Catherine Ogilvie or Nairne did not marry a French nobleman, as was at one time reported. She entered a convent, and remained there until the troubles consequent upon the French Revolution compelled herself and the other inmates to fly to England, where she died. My informant, Mr. Irvine, lawyer at Dunse, tells me that a friend of his saw her tomb, with the name "Catherine Ogilvie" upon it; and that on enquiry, the Superior mentioned that of all the females in the convent she was the most exemplary in every respect.

As for Alexander Ogilvie, on 24th February, 1766, despite being still married to Anne Rattray, he married Margaret Dow, the same young woman who had entertained the Lieutenant in prison. He was arrested on a charge of bigamy on 1st March and his trial set for 4th August. It was reported that Alexander was held in the Tolbooth in Edinburgh 'accused of marrying for a second wife a young girl, who, if fame belies not, was rather too intimate with his brother the Lieutenant while under sentence of Death.'

This surprising denouement elicited a rather prim comment from William Roughead in his book on the case, even though, at the time, Miss Dow, whilst entertaining his brother, Patrick, may not have been in a relationship with Alexander Ogilvie, in which case she was not, in fact, married to him, bigamously or otherwise:

> For Patrick thus to embark upon a fresh affair with his new sister-in-law - albeit an unlawful one - shows, in a person so gravely situated, a singular lack of delicacy and tact.

However, prior to the bigamy trial date, Alexander petitioned the Court for a voluntary banishment from Scotland for seven years' duration, dating from 4th October.

Whether Alexander did, with the aid of Anne Clark, attempt to engineer the deaths of his two brothers - and Katharine - to inherit the Eastmiln estate, he was unsuccessful for it was recorded that the lands of Eastmiln 'now form part of the estate of Kirkhillocks, which belongs to James Small, having been acquired by Francis Rattray of Kirkhillocks'.[69]

Anyone reading an account of this extraordinary case must surely wonder why on earth did Katharine Nairn marry Thomas Ogilvie at a time when divorce was not an option? She made it known from the start that she didn't - and never would - love him. Nor was he a wealthy man; although he owned land and tenant farms the house at Eastmiln was modest in size, isolated and singularly lacking in sufficient space to comfortably accommodate both family members and servants. She could not have expected to inherit vast wealth on her husband's death. Katharine's friends tried to persuade her not to marry him but they proved powerless to prevent it. It may be that she was coerced by her family into marriage with the middle-aged and sickly Thomas Ogilvie on account of her licentious and wanton ways. Had Katharine, in her teens, shown a wayward disregard for convention and already embarked on amorous adventures? She was certainly prepared to exhibit behaviour that was considered outrageous and immoral by her peers and, moreover, without restraint within three weeks of her marriage. If this was the case, marrying her off to Thomas Ogilvie, though he may not have been ideal husband material, would have been a convenient solution - even if the Ogilvie family had its own maverick in the shape of the youngest Ogilvie brother, Alexander.

Clearly Thomas's sexual proclivity may be called into question as he had married late and seemed disinterested in having any sexual relations with his pretty young wife - or it could be that Thomas was simply an impotent and ailing bore. If Katharine had been forced to marry him against her will, could this be the reason she felt entitled - and despised him enough - to flaunt her affair with Patrick under his nose and, moreover, with her mother-in-law also living in close

---

69 From: *Angus or Forfarshire: the Land and People.* Alexander J. Warden. Published Dundee, 1882.

proximity in the house?

By the same token, why did Patrick feel at liberty to have sexual relations with his elder brother's wife with such reckless abandon? He was evidently aggrieved and resentful over the ongoing dispute regarding his late father's legacy, which he felt Thomas was withholding from him but such feuds were not uncommon at a time when it fell to the eldest son to manage the financial affairs of the family, whether he was suitably prudent for the task or, on the other hand, either mad, reckless or parsimonious.

Whatever the reason, Patrick felt entitled to blatantly cuckold his brother - an attitude perhaps coloured by the knowledge that the marriage had been arranged, and was not a love match. Such flouting of the rules, however, actually bedding a man's bride in his own home and in full view of family members and servants suggests that he either despised his brother or, alternatively, that he knew full well that Thomas was not - and never would be - emotionally attached to his wife and therefore she was, to his mind at least, 'fair game'.

What part did Alexander, the youngest of the three Ogilvie brothers, play in the drama? He seemed to have been something of a maverick, a libertine, with a preference for working-class women, respectably employed or otherwise. He was even willing to breach the strict class conventions of the day and co-habit with the likes of the disreputable Anne Clark and even marry, whether legally or not, Anne Rattray and Margaret Dow, both women considered beyond the pale either through their lewd behaviour or their 'low birth'. As this side of his character would have been known it is more surprising that the highly respectable Nairn family agreed to Katharine's marriage into a family with such a renegade in its number.

Was Alexander so angry at the family's disapproval of his marriage to Anne Rattray that he installed Anne Clark in Eastmiln to spy and cause as much friction as possible between Thomas and his new bride? Had the family threatened to disown him and cut him out of any legacies due to him on account of the dissolute lifestyle he had chosen? Did he plan the whole disastrous affair? Did he realise that when Thomas was away at Dunsinnan for those three or four nights soon after the marriage (probably to discuss some form of insurance for Katharine after her brother-in-law, George Spalding, had written to Lady Nairn about his ill-health) Katharine and Patrick would take advantage of his absence and jump into bed together? Did Alexander hope that the reckless lovers would eventually either attempt to remove Thomas Ogilvie or, whether they did resort to killing him or not, their scandalous liaison would, in the eyes of the law, inevitably provide a perfect motive for murder.

If this was Alexander's plan the immediate attraction between Patrick and Katharine, only three weeks after the marriage to Thomas, provided Anne Clark, Alexander's scheming ally, with the perfect opportunity to spread scandalous revelations about the affair, making sure that when he returned Thomas knew what was going on right under his nose within the family home. Yet if financial gain was Alexander's motive his determination to eliminate both Patrick and Katharine as possible beneficiaries, no matter how insignificant the inheritance, defied explanation unless, of course, his family's disapproval of his marriage to Anne Rattray and their rejection of him had affected him, not for financial reasons, but on a very deep emotional level. This was suggested by the lawyer, Mr M'Carty, in his controversial assessment of the case.

Alexander's ally and erstwhile lover, Anne Clark, was surely on a par with Jane Cox, the duplicitous companion of Florence Bravo in the Charles Bravo poisoning case of 1876, for her propensity for malicious meddling.[70] Indeed, it might not be altogether preposterous to suggest an altogether different scenario than the one presented to the court at the trial of Katharine Nairn and Patrick Ogilvie - that Anne Clark, with the connivance of Alexander Ogilvie - may have poisoned the sickly Thomas Ogilvie, in the knowledge that the love affair between Katharine and Patrick would provide

---

70 See author's book, *Murder at the Priory: The Mysterious Poisoning of Charles Bravo*. There is also a chapter on the case in *Deadly Service: Murderous Maids, Devious Housekeepers and Butlers Who Kill.*

Mary Blandy wearing leg irons in the grounds of Oxford Gaol
© Getty Images / Hulton Archive

Captain William Cranstoun
© Getty Images / Hulton Archive

Mary Blandy
© Getty Images / Hulton Archive

Oxford Castle, with the gaoler's house on the right

*John Swan and Elizabeth Jeffries in Chelmsford Prison
from a contemporary pamphlet*

The ONLY True and Authentic

TRIAL

OF

JOHN SWAN

AND

Miss ELIZABETH JEFFREYS,

FOR THE

MURDER

Of her UNCLE,

Mr. *Joseph Jeffreys*, of *Walthamstow* in *Essex*,

AT THE

LENT ASSIZES held at CHELMSFORD,
On *Wednesday* the Eleventh instant,

BEFORE THE

Hon. Sir *Martin Wright* and Sir *Michael Foster*, Knts.
Two of His Majesty's Justices of the Court of *King's-Bench*.

To which are added,

ORIGINAL LETTERS, in which are included their own Confessions; and several Particulars relating to the Murder, never before made public.
Also the WILL of the late Mr. JEFFREYS.

LONDON,

Printed: And sold by *J. Robinson* in *Ludgate-Street*; R. *Baldwin*, in *Pater-noster-Row*; G. *Woodfall*, at *Charing-Cross*; Mrs. *Dodd*, without *Temple-Bar*; and Mess. *Kingman, Cooke*, and *James*, at the *Royal-Exchange*; and by all Booksellers; and of the Hawkers in Town and Country.
M.DCC.LII.   [Price Sixpence.]

Cover of a contemporary pamphlet, 1752

Portrait of Katharine Nairn

THE TRIAL

OF

KATHARINE NAIRN

AND

PATRICK OGILVIE,

FOR THE

CRIMES of INCEST and MURDER.

CONTAINING

The whole Procedure of the High Court of Justiciary, upon the 5th, 12th, 13th, 14th, 15th, and 16th days of August 1765.

EDINBURGH printed: LONDON reprinted, For T. BECKET and P. A. DE HONDT, at Tully's Head, near Surry-Street, in the Strand. M,DCC,LXV.

Left: The Grassmarket, with Edinburgh Castle in the background
Right: Parliament Close, William Nairn's residence

Left and above:
Sarah Gale and James Greenacre in the dock
Courtesy Historical and Special Collections,
Harvard Law School Library

James Greenacre dismembering Hannah Brown, from an execution broadside
John Johnson Collection: Murder and Executions Folder 6 (8). By permission of The Bodleian Libraries, University of Oxford

An execution broadside depicting James Greenacre and Sarah Gale
John Johnson Collection: Murder and Executions Folder 6 (5). By permission of The Bodleian Libraries, University of Oxford

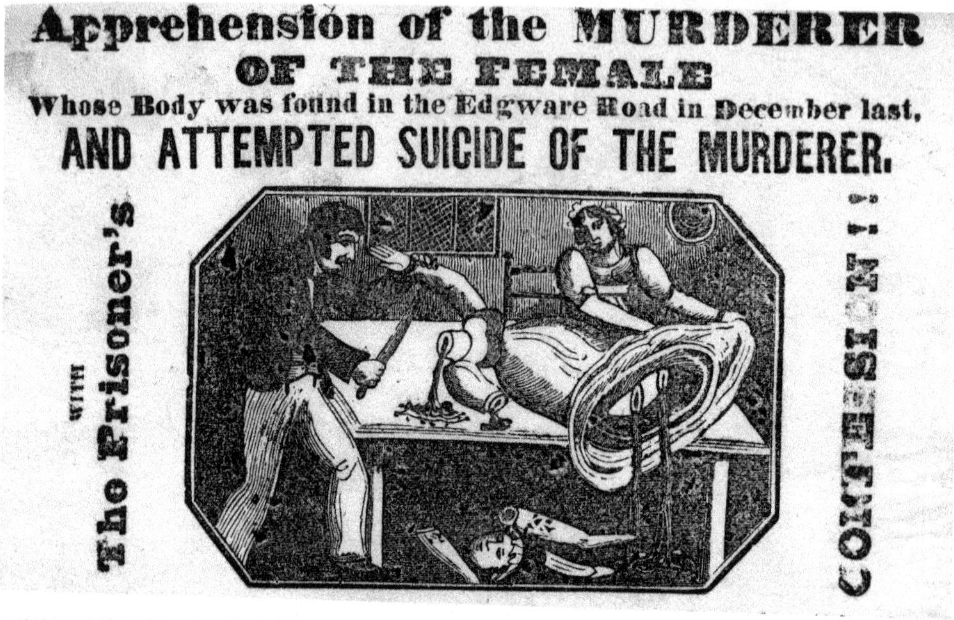

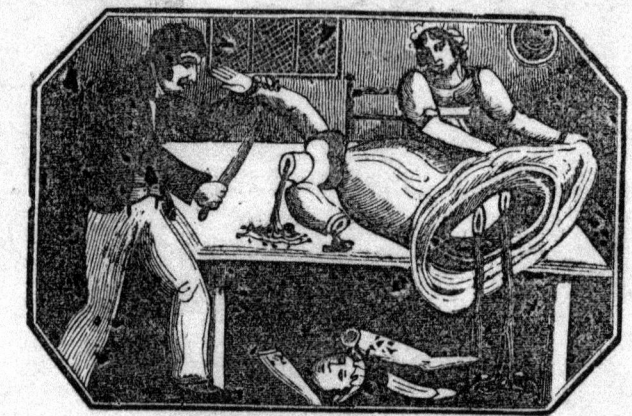

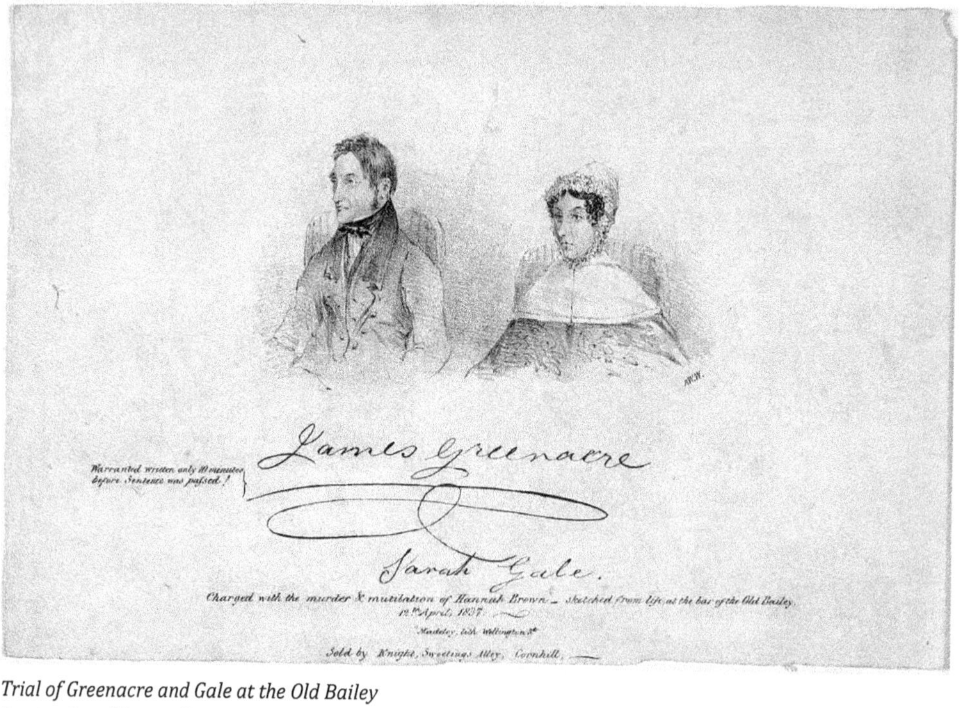

Trial of Greenacre and Gale at the Old Bailey
Courtesy State Library of New South Wales, PXE 910 / a671002

Illustrated Police News, 9th September 1871

Maynard's shop in West Street, Brighton
© *Chris Horlock Collection*

Christiana Edmunds at her trial

a convenient motive for murder - that and the evidence of Patrick's easy access to arsenic (it was readily available for domestic use) and his resentment over the legacy from his father that he felt was being withheld by his elder brother.

If Thomas's death was, indeed, a case of murder, and not caused by either an escalation of his well-documented chronic bowel disease or, as we have seen in similar cases of the 18th and 19th centuries, non-criminal poisoning arising from the presence of arsenic and other toxins in everyday use. Prior to refrigeration, the pasteurisation of milk products and stringent tests for contamination, there was widespread food adulteration. If, however, Thomas was, in fact, murdered, his young bride and the Lieutenant provided the perfect scapegoats, leaving the youngest brother, Alexander, to inherit the entire estate, free at last to enjoy the company of his wife of choice and his erstwhile 'lying whore', formerly so despised by the rest of the family.

Whether or not Katharine did poison her husband by adding arsenic to his morning tea, provided by the Lieutenant, must remain a matter of conjecture. Suffice it to say that their defence advocate, Alexander Lockhart, was, of course, quite right when he declared the trial was a travesty. Had it been conducted today it would surely have been dismissed as 'unsound' and a re-trial ordered. One must surely question the verdict when most of the evidence of the prosecution witnesses was clearly orchestrated and their counsel had been allowed thirty-three hours to present the case for the prosecution whereas the defence lawyers were given merely three hours to plead their case.

It beggars belief that the jurors chose to believe the testimony of Anne Clark, known to be a devious and meddlesome liar who, with Alexander Ogilvie, bore such malice towards the accused that she had actually announced that she 'wished to deprive them of their lives'. If that were not enough, the pronouncements of the maids, whether true or false, would have been generally disregarded as untrustworthy - yet the jurors chose to believe their evidence rather than that given by the medical men and military colleagues of Lieutenant Ogilvie.

Why was this so? Though sexual intercourse between a married woman and her brother-in-law would now be classed as adultery Katharine and Patrick were charged with incest, a crime deemed so degenerate, so appalling and beyond acceptability to the mores of 18th century society (as it remains so today) that the majority of those elected to exercise the law - a jury of fifteen men – could not countenance any verdict other than guilty. Yet Katharine and Patrick must have known that society would condemn them - would they have been so foolhardy as to poison Katharine's husband knowing they would, inevitably, be arrested and tried and, with incest added to the charge of murder, be so vilified and despised that there was not the remotest chance of leniency? Even if they were not guilty of murder they must have known that death would be the only outcome of so scandalous an affair.

The Ogilvie family had an eventful and tragic history in the eighteenth century; some members of which were reckless and morally corrupt in equal measure. Old Mrs Ogilvie's husband, Thomas, had been a Jacobite prisoner in Edinburgh Castle since the 1745 uprising. In April, 1751, in an attempt to escape 'by a net tied to an iron ring, he fell and fractured his skull' having landed on the sloping rock face on the south side of the Castle.

According to a note in the files on the family, quoted by William Roughead, all four Ogilvie sons came to a bad end:

> The eldest Brother of this family grew Delirious & hang'd himself in 48 [1748] in a sheep coat & it was said the place where [he] hang up himself was too low & he came down & Delved below his feet to make it proper for him. William went on board a Man of War carpenter & and was crushed to Death twixt two Ships.
>
> Thomas and Patrick the Lieutenant how they made their Exit is well known. Katharine Nairn's child was overlaid.

Finally, it seems that Alexander Ogilvie's fate was equally unfortunate for Roughead quotes from Alexander J. Warden's book, published in 1882:

Alexander Ogilvy, a younger brother of the poisoned man [Thomas] and of the male poisoner [Patrick] is said to have been the means of bringing his brother and sister-in-law to trial. He was, himself, a few days before Mrs. Ogilvy escaped, convicted of bigamy, and sentenced to banishment for seven years, but he was allowed to remain in Scotland two months to arrange his affairs, and he never left the country. It is said that while leaning over the window of a house in Edinburgh he overbalanced himself, fell over, and was killed.

With such a litany of disaster, mainly generated by reckless bravado, one must surely question old Mrs Ogilvie's mothering skills for she had raised at least two scoundrels who were totally devoid of any moral restraint. Did she choose to turn a blind eye to what was going on in the house at Eastmiln on account of her age or was it through apathy, resignation or diplomacy? Perhaps she had grown weary of their escapades and untimely ends; little wonder that, when her only remaining son, Alexander, was in prison on a charge of bigamy, 'the intrepid dowager' was described in a court paper...

> What add much to the melancholy disasters, the mother of yt [that] Unfortunate family is still alive, though luckily for her, she is formed by nature of too obdurate and unfeeling a dispn [disposition] to be much affected with ye catastrophe of her family.

If this was a fair description of the old woman it might well explain why both Katharine and Patrick were adamant that they did not want her to appear as a defence witness at their trial - they probably realised they could expect little sympathy from a heartless matriarch who had become completely immune to the many tragedies that life had thrown at her.

Sarah Gale and James Greenacre

'As the husband is, the wife is: thou art mated with a clown and the grossness of his nature will have weight to drag thee down...'

By the end of December, 1836, shortly before the young Queen Victoria ascended the throne, workmen had completed the building of five terraced dwellings called Canterbury Villas, in London's Edgware Road. Four of these houses were already occupied and the one that had remained empty housed a watchman. As it was the Christmas period all work had stopped on Saturday 24th December. It was not until four days later, on 28th December, that one of the bricklayers, Robert Bond, returned to the site; in amongst materials stacked in readiness for the resumption of the building work, he noticed a paving slab leaning against the front garden wall behind which someone had tried to conceal a bulky package wrapped in coarse sacking. Moving aside the stone slab he was alarmed to see that copious amounts of blood had oozed from the contents and formed a frozen pool on the ground.

After Robert Bond had fetched the superintendent in charge of the building works it was decided to open the package. Inside was a human torso - the head and legs were missing. It was wrapped in a piece of blue cotton material that looked as if it had been torn from a child's frock, as well as an old towel and part of a small white shawl. Shocked, they called for the assistance of the police which arrived in the form of Constable Pegler who took charge of the gruesome parcel and, finding a wheelbarrow, took it to St James's Workhouse in Paddington.

Once there, the parish physician, Dr Girdwood, examined the remains and established that the torso belonged to a female of about fifty years of age and, judging by the arms and hands, which were rough and unusually muscular, the woman had been accustomed to hard manual labour. He saw no obvious signs of disease that might account for death and in all probability it was a case of murder followed by a hasty dismemberment – the head had been partly severed with a strong, serrated blade, whilst the remainder had been brutally broken off.

An inquest on the body was held at the White Lion Inn, Edgware Road, on Saturday 31st December. Dr Girdwood gave a detailed medical description of the torso but the identity of the dead woman remained a mystery; the jury, therefore, could only record a verdict of 'Wilful Murder against some person or persons unknown.'

The remains were buried in Paddington churchyard and it seemed that the whole gruesome affair would thereafter remain unresolved.

However, within a week, on 6th January, 1837, a human head was dredged up from Johnson's Lock in the Regent's Canal. The lock-keeper, Matthias Ralph, whilst attempting to close the lock gates, found that something was lodged in the way, preventing the gates from closing properly. Reaching for his hitcher, (a sturdy 20 ft long pole with a metal hook on the end) used for hoisting up carcasses, human and animal, he eventually managed to pull an object out of the water. *It was a human head.* The police were alerted once more and took possession of the grim find. It was taken to a surgeon, Dr Birtwhistle, to make a preliminary examination. There were a number of bruises and lacerations clearly visible and the lower jaw was broken though he thought that some of these injuries might have been done by the hitcher as it hauled the head from the water. The recently buried torso in Paddington graveyard was exhumed and it was established by Dr Girdwood, that the head and the torso belonged to the same body. As to the identity of the dead person, that was to remain a mystery for a while longer.

Huge numbers of Londoners came to view the head but, as decomposition had already begun to disfigure the features, it was decided to preserve it in spirits at Dr Girdwood's premises and allow members of the public to view it through the glass.[71]

The legs of the mystery woman's body were not discovered until 2nd February. A labourer, James Page, was cutting osiers[72] in land belonging to a Mr Tenpenny, in Coldharbour Lane, Camberwell, when he stepped over a ditch and saw a partly submerged package wrapped up in sacking. Protruding from a hole in the sack was a human knee. He and a fellow workman un-wrapped the package and found it contained a pair of human legs. These they took straight to Dr Girdwood who was able to ascertain that they belonged to the other dismembered remains - the torso and the head - completing the corpse of a murdered woman.

Despite countless enquiries by the police and citizens alike - the press reported the finding of the body parts in some detail - it was not until 20th March that the identity of the murdered woman was established. Mr Gay, a broker in Goodge Street, Tottenham Court Road, was given permission by Mr Thornton, the churchwarden of the parish of Paddington, to view the decapitated head. He was concerned that the dead woman might have been his sister, Hannah Brown, who he had last seen on the afternoon of the previous Christmas Eve. Other people familiar with Hannah came forward to identify the remains and also to inform the authorities about the relationship between Hannah and a man called James Greenacre. Hannah had accepted his proposal of marriage and, on Christmas

---

71 Prior to the development of photography, the police relied entirely on local knowledge and recognition of the bodies of victims of murder or accidents. In 1726, the decapitated head of John Hayes was displayed on a pole for identification purposes. His wife, Catherine, was eventually burned at the stake for her part in his murder and the dismemberment of his body. See author's book, *Bad Companions*.
72 Cultivated willow for use in basketry and furniture caning. Some reports stated that the package was found in bushes near the osier bed.

Eve, she had left her lodgings in Union Street, Middlesex Hospital, to meet Greenacre at his house in Carpenter's Buildings, Camberwell. They had planned to marry on Christmas Day.

A warrant for the arrest of James Greenacre was issued by magistrates at Marylebone Police Office on 24th March. By this time, Greenacre had moved to lodgings in St Alban's Street, Kennington Road, and when apprehended on Sunday 26th March, he was in bed with a woman called Sarah Gale; Greenacre, Gale and her four year old son, George, were taken into custody.

News of their arrest spread like wild-fire and by the time the pair were brought before the magistrates - Mr Rawlinson, Lord Montfort and Mr Shutt - at the Police Court the following day, Monday 27th March, huge crowds had gathered in Marylebone High Street. James Greenacre was charged with the murder of Hannah Brown and Sarah Gale with being an accessory.

As James Greenacre stood in the dock he was described as a man about fifty years of age and of average height, though a little stout. According to the Champion newspaper, Greenacre 'wore a great coat, tightly buttoned up, and the woman a green cloak, with a white straw bonnet trimmed with blue; the former appeared to be about fifty years of age, and the latter thirty [she was, in fact, thirty-eight] - she was accompanied by her child, a little boy about four years old.'

Sarah Gale seems to have attracted particular attention from the spectators, possibly because she had the child with her. It was noted by several newspapers that Greenacre adopted a casual air, returning the inquisitive gaze directed at him with an air of insolence. His indifference, however, was bravado, for he had already attempted to strangle himself with a handkerchief whilst in police custody. *Freeman's Journal* of 31st March told its readers that Greenacre 'leant his elbow on the iron railing [of the dock] and his cheek on his left hand, and in that position continued throughout the whole of the lengthened investigation; he seemed in a very weak state, owing to his having, shortly after he was locked up in the station-house in Hermitage-street, Paddington, made a most determined attempt to strangle himself in his cell with a handkerchief.'

The *London Standard* also described the suicide attempt stating that once he had been revived he asked for coffee and toast and 'shortly afterwards, the female [Sarah Gale] was brought from her cell into the same room, where some tea had been provided for her; when, seeing her depressed state of mind, he said, "Don't be down-hearted – keep your spirits up." When they had finished their breakfast Greenacre complained that he felt the blood trickling from the place in his neck where he had been bled, and said that they 'had not treated him very kindly.' Asked if he would like a 'fresh plaister on the wound,' he replied, 'with the greatest coolness, "No, let it be until I have washed myself, and have put on a clean shirt."

'On being removed from the bar to the lock-up, he requested to be placed in as comfortable a one as possible, as he felt very cold.'

The first court appearance on Monday 27th March was widely reported. The *London Standard* told its readers:

> At an early hour the greater portion of High-street, and every avenue leading to the Marylebone-office were thronged by a crowd who were anxiously awaiting the prisoners' arrival, which, according to an arrangement made by the magistrates, and communicated to Inspector Feltham, was delayed until after twelve o'clock, when, in order to avoid confusion (and there could not have been, between eleven and twelve, no fewer than 4000 or 5000 people congregated in Grotto-passage, Paradise-street, and in front of the office private door), many of the tradesmen deemed it necessary, so great was the curiosity of the crowd, and their eagerness to force their way towards the justice-room, to put up their shutters and a great many policemen of the D division were on duty to keep the road and footways as clear as possible.
>
> At a quarter past twelve a hackney-coach was seen to come down Paddington-street, followed by a mob of several hundred persons, and in a moment all eyes were directed towards the vehicle, which, on its approach, was found to contain the two persons accused together with the inspector above-mentioned and a police constable.

A number of witness statements were presented, all of which would be repeated at the subsequent murder trial. At the end of the day's proceedings, Greenacre was taken to Clerkenwell Prison, to return for the next court hearing on the following Saturday, 1st April. Sarah Gale and her young son were taken to the House of Correction[73] at which place on being set down by the officer who went from the High Street office with the van, Greenacre said to her, "Don't be down-hearted, my dear, you know nothing about it, and will be discharged on Saturday; you must, my dear, then call and see me."[74] 'On the road to their destination they several times shook hands with each other and shed tears...they seemed much inclined to keep up a conversation with each other, but they were very properly prevented from doing so by a constable who was placed between them in the vehicle.'

There was still an immense crowd gathered in the streets surrounding the police office to watch them being driven away.

Several newspapers reported the rumour that Greenacre had 'done away with' a child born to Sarah Gale whilst she was living with him in December, 1834; that he had dumped the newborn infant on the doorstep of a Mr Dale, in Rupert Street, Haymarket. It was then taken to St James's Workhouse where it died. Rumours were soon rampant amongst the neighbours in the closely-knit community in Carpenter's Buildings but when they had asked about the whereabouts of the newborn they were given totally different stories by Greenacre and Gale. However, when Sarah Gale was subsequently questioned by the sheriffs in her cell at Newgate she admitted that *she* had left the child on the doorstep, not Greenacre. She could, of course, have been lying to protect him as, by that time, he had already been convicted on a murder charge and any further indictments would have demolished any chance of a reprieve.

The suspicions of the neighbours seemed to indicate that Greenacre had a chequered past, was considered untrustworthy, suspected of infanticide and any number of other felonies.

---

73 Bridewell Prison and Hospital (also known as Tothill Fields Prison and Westminster Bridewell) was established in 1553 to house the 'miscreant poor' and homeless children. As well as being a House of Correction, it also trained young apprentices referred by magistrates and parish officials who were anxious to off-load responsibility for impoverished adolescents in their care.

74 *Buck's Herald,* Saturday 1st April, 1837

As the crowds in Marylebone and Paddington continued to gather, causing considerable disruption, it was decided to hold the last session, on Wednesday 5th April, not in the Police Office but in the New Prison, Clerkenwell, where James Greenacre was being held. Not to be cheated of a chance to gawp, the crowds surged towards Clerkenwell hoping to see Sarah Gale as she arrived at the New Prison from the House of Correction at Bridewell, where she had been incarcerated.

The *Staffordshire Advertiser* described the scene for its readers:

> The crowd outside evinced symptoms of impatience at the non-arrival of the female prisoner, until a coach, which brought her from her place of confinement, drew up to the New Prison gate, followed by a number of men and women: some by clinging to the windows, and others attempting to get up in front, narrowly escaped being knocked down and run over. On reaching the gate the coach door was opened, and the turn-key having first alighted, the woman Gale, who trembled from head to foot, descended the steps, followed by her child. She looked exceedingly pale, and it was apparent that her mental sufferings were great. She was led away to a lock-up room in the yard, the child holding tightly by her hand and, in happy ignorance of its mother's fearful situation, smiling as it tripped along.

During this last session before the magistrates all the evidence given thus far was summarised and James Greenacre and Sarah Gale were permitted to make statements in their defence. Greenacre took this opportunity to contest the evidence of Mrs Davis (which will follow in an account of the subsequent murder trial) and rose to address the magistrates in a clear and unemotional voice:

> I have to state that in the evidence given there are many direct falsehoods. I distinctly told Mrs Davis that we had had no words at all of consequence – that is, no quarrel. What I mentioned to her was that I had found out Mrs Brown had no money at all, and had tried to set up things in my name at a tally-shop. I merely argued the point with her, but there had been no dispute worth speaking of. There may have been duplicity on both sides. I represented myself to her to be a man of property, as many other people do; and I found out that she was not a suitable companion for me, which may fairly be concluded from her conduct towards her brothers and sisters. I'll

adhere strictly to the truth in what I am saying, although there are circumstances in the evidence combining together against me, and which may perhaps cost me my life.

One of the witnesses has said that I helped to move the boxes on the Saturday; that is true, but I will precede that remark by stating that I had this female (the other prisoner) in a room at the time, where she was lodging, and did my cooking for me. I gave her notice to leave previous to Mrs Brown coming home, and she left accordingly.

On the Saturday night before Christmas Day, Mrs Brown came down to my house, rather fresh from drinking, having in the course of the morning treated the coachman, and insisted on having some more rum, a quantity of which she had had with her tea. I then thought it a favourable opportunity to press upon her for the state of her circumstances. She was very reluctant to give me an answer, and I told her she had often dropped insinuations in my hearing about her having property enough to enable her to go into business, and that she had said she could command at any time three hundred or four hundred pounds.

I told her I had made some inquiry about her character, and had ascertained she had been to Smith's tally-shop, in Longacre, and tried to procure silk gowns in my name. She put on a feigned laugh, and retaliated by saying she thought I had been deceiving her in respect of my property, by misrepresenting it. During this conversation she was reeling backwards and forwards in her chair, which was on the swing, and as I am determined to adhere strictly to the truth, I must say that I put my foot to the chair, and she fell back with great violence against a chump of wood that I had been using; this alarmed me very much, and I went round the table and took her by the hand, and kept shaking her, but she appeared to be entirely gone.

It is impossible to give a description of my feelings at the time; and, in the state of excitement I was in, I unfortunately determined on putting her away. I deliberated for a little while, and then made up my mind to conceal her death in the manner already gone forth to the world. I thought it might be more safe that way than if I gave an alarm of what had occurred. No one individual up to the present moment had the least knowledge of what I have stated here. This female [Sarah Gale] I perfectly exonerate from having any more knowledge of it than any other person, as she was away from the house.

As for Sarah Gale, she told the magistrates that she had nothing to do with the death of Hannah Brown.

> Mr Greenacre told me to leave his house a fortnight before Christmas,' she told the court, 'but I did not then leave, as I could not suit myself with lodgings, and I went away on the following Thursday. On the Monday week after that I returned to the house, and he told me that the correspondence between him and Mrs Brown was broken off. That's all I have to say.

When asked to sign her written statement, Sarah seemed confused and reluctant and her hand was trembling. Greenacre said to her: 'Sign, sign; don't frighten yourself at what people say about your going to be hanged, and all that sort of stuff!'

The magistrates, having considered all the evidence, ordered that both prisoners were remanded in custody and taken to Newgate Prison to await trial for the murder of Hannah Brown. Before leaving, James Greenacre issued the following statement to the reporters at court for them to publish in the newspapers.

> To a humane and enlightened public.
> New Prison, Clerkenwell, April 5.

> Everything that ingenuity and malice could invent to influence the minds of the ignorant, and to fill the minds of the good and religious with awe, has been the result of newspaper comment against me. It is said that the finger of God is manifested in bringing this horrid and wilful murder to light, the day only before my flight to America! I contend that this manifestation of Divine Providence is to serve my case, or the cause of a suffering mind, to prevent me from the life of continual dread of being fetched back from America on this awful charge, and which would certainly have been the result, if the deceased had not been recognised until I had departed; thus it may be shown that Providence is on my side.

> Again, if my crossing the Atlantic, or by any other means, my death had ensued, the fatal conviction of an innocent female would certainly have been the result – suspicion would have been too strong against her to have saved her; it was for God, and God only, to prevent this fatal termination – no human mind could have discerned anything in her favour, if my death had preceded this investigation. God is just; and God be praised for this timely interference to prevent my premature

death through either my crossing the seas, or the distracted state of my mind. I hope, therefore, that my unfortunate situation may not be prejudiced by malice and perverted comments.

Whilst awaiting trial, Greenacre also wrote a statement for his defence counsel, Mr Price, and then penned the following autobiographical account for him to publish:

> Having furnished my counsel and legal adviser with every true and particular statement in my case, I conceive it to be my necessary duty towards myself, my family, and a reflecting public, to pen a brief outline of my history, in the hope of counteracting the vindictive feeling and public prejudice which have been excited against me, through falsehood and exaggerated statements that have appeared in the public newspapers, and which it is my duty to refute, by immediately committing this narrative to paper, to prove to the world that I am not that bloody-minded character in the minds of those persons in whose hands my life is placed.
>
> I am not immaculate; neither am I without many sins of commission and omission; but that truth may appear, and that justice may be done to my name when I am no more, should the prejudice of my jury prevail over the extenuating facts of my case, I proceed to state the circumstances of my life.
>
> I was born in 1725, in Norfolk, of honest and industrious parents, who were farmers. I only, of a large family, relinquished the business of a farmer, and was put into business in the grocery line, in the parish of St George, in the Borough, by my parents, at the age of nineteen. From the moment I became a landlord, no tenant of mine ever questioned the kindness of my disposition; I have been many years in the possession of three cottages, which I built in Jane-place, Old Kent-road, and have had many tenants, but never distrained upon any of them for rent, but have always taken pleasure in assisting them in any difficulty, and have often, very often, given up to them their back rents or arrears that unavoidably happen to poor persons in cases of sickness, and the want of employment.
>
> I have also eight cottages in Bowyer-lane, Camberwell, but have never once distrained upon a tenant in my life, but have absolutely felt all the sympathy of a near relative, when my claim for rent has been met by an apology through sickness, in times of accouchement, and other

causes of distress. I can with perfect safeness say, that these eleven cottages, and those two in Carpenter's-place, I never distrained upon a poor tenant in my life.

Now, as regards my domestic history, I will just refer to a few demonstrations of my disposition and general character, as a husband, a father, and a respected friend. I have been a man of affliction, in losing three amiable companions, with whom I always lived in the most perfect harmony. It may be added, that I was no fortune-hunter in these cases; but I always sought after the prospects of my issue, by forming an alliance where my children might reap the advantages of their mother's dower on the death of their parents; and I have much consolation in finding that my children, by each of my wives' parents, are amply provided for by legacies. Before I pass over this trait in my character as a husband and father, the scandalous reports of my enemies make it necessary for me to refer to the deaths of my wives.

The first was the daughter of Charles Ware, of the Crown and Anchor Tavern, Woolwich, to whom I was married at the age of nineteen; my wife eighteen. I was then in business in the grocery line, by the assistance of my own parents, who were farmers in Norfolk. My wife died suddenly of putrid sore throat. She was attended by that eminent physician, Dr Blackburn, who, and whose assistants, admonished me not to go near my wife to receive her breath; but such being the result of my feelings that I could not resist the force of affection, and there are many persons now living who can bear testimony to the fact, I took the complaint, and it nearly cost me my life. I engaged a respectable woman as housekeeper, who, as nurse and housekeeper, has since been in my service at intervals for a period equal to thirteen years, and who is now living.

My next wife was the daughter of Mr John Romford, a considerable landowner in Essex. By this lady I also had two children. This wife died of brain fever, brought on by exerting herself, I believe, riding on horseback, whilst on a visit to her relations; and having an infant at the time, her milk was affected by the fever, which caused her death. Mr Culthred, now residing in the Borough, attended her. My old housekeeper, who nursed my wife in each accouchement, now became my housekeeper again.

I continued a widower fifteen months, and married Miss Simmonds, of Long-lane, Bermondsey, with whom I also lived in harmony and affection up to the time I went to America (May 1833). This amiable

> companion, with whom I had arranged to come after I had provided a home for her, died in London of the cholera about three weeks after my departure. By this wife I had seven children, two only of whom are living.[75] My old housekeeper always attended as nurse to all my wives, and upon all occasions of sickness, making a period of near thirteen years. As a sober and affectionate husband, no person living can deny but this has uniformly been my character. I have always abhorred a public-house, and the babble of drunken men. The society of my books, and wife, and children, have always been to me the greatest source of delight that my mind could possibly enjoy.

The statement then articulates Greenacre's kindly treatment of various apprentices he had employed in his business, after which he continues to condemn the press coverage of his case:

> Now, as a friend, I think I can give the most incontrovertible testimony; and had it not been the infamous lying and slandering newspapers, who glory in any crime for the sale of their dangerous weapons, I might have received the visits, advice, and assistance of hundreds of friends, but all are frightened by those horrifying falsehoods. I have received anonymous letters whilst in jail, which I have shown to the governor of the prison, and have handed to my solicitor, wherein the writers express their wishes to aid me, but durst not avow their names. My counsel also have received instructions to aid me by the receipt of anonymous letters enclosing money, with the like expressions of the writers' fear that their names may be known. Thus it is that I am compelled to give this brief outline of my life, in the hopes of defeating the power of falsehood and slander.

By way of demonstrating his popularity in the St George's district he recounted his election as an overseer in 1832, with a record number of parishioners voting for him. He admitted that he was £150 in debt when he went to America, which he referred to as 'trifling', but had left invoices and cash for his wife to settle the debt in his absence. But her sudden illness and death from cholera meant that the debt was not paid and his creditors, no doubt believing he

---

75 The *London Standard*, dated 28th March, 1837, reported a statement by Greenacre's sister and her husband, Mr and Mrs Ogleby, stating that the two remaining children were being cared for by a relative, Mr Blower, a fish salesman, of Bermondsey.

had absconded to America to avoid payment, had him declared a bankrupt. In his statement, however, Greenacre makes the valid observation that, had it been his intention to renege on his debt and remain in America, he would surely have accrued a far larger sum from his creditors. His financial situation dealt with, Greenacre finishes by some more on his character:

> I have mentioned my abhorrence of public-houses; I trust, therefore, that the vice of drinking, the foundation of error and crime, may not be considered the cause of my unhappy accident and subsequent resolve to put away the body, which has produced my disputable notoriety. It was the horror of my feelings, and fear only that took possession of my mind. I was actuated by no feelings of a felonious or malicious kind. The unfortunate deceased was evidently very much in liquor when her chair went backwards; and had candidly avowed her poverty when I talked to her on the consequences of our marrying in deception, and of her having been to a tally-shop to obtain a dress upon credit in my name. Felonious intentions cannot be attributed to me, since it is well known that if she had property it might have been mine in a few hours' time by the legal right of marriage.

Still very much in denial, three days before his trial for murder Greenacre wrote the following letter to W. Greenacre, farmer, North Runston, near Lynn, Norfolk, from his prison cell:

> Chapel-yard, Newgate, April 7, 1837
>
> Dear Brothers and Sisters, - I wrote to you last week to beg of you to advance me some pecuniary assistance at this critical moment. It certainly is the most extraordinary thing that I have not heard from you either by a remittance, or by letter, or by personal visit; but I suppose you have believed all the lying reports of the newspapers, and, taking them to be true, you are all deterred from interesting yourself about my fate. Now it is a cruel thing that any man should believe any thing before he has any proof of the truth or falsehood of the report. My lawyer and counsellors have desired me not to send any thing to print, to counteract the falsehood that has been published to the world; lies, they justly observe, can only injure for a short time; the tide will soon return in my favour, when the truth appears...
>
> You suppose, from report, that I shall be hanged, and therefore you

suppose that it is not worth your while to waste money in defending my life and the name of Greenacre from that inevitable disgrace; that is, however, a shocking, awful instance of prejudice; but, thank God, I have found many friends in the higher class, who visited me at Clerkenwell, and many gentlemen in the city now visit me in Newgate, and have ordered me additional counsel. The prejudice, I know, has been very great; but men of talent and reflecting minds are not easily carried away by newspapers, whose trade is to fill up their columns with any thing to stir up the minds of the people for the next addition of their papers. You may have heard many reports which, if they were true, I agree that I should very justly deserve to be hanged; but should prejudice prevail over the minds of the jury on Monday next why then I must make up my mind to meet my fate, and to learn the grand secret that has always been a subject of cavil and dispute of men since the world began, each disputant professing to know all about it, but which I contend can only been known through death. Had you come to London, I meant to have assigned over to you my cottages, and my boxes of goods, including a good working model of a new invented washing-machine, which may now be turned to good purpose; and if I be hanged, the sale of the machine would certainly become most extensive; indeed, I believe that it would be a better and safer competence than any farm [form] in England – the model I meant to have given you; and should I be fortunate enough to escape I will not lose the chance that this unfortunate unpopularity has opened for my future prosperity, by pushing forward the machine.

Yours, affectionately,
JAMES GREENACRE.

Such were James Greenacre's versions of events but the full story of the days leading up to the murder began to unfold before a rapt audience gathered in the Central Criminal Court, Old Bailey, on 10th April, 1837. The scene that day was widely reported:

> ...as early as seven o'clock the doors of the Court were literally besieged by persons anxious to gain admittance. By a prudent regulation, however, none were admitted but by orders previously obtained, and these only by the side doors, the principal entrance by

the gates in the Old Bailey being kept closed, except for the admission of City Functionaries, etc.

Almost immediately after the Court was opened, at nine o'clock, every available seat was occupied; and so desirous were the public to get a sight of the prisoners, and to witness the proceedings of the day, that in the course of a very short time the gallery was completely filled, the exorbitant price of 10s. 6d. being demanded as the entrance money. The class of person in the inside of the Court was apparently highly respectable, while many of those who did not possess sufficient influence to procure tickets of admission, and were more chary of their money than to pay the required fee for admittance to the gallery, and who were waiting outside, were apparently of equal respectability. Many of them, however, were of the lower order of persons, who, although they could not expect to obtain a sight of the prisoners, yet remained in waiting, to gain the earliest intelligence of the proceedings of the Court.[76]

Shortly before ten o'clock in the morning both prisoners were arraigned. James Greenacre was charged with the wilful murder of Hannah Brown whereas Sarah Gale was charged with 'having guilty knowledge of the matter after the act, and with continuing to aid, comfort, and assist the murderer.' Greenacre looked around the crowded courtroom with 'a grave, quiet, unabashed look, and pleaded 'Not Guilty' in a strong, clear voice.'[77]

As for Sarah Gale, she 'appeared to feel her awful situation very keenly. She never looked up, except to cast a furtive glance at any particular part of the court. She pleaded 'Not Guilty' almost inaudibly. She was accommodated with a chair during the trial.'

At precisely ten o'clock, Chief Justice Tindal, Justices Coleridge and Coltman, and the Recorder, took their seats on the Bench.

The prosecution was represented by Messrs Adolphus, Clarkson and Bodkin and for the defence - Mr Price and Mr Payne. Addressing the jury, Mr Adolphus began to outline the facts of the case which would be reiterated later in the words of the witnesses called to give evidence. But before proceeding he reminded the jurors to 'dismiss

[76] *Coventry Herald,* Friday 14th April 1837.
[77] Unless otherwise stated quotes are taken from the pamphlet, *The Trial of J. Greenacre, and Sarah Gale, for the Wilful Murder of Hannah Brown,* distributed within days of the trial.

from their minds anything they had read or, and to judge impartially upon the evidence that would be laid before them, according to the directions they would receive from the learned Judges.'

The first witness to be called that morning was the policeman, Constable Samuel Pegler, who, when questioned by Mr Clarkson, had this to say:

> On the 28th Dec I was in the Edgeware-road with a person named Bond. I went to a place pointed out by Bond, and found a sack containing the trunk of a human body. The arms were tied with part of cord... I found some pieces of rag lying near, and upon the bag. There was a flag-stone covering it. The stone was in a slanting position, leaning against the wall. On examining the bag I found some mahogany shavings or scrapings. On the 27th [26th] March, in consequence of hearing of the apprehension of a person I accompanied Inspector Feltham to a house, No. 1 St Alban's-street, Lambeth, and in the back room, ground floor, I found a child's twilled cotton frock, patched with nankeen, [a coarse buff-coloured cotton material] which was also the case with the rags I found near the sack. The shade of the nankeen patches is alike in both.'

He also informed the court that the sack belonged to a Mr Ward, a worker in mahogany, in Tottenham Court Road who had employed James Greenacre for two or three days prior to the murder.

At this point the jurors were shown the rags found near the sack, and the frock found in the house in St Alban's Street. Two workmen, James White and Ezekiel Higgins (some accounts gave his name as Dickens) were then questioned briefly by Mr Bodkin. Both men had seen the paving-slab and the bundle hidden behind it on 28th December, but Higgins told the court that the sack wasn't there when he passed the site on 24th December.

Next to give evidence was Matthias Ralph, the lock-keeper at Johnson's Lock, Regent's Canal, Stepney. He had this to say:

> About half past eight on the morning of 6th January, I was called by a bargeman, who said there was something which prevented the gates closing. I procured a hitcher, and raised something which I thought was a dead dog, but which turned out to be the head of a human being. The water was about five feet in depth. On examining the head

> which had been taken up by the hair, I found that the right eye had been knocked out by a stick or some other weapon. The flesh was soft and puffed. The left jaw-bone had been broken, and the bone protruded through the skin. The left ear had a seam, as if the earring had been torn out in the youth of the person and that it had grown up again. The hole in the other ear was perfect. The head seemed to have been some days in the water. I did not examine it any further.

Cross-examined by Mr Price, Mr Ralph suggested that the wound over the right eye had *not* been caused by dredging with the hitcher as it was not a fresh wound but he conceded that some of the other damage to the head might have been caused as he tried several times to hoist the head from the water. The court was told that he took the head to the bone-house or charnel where a number of people inspected it before it was passed to a police officer.

James Page was next in the witness box and had this to say:

> I am a labourer, and on the 2nd February I was working at an osier bed in Coldharbour-lane, near Camberwell. I found a sack among some bushes, and found in it the legs and thighs of a human being. A man who was with me pulled the sack open. They were taken to the station house and the police took charge of them. The legs remained there till after an inquest was held on them.

The next person to give evidence was Evan Davis, a cabinet maker and upholsterer, of 45 Bartholomew Close, who had known the murder victim, Hannah Brown, for about five years.

> I heard shortly before Christmas last, that she was going to be married. About nine days before Christmas I was called down from my workshop, and found Mrs Brown and her beau. The prisoner at the bar is the man. Mrs Brown introduced him to me. They remained about three quarters of an hour and the prisoner and myself adjourned to a public house [the Queen's Head] where we had some drink. He had a deal to say about America and said he had a large farm of about 1,000 acres at Hudson's Bay - that he had returned from it four months previously and was returning about three weeks after Christmas. On the 22nd December I saw him again, and we had some drink at the Queen's Head. He then also spoke about America, and we returned to my house. Mrs Brown was there and they sat together on the sofa.

It was at this point, said Evan Davis, that Greenacre announced that he and Hannah Brown were getting married on the Sunday morning at the church of St Giles-in-the-Field, Camden - furthermore, he said he wanted Mr Davis to give her away and would like his eldest daughter, Hannah, to be a bridesmaid. This settled, Greenacre and Hannah Brown stayed for dinner and it was arranged that on the day of the wedding they would all meet at the Angel public house which was near the church. The visitors left about quarter past ten that evening and Mr Davis never saw Hannah Brown alive again.

When he went to view the head dredged from the canal which was on display at the Paddington Workhouse he could see the resemblance to Mrs Brown. 'The forehead was flat, and the eyebrow was straight, exactly like that of Hannah Brown. In my opinion it was her head. The teeth were like hers, and the eye was the same colour.'

Mr Price, for the defence, rose to cross-examine the witness and evidently suggested that the victim, Hannah Brown, was a heavy drinker for Mr Davis replied:

> I accompanied the prisoner and Mrs Brown about one hundred yards the last time they were at my house. I don't recollect Mrs Brown asking us to have something to drink on the night after they left. I never knew a more sober woman. There was not a more pleasant, agreeable, or sober woman in London.

Called to give evidence, Catharine Glass, the wife of a plasterer, told the court that she lived in Windmill Street, Tottenham Court Road, and had been a friend of Hannah Brown. In fact, she had been with her on Christmas Eve until midday and it had been planned that Hannah should return to the house by nine o'clock that evening and sleep there prior to her wedding the following day. When she was at her house that day, Mrs Glass assured the court that Mrs Brown did not have any marks or bruising on her face. The witness also testified that Mrs Brown had been a 'perfectly sober woman'.

When cross-examined by Mr Payne, Catharine Glass said both she and Hannah Brown - who lived close by - had 'kept a mangle', implying that they both took in laundry for a living.

The next witness was Hannah Davis, wife of Evan Davis, who had known Hannah Brown for about five years. She had last seen the victim on 22nd December but on the evening of 24th December, James Greenacre had come to her house and asked if Hannah Brown had been there. He seemed 'very much agitated' and remained on the doorstep; he then informed her that the proposed marriage would not take place as he had discovered that Hannah Brown did not have any property and it would be unwise to 'plunge themselves into poverty' by marrying as planned.

Asked to describe her friend, Hannah Brown, Mrs Davis said she 'had a high forehead and longish features. She had white even teeth. There was a slit in one of her ears. Her hair was brown intermixed with grey. She was fair complexioned. Her hair was very long at the back. She was a tall, genteel, fine, respectable looking female.'

Cross-examined by Mr Price, Mrs Davis told the court that Hannah Brown had lived in Union Street for about a year and a half and they had seen each other on numerous occasions. She described Hannah as being a 'sober, industrious and agreeable woman'. She had previously lived at Oliver's, the anchor-smith, at Wapping, and had talked about having 'a little shop to sell fruit and pastry' although Mrs Davis had never seen it. For a couple of years she also worked for a Mr Perring, a hatter in The Strand. Whenever she had been in the company of James Greenacre and Hannah Brown they seemed on the best of terms and eager to be married and they talked about their proposed trip to America after the wedding.

Mrs Davis's place in the witness box was taken next by Elizabeth Corney, who introduced herself as the wife of John Corney, a shoemaker of 46 Union Street, Middlesex Hospital. Questioned by Mr Clarkson she had this to say about Hannah Brown:

> She occupied the front kitchen of a house of mine at No. 45. She got her living by washing and mangling. I saw her last on December 24th. I understood she was then going to be married. She had household furniture and little things of her own, quite sufficient for her use. She sold those things before the 24th December. She said Mr Greenacre wished her to sell them for pocket-money. She disposed of her mangle.

Questioned further by Mr Clarkson, Mrs Corney said that Hannah

Brown had left her house on the 24th of December, between the hours of twelve and three o'clock.

> A hackney coach had been waiting for her which I saw her enter. She took her boxes with her... I believe the prisoner [Greenacre] to be the man who went with her in the hackney coach. Greenacre and the coachman helped her out with her boxes.

As Mrs Brown's tenancy still had a few days to run it was agreed that she should keep the key to her room so she could collect a few remaining items and return it at the end of the week. When she left her premises Hannah Brown had no bruises or injuries of any kind and that was the last time Mrs Corney had seen her alive.

It was now one o'clock and, having heard Mrs Corney's testimony, the court officials and jurors retired for refreshments. The two prisoners in the dock were also allowed to leave the courtroom but within half an hour all parties returned and the trial resumed.

Hannah Brown's former landlady, Mrs Corney, was recalled and questioned further about the key to Hannah's room. She said that one of her other lodgers, Mrs Oxford, had been given it by a young boy. She indicated that there was still some rent owing on the room which, when she and her husband went to inspect it they found it contained only 'an empty bird cage, of no value'. She had viewed the severed head on display at the Paddington Workhouse and was of the opinion that the appearance of the hair and the teeth was very similar to that of Hannah Brown.

The next witness was William Gay who, questioned by Mr Bodkin, had this to say:

> I live in Goodge Street, and am a broker, I am shop-man to my mistress [his employer, Mrs Blanchard]. The deceased was my sister. Just before her death we were not on friendly terms. I saw her the Thursday before her death. She was alone. I saw Greenacre on the Tuesday night following, it was about seven o'clock. He came to our shop. My mistress was in the shop when he came. I heard him tell her the wedding was put off, and that Mrs Brown had no property. He

said that she had run him in debt at a tally-shop, that they had had a few words, and were not going to be married, and that he was going to take a shop instead of going to America.

William Gay went on to tell the court that Mrs Blanchard had known his sister, Hannah, since childhood. When she told Greenacre that William Gay was Hannah's brother, Greenacre's countenance changed completely, he seemed flustered and, declining an invitation to come into the house, hurried away.

Questioned further, Mr Gay said that Hannah Brown had cared for a girl belonging to one of her sisters and always referred to her as her daughter although she had no children of her own.[78] He was positive that the head on display at the Paddington Workhouse was that of his sister, Hannah Brown. He described her as 'a tall woman, a middle-proportioned woman, not the stoutest nor the thinnest' and had recognised his sister's light hair, mixed with grey, the colour of the remaining eye and the healed over slit in her left ear.

The next witness was Maria Gay, the wife of the previous witness for eighteen years. She had known Hannah Brown for the same length of time and had first known her in Norfolk. She described her as 'tall and stout, with large hands and long fingers, fair and delicate. There was a particular mark on her left ear occasioned by her earring having been pulled out by a fellow servant many years ago.' She went on to describe the dead woman's face:

> 'The nose was flattened, but she had a flat nose. The face was very much fractured. She got her living by hard work. I should say she was much stronger than I am. She had a very delicate skin, and was very high chested, much more than most women.'

That evening her husband had told her how Greenacre's face had changed colour when he realised that he, William Gay, was Hannah Brown's brother during the visit to Mrs Blanchard's shop.

The next witness to be called was Mrs Susan Dillon who lived in

---

78 It later emerged during the evidence of one of Hannah Brown's sisters, Rebecca Smith, that the girl, Mary Ann Bale, was the daughter of her other sister, Sarah Gay; Hannah was her godmother and brought her to London from Norfolk and regarded her as her own daughter. She was a straw hat-maker in the Strand.

Carpenter's Buildings; she was questioned about Sarah Gale:

> I knew the prisoner Gale as Mrs Greenacre. I live now in the house he lived in at No. 6. I then lived about 20 yards from and opposite Greenacre's house. He took it last August twelvemonth, and first saw Mrs Gale in the following October. On Boxing Day I saw her child crying. About seven o'clock I saw Mrs Gale in the front garden coming from the house.

There was snow on the ground, she told the court, and the child, a boy of about four years old, wasn't wearing a hat against the cold and was trailing behind Mrs Gale and crying violently.

A surveyor, Mr Charles Thatcher, was brought into the witness box to dispute Greenacre's version of the events of Christmas Eve as given in his defence statement - that Hannah Brown's death had been accidental when she fell backwards in her chair, smashing her head on the floor. He produced a plan of No. 6 Carpenter's Buildings, and it became clear that the dimensions of the house were small - in fact, the parlour in which Hannah Brown had died was only 10ft x 8ft - dimensions that were typical of the 'two-up, two-down' working man's terraced cottages in London at the time. The surveyor was of the opinion that as the chair by the fireplace had been so close to the wall it was most unlikely that Hannah could have fallen right back and died from her injuries. There followed questions about the distance between the fireplace and the adjoining door to the kitchen after which Mr Price rose to suggest that the victim had fallen backwards, through the door to the kitchen, which was at a lower level. The surveyor, however, thought this scenario unlikely as the victim had been sitting in a chair facing the kitchen door.

Henrietta Headlands, who lived at 5 Windmill Lane, Camberwell, almost directly opposite No. 6 Carpenter's Buildings, testified that she had seen Sarah Gale - whom she knew as Mrs Greenacre - in the garden of Greenacre's house on the Christmas Eve between half ten and half eleven, the day that Hannah Brown was due to call in the afternoon. She had seen her there again on Monday, 26th December, Boxing Day, and her little boy was 'screaming violently'. Sarah had lifted him up - her bonnet was askew - and told him he was 'a naughty, cross child'. Most mornings in the week after Christmas day the shutters of the Greenacre house had been kept closed and Miss Headlands had seen Greenacre leaving the premises carrying a blue merino bag (a rucksack commonly used by labourers).

A couple of weeks later, when Greenacre had moved to St Albans Street, the witness accompanied Mrs Dillon, with whom she was lodging, to view the property which was to let, Sarah Gale and the little boy were there and the house smelt strongly of brimstone as though it had been fumigated, so much so that it had made her cough violently.

Another witness, Mr Edmonds, who lived at 5 Windmill Lane, said he had seen Sarah Gale in the garden of No. 6 Carpenter's Buildings between ten and eleven o'clock on Christmas Day and he had seen her and Greenacre together a number of times. When Greenacre moved to lodgings in St Alban's Street and No. 6 was to let, he and Mr Dillon went to inspect the property. He confirmed that Sarah Gale and the child were there and there was a strong smell of brimstone.

Frances, the wife of Joseph Andrews, a shoemaker, living at No. 11 Carpenter's Buildings, was questioned next and provided some crucial information – that Sarah Gale was back at No. 6 Carpenter's Buildings on Boxing Day and during the remainder of that week when the body of Hannah Brown was being dismembered and the house was scrubbed clean. She told the court that she knew both prisoners and knew Sarah as Mrs Gale while she was living at No. 6, on the opposite side of the street. As there was only a water supply on Mrs Andrews's side of the street, she often let Sarah Gale use her water outlet whenever it 'was on'.[79]

On Sunday, 18th December, when she lent Sarah Gale an iron, she 'saw a tall, stout woman go into Greenacre's house - she had on a pea green gown' but, she told the court, she hadn't seen her since. The shutters at No. 6 were closed on Christmas Day and she saw Sarah

---

79 Early Victorian water supplies were scarce and intermittent, probably consisting of localised systems to re-direct water from tanks and water-butts. The murderess, Elizabeth Brownrigg's husband was a plumber and had rigged up a water-pipe into the kitchen, on which Brownrigg would tie her maid-servants before flogging them. See author's book *Bad Companions*.

Gale there again on Boxing Day when she took over some plum pudding for the little boy.

On Wednesday, 28th December, three days after Christmas day, Mrs Andrews had gone over to No. 6 to tell Sarah Gale that the water was on if she needed some. Greenacre had given her some whiskey and later that morning Sarah asked her to look after her little boy - leaving some bread and bacon for him to eat - as she needed to go out. She returned for him later that evening, after it was dark.

Thomas Clissold, a shoe-maker, of 1 Pitt Street, Camberwell, entered the witness box and described a chance meeting with James Greenacre in the Christmas week. He'd hired him to move pieces of furniture and belongings from 6 Carpenter's Buildings on his cart - described in the newspapers as 'painted red with green wheels'. Although Greenacre had helped him tie up the boxes he seemed 'very much agitated' and 'trembled exceedingly'. He and Sarah Gale walked on either side of the cart – though Sarah Gale went off somewhere when they reached Walworth Road - as far as the Elephant and Castle at which point Greenacre said he was going to sell the furniture. He paid Thomas Clissold 6d and the boy 3d before dispensing with their services.

Next came Thomas Higgins, who had this to say:

> I work for Mr Ward, a mangle maker in Tottenham-court road. I know the sack produced. The one in which the body of the deceased was found. I knew it from a piece of string attached to it, which I had taken from my apron...

The sack had belonged to his employer and Mr Higgins had used it to carry wood shavings - of beech and mahogany – although, he admitted, there were some holes in it made by his children. James Greenacre had been working for Mr Ward in the week before Christmas and it was during that time that the sack went missing.

Cross-examined by Mr Price, Higgins said that Hannah Brown had known his employer, Mr Ward, and a boy delivered shavings in a sack to her home in Union Street - possibly for fire kindling needed to heat water for the laundry she took in - although the witness said that the finest shavings were usually sold to bakers.

Henry Wignell, of 56 Portland Street, Walworth, told the court that on 22nd December, Sarah Gale had rented the back parlour and she slept there that night. In the days that followed Greenacre slept there on several nights. On 1st January, Mr Wignell saw the account of the finding of the torso in Edgware Road in a newspaper and read it out loud to his wife. Greenacre and Gale must have heard him but although they said nothing at the time, they left their lodgings that same day.

Questioned by Mr Price, Wignell said that Mrs Gale was at home on Christmas Day but went out for a short time in the evening. Greenacre had called round about between one and two o'clock. This evidence contradicted that given by Mr Edmonds, who said that she was at Greenacre's house on that day.

> She was a very quiet, well-behaved person. I did not see any alteration in her manner during the time. I did not approve of him coming to my house. I gave her warning to quit, because she went out all boxing night. That was a very inclement night.

His wife, Mrs Sarah Wignell, had more to say about her lodger, Sarah Gale:

> I let the lodging to the prisoner Gale. She said she was a widow woman, but she did not give her name. Greenacre came the same evening, and helped her furniture in. The next day he came with a handkerchief bundle, about the size of a quartern loaf. She was out all boxing night. A little boy she had brought with her she locked in the room. She returned the next day between seven and eight. I then gave her notice to quit.

Under cross-examination she said that Sarah Gale 'lived abstemiously. On Christmas Day they had about a pound of scrag of mutton and turnips for dinner. Greenacre came about one o'clock. He remained till between nine and 10 o'clock, when he went away alone. I cannot recollect whether she went out.' To this she added that when the child was locked in the room on the night of Boxing Day she had heard the child crying, 'Mother', about eight o'clock, after she had gone, and several times during the night, the child cried out 'Mother.' She also heard him cry out 'Mother!' when Sarah

Gale had returned the following morning.

A pawnbroker, Joseph Knowles, of Bolingbroke Row, Walworth, was next to give evidence:

> On the 17th of January some articles were pawned at our shop by a female, I believe to be the prisoner Gale. I produce a pair of shoes, two veils, and a handkerchief, wrapped up in an old silk handkerchief. There were holes in the handkerchief as it had been burnt, and there were marks of blood upon it. I lent 2s on the articles, they are not worth more.

Next to be questioned was Inspector George Feltham, who was asked to recall the arrest of Greenacre and Gale:

> I went on Sunday, the 26th of March, to No.1 St Alban's street, Kennington-road. The street door was open. I first saw the landlord. It was between 10 and 11 o'clock at night. I said I wanted Mr. Greenacre. A voice from within answered, "What do you want?" That was Greenacre's voice. I said, "I want to speak to you." He said, "Wait a bit till I strike a light". But I did not wait. I heard a noise as of a person getting out of bed. I lifted the latch and went in. He asked me, "What do you want?" I replied, "I want you upon a warrant for the wilful murder of Hannah Brown".
>
> The landlord then brought a candle up. I asked him if he knew Hannah Brown. He said he did not. I asked him if ever he was asked in church with Hannah Brown [the reading of the banns]. He said "we were". I asked "Where is Hannah Brown?" He answered "I don't know - you have no right to ask me these questions". I replied, "I do not intend to ask you any more questions, and whatever you say to me I shall have to repeat elsewhere".
>
> He put on his stockings and while he was putting on his trousers I saw Gale. I said, "What woman's that?" He said, "A woman that's come to sleep with me". I told her she must get up and dress too as she must go with us. I than heard the rattling of a watch chain in Gale's hand, which I took from her, as well as two rings from her fingers, also two cornelian earrings set in gold, and 2s.6d. from her pockets, and some duplicates, [pawn tickets] amongst them one for a pair of shoes and two veils, pawned on 17th January, at Mr Knowles's pawnbroker, 19 Bolingbroke row, Walworth road, in the name of Mary Stevens.
>
> When the prisoners were dressed I sent for a hackney coach. Gale

said, "There is a child in the next room, and I can't go without my boy." The child was sent for. Greenacre then asked for a great coat, which I got out of a corded box, and gave to him. He said to me, "It's lucky for you you came to-day, for I should have been on my way on the sea tomorrow morning". But he did not say where he was going to.

I took five boxes away to Paddington station-house, and there opened them, and took such things as I considered necessary.

The jurors were then shown a boa, a dress, a small neck shawl upon which there were some drops of blood – a collar and other articles which were afterwards identified as belonging to Hannah Brown. In addition, he produced 'a saw, a French knife, some bullets newly and roughly cast'.

When cross-examined by Mr Payne, the Inspector also said he had found a pistol at the lodging house, which had a small quantity of powder in it, about the third of a charge. 'I found it in one of the boxes. It had a percussion cap on.'

After Greenacre and Gale had been taken into custody, Inspector Feltham returned to their lodgings at St Alban's Street with some of Hannah Brown's friends and they identified a collar found in the room in which the child had been sleeping. There were two boxes containing women's and a child's clothing.

Mr Payne suggested that the stains on the shawl were caused by port wine but Mr Adolphus for the prosecution disputed this, declaring that they were blood stains.

Two witnesses were able to identify the shawl as belonging to Hannah Brown - young Hannah Davis, who was to have been her bridesmaid, her mother, Mrs Davis, and Sarah Ellerthorn, also recognised Hannah's cornelian earrings.

Before the trial ended on that first day, Mr Taylor, the parish clerk of St Giles-in-the-Field, confirmed that, in readiness for the marriage of James Greenacre and Hannah Brown, the banns had been read on 27th November, and again on the 4th and 11th of December.

By this time it was eight o'clock in the evening and the court was adjourned until the following day.

On the second day of the trial Police Sergeant Michael Callow Brown took his place in the witness box and described the events of the evening of 26th March, 1837, when the two prisoners had been arrested and brought to the police station by Inspector George Feltham. He put them in separate cells and went to fetch the Charge Book. When he returned with it to charge Greenacre he found him lying on his back with a noose made from a silk handkerchief around his neck and another around his right foot. Sergeant Brown described him as stiff and apparently dead. The police surgeon was sent for and bled him and after about three hours he had fully recovered.

> The first words he made use of were "I don't thank you for what you've done. Why did you not let me die? I want to die. Damn the man who is afraid to die – I am not!"

Another policeman, Thomas Tringham, described a conversation he had with James Greenacre in his cell on the morning of 1st April, before the second magistrate's hearing. He talked of the number of people who came to gawp at him and how they got certain aspects of the story all wrong. He had moved the torso in a cab, not a cart, as was commonly stated, between two and five on the Monday morning, Boxing Day. It was also rumoured, he said, that the head had been thrown over a tunnel at Maida Vale. 'However,' he told the witness, 'I don't want to satisfy public curiosity.'

The surgeon, Dr Birtwhistle, from Mile End Road, confirmed that on 6th February he had made a preliminary examination of the head that had been dredged from the Regent's Canal before it was taken to the Paddington Workhouse. This was done in the graveyard of Stepney Church. There was a severe wound to the right eye which had ruptured the orb.

'The face was cut in various places - the eye remained in the head, devoid of humours.'

In his opinion, all the bruises and lacerations - except the injury to the right eye - were inflicted after death; some may have been caused either whilst the head was in the canal or it was being hauled up by the lock-man's hitcher. He and the other surgeon, Dr Girdwood, made a more detailed examination after the head was taken to the Paddington Workhouse.

It was during this examination that the skull was opened and showed a significant injury inside at the back which had not been evident from the outward appearance of the head. He noted that the head was devoid of blood which indicated that the decapitation had occurred before death. However, when cross-examined, he agreed that it was possible for blood to continue to flow after a sudden death, at least whilst the body remained warm for an hour or two.

Introduced to the court as the parish surgeon for Paddington, Dr Gilbert Finley Girdwood gave evidence next. He confirmed that he had examined the severed head on 8th February at the Paddington Workhouse in the presence of Dr Birtwhistle and other surgeons. He agreed that the wound to the eye had been inflicted before death, probably by a heavy blow with a fist, not a weapon, as there were no abrasions to the skin. The victim had probably been knocked unconscious by the force of the blow. In his opinion, the injury inside the back of the skull had been caused by that same blow to the face in conjunction with resistance behind the head. The neck had the appearance of being repeatedly cut in order to sever it from the body and the witness described the wounds as 'ragged'.

There followed a detailed description of the condition of the body, the bruising and the other effects of trauma on blood and tissue. It was emphasised that the head and parts of the torso were devoid of blood which might indicate that the head was severed before death. However, the surgeon agreed with the previous witness that there had been experiments to prove that 'where death is occasioned by any sudden violence, blood will flow from a divided vessel for sixteen hours after death.'

Questioned about the examination he had made on the torso on 26th December, he said;

> The appearances of the cut incisions were such as to induce me to

suppose that the other parts had been separated immediately after death, the muscles being very much contracted. I also inferred that from the bloodless state of the body. I opened the stomach, there was no injury internally. I found in it some indigested food - it had a spirituous smell. The person appeared to me to have been a female about five feet eight inches. She was well-formed externally, strong, and in perfect health.

Mr Bodkin, for the prosecution, then asked:

Looking at all the circumstances, and after your minute examination of the body, what, in your opinion, was the immediate cause of death?

Dr Girdwood replied:

On looking at all the facts, first, the very severe blow on the eye, and that indicated during life, and looking at the corresponding bruise at the back part of the head... such an injury would be mortal.' To this, the witness added an obvious proviso: 'But certainly if it had not been so, the cutting of the neck would have necessarily caused it.

Next to give medical evidence was James Hunter Lane, a physician and lecturer on chemistry.

I examined the stomach of the deceased. On opening the stomach I found it to contain a quantity of meat, which I supposed to be either pork or beef, potatoes and some pastry. There was a quantity of fluid, the whole mixture having a spirituous smell. I could not come to the conclusion that the spirit in the stomach was neither whisky nor rum. Upon exposing either whisky or rum to the atmosphere it will lose its odour, but common gin will not. There did not appear to me to be sufficient spirits in the stomach to produce intoxication. The digestion appeared to have gone through half its progress. I should conceive the death to have been sudden.

When the last witness had stepped down, Mr Adolphus declared that his evidence had concluded the case for the prosecution. As it was then a quarter to three in the afternoon the jurors and other court officials were permitted to retire for refreshments. At twenty-five minutes past three they returned and the trial was resumed.

Mr Price, for the defence, rose to address the jury on behalf of the two prisoners. After referring to the difficulties of the case he said that he was 'quite sure that, from the moment of having come to his senses, the male prisoner, had bitterly regretted and repented his offence against decency, and against the respect which was due to the dead. He was sincere in what he was saying and was not using the language of a mere advocate because he knew, and was proud to say, it was not in human nature to feel otherwise than he had.'

He entreated the jurors to disregard any press reports concerning the case, saying:

> The current of justice had been perverted, the stream of truth, which ought to flow pure in all its channels had been so blotted and so basely corrupted by a large proportion of the British press, that none could scarcely see through it. But they must take the case as they found it, and notwithstanding all the difficulties surrounding it, their duty must be discharged.

Mr Price proceeded to insist that although Sarah Gale had knowledge of the atrocious crime *after* it had been committed, she was not involved in the death and was entirely innocent of the charge against her. As for James Greenacre, the jurors must consider the veracity of his statement in which he declared the death of Hannah Brown was not a case of premeditated murder but a terrible accident that he, perhaps inadvisably, with hindsight, in a panic, had decided to conceal.

Before closing, Mr Price called John Freeman, a stone-mason from Millbank, who told the court that Sarah Gale had lived with his family for a year, employed as a wet-nurse and behaved 'with affection and attention during the whole time', so much so that his wife gave her a very favourable character reference after she had left.

It was the intention of Mr Price to call a witness to speak for the character of James Greenacre but when Mr Adolphus reminded him that if he did so, as prosecuting counsel, he, Adolphus, would claim his right to reply. For some reason - possibly because it was already a quarter past six in the evening, it had been a long day and the Judge had yet to deliver his summary - Mr Price, no doubt much to the relief of many, declined to call anyone on Greenacre's behalf.

The Lord Chief Justice began his summing up by reiterating the facts of the case fully covered in the magistrates' court and the trial.

He remarked on a discrepancy of evidence in which one witness said Sarah Gale was seen at Greenacre's lodgings in Carpenter's Buildings on Boxing Day whereas another witness said she was at another house some distance away in Walworth on that day.

The fact that Greenacre had dismembered the body of Hannah Brown in order to dispose of the evidence did not necessarily mean that an accidental death was out of the question and it could be that he was innocent of murder.

> A strong minded man would, under the circumstances in which the prisoner was placed, naturally have made the accident known – but there were others who would take the crooked path instead of the straight path although not actually guilty.

In conclusion, the Judge said the jury 'were to consider first, had the prisoner been guilty of a wilful and premeditated murder, or could they view it in the light in which the prisoner stated it, the offence of manslaughter, or was death occasioned accidentally by a wanton act. Lastly, whether they found the prisoner guilty of the higher offence of murder, or the minor one of manslaughter, it would be their duty to consider whether the female prisoner was guilty of harbouring-aiding, and comforting the male prisoner, Greenacre, she knowing at the time that he had been guilty of committing the murder with which he stood indicted.'

By the time the Judge had finished his address and instructed the jurors to retire to consider their verdict, it was a quarter past nine in the evening. They made their way to the London Coffee House but mercifully, the anxious wait for the two prisoners and their defence counsel was short for the jurors filed back within a quarter of an hour. In the light of the Judge's favourable assessment of Sarah Gale's part in the death of Hannah Brown, many expected an acquittal yet the jury found both prisoners guilty as charged.

One can do no better than to refer to the anonymous account of the events that followed:[80]

---

80 'The Distribution of Hannah Brown' in *The Christmas Murders*; edited by Jonathan Goodman.

As they passed to their box, Greenacre surveyed each of them with a keen, searching, and eager glance, as if to read in their expressions the fate which awaited him, and of which the jury were now the arbiters. His countenance, however, remained unchanged; and he still appeared to preserve the same degree of firmness and self-possession which distinguished his demeanour throughout the whole of the trial, and seemed as a man who had already anticipated his fate, and whose mind was made up to the worst that could befall him.

The prisoner Gale, on the contrary, seemed lost and bewildered, and almost unconscious of her awful situation; but with that feeling of attachment for her paramour which women will evince even under circumstances of misery, shame and peril, she fixed her look during the painful interval of suspense and agony upon the countenance of him to whose fate she appeared to cling, even in this trying moment, when life or death was about to unite them once more, or sever their unfortunate connexion [sic] for ever.

After he had read out the names of the jurors, the clerk of arraigns asked:

'Gentlemen, how say you: do you find the prisoner at the bar, James Greenacre, guilty or not guilty of the felony of murder with which he is charged?'

The foreman of the jury answered: "Guilty."

When asked the same question regarding Sarah Gale, the foreman replied: "Guilty."

The countenance of Greenacre remained unaltered. He exhibited no emotion, but leaned back in his chair and seemed perfectly indifferent to what might follow. Gale appeared almost unconscious of what was passing around her.

Once the huge crowd outside the Court heard the announcement of the verdict there arose a deafening roar, cries and cheers and some spectators tossed their hats into the air in jubilation - scenes that would, no doubt, be repeated the following day, 12th April, when the prisoners were brought back to court to receive their sentence. Before the sentence was pronounced, Greenacre was permitted to make a statement which he did in a firm tone:

> My Lord, my unhappy condition in this unfortunate affair has given rise to abundance of evidence against me, such as might be collected in any pot-house or gin-shop, owing to the reports spread abroad to my prejudice, upon which the jurymen have acted. It is contrary to reason and common sense to suppose that I should have meditated the death of the woman, much less that I should effect it in the manner described, because of the property she had. If that had been my object, I could have had it all on the morning, when our marriage was to have taken place, and then it would have been mine. What, then, was my motive for murdering of her?

At this point, the Recorder rose to interrupt Greenacre:

> This is all very proper a matter to have been urged by your counsel at the trial, but should not be pressed upon the Court now. The only question now is, as to the matter of law. If there are the slightest grounds for questioning the verdict of the jury, your only course is to apply to the Secretary of State, the court having no power of itself to interfere. Have you anything more to say?

To this, Greenacre replied:

> In the next place, my Lord, I beg to say that this woman was utterly ignorant of the affair up to the time of my being taken to the police-office. She had no knowledge whatever of it, and is as innocent as any lady or gentleman in this court. This I say, as I am going into my grave - that she is innocent. I invited her back to the house after the body was removed, and she never knew anything of it. I deem it a religious duty to exculpate her from having any concern in this unfortunate affair. I have no more to say.

Turning to Sarah Gale in the dock, the Recorder said this:

> I shall make the same observation to you, Gale, that I have just addressed to the other prisoner. If there be any ground for a further inquiry into your case, you must apply to the Secretary of State, who will exercise his best discretion upon the subject, under the advice of the responsible officers of the Crown.

The prisoner Gale was then led to a chair at the back of the dock, and the usual proclamation for silence, preparatory to the passing of the sentence of death.

The Recorder, in a solemn and impressive tone, proceeded to

address the male prisoner in the following words:

James Greenacre, after a protracted trial, which endured for two entire days, upon a patient and impartial investigation of all the circumstances connected with your case, a jury of your country have found themselves inevitably compelled to find you guilty of the dreadful offence for which you were indicted.

You have been convicted upon evidence, indeed the most satisfactory, of the crime of wilful murder. The appalling details of your dreadful case must be fresh in the recollection of all who now hear my voice, and will long live in the memory and in the execration of mankind; and generations yet to come will shudder at your guilt. You have, indeed, acquired for yourself a revolting celebrity; an odious notoriety in the annals of cruelty and crime.

The means to which you were prompted to resort, in order to conceal the mangled and dismembered portions of your victim, were for a reason attended with partial success. You disposed of her remains, as you thought, in places secure from discovery, but that course availed you not; for after a short interval accumulated evidence and irrefragable proofs of your guilty contrivance became apparent. The amputated limbs and the dissevered body were united to the bloodless head of the murdered woman, and every injury by you inflicted after death has afforded the means of proving by comparison, beyond doubt, that the wound on the eye was inflicted by you while your victim was in life, and strength, and health.

Horrible and revolting to humanity as was the spectacle presented by the mutilated trunk and mangled remains, fresh details and discoveries suggested both the means and manner by which you accomplished the destruction of the deceased. Both surgical skill and medical science came to the assistance of common observation; and it was clearly and beyond all doubt demonstrated that the wounds on the eye and skull were sufficient to produce death; and it was still further proved that while the blood was yet in a fluid state, and circulating through the veins and arteries, you accomplished your horrible object, by severing the head from the body.

Stupor of the senses and suspended animation were the effect of your blows; and then you imbrued your hands in the gushing life's-blood of the wretched and unhappy being who was stretched senseless and unconscious at your feet. The still warm corpse was then barbarously mutilated and mangled by you, in the hope that the eye of man would not detect your guilt; but the eye of God was upon you. The natural disgust and horror which your conduct in this respect excites, compels me to throw a veil over the frightful and appalling particulars of that hideous scene.

But even that scene, revolting as it is, may be useful in a moral point of view, for it shows how the hand of Providence points out the guilty, and proves both the means of detection and the certainty of punishment. The certain but unseen agency of Providence is exhibited in the development of the peculiar and complicated circumstances of your case. The curiosity excited, the alarm produced, and the peculiarity of each succeeding discovery of the mangled members of the body, and the seemingly impenetrable mystery in which the circumstances of such a murder were shrouded, all conspired to awaken suspicion, renew inquiry, and excite to fresh exertion, until at last the mystery was developed by the family of the deceased. The embalmed head was identified, the name of the murdered woman came to light, and sufficient evidence was produced to point out you as the author of her death, and bring you before the tribunal of public justice.

The circumstances attending the discovery of this murder lead to the inevitable conclusion that neither cunning nor ferocity can shelter and secure a murderer; for although the crime may be hidden for a time - although delays may occur, and the mystery of the transaction almost preclude the hope of its discovery, yet the all-seeing eye of God is cognizant of the deed, and man becomes the agent of its discovery. Indeed, instances of escape from such a crime are so rare that the detection is almost as sure as the punishment is certain.

It is plain from the attention with which I perceive you are listening to what I now say that I am addressing an individual not devoid of education, of reasoning faculties, and strength of mind. The occasion you must indeed beware of, as regards yourself, standing where you do, and under the circumstances in which you are placed, awful and solemn to the last degree, both as regards your faith in this world and the world to come. I will not draw arguments from my own feeble resources alone to endeavour to induce and implore you to repent before it is too late.

Let me then, before I proceed to pass upon you the dreadful sentence, entreat you to consider well your past life, and the chances which await you in the life that is to come... The limits of time and the span of this present life furnish no obstacles in the way of a repentant sinner. Turn, therefore, I implore you, with an humble and penitent heart, to the source of all hope and mercy - the blessed Redeemer of mankind - and employ the brief interval which it is yet left to you on this side of eternity in penitence and prayer, as the only means of obtaining that mercy hereafter which the laws of God and man deny you in this world.

It now only remains for me to pass upon you the dreadful sentence of the law; and that sentence is that you be taken from hence to the prison from which you came, and from thence to a place of execution, where you shall be hanged by the neck until you are dead, and that your body be then buried within the precincts of the jail; and may the Lord God Almighty take compassion on your sinful soul.'

It was noticed by those assembled in the court that the Recorder appeared to be deeply moved by his address and seemed close to tears. Yet, although Greenacre had listened intently to the Recorder's words, he showed no emotion. He was led to the back of the dock and Sarah Gale was brought forward to hear her sentence.

'Sarah Gale,' the Recorder began,

I will not aggravate the sufferings which you must now endure with any observations tending to increase those sufferings. The unhappy man who a short time ago stood beside you at that bar has declared that you had no guilty knowledge of the transaction in which he was involved. I cannot but observe, however, with regard to that remark, that you had united yourself to him, sharing his society and bed, and comforting, assisting, and sheltering him without being joined to him by any moral or religious tie. As he has stated that you were ignorant of the dreadful transaction, I think it right to remind you that the earrings found in your pocket had belonged to the unfortunate woman who had been slaughtered by his hands; that duplicates [pawn-tickets] of property which belonged to her were also found in your possession; and that in an adjoining room a box was found, proved to have been hers, besides other property.

I cannot, therefore, as at present advised, entertain and doubt but that the verdict of the jury in your case was well and justly grounded. How far your attachment to the prisoner induced you to continue your intercourse with him, notwithstanding his possession of the property of the deceased under circumstances which I should think must at least have excited suspicion in your mind, it is not for me to judge. Perhaps you considered that what had been done could not be undone; but whatever feeling actuated your conduct in connexion with the circumstances of the case, I feel that I am bound to pass upon you the full sentence directed by the act of parliament; and if upon further investigation of your case, should you be disposed to apply to the Secretary of State for a revision of your sentence, any favourable circumstances should arise, that matter will be considered and disposed of by the competent authorities.

At present I have only to pronounce upon you the sentence of the law: and that sentence is, and this Court do adjudge, that you be transported beyond the sea to such place as His Majesty, with the advice of his privy council, shall direct and appoint, for the term of your natural life.'

Greenacre had remained impassive as his sentence was read to him but his composure collapsed when Sarah was sentenced and he had to grasp the iron railing of the dock to steady himself.

With more than 200 crimes carrying the death penalty at the time – and even petty felonies incurring terms of imprisonment - the prisons were grossly over-crowded. In 1718, transportation was introduced as an alternative sentence available to the courts for minor crimes. In view of the waiting hulks - or floating prisons - the notoriously grim conditions on the long sea voyages out and the harsh penal colonies that were waiting for them, many convicts considered death on the gallows as a more humane – and at least immediate – option.

On leaving the courtroom, Greenacre was *not* taken to the condemned cell deep in the basement of Newgate prison which was the usual practice; he was held in a cell situated higher in the building as it was felt that, as the weather was particularly harsh, this would be more agreeable to the turnkeys assigned to watch him around the clock to prevent him trying once again to take his own life. He was also given a fire in his cell after complaining of the cold.

Greenacre's demeanour remained calm and, having been given paper, pen and ink, he spent several days writing page after page though most of the drafts he produced he chose to burn. It was to the sheriffs who visited him in his cell soon after he had received his sentence that he issued a verbal statement, one that detailed his killing of Hannah Brown more fully than the previous statements he had made when he was arrested and stood trial for murder. On 22nd April, *The Times* reported that:

> He commenced by a distinct admission, that the statement he made at Marylebone Police-office was untrue in many important particulars. The account he gave on Thursday was, almost to a word, as follows:
>
> "When Hannah Brown came to my house on Saturday evening (Christmas Eve), we had tea together. We talked over various matters relating to our intended marriage. I reproached her with having deceived me as to the value of the property which she had given me to understand she was possessed of. There was deception on both sides. She was then washing up the tea cups. I had risen from the table, and was walking too and fro in the room. Mrs Brown, when retaliating the charge of deception, made use of some expressions which irritated me. I caught up a piece of wood, such as is used for rolling silk upon, and threw it at her, (the other accounts state that he struck her with it) and coming with considerable force against her eye, she dropped back upon the chair, in a state of total insensibility. She would have fallen on the floor had I not caught hold of the chair. I then took a common table-knife, and cut her throat. She was incapable of resistance. The blood I wiped up with two pieces of flannel, and threw them down the privy.[81]
>
> When the flow of blood had partially ceased, I laid her on the floor, and paused a few moments to consider what I should do with the body. I ultimately resolved in my own mind to carry it away piece-meal. I then cut off the head, which I put into a piece of sacking, and wrapping it up in a pocket-handkerchief. I took it with me, having locked up the house.
>
> Having got into the Camberwell-road, I took a seat in an omnibus to the Mile-end-gate, where I got out, near the Globe Tavern, and walked on by the bank of the canal, until I got near the lock. Finding that there was no person within view or hearing, I shot out the

---

81 In another statement, Greenacre expressed surprise that these items were not found when his house was searched.

head into the water, within a few yards of the spot where it was afterwards discovered. I then proceeded to the house of Mr. Davis, in Bartholomew-close, and told them that the match was all off between me and Hannah Brown: after which I returned to my own house, where I slept that night.

Next day I cut off the legs and took them to Coldharbour-lane, Brixton, and placed them in the osier ground. The same night (Sunday) I slept at Mrs Gale's lodgings, but she knew nothing of what passed on the previous evening. She saw some of Hannah Brown's property subsequently at my house and asked me how came it to be there? But I told her that it made no matter...

The following day I packed up the trunk in a canvas sack, and carried it into the Camberwell-road, to procure a conveyance. I saw a carrier, of the name of Wood, whom I knew, and asked him to allow me to place the parcel on the tail-board of his cart. The carrier said I might put it inside; but I said it would do very well behind. I got up in front and rode to the Elephant and Castle. When waiting there, a person asked me what the sack contained? I replied, "butcher's meat". The carrier being detained, I took a cab, and with the parcel proceeded to the Edgware-road, and when near the Pine Apple-gate, I got out, and placed the trunk where it was afterwards found. Mrs Gale knew nothing of these circumstances until after we were taken into custody and then only from the statement I made at the Marylebone Police-office'.

The Times continued its report with another of Greenacre's statements to the sheriffs:

I returned in the afternoon to Mrs Gale, and asked her to come to my house to make a giblet-pie; this she did, and stayed with me that night. Mrs Gale observed the boxes under the table by the window and made some remark. I told her that Mrs Brown had hired a porter and took away what goods she wanted and had left these boxes to call or send for another time. The next day (Tuesday or Wednesday) I was at Mrs Gale's and the report of the Edgware-road murder was in the paper, and very exactly described to me Mrs Brown (or at least it appeared to be so to me). Mrs Gale expressed her horror at the report and when she found that the things of Mrs Brown were not fetched away, she began to express her doubts whether the man who helped to take Mrs Brown's box on the Saturday night (as I had told her) had made away with the woman. I encouraged this suggestion, and as no one sent for the goods the fear of Mrs Brown being murdered by the unknown porter gained a strong belief in the mind of Mrs Gale who expressed her fears that I should be suspected of the murder and that if her goods [Hannah Brown's] were found upon me it would be a shocking thing for me. I encouraged the suggestion and thus did I account to her for my most obvious state of fear and anxiety, which she, poor innocent woman, endeavoured to assuage by assisting me to put away the goods; she never knew or suspected that the fatal tragedy had originated from me.

I now beg leave to refer to the very many reasons to show the great improbability of my contemplating the death of Mrs Brown:

First, then, can it be supposed that I could do it for plunder when the whole of the property, little or much, would have been my own by the legal right of marriage the next morning?[82]

Secondly, - If I had been wicked enough only to want the property and not the wife, could I not have possessed myself of one and got rid of the other by going to America?

Thirdly, - If I had been capable of devising the death of Mrs Brown, can it be supposed that I should have betrayed such decided proofs of a frenzied mind, as is evident to the world by the act of putting away the body instead of the completely destroying or burying it...'

Fourthly, - As a proof that Mrs Gale was not going with me to America, I took three places on board of the Neptune, lying in London Docks, in the name of Henry Thomas and wife, and James Thomas (meaning myself). Mr and Mrs Thomas sailed, I suppose, the morning after I was arrested. I took the places and signed the Dock books on the 22nd or 23rd of March; and as an additional proof that Mrs Gale was not going with me, I had just disposed of all my furniture, and Mrs Gale had not disposed of any of her's.

Fifthly, - As a proof that Mrs Gale was not an accessory, or a felonious receiver of the clothes of Mrs Brown, the only things of value - the boa, the shawl, and the cloak - were in my box, with the model of my washing-machine, and carpet-bag, etc, corded up ready to start the next morning. The watch was also found in my trowsers [sic] pocket.

82 The Married Women's Property Act was introduced in 1870; until that time a husband was entitled to all his wife's assets. The new act allowed a wife, through a legal settlement, to retain her own assets, separate from those of her husband.

This statement absolved Sarah Gale from any involvement before or after the murder yet does not explain the evidence of Mrs Andrews in which she maintained that Sarah Gale had spent many hours cleaning the scene of the crime, over several days following the murder, openly accepting buckets of water during the process. Further evidence was given by Mr and Mrs Dillon and Mr Edmonds who remarked on the strong smell of brimstone as though the house had been fumigated.

At this point, Greenacre complains about 'false conjectures' on the part of some of the witnesses who testified against him and states that 'it is out of my nature to contemplate the awful thought of murder'.

The Times report then reminds its readers that James Greenacre changed his version of the events leading to Hannah Brown's death several times and only after his conviction - and the evidence of the medical witnesses - did he admit that the version he gave at the magistrates' court and the murder trial - that Hannah Brown had fallen backwards and suffered a blow to the back of her head - was untrue and that he had struck her with the heavy wooden silk rolling pin, inflicting the blow to the eye that killed her. It was noted that Sarah Gale said there was no such silk rolling pin in the house; informed of this, Greenacre said he had taken it from one of Hannah Brown's boxes.

Whilst awaiting execution in Newgate, James Greenacre seemed more bent on writing versions of his confession which he later destroyed than accepting the ministrations of the prison ordinary, the Rev. Horace Cotton.[83]

Although he told the turnkeys that he didn't want any visitors, except for Mr Price and Mr Cotton (and then only under sufferance)

---

83 Rev. Horace Cotton, Newgate ordinary, an Anglican chaplain active in extracting confessions from convicted prisoners and providing evidence of contrition. He was especially persistent in his attempts to get Eliza Fenning to confess - see the author's book, *Bad Companions*. The prison ordinary would often write accounts of those executed, later used in the *Newgate Calendar*, in part to illustrate the wickedness and weak character of offenders and, hopefully, to deter potential criminals. Cotton was eventually censured for over-doing the hell-fire rhetoric in his pre-execution sermons.

he seemed to have formed some sort of relationship with the prison doctor, Dr M'Murdo, for he wrote the following letter on 18th April, printed in the *Bucks Herald*:

> Honoured Sir, I return you my sincere thanks for your kind consideration of my feeble and exhausted state and my unhappy situation, by allowing me a pint of milk and beer. I feel the more grateful for this set of kindness, because I find that my constitution would sink under this heavy affliction and from the extreme loss of blood which I have sustained, were it not for the sustenance which you have so kindly directed to be allowed me.
>
> "I have taken, Sir, a final farewell of this world, of a misguided public and treacherous friends, and am desirous that my mortal remains to be given to the surgeons for dissection[84], for the advancement of science and the benefit of society, as the only atonement I can make for that act of concealment into which I was propelled by a frenzied state of mind. I cannot say that I shall be able to tranquilise my mind, since it is impressed with the awful reflection that my name hereafter will have the odious notoriety of a wilful murderer, than which nothing can be more remote from my soul's guilt among all the sins and follies of my life.
>
> "My object, Sir, in addressing this letter to you is to give you the disposal of my remains, if you think proper to accept this humble mark of gratitude, from Sir,
>
> Your devoted, obedient, and humble servant,
> J.GREENACRE.
>
> P.S. I have just ascertained that the most monstrous falsehoods are still being published to incense and prejudice the minds of the public against me; that I am charged with being an Atheist; that I am charged with being concerned in the Cato-street affair,[85] and charged

---

[84] The Murder Act of 1751 allowed the corpses of executed murderers in London – a maximum of ten per year – to be used for dissection by anatomists. Post 1834, the bodies were buried in unmarked graves within the place of execution.

[85] In 1820, the Cato Street Conspirators, a group of political dissenters in London led by Arthur Thistlewood, were arrested in a house in Cato Street, near Edgware Road. Their aim was to overthrow the government by assassinating the Prime Minister and the entire cabinet. The plot failed: five of the conspirators were transported and five were hanged at Newgate Prison. It had been rumoured in the press that Greenacre often expressed radical political views and it was even suggested that he had been, in his youth, the member of

with the murder of Mrs Gale's baby, which was taken to St James's Workhouse. These and many other diabolical falsehoods that have no foundation in fact are now invented and put forward as truths.

He was indignant about the reports in the newspapers and strongly denied the rumour that he had killed one of his children. Indeed, there were also rumours in the press about the death of a new-born infant though whether it refers to the one deposited on Mr Dale's doorstep or another child is uncertain. The *Staffordshire Advertiser*, on 22nd April, had this to say:

> It will be recollected that it was stated by Mr. Price, the counsel for the prisoners, that the child with the convict Gale was not her own offspring. We are, however, informed that that statement is not correct, but that in the year 1833, while living with a man named Thomas Gale, who was not her husband, and lodging at the house of Mrs. Riches, No. 69 Lyon-street, New Kent-road, near the Elephant and Castle, she was delivered on the 30th of January in that year, by Mr. Hareby, a surgeon residing in Walworth, of the child in question, who was afterwards called George, and is now, therefore, turned four years of age.
>
> Shortly after Greenacre's return from America she formed an acquaintance with him, and in the October of 1835 went to reside at his house in Carpenter's-place. About five o'clock on the morning of February 17, 1836, Greenacre called up Mr. Hareby, and requested his assistance to his wife, as he alleged, whom he stated to be in labour. Mr. Hareby, in about ten minutes afterwards arrived at Greenacre's house, No. 6 Carpenter's-place, when he found Gale was already delivered of a male child which was lying on its face, and nearly suffocated. He immediately inflated its lungs and used the other usual means for restoration and left the child doing well. He visited Gale on three following days but from the first visit he never again saw the child. On the third day he called he found Gale up and appearing as if nothing had happened but the child was not with her, nor did he on any occasion see another female in the house, the only person besides Gale being Greenacre – a circumstance which, at such a time, excited his astonishment.

the group that had escaped capture. He was buried within the prison grounds close to the five executed conspirators.

> On the 21st of the same month the body of a male infant was discovered secreted under a clod of grass near the well-known gate called the Halfpenny-hatch. It was examined by a surgeon who was passing at the time, who gave it as his opinion that it had been born alive, was about three days old, and had been secreted about twenty-four hours. It was then removed to Bermondsey Workhouse, where an inquest was afterwards held on the body, and the jury, from there being no marks of violence visible, returned a verdict of 'found dead'.
>
> The sudden disappearance of Gale's child, and the circumstances of the finding of a body as above described, occasioned many rumours on the subject to be circulated about the neighbourhood, and on Mrs Gale being informed by a neighbour that either she or Greenacre had murdered her child, she repelled the accusation with great warmth, saying that it was alive and doing well at the house of a friend in the Old Kent-road. Greenacre was also about the same time questioned on the subject, when he also said it was doing well, but alleged it was at the house of a friend of his in the Edgeware-road: and to another person who questioned him about a fortnight afterwards he declared the child was dead.

Not only that, the article also suggested that the statement that Greenacre made whilst awaiting trial - that his third wife, described as 'a young woman of considerable personal attractions'- had died of cholera while he was away in America - was incorrect. It states:

> This fact has, since his conviction, been ascertained by a gentleman who is acquainted with her family, calling on Inspector Feltham and acquainting him with the circumstance, and who at the time informed him that she and Greenacre's son by his first wife were at New York in a state of distress, Greenacre having parted from them at the corner of a street, without giving them the slightest idea that he was coming back to England.
>
> That information is corroborated by a printed circular issued by Greenacre, head, "England and America: an extraordinary and important discovery:" in which he professes, while in America, to have discovered a herb, the juices of which, when combined with the English coltsfoot, forms an "amalgamated candy", most efficacious in the removal and prevention of "coughs, colds, sore throats, hoarseness, asthma, and shortness of breath". He then states that "some difficulty has been experienced in obtaining a regular supply of

a well-selected quality of the coltsfoot to meet the increasing demand of the public, and to obviate this inconvenience, J.G. has returned to England, where he intends to manufacture his amalgamated candy and supply his own family in America with it wholesale, who will transmit the American exotic to him in London.

Evidently, contrary to Greenacre's statements, his third wife was still alive, whether in England or America, so when he proposed marriage to Hannah Brown he was not, in fact, legally in a position to do so. The other information in the report simply illustrates that James Greenacre was one of the thousands of 'snake oil salesmen', a 'quack' and a purveyor of the fabled elixir of life, taking advantage of gullible people who were unable to access professional medication for their common ailments.

The article continues with the information that the turnkeys were on suicide watch in his cell and at night fixed a type of strait-jacket to pinion his arms. As for Sarah Gale, the report says that 'she continues in a very dejected state. Her child is with her, but with no other person, the woman who was her companion in the cell having been removed into the infirmary'.

Finally, the reporter informs his readers:

> It is well known that crowds have flocked to Camberwell and disbursed their three-pences to inspect the cottage of the prisoners. But will it be believed that the kitchen in which poor Mrs. Brown used to reside in the vicinity of the Middlesex Hospital has also been visited by hundreds of gaping sightseers, although it might puzzle the most enthusiastic of the visitors to give a reason for their enthusiasm, or decide what they expected to see. Nay, it is said that the identical mangle which the unfortunate creature was in the habit of using is being exhibited to the curious for a consideration, and that the fortunate purchaser has no reason to regret the investment of his cash.

The following announcement appeared in the *Champion* of Sunday 23rd April:

> REWARD FOR THE APPREHENSION OF THE CONVICT GREENACRE
>
> On Wednesday, Gay, the brother of the unfortunate Hannah Brown,

who gave the first clue to the apprehension of the murderer, applied to Mr. Rawlinson, the sitting magistrate at Marylebone-office, respecting the rewards offered – namely 100l. [£100] by the Secretary of State, and half that sum by the parish of Paddington. After some remarks upon the delay in giving the information, Mr. Rawlinson told him that as there were several claimants to the reward, he had better memorialise [petition] the Secretary of State, who would doubtless do what was right... A few days ago an apprentice to Greenacre applied upon the same subject, asserting that he had given important information in the matter.

The date set for the execution of James Greenacre was Tuesday, 2nd of May, 1837. The *Bucks Herald* carried this announcement:

> ...the execution will take place in the Old Bailey, and arrangements will no doubt be made to prevent the recurrence of those scenes of confusion which on former occasions, in cases of excitement, were productive of fatal consequences. [possibly persons trampled to death]. The expression of the public feeling at the conclusion of the trial necessarily leads to the anticipation of an assemblage of more than ordinary magnitude; and even now we hear that persons taking an interest in such painful exhibitions have actually commenced negotiations to obtain situations in the houses opposite the gaol, from whence they can command a view of the final sufferings of this atrocious criminal.

When informed of his fate, Greenacre seemed sanguine and declared that he was not afraid of death although he still felt angry that he should be branded a murderer when in fact, as he had always insisted, Hannah Brown had died accidentally, and his only crime was the dismembering of her body and concealing the remains. Even at this late hour, he declined the prayers of the prison Ordinary, the Rev. Horace Cotton. He spent his time writing letters and, although he professed to debunk the tenets of Christianity and even questioned the authenticity of the New Testament, the letter he wrote to his children does contain some reference to religious dogma:

Sarah Gale and James Greenacre

Chapel-yard, Newgate, May 1, 1837

My Dear Children,

It grieves me to inform you that the die of your father's fate is cast. His hours are numbered, and all his fond Hopes of seeing you in manhood and prosperity have departed from him.

And as I shall never see your faces again in this world, I have penned this Letter for your future guidance. But as it regards the untimely Fate of your Father, no precaution can be to any avail, for that which has happened to me may prove the Fate of any man. To detail the catastrophe, I can conceive to be unnecessary, for that is now universally known; but never was there a more decided accident in the moment of anger in the world; it was alas! The subsequent proceedings into which I was propelled by an aberration of mind! This it was that involved the accident in misery and has terminated the Life of your Father in the odious charge of WILFUL murderer.

To avoid such a Fate I might admonish you never to throw at any person, nor to yield to passion. But in case of an accident with a gun or otherwise (as that of your Uncle, Samuel Greenacre, killing your Grandmother, and shooting off your Aunt Mary's Head) in cases of death, if terror should seize the mind, and suspended Reason ensue. No charge can be laid to any act under a state of mind. Such, however, was my state of mind, as that God is just and True, before whom I must soon appear.

Now, my Sons, in directing your mind to your future interests, I would have you blend in your Hearts' Study, your Worldly as well as your Spiritual welfare; for be assured that upon your Temporal circumstances depends your happiness or your Wretchedness in this life, as much as the fate of your soul depends upon the moral rectitude of your character.

This conclusion is most obvious to me by much experience, and by recent observations upon the wretched and woe-worn countenances of those who form the assembled congregation in the chaple [sic] of Newgate; there I beheld an Index of the Heart which excited my sympathy and pity, as delineated in the Faces of Men and Children of all ages, which more than proclaimed Necessity to be, the Soarce [sic] of their Crimes.

I will call your attention to a text which I have no doubt but you have many times repeated, 'From our enemies defend us, O Christ!'

There are many ways to dilate and expound almost every passage in Scripture, since the various and clashing opinions of vain and voluminous commentators; but my sons, exercise on these, and all other matters (where faith is determined) that best gift of God to man, your own reason and reflection.

'From our enemies defend us, O Christ!'

Be you assured, my dear boys, that there is no enemy to man equal to that of poverty; it is poverty fills the country with sin and crime – poverty fills the jails, the workhouses, and the streets, with the forlorn, the wretched, and the distressed; Poverty, it is true, is too often the consequences of those snares and traps of our personal enemies, as spoken of in the text; but be you assured that God never assists those who bury in the earth, or lay up their talent in a napkin; that is, those who do not exercise their reason and discretion to help themselves; and herein is the chief use of those talents, to distinguish your enemies from your friends.

God has made man the head of the creation, and by his peculiar understanding and faculty for art and cunning, is thereby enabled to render all animate and inanimate nature subservient to his will; so, also, are those faculties for art and cunning in daily practice by man against man. The chief of danger is not the petty thief, the highwayman, or house-breaker; these, though bad enough, are under the vigilant constraint of the law. The danger against which I would caution you, my sons, is that of a falling into the society of designing knaves, who, under the garb of sanctity or Friendship, will spare neither Time, Pains, nor expense, to ingratiate themselves to accomplish the swindling and ruin of their fellow-man. I speak this advisedly, having sustained great losses by the same means.

You have each an ample legacy to start you in business, and to carry you through life in ease and comfort with attention and care. The baneful vices of drunkenness, and gambling, and senseless pleasures, I beseech you to shun. And let your books be miscellaneous, not all religious; lest Enthusiasm usurps the power of Reason, and you become like some infatuated creatures whose minds are absorbed by an ardent thought upon one thing.

Wishing you health, happiness, and prosperity through life. I remain your affectionate Father,

JAMES GREENACRE

Greenacre also wrote a letter to his solicitor, Mr Hobler, in which he insisted, yet again, that the death of Hannah Brown was an accident. On the eve of his execution he issued the following request:

> I hereby request that the watch, chain, and key, be given to my solicitor, Mr. Hobler. It is my property and used by me up to the time that I was taken into custody by the officer Feltham, who returned it to me by order of the Lord Chief Justice Tindal. Silver hunting watch, No. 513 Presbury, London; fine gold chain and slides, plain seal, one large key.

On the Sunday preceding the day of execution the Rev. Horace Cotton conducted the customary ceremony for the condemned in the prison Chapel. As visitors were allowed admission to witness at close hand the shame and terror of those about to die, the clamour for entrance was intense. The *Morning Post* informed its readers:

> Yesterday what is usually called the condemned sermon was preached in the chapel at Newgate by the Rev. Dr. Cotton, the Ordinary, the service commencing at 11 o'clock. So anxious were the public to gain admission to the chapel that hours before the service commenced the felon's door was besieged by respectable inquirers, who were told that no person could have ingress without a written order, and that those who had them must enter through the Governor's house; and through that medium nearly one hundred persons found their way to the northern gallery... the front seat in the gallery was reserved for those admitted through the chief magistrate.

Although for the most part, Greenacre behaved well during the service, when Cotton referred to him as a murderer in his sermon, Greenacre could not disguise his anger and complained to the cleric afterwards.

He was invited to partake of the Holy Sacrament on the night before his execution but declined and by way of explanation declared that, although he believed in God, he did not believe that Christ was divine. He also felt that his sufferings in this world would atone for any faults of which he was guilty - not what the zealous ordinary wanted to hear.

Greenacre had one final letter to write on the eve of his execution - to Sarah Gale, whom he addresses as Susan - which was either the name he preferred to call her or a mistake on the part of the pamphleteer, as she and her young son awaited transportation:

> Dear Susan, - I am happy to be able to send [this letter] to you by Mr. Alderman Humphery. I should have been glad to have seen you before I leave this world, but I am denied this favour. I have continued, as in duty bound, to declare your innocence of all knowledge of the offence for which you are to be banished the country; but I do not despair you will be better off there than you are in this country, particularly if you take George with you. He will be a support to you in your old age, and will be as a native of the country. Take him with you by all means. Do not fret on my account. I heard you were very much affected on Sunday last at the misrepresentation of Dr. Cotton's sermon. Adieu, I hope you will keep up your spirits. It will be all over by 9 o'clock to-morrow, and I hope you will not make yourself unhappy about me. I should advise you to make a good use of your time when abroad, for there females are very scarce, and a good wife is a great treasure and thought more of than in England.
>
> I have no more to say, but to wish you health and happiness.
>
> Yours truly, James Greenacre.
>
> 'I will send you my spectacles to-morrow morning. Adieu.'

That night, Greenacre slept well for several hours and rose at four in the morning, dressed himself and then settled down to write some letters to relatives and some members of his defence counsel. At seven o'clock he was given breakfast after which his composure began to crumble and he was seen to cry. By eight o'clock, the time set for execution, he was in state of extreme agitation although he submitted to having his arms pinioned without resistance. He expressed a fear of being exposed to the rapacious crowds already gathered outside the prison, ready to gawp, shout and cheer whilst watching him hang. Indeed, he must have been fully aware that a raucous mob had already started to gather outside the gaol the night before and had swelled to thousands by the time the sun rose on the following day.

According to Charles Hindley's book, *History of the Catnach Press*, (1886), the canny street ballad printer, James Catnach, sold

1,655,000 broadsides at the time of Greenacre's execution, some of which included grisly illustrations depicting the murder and dismemberment of Hannah Brown's body for full effect.

At four in the morning, when workmen wheeled out the portable gallows, huge cheers rose from the crowds below. Similar deafening applause erupted when the final piece – the horizontal beam – was put into place, ready to accommodate the noose around Greenacre's neck. Such was the frenzied excitement of the vast crowds swarming around the site of the gallows that several people were carried away insensible and no doubt the usual pick-pockets were kept busy plying their lucrative trade.

As the bell of the nearby St Sepulchre's Church[86] began to toll there was another surge amongst the crowd, jostling to position themselves in front of the gallows, allowing them a view of the face of the condemned as he was, in the parlance of the day, 'turned off'.

Before Greenacre stepped into public view he requested that his spectacles should be given to Sarah Gale after which, still ignoring Cotton's attempts to include him in the reciting of prayers, he joined the procession to the gallows. As he stepped up to the scaffold a huge, triumphant roar rose from the crowd but before Cotton had finished reading the first part of the burial service, the executioner pulled back the bolt and Greenacre fell, his neck broken, the only perceptible movement being a slight 'grasp of his hand'.

At nine o'clock, Greenacre's body was cut down accompanied by a tumultuous cheer from the crowds that had remained to watch the finale of this gruesome piece of theatre. His body was buried later that day within the gaol, close, it was said, to the bodies of Thistlewood and his cohorts, The Cato Street conspirators, hanged for high treason.

---

86 The hand bell at the nearby St Sepulchre's Church was first rung on the eve and again on the morning before the execution. Prior to 1868, when public executions were abolished, the condemned were taken by cart or dragged on a sledge to the gallows at Tyburn. On their way they would stop at the church to hear prayers. The Rev. John Rogers, vicar of St Sepulchre, was the first martyr under the rule of Queen Mary Tudor; he was burned to death in the churchyard in 1555.

It is scarcely believable, but nonetheless true, that Greenacre had advertised for a partner barely a month after he had bludgeoned Hannah Brown to death because he found her relative poverty unacceptable in a prospective wife. He was determined to find either a fourth wife with means or devise some other way to supplement his income. Within four weeks of disposing of Hannah Brown as unsuitably impoverished he placed the following advertisement in *The Times*, on 23rd January, 1837:

> Wanted, a partner, who can command £300, to join the advertiser in a patent to bring forward a new-invented machine, of great public benefit, that is certain of realising an ample reward. Applications by letter only (post-paid), for J.G., at Mr Bishop's, No.1, Tudor-place, Tottenham Court-road.[87]

Apparently, a lady of some means did contact Greenacre but, after several meetings, avaricious and incorrigible as ever, he decided it would be more fortuitous to propose to her, which he did in a letter written on Saturday, 4th February, 1837, the day of the inquest into the death of Hannah Brown. It was published in a number of newspapers and read:

> February 4, 1837.
>
> Dear Madam,
>
> Having had several letters in answer to my advertisement, yours is the third to which I have applied for an interview, and is the last I shall answer. I advertised in the 'Times' newspaper on the 23rd of January for a partner with £300. to join me in a patent to bring forward a new invented machine, of which I have enclosed you a printed specification from scientific gentlemen of property, each anxious to co-operate with me in it; but upon mature consideration, and by the advice of my friends, I have determined not to throw away the half of this most important discovery for the trifling sum of £300., as it is certainly worth as many thousands.

---

87 This so-called new invention was an apparatus for washing linen; there was a descriptive article on it in Greenacre's possession when he was arrested for the murder of Hannah Brown.

It is, therefore, my wish to meet with a female companion, with a small capital, one with whom a mutual and tender attachment might be formed, who would share with me in those advantageous pecuniary prospects which are now before me. And thereby secure the advantages of my own production.

No man can have a greater aversion than myself to advertising for a wife; nevertheless, this advertisement was intended to give an opportunity, by which I might take propositions of an honourable nature to one whom I might prefer as a companion for life. It may be, however, that the first impression from our short interviews has left very different feelings towards me than those by which I am influenced to write this letter to you; I hope however otherwise, or at least that you will not yield to any unfavourable conjectures relative to the moderation of my views, as regards the sum of money I named in my advertisement. It is, I think, sufficient to convince you, or any of your advisers and friends, that property forms but a small share of my hopes and object, in turning my attention towards a partner for life.

I am a widower, thirty-eight years of age, without any incumbrance [sic], and am in the possession of a small income arising from the rent of some houses. I was sixteen years in a large way of business, which I relinquished about three years ago, but have lost much of my property by assisting others and confiding too strongly in the professions of pretended friends.

Under these circumstances, I am induced to seek a partner, or a companion with a small sum, to co-operate with me in securing the advantages of this machine, which will be a great public benefit, and which has long been attempted by many scientific persons, and is certain of realising a competency.

Having given you this plain statement of my situation, I beg leave to add, that my mind is thoroughly fixed upon making you the future object of my affections and constant regard. If you should feel disposed to favour my sincere and honourable intentions, I shall take the liberty of calling upon you, and hope that you will divest your mind of any idea beyond that of the most sacred candour and honourable intentions on my part.

Should you feel disposed to communicate any remarks on the subject by letter, I hope that you will do so. Excuse the dissimulation by which I have obtained an introduction to you, and believe that my present proposal is dictated by every honourable and affectionate feeling towards you.- I am, dear Madam, yours most sincerely,'

James Greenacre.
"No.6, Carpenter's –place, Camberwell, Surrey."

The lady, it seems, declined to take the matter further, and survived.

The following comment appeared in the *Hereford Times* on Saturday 27th May, 1837:

> DEPRAVITY of TASTE: - The morbid hankering after every, the most trifling particular, descriptive, biographical, and pictorial, respecting murderers and their victims, prevailing at the present moment, amongst all classes of persons, high as well as low, has reached a disgusting height. Far, however, as the caterers of this depraved taste have hitherto gone in supplying food for this growing appetite, all other efforts are completely cast into the shade by the superior genius of a confectioner in the neighbourhood of Leicester-square, who, absolutely it will scarcely be believed, exhibits in the show-window a sugar composition bust of that monster Greenacre – Greenacre and confectionary! – sweetmeats and murder! – jellies and blood! No one, we should think, could purchase, much less eat, even a macaroni, in a shop glorying in the effigies, albeit composed of flour and sugar, of an abhorred and executed cut-throat...

Greenacre's notoriety was such that his death mask now rests in Norwich Castle and, in 2011, a commemorative coin, dated 2nd May, 1837, with the name Greenacre beneath the image of a man hanging from the gallows, was sold at auction for £420.

What sort of man was James Greenacre? In his autobiographical statements he described himself as a man of property, a man of sober habits, a father of numerous children by three wives, all of whom died tragically. Yet this was a man who delivered such a sudden and violent blow to Hannah Brown's head that it burst her right eyeball and knocked her senseless. This loving husband and father then systematically severed Hannah's head from her body, first with jabbing cuts with a knife and then, in desperation, wrenching off the remaining tissue and fractured bone to free it from the body.

Was his desperate desire for the property he thought Hannah owned so great that his frustration when he realised he had been duped let loose such a rampant form of violence? His sudden rage reveals that he was a man consumed by the need to make money; he had debts of £150 and had already faced bankruptcy, despite having a number of houses which presumably provided a reasonable income from rents. He may well have funded these acquisitions using assets provided by his wives' families but it's unclear whether he had ever helped to maintain any of his children; the two from his last marriage were cared for by relatives. If the self-congratulating statement he wrote for publication can be believed he enjoyed married life and took pride in providing for his legitimate children though not averse to disposing of any illegitimate progeny. In an age when both birth rates and infant mortality were high, sickly or unwanted infants were often dumped in privies, ditches or alleyways. Others were handed over to the notorious 'baby-farmers', vile women who took advantage of mothers who, either through extreme poverty or shame, couldn't care for their children. Once the fee had been paid, those involved in this evil trade would sometimes starve or strangle the baby and then await the next lucrative knock on the door. At least Greenacre made sure his children were provided for though he obviously had a hand in the depositing of one, and maybe two, of Sarah Gale's new-born babies. It is perhaps surprising that there was an inquest, complete with jury, on the death of the baby found dead which illustrates that the society into which it was born may not have been as heartlessly dismissive of child fatalities as is sometimes supposed.

James Greenacre was certainly a complex character - self-centred, avaricious and totally ruthless if thwarted. It is evident from the differing versions of the death of Hannah Brown that James Greenacre was an inveterate liar and a fantasist with delusions about the viability of his speculative money-making schemes. Clearly he was involved in various entrepreneurial ventures and scams and was so determined to launch the patent on his new washing-machine that he even suggested in his letter to his relatives whilst awaiting trial that his notoriety might help its promotion![88]

One wonders why the exemplary landlord, husband and father as depicted in Greenacre's autobiographical statement, didn't manage to rustle up a few friends, business colleagues or grateful tenants – for whom, he assured his readers, he had so often waived aside rent arrears in cases of hardship - to speak on his behalf at his trial. Greenacre, of course, as seen in his letter to his relatives, attributed this lack of support to the fact that, on account of the grisly nature of the crime with which he had been so falsely charged, his friends had preferred to remain anonymous and give the Old Bailey court-house and the gaol at Newgate a wide birth.

Clearly, his position as an overseer and his public persona as a man of property was extremely important to him but as a type often, perhaps unfairly, regarded as a typically Victorian gentleman, he lived by double standards and his attitudes were steeped in hypocrisy concerning the denigration of the sort of woman he considered was born to be of service and bear his bastard children. James Greenacre apparently didn't see Sarah Gale as someone worth marrying - she was, or had been, after all, an 'unfortunate' or prostitute – though, of course, he was quite happy to live with her and allow her to cook, clean and have sex with him. We cannot guess whether Sarah Gale was willing to accept being used as Greenacre's sexually available drudge but perhaps she was just grateful for his protection, providing her and young George with somewhere to live. He readily admitted that, at the time of his arrest, he had fully intended to return to America without Sarah.

He did, however, in his writings from the time of his arrest, trial and whilst awaiting execution, emphasise that Sarah Gale did

---

[88] James Greenacre achieved further notoriety for, according to Jonathan Goodman's editorial note in *The Christmas Murders*, he states that 'when stevedores in the London docks let fall a case of soft fruits, with the result that the case split open and the fruits rolled (the unblemished of them to be picked up and pocketed as perks), the object of the accident was referred to as "*a Greenacre*".

not participate in the murder nor even help him dispose of the dismembered body parts - this, despite the fact that witnesses testified to her cleaning up his house after the slaughter. Whether she was guilty or not, he could so easily have implicated her and made sure she joined him on the gallows. The fact that he asked Cotton to give his spectacles to Sarah Gale after his death was rather touching for clearly her eyesight was not good and she could never have afforded to buy a pair of glasses of her own.

Meanwhile, what became of Sarah Gale, the other protagonist in this grotesque drama? Not surprisingly, she fell into a stupor of despair whilst in Newgate. She had been refused permission to speak to Greenacre again and, in addition to her grief at his execution - she must have heard the terrible roar of the crowds outside the prison - she faced the prospect of transportation to a notoriously brutal penal colony on the other side of the world. Some of her friends rallied behind her with pleas for mercy but these were ignored and on 26th June, Sarah and twenty other female convicts, were removed from Newgate and taken to the hulks or floating prisons at Woolwich and from there to the south coast awaiting transportation to New South Wales. She was one of 140 women transported on board the ship, *Henry Wellesley*, which sailed from England on 17th July, 1837.[89]

She did, however, survive the hazardous and harrowing journey to the penal colony, arriving on 22nd December that year, a destination fraught with danger, desperation and fear of the unknown. One cannot help wondering what became of Sarah Gale from the time she left the transportation ship, *Henry Wellesley*, in 1837, and landed in New South Wales. Having arrived in such a far off colony with no money, friends or prospects, how did she survive? Women were

---

89 Ellen Paul, Jane May, Eliza Campbell, Bridget Walker, Mary Spencer, Mary Jackson – just some of the women on board the *Henry Wellesley* with Sarah Gale. Their crimes were probably petty theft, drunkenness, public disorder and affray, concealment of a birth, etc. Transportation to New South Wales continued until it was abolished in 1850.

treated atrociously, considered sexually fair game for government officials, guards and convicts alike, to be used, discarded and even sold on as chattels.

Post-transportation records of Sarah Gale (sometimes referred to as Sarah Farre) can be contradictory as she often changed her name and age when dealing with officialdom. On arrival in New South Wales she was described in the Convict Registration documents as:

'...a bonnet-maker and nurse, 5 feet 4 inches tall, sallow complexion, brown hair and eyes, could read and write, Protestant, single, front teeth missing and a cast in her left eye.'

There is no record of Sarah's son, four year old George, in the passenger listings for the *Henry Wellesley* or the Convict Register list, though minors may not have been included. Children as young as ten years old were transported as punishment for theft, more often than not from their employers. On arrival, infants belonging to convict mothers were deposited in orphanages until such time as the mothers' sentences had been completed and they were free to collect them.

This may have been the case with young George or he may have been left behind in England; it seems that Sarah had not decided whether to take him or not as in his last letter Greenacre tried to persuade her to have him with her. Did she think the youngster would never survive the rigours of the journey to New South Wales, a five month voyage that was fraught with danger, especially for a young child? She may, of course, have felt that having a child would hamper her chances of finding a husband in New South Wales and, if she was working as a prostitute, become an unnecessary encumbrance.

Female convicts were sometimes sent to work as domestics in the households of early settlers or free men and, of course, those chosen for the job were usually the younger and more attractive of those on offer. In November, 1843, Sarah applied for permission to marry a fellow convict, John Fay. He had been sentenced to seven years' penal servitude but by the time he and Sarah planned to wed, he was a free man though Sarah, who gave her age as forty-six, was still in bond. However, there is no record of the marriage ever taking place.

An announcement appeared in the *Newcastle Courant* on 12th January, 1844, entitled: THE GREENACRE TRAGEDY:

> SARAH GALE. The companion of the notorious Greenacre, and who, for the robbery of his unfortunate victim, was sentenced to transportation, is living in Port Philip, [where there was a penal colony] an assistant in a confectioner's shop. She is described by a person who recently saw her in that colony as having regained her health and looking very comely; her haggard appearance at her trial showing the relics of a countenance of considerable prior attractions.

On 28th May, 1849, Sarah again applied for permission to marry a fellow convict - this time to a forty-three year old man called Job Noon, who, at the age of twenty-four, had been convicted of sheep-stealing in Lincolnshire, and, like Sarah, had been sentenced to transportation for life, arriving in New South Wales on the ship, *Bengal Merchant*. On this occasion, she gave her correct age as fifty-one. This marriage *did* take place and, a year later, on 1st October, 1850, Sarah Gale, having completed thirteen years of her sentence, received a Conditional Pardon, the condition being that, as she has been sentenced to transportation for life, she must remain in Australia and should not enter the United Kingdom of Great Britain and Ireland; the penalty for breaching this condition being that the Pardon would become null and void and the convict's bonded sentence would be resumed.

It appears that Job Noon, who had been also been granted a Conditional Pardon in 1849, died in New South Wales, in 1865, but Sarah Gale's movements since she received the Pardon remain uncertain.[90] It has been suggested that Sarah Gale died in Australia in 1888 yet the following account of her death in 1858 appeared in

---

90 Although it is recorded that a man called Job Noon died in Warwickshire in 1888, aged seventy-eight, this is unlikely to be the Job Noon of this narrative as the latter was subject to the restrictions of his Conditional Pardon. The Job Noon who died in 1865, in Maitland, NSW, aged fifty-nine, is more likely to be the ex-convict Sarah married in 1849. Coincidentally, The British Census Record for 1861 lists a Job Gale, fifty-five, and Sarah Gale, fifty-four, living in Bridport, Dorset.

The Empire, entitled 'Remarkable Incidents in the Experience of a Medical Man', published in Sydney, New South Wales, on 4th June, 1861, and reprinted in a number of English newspapers, including the *York Herald*, the *Louth and North Lincolnshire Advertiser*, *The Times* and *Lloyd's Weekly* in October of that year. The writer informs his readers:

> Of the murderer himself, and of the particulars of his trial and execution, I shall here say nothing. The circumstances which I am about to relate has no further connection with him and his history than that it refers to the ultimate fate of the wretched woman who was his paramour and accomplice, who assisted him, if not in the actual murder, at least to conceal the evidence of it, and who was to have shared the proceeds of his guilt.
>
> Sarah Gale, the woman alluded to, became, if possible, an object of greater execration than the murderer himself. She was admitted on the trial to give evidence against him, and by this means to preserve her worthless life for the fate which befell her many years afterwards in the far interior of this country.
>
> In the year 1858, the writer, who is a medical man, and lived in the remote part of the colony, was summoned to attend a woman who had been thrown from her horse against a tree. The messenger informed me that if I made haste and could save the patient I should be handsomely rewarded, as she was very rich, having some thousands of cattle and stations half as big as England itself; that fresh horses would meet us, and that if I rode well we could do the distance in something like five hours. This gratuitous information he gave me while hurrying on my clothes. In 20 minutes, I was on my way to the Big River, across arid plains, with not a tree or shrub in sight. After a ride of six hours and ten minutes we arrived at the homestead, or head station.
>
> After running the gauntlet through a dozen kangaroo dogs I reached the patient's bed-room. On approaching the door I saw the bed directly opposite; it seemed a huge pile of something in the centre. On going close to the bedside I found my patient to be a woman of vast size and weight – certainly not less than 16 stone and the heap I had noticed on my entrance was her very extensive and respectable corporation.

On examination I found she had suffered both from external and internal injuries to such an extent that I feared the case was hopeless. She turned to look at me. I begged she would not disturb herself.

'Not disturb myself,' she interrupted. 'It is easy to say so, but why do you not give me something to relieve this dreadful pain? Give me something, I pray, or I must go mad.'

At noon next day a marked change for the worse had taken place. The period had arrived for me to perform an unpleasant duty. I broke the news to the unfortunate woman with as much caution as possible, telling her to prepare for the worst, and to arrange any affairs she might wish to have settled before her final departure from this world. She told me the whole cause of the accident, in a calm, collected manner, and begged I would be kind enough to draw up a will for her, as she informed me the whole of the property was hers and that she was living with J..., but not legally married to him, therefore she could dispose of her property as she liked, which she did.

The will being finished, I wished her to sign it in my presence, and in that of other witnesses; she had a marked repugnance to do this, which seemed dreadful to her, as a last act. I showed her the necessity of doing so while in possession of all her faculties or before derangement took place. She refused to sign it but in the presence of two persons, whom she named, her husband and myself. I ordered the room to be cleared, and gave her the pen, putting at the same time the usual questions. She hesitated a long time – there was a stillness that was fearful to me for some ten minutes; at last she summoned sufficient resolution to commence, but stopped at the first letter, 'I am thinking, thinking, thinking, of times long past,' and as she seemed talking more to herself, as it is called, than addressing us, I made no reply.

Her husband, who was not sober, witnessed this death-bed scene with evident emotion.

'James,' said the woman, 'I should like to be alone with the doctor for a little while. I have something to tell him, but nothing I have to confess that you do not already know.' The husband then left.

She then told me what I was never, never to tell again. I was at first absolutely paralysed. There in that remote solitude, did that dying woman reveal facts so dreadful, and so connected with my painfully distinct recollection of by-gone days, that I absolutely shook with agitation. It seemed more like a horrible dream than a waking reality. She recalled me to my senses by her despairing appeals to heaven for forgiveness. She seemed completely hopeless of pardon. I tried at length to comfort her, and I bade her not despair;

'How glad I am you are here, doctor; you shall be well paid for all this. Do you know I feel happier now since I have told you all. Oh, if I could have seen a clergyman, but there is none nearer than 150 miles. Too late! Too late! I shall soon be elsewhere. Ah, where?'

I begged her to sincerely repent of her faults, and seek hope for the future; she clasped her hands together, sighed deeply as though her heart too was oppressed, and she was at a loss for words; she spoke at last with effort and evident fatigue.

'Call him in,' she said. I did her bidding; in the presence of her husband I gave her the pen; she took one look of despair and anguish, signed the will, and I witnessed at once the death and signature of "Sarah Gale"

As it was too late to start for home the same day on which Mrs Gale died, and to sleep was impossible, I made a memorandum of the circumstances an hour or so after her death took place. I have said all that I feel at liberty to divulge of a story which will ever haunt my memory.'[91]

The article ends with the following information:

The weapons with which Greenacre destroyed Mrs. Brown were not found until quite recently. In making the railroad from Dulwich to the Elephant and Castle, the excavators had to empty the cesspool of Greenacre's house and therein they found a butcher's knife and two-foot crowbar, with which he is supposed to have committed the murder.

The Australian doctor's account was also published in the *York Herald* on 5th October, 1861, but began with a few ghoulish reminders concerning the murder of Hannah Brown:

Most people whose memory carries them back a quarter of a century will remember the leading features of an extraordinary crime which

---

91 There was no mention of Sarah's son, George, who would have been twenty-five years old at the time.

took place in London about the commencement of the 1837, and which probably excited in the public mind a great deal of horror as any deed of guilt ever committed in the metropolis. I allude to the murder by Greenacre of Mrs Brown...

The article then elaborates the story by informing readers that Greenacre

...actually rode about London in cabs and omnibuses, for two or three days, with the head under his arm, wrapped in a silk handkerchief, telling friends and acquaintances who happened to inquire as to the contents of the bundle he seemed so careful of, that it was only a cabbage!

If the doctor's account of Sarah Gale's death is true how would she have been able to accumulate such wealth and become the owner of 'some thousands of cattle and stations half as big as England itself' during the eight years between her freedom from bondage and her death? Though land in the outback was then cheap it must surely have been through sheer cunning, theft or perhaps by way of a fortuitous 'marriage' partnership that she acquired so much territory either with an official or, more likely, with a fellow convict with some knowledge of farming.

An entry in the *Newgate Calendar* states that Sarah Gale, née Farre, 'received a moderate education' and at one time, under the name of Sarah Wiston, (Wilton?) was part of a theatre group in the East End of London. At that time actresses were, in the eyes of society, little more than prostitutes and Sarah did subsequently resort to working as an 'unfortunate' as they were called, in and around the Strand and Haymarket, the bustling theatre areas of central London.

The account states that Sarah 'became acquainted with a member of the legal profession, with whom she lived for a considerable time, and by whom she had one child which died in its infancy'. When the relationship with her 'protector' ended he set her up in a chandler's shop in Southwark and she married a hackney-coachman who, it was said, left her, having caused her to become destitute once more. It was understood that the child, George, was her husband's son. Two years after her husband's desertion, Sarah began the disastrous relationship with James Greenacre. Charming and plausible, he presented himself as a London landlord and the owner of a large farm in Hudson Bay. Desperate and gullible, Sarah must have considered an alliance with him to be a more than lucrative proposition. Little could she foresee that it would lead to a terrible murder and drastically change the course of her life.

It is quite possible that Sarah Gale continued to work as a prostitute once she reached New South Wales and, perhaps, as before, through a prosperous client, was helped to not only subsist but even to accumulate the wealth mentioned by the doctor who professed to have witnessed her will and death. Or she might have married well though her only officially recorded marriage was to the sheep-stealer, Job Noon. As Greenacre had said in his last letter to her, in such a sparsely populated country, women were at a premium and much sought after, not only to bear children but also to share the load of manual work on the farms.

Many others transported to the colonies and forced to start life again in a foreign country did well, became entrepreneurs, amassed wealth and attained positions of influence.

Finally, what of Hannah Brown, the victim in this tragic affair? She was born Hannah Gay, in 1780 (1790 in some reports) near Norwich, of respectable parents. At sixteen she went into service for Lord Wodehouse, at Crimley Hall, but four years later she headed for London and continued in service until she married Thomas Brown, a shoe-maker. According to the *Newgate Calendar*, the marriage lasted for only two years and her husband, whilst travelling to Jamaica to settle some inheritance, was washed overboard and, unfortunately, Hannah was unable to claim her husband's legacy. She went back into service for four years as a cook with Mr Deputy Greenaway, a hat-maker, in Bishopsgate, and from there she went to work for Mr C. Barclay, a well-known brewer. Next, she went to live with two maiden ladies named Potter, in the Old Kent Road and after that, with Mr Oliver, an anchor-smith, near London Docks. Her next job was with Mr Perring, another hat-maker, in the Strand. By this time, Hannah had managed to save enough money to buy a mangle so she could earn a living by taking in washing at her new lodging at No. 45 Union Street. It was rumoured that, through sheer hard work, she had managed to accrue some substantial savings but, it was said, 'she was a person of reserved disposition and communicated with few as to her position in life'.

How she became acquainted with James Greenacre about three months before her death is unknown - although they were born only a few miles apart in Norfolk - but she may have responded to one of his advertisements for a wife with money.

It is notable that the Judge, Recorder and even the prosecuting counsel at the trial of Greenacre and Gale rarely referred to Hannah Brown by name, using the term 'the victim' instead. Nor did James Greenacre use her name in his statements yet there were many witnesses willing to testify that she was a good woman, hardworking and respectable and, despite Greenacre's attempt to insinuate that she was a heavy drinker, a woman that was never seen to be drunk. A small amount of gin was found in her stomach at post-mortem but it seems far from remarkable that she should celebrate with a glass of gin on the eve of her marriage to James Greenacre, who she thought was a conscientious property owner and entrepreneur who had promised to release her from the drudgery of the mangle and introduce her to a new life in America. If she had ever harboured any doubts about James Greenacre these were terrifyingly confirmed the split second she saw him brandishing a piece of wood above his head poised to deliver the violent blow that would kill her.

Christiana Edmunds and Dr Charles Beard

*'And most of all would I flee from the cruel madness of love,
The honey of poison-flowers and all the measureless ill.'*

The setting for the drama of The Poisoned Chocolate Creams, one of the strangest murder cases of the nineteenth century, was the fashionable south coast resort of Brighton. One can imagine the scene in 1870, as holiday-makers strolled along the Promenade, marvelling at the sight of the West Pier in the distance, one of three that thrust far out into the English Channel; the bathing machines parked at the water's edge; the air rent with the shrieks of excited children echoed by flocks of greedy gulls circling above, drawn by the smells wafting from the rows of makeshift food stalls below; the clatter of the horse-drawn omnibuses and private carriages; the cries of the sharp-eyed street vendors and beach photographers touting for custom from the ladies who were taking the sea air, gloved and weighed down, even on hot days, by long, heavily draped dresses, their hats flamboyantly veiled and festooned with silk flowers and feathers - and, as they picked their way through the crowded beach, booted and buttoned, many with a weary young maid in tow.

Above all the noise could be heard the jaunty strumming of a black minstrel band entertaining the visitors to this most fashionable of seaside resorts which, since its popularity in the Regency period and the patronage of the Prince of Wales, had afforded sightseers the magnificent spectacle of the Brighton Pavilion. Little wonder that it had become a magnet for the hordes of London day-trippers in the months of July and August; and once they had returned to their labours in the kitchens, parlours and city workshops, Brighton drew the pleasure seekers from the wealthier, more leisured classes.

One such day in September, 1870, a smartly dressed woman, gloved, bonneted and heavily veiled, was making her way the short distance from her home at 16 Gloucester Place, to the residence of forty-three year old, Dr Charles Izard Beard, and his wife, Emily,[92] at 64 Grand Parade, an imposing Georgian town house large enough to accommodate not only the doctor, his wife and their four young children – their eldest son, Hugh, was at school - but also a boarder and five live-in servants. The name of their lady visitor was Christiana Edmunds and she had in her pocket a small token of friendship - some chocolate creams - which she had purchased from Mr Maynard's large, double-fronted confectionary shop in West Street.

For several years she had been a friend and regular visitor to the Beard family home, for both belonged to the well-heeled, respectable stratum of society in Victorian Brighton, a town in which class divisions were clearly defined and largely accepted without question.

Christiana's behaviour that afternoon, however, was to cause the doctor and his wife considerable alarm and subsequently engendered enquiries that would culminate in tragedy. Christiana had, for some time, harboured a secret passion for Dr Beard, bombarding him with emotionally charged letters - inappropriate, to say the least, for not only was she masquerading as a close friend of Emily Beard and her family, but she was also one of the doctor's

---

[92] Dr Charles Izard Beard: Cambridge graduate and member of the Royal College of Practitioners: in addition to his medical practice in Brighton he travelled extensively in his position as Government Inspector of Vaccination in the Midlands. He and his wife, Emily, were cousins and had known each other since childhood.

patients. She was an accomplished draughtswoman and had, a local doctor, Nathaniel Blaker, recalled later, collaborated with Dr Beard on producing anatomical drawings for display in the Library of the Sussex Hospital. Whether Christiana's passion was ever returned or even encouraged by Dr Beard - who may well have been flattered by such an ardent infatuation - was never fully addressed. It seems, however, that he may have responded to some degree, though when asked at a later date whether he had ever written letters in reply, he denied it.

During her visit to the Beards' home that afternoon Christiana offered Emily Beard some chocolates for her children, but they were elsewhere - their mother said they were in bed. Instead, Christiana teasingly popped a chocolate into Emily's mouth. Fortunately, as it tasted so bitter, she promptly left the room and spat it out. Her guest's behaviour would have been socially unacceptable in a class that adhered so strictly to the observance of manners, etiquette and personal boundaries. They might have expected their kitchen maids to behave in this over-familiar way but not two respectable, middle class women.

As a consequence of this *faux-pas* Dr Charles Beard, concerned and annoyed, called on Christiana and her seventy-one year old mother, Ann, and insinuated that Christiana had attempted to poison his wife with the chocolate cream. Both Christiana and her mother reacted angrily, threatening to 'bring a charge' for defamation against the doctor unless he retracted his words. Not to be intimidated, the doctor stipulated that Christiana would no longer be welcome at his house and, furthermore, he insisted that all contact between her and his family must cease. However, unable to prove attempted poisoning Dr Beard returned home, feeling powerless to resolve such a socially awkward situation. After all, both Miss Edmunds and her mother were law-abiding citizens, well-liked and respected in the town; their behaviour had never caused the slightest concern. However, when suspicion was subsequently focussed on Christiana, police investigators soon became aware that several of her relatives had been certified insane – some of this information being given to the police by a Dr Humphrey who had recently treated Christiana.[93]

It transpired that, a few months later, in January, 1871, unsettled by the continued flow of love letters from Christiana, Dr Beard asked her once again to stop, at the same time informing her that he had not only told his wife about her infatuation for him but had also shown her the letters. Christiana reacted badly to this and, on reaching home, had, according to her mother's later testimony, paced the floor, highly agitated and convinced she would go mad - which, unfortunately, proved to be a remarkably accurate prophecy.

On 12th June of that year, Mr Albert Barker, a silversmith from Clapham, was on holiday in Brighton with his family; the party included his wife, Leticia, their young son, Sidney, and Albert's two young brothers-in-law, eighteen year old Charles and seventeen year old Ernest. They were lodging with Mrs Woodham, in West Street, and Charles Miller bought some chocolate creams from Mr Maynard's shop nearby to give to his nephew, four year old Sidney Barker. The child ate some without any ill effect but later in the day, having sampled another, he became very ill and within twenty minutes he was dead.

There was an inquest, of course, which was held at the Carpenter's Arms, in West Street, and a Brighton surgeon, Dr Richard Rugg, was called to describe the sequence of events:

> I recollect being sent for on the 12th of June to Mrs Woodham's to see the little boy, Barker. It was soon after four o'clock in the afternoon. He died in about 10 minutes after.
>
> Next day I made a post-mortem examination of the body. The child was in strong convulsions on my arrival and continued so until his death which was very sudden. In the post-mortem examination I found the body in a very healthy state generally. The brain was slightly congested but no more than one would have expected in the case of a child dying from convulsions.

[93] Christiana's father, a prominent architect in Margate, had designed and built the Lighthouse at Margate and other civic buildings in the town. In middle age he was confined to the Peckham Asylum, where he died in 1847. Details of other family members similarly afflicted would eventually be made known.

> At the request of the coroner I had the stomach, with its contents, taken out and it was given to Inspector Gibbs. There was nothing in the appearance of the organs of the body to cause death. The whole body was in a state of rigidity. There was nothing else to be seen to account for death.

The jar with the stomach was sent by Detective Inspector Gibbs to Dr Letheby.'

Dr Henry Letheby described the outcome of his analysis:

> I am professor of chemistry at the London Hospital and reside at No. 17 Sussex-place, Regent's-park. I recollect that on Friday evening, the 16th of June, Inspector Gibbs gave me a parcel containing a sealed jar together with two small packages containing chocolate creams. The jar contained a child's stomach and a piece of liver. I submitted the stomach to careful examination. It did not contain any mineral poison but contained strychnine to the amount of about a quarter of a grain which was enough to kill a child of that age. The contents of the stomach had an odour of chocolate.
>
> The symptoms of the child's illness were the symptoms of poisoning by strychnine. I examined the liver but there was nothing about it to command my attention. In one of the parcels of chocolate creams I found strychnine but in the other I found no strychnine or other poison.
>
> A day or two afterwards I received a third parcel from Inspector Gibbs which contained a large quantity of strychnine...'

Christiana Edmunds was also called as a witness and she testified that she, too, had been made ill after eating chocolates bought from Mr Maynard's shop. Furthermore, she had taken the extraordinary step of sending samples to a local chemist, Mr Schweitzer, for analysis and he had confirmed that strychnine was present in some of the sweets.[94]

The result of the inquest on young Sidney Barker was that whilst it had been established that strychnine was found in some of the

---

94 The Marsh test, devised in 1836, could detect arsenic but a more accurate analysis would have been obtained using the Reinsch test, of 1841, which could detect even small traces of antimony, strychnine, arsenic, mercury and other poisons.

chocolates bought from Mr Maynard's shop, there was no indication as to how the poison had got there. It had been suggested that strychnine may have contaminated the chocolates during the manufacturing process. This was a possibility as such poisons were used in the warehouses where cocoa beans were stored to deal with rat infestation. However, a verdict of accidental death was recorded.

After the inquest three anonymous letters were sent to the child's father, Mr Albert Barker, at his home in Clapham, London, urging him to sue Mr Maynard for causing the death of his son.[95] They were posted from different parts of Brighton, one on 27th June, another on the 28th June and another on the 1st July. The letters expressed sympathy with the parents and pointed out that the poison could have found its way into the sweets only in Mr Maynard's shop; they urged Mr Barker to instigate further inquiries, saying that the public was dissatisfied with the results of the inquest and expressed a hope that Mr Maynard would be prosecuted.

At this stage the police investigations began to throw suspicion on Christiana Edmunds, but some incriminating evidence was needed. Inspector William Gibbs sent a letter to Christiana concerning her illness after eating chocolate creams and received a reply the same day. He sent this letter to a handwriting expert who was able to compare the handwriting with the notes sent to Sidney Barker's parents.

Shortly after the inquest Christiana wrote the following letter to Dr Beard, signing herself, DOROTHEA:

CARO MIO,

I have been so miserable since my last letter to you. I can't go on without ever speaking to you. What made me write so! I thought, perhaps, it would be better for both of us, but I have not strength of mind to bear it.

We met La Sposa the day after her return and were glad to see her back again. La Madre thought she looked very thin and careworn;

---

95   These letters were later produced in court and a handwriting expert, Mr Netherclift, testified that, in his opinion, they were all written by Christiana Edmunds.

I hope she will feel the good now from her change. You must have missed her. I didn't enter into the poisoning case in the street, but I called and told her that I was obliged to appear at the inquest in a few days and I hope she would send you a paper and let you know, but she said No, she did not wish to unsettle you. However, dear, I mean you to know about this dreadful poisoning case, especially as I had to give evidence; and I know how interested you were in it as you told me you would give anything to know what La Sposa swallowed. I sent you the analysis and have no means of knowing if it was sent to you. Yes, through my analysis the police found me out and cited me to appear. You can fancy what I felt: such an array of gentlemen; and that clever Mr Letheby, looking so ugly and terrific, frightened me more than anyone; for, if I gave wrong symptoms, of course he would have known. You can fancy my feelings, standing before the public, looking very rosy and frightened as I was. When I saw the reporter's pens going and taking down all I uttered, Burn's lines rushed to my memory, 'The chiel's amang them taking notes and faith he'll prent it'.

I did the best I could, thankful when I had finished. It seemed so long and my evidence was useful. As the jury had nothing to say, my heart was thankful. When Mr Gell and Penfold attacked me – Mr G: 'Why didn't I show Maynard the analysis?' – it was so sudden, my ideas all left me, and I merely said, because I found Mr Maynard so sceptical and prejudiced, and I thought I had done sufficient. Oh! Why didn't I say as I meant. Because, I suppose Mr M would take the same steps as I had done or else destroy his stock, and that, if those sold to Mr Miller were from the same stock, I had warned him against these – he was answerable.

If I had only said that, for I had no friendly feelings towards Mr M. That man's chocolates have been the cause of great suffering to me. The Inspector said he wished I had spoken as I felt and as I did to him when he came to me, earnestly and energetically. But La Madre told me I should be thought flippant, so you see I was subdued. It was unfortunate the woman Cole's case was dropped. The Inspector told me that Dr Letheby took one of the chocolates from the bag and said, 'Good God! This is filled with strychnine'. He felt the effects of it all day: it was rash of him. You see there were two poisons. Zinc was in La Sposa's case and mine. I was troubled to describe the taste. The reporters smiled when I said castor oil and brandy. The Coroner said, 'Ah! Your usual remedy'. I was stupid. He is so deaf. I was told to stand close to him. I took care to turn my back to the jury and on all

I could. They were all very polite to me, even that fierce Mr Penfold. Dr Letheby's evidence was so interesting, and showed the different sweets in one glass tube, yet separated. His physique is large and grand, like his mind.

Now, darling, rest assured through the whole affair I never mention your name or La Sposa's, and if I had been asked to mention a friend I should say Mrs Dix. She is very kind and fond of me, and would have come forward had they wanted her, to help me. No, the rack shouldn't have torn your name from me, and the only reason I said September was, that you might see I had concealed nothing.

My dear boy, do esteem me now. I am sure you must. What trial it was to go through, that inquest! La Madre was angry I ever had the analysis; but you know why I did it – to clear myself in my dear friend's eye. She always says nothing was meant by you. No, darling; you wanted an excuse for my being so slighted. I never think of it; it was all a mistake. I called on La Sposa and told her how I got on. She said my evidence was very nice. She didn't ask me to come; but perhaps she mustn't. Now there is no reason. La Madre says if you were at home, she was sure you would ask me just the same as ever.

Come and see us, darling, you have time now. La Madre and I have been looking forward to your holiday to see you. She wants to know how you get on and like the North. Don't be biased by any relatives; act as your kind heart tells you, and make a poor little thing happy, and fancy a long, long bacio from DOROTHEA. [96]

I haven't taken back your etchings yet, and I'll not call while you are not here, as I have just been and it will be better and right for you to come to us.

Clearly, the object of this letter was to deflect suspicion from herself and towards Mr Maynard. As the chocolates sold by him had been found to be at fault in that instance, thereby proving her

---

[96] It is not known why Christiana chose to call herself Dorothea unless she identified herself with some legendary romantic heroine – perhaps St Dorothea of Caesarea, a 4th Century Virgin Martyr or the 19th Century campaigner, Dorothea Dix, who dedicated her life to social reform for prisoners and the mentally ill. Or Dorothea may have simply been a character in a popular novel or ballad that had some relevance to her emotional situation at the time. The 'Mrs Dix' referred to in the letter does not appear in any of the contemporary press coverage of the case.

innocence regarding the chocolate she had given to his wife, might she and the doctor become friends once more? Not surprisingly, this request was refused and it seems that any connection between Dr Beard and Christiana Edmunds ceased from that time. Christiana's vendetta against Mr Maynard continued, however, whether from sheer spite or in an attempt to further deflect suspicion from herself.

Disturbingly, after the inquest, there were more poisoning episodes. On Thursday, 10th August, 1871, several prominent Brighton residents, Mrs Emily Beard, Mrs Elizabeth Boys, Mr William Curtis, proprietor of the *Brighton Gazette*, Mr George Tatham, a local surgeon and magistrate, and the chemist, Mr Garrett, all received parcels of poisoned cakes, sweetmeats, gingerbread nuts and crystallised fruits; some had been posted locally in Brighton, whilst others were delivered pre-paid by rail from Victoria Station in London. All the recipients became ill after sampling the contents of the parcels; in the case of Emily Beard's box, she and two of her servants sampled the fare and one of them became extremely ill and required medical attention. In this last case, a surgeon, Mr Nathaniel Blaker, was called in and found his patient vomiting and suffering as if from the effects of some irritant poison.

A note in Emily Beard's box said this:

> A few home-made cakes for the children. Those done up are flavoured on purpose for yourself to enjoy. You will guess who this is from. I cannot mystify you, I fear. I hope this will arrive in time for you tonight while the eatables are fresh.

Mrs Boys, the wife of a retired solicitor and magistrate, and a friend and neighbour of the Beards in Grand Parade, received a similar box by rail, direct from Victoria Station; it contained cakes and a note simply signed with the initials 'G.M'.

Christiana Edmunds also received a parcel, a small green box which was handed over to Inspector Gibbs by her mother three days later. When he subsequently called at 16 Gloucester Place during his enquiries he found Christiana lying on a couch, looking pale and ill. She said: 'Here I am again, Mr Gibbs, nearly poisoned.'

She said that someone had sent her the box of fruit on the evening of Thursday, 10th August, bearing a Brighton postmark; but she doubted if it was from anyone she knew as they had spelt her name incorrectly and the address had been given as number 17 instead of 16. The box contained, she said, strawberries, two apricots and a pair of new gloves. She said, 'My mother ate the strawberries. I ate one apricot and that was all right. I bit the other but it was terribly bitter and I spat it out and I have been ill ever since.'

To this she added, 'I hear Mrs Beard has got one. How very strange; I feel certain you will never find it out.'

Dr Beard, having kept quiet as to his suspicions about Christiana, probably for fear of her infatuation for him becoming public knowledge - especially if it was in some small way reciprocated - became increasingly anxious for his wife and other members of his household. He informed the police that he suspected Christiana might have been responsible for the recent spate of attempted poisonings in the town and he handed over the letters she had sent him, presumably to illustrate the deluded state of her mind.

The full extent of Christiana's poisoning spree, however, emerged a week later, when Inspector Gibbs had fully investigated the six boxes of poisoned sweetmeats and had them analysed. He also managed to trace and question several boys who had purchased both strychnine and arsenic on Christiana's behalf from Mr Garrett, the chemist in Queen's Road - and, it was subsequently proved, another chemist, Mr Samuel Bradbury, who had since left the town.

On Saturday, 12th August, Chief Constable George White was acquainted with the witness statements and also with the fact that most of those who had partaken of the contents of the boxes had suffered similar symptoms of poisoning. The following notice was issued locally:

> Brighton residents are hereby informed that some evil-disposed person has lately sent to different families in Brighton parcels of fruit, cakes and sweets, which have been found to contain poison. A notice has been issued by the police that whoever would give such

information to the chief constable as should lead to the apprehension and conviction of the offender will be paid a reward.

All these factors, including the evidence of the handwriting expert, culminated in the arrest of Christiana Edmunds on 17th August, 1871. She was charged with 'attempting to administer poison to Emily Beard, with intent to murder.'

Her case came before the stipendiary Magistrate, Mr Merrifield, at the Police Court, Brighton Town Hall, on Thursday, 24th August, 1871. Mr William Stuckey was enlisted to lead the prosecution, Mr Charles Lamb for the defence, and Mr John Penfold watched the proceedings on behalf of the confectioner, Mr Maynard.

The following report from the *Daily Gazette for Middlesbrough* was one of many in both the local and later the national press that provided copiously detailed accounts of the proceedings; these eventually went through three weekly adjournments and lasted from 24th August to 8th September of that year.

> The case is a most extraordinary one of its kind and has created an immense amount of excitement in Brighton and the neighbourhood.
>
> The prisoner, who is 35 years of age – [she was actually 42 at the time] – rather good-looking and extremely lady-like in her demeanour, resided in Brighton, and was on intimate terms with Mrs Beard, one of the ladies against whose life she is alleged to have plotted.
>
> Some time ago it was discovered that six different families had received boxes of confectionary from an unknown person, but luckily suspicion was aroused and on examination the sweets and cakes turned out to be laced with arsenic and other poisons.
>
> One of the persons favoured with the deadly gifts was Mrs Beard, wife of Dr Beard, at whose house the prisoner had once been in the habit of visiting. She had, however, on more than one occasion presented poisonous chocolate drops to Mrs Beard and the children and, in consequence of the suspicions aroused, Mrs Beard quarrelled with her and declined to receive her as a friend.
>
> Despite this quarrel, the prisoner entered into an extraordinary correspondence with Dr Beard whom she pestered with letters full of terms of endearment, although he repeatedly told her to desist.

The Chief Constable of Brighton offered a reward for the sender of the mysterious presents of confectionary and the result was that on the story of Miss Edmunds's antecedents becoming known, that lady was arrested.

Brought into court shortly before eleven o'clock, Christiana Edmunds was allowed to be seated during the proceedings. It was widely reported that the case had excited a great sensation in Brighton and the courtroom was crowded with 'privileged persons anxious to hear the inquiry' and the street in front of the Town Hall was crowded with eager spectators.

The *London Daily News,* of 23rd August, 1871, said that Miss Edmunds,

> ...sat in a corner of the ordinary prisoner's dock, being attired in a black silk dress, black lace shawl and black bonnet with a veil. Her demeanour throughout was quiet and self-possessed; but she occasionally glanced around the court with evident interest in the scene.

Reporting on a later court appearance, *The Times* of 1st September noted that:

> ...She is a self-possessed woman, fair, and well-dressed. She sat in a corner of the prisoner's dock, and not infrequently smiled as the descriptions were given of the pains to trace the hand administering the poisons.

On Tuesday 16th January, 1872, the *London Daily News* issued a far from flattering description of Christiana in the dock of the Old Bailey:

> There is considerable character in the upper features, in spite of the plainness; the quick flash of the large dark eyes, once noted, suffices to block out the first conception of common-place. But the character of the face lies in the lower features. The profile is irregular, but not unpleasing; the upper lip is long and convex; mouth slightly projecting; chin straight, long, and cruel; the lower jaw heavy, massive and animal in its development. The lips are loose – almost pendulous – the lower one being fullest and projecting, and the mouth is exceptionally large. From the configuration of the lips the

mouth might be thought weak, but a glance at the chin removes any such impression.

A lengthy and detailed report in the *Brighton Daily News* for Tuesday 22nd August informed its readers that:

> ...the police have already found two of the boys who were employed to obtain considerable quantities of poison from the chemist, Mr Garrett, on the faith of forged orders. Their evidence on Thursday next will, doubtless, be looked forward to with much interest but until then it would manifestly be unfair to say any more on the subject.
>
> It has been stated that the present accused is the person who volunteered to come forward at the inquest in June on the body of a little boy, named Barker, who died from eating poisoned chocolate creams said to have been purchased at Mr Maynard's, in West Street, and whose death, under these singular circumstances, created a considerable sensation at the time.
>
> This, however, is not quite correct, as Miss Edmunds did not volunteer to come forward but the police authorities, having heard that she had had an analysis made, cited her to appear, as she said in her letter to Dr Beard.
>
> As her connection with the affair promises to be of considerable importance, our contemporary prints a summary of the proceedings [at the inquest] on that occasion in order that its readers may be enabled to understand the bearings and importance of facts which have been or may be elicited at the present inquiry and without which it would be impossible for them to do.
>
> Dr Letheby then gave evidence to the effect that he had examined the stomach of the deceased and that he found quite enough strychnine therein to account for death. He also stated that three out of four packets of sweets sent to him were free from poison but the fourth contained strychnine. Miss Christiana Edmunds, of 16 Gloucester Place, (the present accused) then said that in September last she had bought some chocolate creams at Mr Maynard's establishment.
>
> On that occasion she ate two of them and about an hour afterwards, was seized with violent internal pains and a burning in the throat which lasted twenty minutes. On the same day she took back the remainder of the chocolate creams to Mr Maynard and told him what

had occurred. He assured her that she was mistaken in supposing that it was the chocolate creams which had affected her. Some more were bought and tasted but they seemed all right. Mrs Maynard also tasted one of those which the witness originally bought and found that there was nothing the matter with it.

In the course of his evidence Mr Maynard stated that Miss Edmunds's complaint was the first of that character that he had received and that his youngest boy was in the habit of continually eating these very chocolate creams without any ill effects. As it could not be proved that any of these creams were bought at Mr Maynard's shop the evidence was irrelevant for the purposes of the inquiry and that part of the case was dropped as related by Miss Edmunds in her letter to Dr Beard.

The following account of the Magistrates' hearing is from the *Nottingham Guardian,* dated Friday 1st September, 1871:

Chief Constable White said he would concentrate on ONE of six cases of attempted poison [that of Emily Beard]. Six parcels had been sent to females living in Brighton, some by post, and some by railway train.

Emily Beard, the wife of Dr Beard, residing at 64 Grande Parade, Brighton, produced a box, about a foot long, wrapped in brown paper which was sent to her and delivered at her house on Thursday evening last [10th August]. It contained cakes, preserved fruit, and ginger-bread nuts, also a piece of note paper on which was written:

"A few home-made cakes for the children; those done up are flavoured on purpose for yourself to enjoy. You will guess who this is from. I can't mystify you, I fear. I hope this will arrive in time for you tonight while the eatables are fresh."

This note was wrapped round a small plum cake about the size of a tea cup. Mrs Beard cut the cake open about noon on Saturday and she observed inside something looking like unbaked flour. She cut that piece out and after making some observation to her servant regarding it she told her to take it away.

Two of her servants, Margaret Knight and Emily Agate, who partook of the cake, were subsequently unwell. She (Mrs Beard) and others in the house partook of some of the contents of the box, but felt no ill effects from it.

She had been acquainted with the prisoner between five and seven years. She had been a patient of Dr Beard's and was at one time on terms of great intimacy with the family but this intimacy ceased about a year ago in consequence of a circumstance that took place in Mrs Beard's drawing room. Upon that occasion Miss Edmunds took some chocolate from her pocket and said she had brought them for the children. The children had then gone to bed but Miss Edmunds put one of the chocolates in Mrs Beard's mouth which she instantly spat out in consequence of its peculiar metallic flavour. It produced a great deal of saliva in the mouth during the night and also an attack of diarrhoea. Mrs Beard mentioned this circumstance to her husband a few days afterwards.

The evidence of Dr Charles Beard was eagerly awaited as rumours about Christiana Edmunds's inappropriate infatuation with the doctor must have been rife in the town. The court was shown a letter he had received in July and he admitted he had received many letters from Miss Edmunds. She had written to him from the middle of 1869 to 1870 and there had been a few letters since. He last met the prisoner three weeks ago when, to the best of his belief, he said to her; "This correspondence must cease. It is not good for either of us."

When he told her that he had mentioned the whole circumstance to his wife, Christiana had exclaimed: "Surely you have not shown my letters to her!"

When he said that he had - in fact he had shown her every letter since the 3rd October the previous year - Christiana Edmunds said she would stop the correspondence if he wished it. He told the court how he had gone round to Miss Edmunds's house and mentioned to her and her mother the illness of his wife and two servants after eating the chocolate given to them by Christiana. As he could not prove anything, he said, he had alluded to the matter in a rather light-hearted way and he did not actually accuse her of trying to poison his wife. Instead, he mentioned the fact that it was now possible, with the use of a spectroscope, to discover the smallest amount of poison in animal tissues.

Christiana had denied making any attempt to poison the doctor's wife and reminded him that she, too, had been ill after eating chocolate bought from Mr Maynard's shop. She went on to say that she wished to remain friends with the doctor and his family and when the doctor declined she asked to know why.

Questioned further, Dr Beard admitted that Miss Edmunds was very indignant and she and her mother called upon him the following morning to reprimand him. Practically, he could prove nothing and the ladies made it quite clear that, unless he retracted his suggestion, they would consider taking legal against him. He told the court that he had not written any letters to Christiana Edmunds or destroyed any of her letters during the last four months. He had received about twenty letters since 20th October, 1870 and would produce them if required.

Mr Isaac Garrett was called next and testified that he was the owner of a chemist's shop at 10 Queen's Road. Although he had known the prisoner as a customer for about four years, he did not actually know her name until March that year. He gave the following testimony:

> She was only an occasional customer until the beginning of this year when she became a more frequent customer. She came to my shop on the 26th of March last when she purchased several toilet articles. She used to have a great deal of quinine and iron mixture and used to talk of going back by the train as she lived in the country. The accused usually came into the shop about nine or ten in the morning.
>
> On the 28th March she requested me to supply her with a small quantity of strychnine to destroy the cats that infested her garden and said her husband and herself were anxious to get rid of them. I declined to supply her. She assured me that no harm should possibly happen, as there were no children, and it would pass into her own and her husband's hands.
>
> I then told her that I should require a witness known to both of us. She then said the only person she was well-acquainted with in the neighbourhood was Mrs Stone, as she was in the habit of dealing with her. She then went and fetched Mrs Stone and when she returned the prisoner told me to fill up the certificate in the register for *Mrs Wood, Hillside, Kingstone*. I did so and Mrs Stone signed it as the witness.

The prisoner also signed it *'Mrs Wood'*. Ten grains of strychnine is the amount I supplied.[97]

He then told the court that between 28th March and 15th April Christiana Edmunds visited his shop several times and that until he heard that the prisoner was in custody he believed her to be a married lady called Mrs Wood. She always kept herself closely veiled when she came to his shop, saying that she suffered from neuralgia, for which complaint she was prescribed quinine and iron.

The court heard that, on the 15th of April, Miss Edmunds had gone back to Mr Garrett's chemist shop to buy more strychnine as the other 10 grains he'd sold her hadn't worked on the cats and they were, she said, 'as numerous as ever'. Once again she reassured him that there was no danger as only her and her husband would handle the poison; she went again to fetch Mrs Stone to vouch for her. He sold her another 10 grains of strychnine - here the Court was shown the Poison Register - both sales were registered on different dates and signed in the name of 'Mrs Wood'.

On 11th May, Christiana went again to the shop and told him she and her husband were moving to Devon and needed to kill an old and diseased dog as they didn't like to leave it behind. He supplied the strychnine but this time he didn't request Mrs Stone's signature as witness.

Mr Garrett went on to tell the court that subsequently, on 8th June, 1871, a boy brought a note in a sealed envelope; it read:

> Messrs. Glaisyer and Kemp will be much obliged if Mr Garrett could supply them with a little strychnia. They are in immediate want of half an ounce, or, if not able, a smaller quantity will do. Will Mr Garrett send it in a bottle and seal it up? The bearer can be safely trusted with it. Glaisyer and Kemp, 11 and 12, North-street.

Garrett did not send the poison but wrote a note to Glaisyer and

---

[97] In an attempt to reduce the number of accidental deaths from readily available poisons for domestic use – arsenic and lead were also ingredients in many products such as flypapers, green dye, paint, face washes, etc. The Pharmacy Act of 1868 required chemists to keep a register of sales, including the purchaser's name and address, the substance sold, the date of the purchase and a signature of a witness.

Kemp, saying that he could not supply the strychnia without an order and not a quarter of an ounce as he only had a drachm in stock. He gave the note to the boy who came back within the hour with 2s.6d for the poison and a sealed note which read:

> Messrs. Glaisyer and Kemp will be satisfied with a drachm of strychnia till their own arrives and thank Mr Garrett for supplying them. Their signature always being sufficient before in their business transactions. Should Mr Garrett feel the least hesitation in supplying them they must apply elsewhere.
>
> Glaisyer and Kemp, 11 and 12, North-street.

Mr Garrett then supplied a drachm of strychnia in a bottle, sealed it, labelled it '*Poison*', put his own name and address on it and gave it to the boy. He enclosed 1s.3d change.

On another occasion, a boy called Adam May brought the following note:

> Sir, - I shall be much obliged if you would allow me the loan of the book wherein you register the poisonous drugs you sell. It is merely in furtherance to an inquiry I am making as to the sale of certain poisons and bears no reference to anything you have sold or any irregularity in selling but only to aid me in my investigation. You will tie up your book and send it at once by the bearer; it shall be returned as you may need it.-
>
> Yours truly,
D. Black, Borough Coroner.

Mr Garrett testified that he'd wrapped the Poison Register in a piece of paper and sent it by the boy. That was shortly before 19th of July. The book was brought back by the same boy within an hour and in the same wrapping paper. Garrett thought the book was intact at first but later discovered that some pages were missing. The leaves which had been torn out of the book related to transactions between 28th July, 1870 and the end of July, 1871.

An eleven year old boy, William Booth, was called next and told the court that he had met the lady in the dock in the street on 19th July in North Road. She had asked him to take a letter to Mr Garrett and to say that it came from Messrs Glaisyer and Kemp, the chemists in North Street. There was a shilling inside the envelope and the note read as follows:

> Messrs Glaisyer and Kemp will be much obliged if Mr Garrett could supply them with two ounces of arsenic or three ounces if he can. So please send back directly. Their signatures will be sufficient.

Recalled to the witness box, Mr Garrett said that he had refused to supply the arsenic and sent a note to Glaisyer and Kemp, returning the shilling. When he didn't receive a reply to his note he became suspicious and went to see the two chemists at their pharmacy the same day. They both denied sending any notes or letters requesting poisons at which Mr Garrett, now deeply concerned, went to the police to make a voluntary statement.

Mr Garrett went on to identify a small box and an accompanying envelope which he had received on 10th or 11th of August. He said that the box contained two peaches and enclosed in a piece of paper, half a sovereign. On a slip of paper were the words:

> The last of my debt and the first of my fruit from my garden.

He had given the box to Inspector Gibbs during his preliminary investigations but had kept the half sovereign.

Inspector Gibbs was then sworn and told the court that shortly after the inquest on Sidney Barker, as part of his investigations, he had written to Miss Edmunds about her reported illness, hoping to receive a reply which would enable him to compare her handwriting with the letters sent to Dr Beard, Mr Garrett, Albert Barker and the recipients of the mystery boxes. She sent this reply the same day:

> Miss Edmunds begs to inform Mr Gibbs that she bought the last lot of chocolate creams at Mr Maynard's on the 16th of March, and had them analysed the same day at Mr Schweitzer's.

Having consulted a handwriting expert - who would later be called upon to give evidence - Inspector Gibbs, Chief Constable White and Inspector Terry went to Christiana Edmunds's home at 16 Gloucester Place on the afternoon of Thursday, 17th August. Miss Edmunds was in a back room, looking unwell. When Inspector Gibbs produced a warrant for her arrest and charged her with attempting to poison the doctor's wife, Emily Beard, she protested, saying;

> Me poison Mrs Beard! Who can say so? I have been nearly poisoned myself.

Further witnesses were called during the protracted Magistrates' Court hearings and much of the evidence was repeated in part, and in full, but the following summary of further evidence given during the proceedings may suffice:

One of the first witnesses to be called was Dr Beard's cook, Emily Agate. She said that she remembered Margaret Knight, the housemaid, bringing a cake down to the kitchen on Saturday 12th August. She ate a small piece of the cake and about an hour later she felt giddy and sick and very hot in the throat but she was not actually sick. She was also attacked with diarrhoea about two and a half hours later.

When eleven year old, Adam May, had been required to give evidence he was so small he had to stand on a chair to be seen in the witness box. Though unable to positively identify the lady in the dock - she had probably been heavily veiled when she met the boy in the street - he told the court that he 'saw a lady in King's Street about 5 or 6 weeks ago. She said she wanted me to go up to Mr Garrett's on the Queen's Road to get a book; she gave me a note'.

After the boy had asked his mother for permission to run the errand, the lady walked some of the way with him and told him to meet her with the book in Duke's Street. The chemist, Mr Garrett, read the note and gave him the Poison Register. The boy went down to Duke's Street as instructed and saw the lady walking up and down near the Post Office. He gave her the book and she gave him four and a half pence for his trouble.

Also called as a witness was Harriet Elizabeth Cole, wife of Samuel Cole, a greengrocer, living at 32 Church Street. She said she knew the boy, Adam May, and the prisoner. She testified that as she stood in the doorway of her shop that day she saw them talking together in the street and she watched them walk up Church Street and turn left into Queen's Road, where Mr Garrett had his chemist shop.

On one occasion Christiana Edmunds came into the shop and bought a few articles but after she had gone Mrs Cole noticed that she'd left a bag of chocolate creams. They were in a paper bag with Mr Maynard's name on it. The bag contained small and large chocolates and three lemon bulls' eyes. She had eaten two of the bulls' eyes and her daughter sampled one of the chocolate creams but spat it out because it tasted bitter. She had then wrapped the sweets up again and the next day she gave them to a boy called Henry Walker. Mrs Cole went on to say that some time in March the prisoner had again purchased a few articles in her shop and she had found a bag of chocolate creams on the counter after she had left. Once again, they were in a bag with Mr Maynard's name printed on it and her daughter and another young woman ate some of these without any ill effect. She was then asked to recall the inquest on Sidney Barker.

> 'I attended the inquest on the body of the little boy Barker,' she informed the court. 'I saw the prisoner there and I asked her if she had dropped some chocolate creams when she came to my shop. She said, "No".'

The ten year old lad, Henry Walker, told the court that he had taken the bag of sweets that Mrs Cole had given him home to his mother, Caroline Walker. She was the next witness to testify, stating that she had eaten a piece of chocolate cream and within ten minutes had become very ill. She described 'a strange sensation' in her head, loss of use of her limbs and great prostration. She had given the remainder of the chocolate cream to the police who sent it to Dr Letheby for analysis.

The court heard that Mr William Curtis, publisher of the *Brighton Gazette*, had also received a small box on Thursday 10th August which contained crystallised fruit. Five or six persons ate the fruit and, in consequence, some became very ill, his son included. To help with their enquiries he handed the box over to the police for analysis.

A dressmaker, Mrs Caroline Stone, described how Christiana Edmunds, wearing a lace veil, had come into her shop and bought a Shetland veil – popular with ladies who suffered from neuralgia to protect them from the cold air. She had then asked Mrs Stone if she would accompany her to Mr Garrett's shop and sign the Poison Register as she wanted some poison to stuff birds, saying that she and her husband were naturalists. When Mrs Stone had asked her name she was told it was Mrs Wood, of Kingston. Christiana Edmunds had returned to the shop on 15th April to buy another veil and, once again, asked her to sign the book at Mr Garrett's shop.

In order to provide evidence that it was Christiana Edmunds who had sent the six parcels of poisoned sweetmeats to residents of Brighton on 10th August, a young housemaid, Adelaide Ann Friend, was called. She told the court she worked for a Mrs Bearling, in Margate, who let rooms. She testified that Christiana Edmunds had arrived at the house in the evening of Tuesday, 8th August, and rented a room for two nights at half a crown a night. She had with her a black leather bag and a square parcel, done up in brown paper and string. The maid then admitted that she had opened it and seen two peaches inside. Miss Edmunds had left early on the Thursday morning saying she was going to catch the eight o'clock train to London. She'd left a piece of cake behind and, when asked what became of it, the maid said she had eaten it - a remark that caused some laughter in court.

Further evidence was given by the maid, Charlotte Elizabeth Petitt, who worked at the home of Christiana Edmunds and her mother at 16 Gloucester Place. She remembered Miss Edmunds leaving the house early on the 8th of August, saying she was going to Margate to visit her sister's grave and she had returned about half past six on the Thursday evening. Before she went out the next day she gave the maid some powders in packets - they were partly undone and the labels had been torn off. The maid was told to 'take them away'.

She had kept one of the packets thinking it contained powdered myrrh but later gave it to Inspector Gibbs. She had thrown the rest away. She told the court that the household had never been troubled with stray cats and had never heard Miss Edmunds make any complaint about cats.

The court then learned that on 27th May, the much-loved dog belonging to Miss Taylor, another lodger at 16 Gloucester Place, had died suddenly and in great agony. Shortly before it collapsed, the maid had seen Miss Edmunds playing with it. Minutes later she had seen it twisting about on the landing as though it was suffocating or choking. The dog was taken away to a taxidermist, Mr Swaysland, to be stuffed.

The evidence against Christiana Edmunds was mounting and the *Leeds Times*, on Saturday 26th August, 1871, announced that:

> The case has been further remanded to give time for analysis of certain articles. The police have discovered an important clue. The symptoms experienced by Mrs Beard's servants were those of arsenical poisoning rather than of strychnine, with which latter poison the accused was alleged to have dealt. Some person is now shown to have procured 3oz of arsenic about that time by a forged order from a chemist named Bradbury, who has since left the town. A reward has been offered for the discovery of the boy who took the order to Bradbury.

However, on Saturday 2nd September, 1871, the *Bristol Mercury* had this to say:

> Mr Stuckey [prosecution] said that he now he proposed *three* charges against Christiana Edmunds – namely, for attempting to administer poison to Mrs Beard, with intent to murder: in the second place with attempting to poison Mrs Boys and Mr Garrett: and thirdly, with being the cause of divers other persons taking poison by which they had sustained bodily harm. These charges would be substantiated by evidence.

Mr Lamb, solicitor for the defence, immediately rose to object, demanding that the prosecution stick to the first charge only but after a 'warm discussion' the presiding Magistrate, Mr Merrifield, ruled that any evidence bearing directly or indirectly on the acts of Christiana Edmunds was admissible.

Henry Swaysland, described as a 'bird-fancier and stuffer',

confirmed that he had fetched the body of a dog from the Edmunds's home at 16 Gloucester Place on 28th or 29th of May and handed it over to a taxidermist called Mr Robert Brazenor who used arsenic as a preservative.

When questioned on the condition of the dead dog, Mr Brazenor, who described himself as 'a bird, reptile and fish stuffer' working from 39 Lewes Road, Brighton, said that when he opened the body he found that the dog had been poisoned, but not with prussic acid. He testified that,

> The muscles were limp and the backbone was curved inwards. I never had a case like it before. I have been at the business for thirty years and never saw such a case before. There was also an objectionable smell from the throat.

Frederick George Netherclift, of 18 Golden Square, London, was also called to give evidence. He described himself as an expert in handwriting for thirty years and had often given evidence in courts of law in disputes over the authenticity of wills.

Mr Stuckey asked him to look at the sample letter which Christiana had written to Dr Beard and compare that handwriting with the note with the words 'specially flavoured for Mrs Beard herself' in the box sent to Mrs Beard. The witness testified that, in his opinion, the writing in the sweet parcels, the letters to Mr Garrett, the signature 'Mrs Wood' in the Sale of Poison Register and the letter to the chemist, Mr Bradbury, requesting arsenic, were all written by the same hand – that of Christiana Edmunds.

The surgeon, Dr Nathaniel Payne Blaker, was also called and said that he had handed the vomit of the Beard family's servant, Margaret Knight, to Inspector Gibbs. When recalled, Inspector Gibbs confirmed he had received two sealed jars of vomit from Dr Blaker which he numbered 2 and 3 and some cake and preserved fruit from Mrs Beard on the 13th which he labelled no 1, and a handkerchief which he marked 4, and gave them all to Professor Rodgers for analysis.

When the Court reassembled on Thursday 30th August, Professor Rodgers,[98] of Sussex Street, Warwick Square, London, was called to give evidence and confirmed that he had received the items listed from Inspector Gibbs. His evidence gave a clear indication that the arsenic had been added to the cakes and fruits after baking and was therefore intentional as opposed to being a fairly common case of accidental poisoning of the ingredients:

> I have carefully analysed all these articles and the contents of the jars and have particularly tested them. Jar no 2 contained arsenic in most decided quantities. Jar no 3 contained arsenic but in less quantities. The handkerchief yielded traces of arsenic. There was no other poison but arsenic in these 3 articles. One of the cakes had on it a large and a most dangerous quantity of arsenic. It was sprinkled over the cake. A second cake had a little less arsenic. There were traces of arsenic on the other 2 cakes. I examined the four preserved fruits. They all had arsenic on them and one was literally stuffed with it. This was enough to destroy the life of anyone. I have analysed the two peaches sent to Mr Garrett and found them covered with strychnine which was enough to cause death.

Mr Glaisyer, of Glaisyer and Kemp, the Brighton chemists, and Mr David Black, the Coroner for Borough of Brighton, both denied that letters given to the chemist, Mr Garrett, requesting poison and authorising the sending of the Poison Register, were in their handwriting.

Another witness was Emma Helsey, a parlour maid to Mrs Boys, of 59 Grand Parade. She recalled a parcel arriving by the 'railway van' on 10th August about half past six. It was a pre-paid square parcel wrapped in brown paper and addressed to Mrs Boys. Mrs Boys came back from a trip to Tunbridge Wells about nine thirty that evening.

The next day she saw the nurse taking some cakes from a parcel and putting them in a dish. There were two ginger breads, two cheese cakes, two macaroons, two plum cakes and two tartlets done up separately for Mrs Boys. A piece of paper was wrapped around them with Mrs Boys's name written on it. The nurse broke one of

---

98 Julian Edward Disbrowe Rodgers, Professor of Toxicology at the London Hospital.

the tartlets in half. She ate part of it and the maid ate the other part. After about ten minutes the witness and the nurse felt very sick with a burning sensation in the throat and they were both ill for about a week.

Called to the witness box, Mrs Elizabeth Boys confirmed that she received the parcel on 10th August:

> There was a piece of paper around the cakes and written on it were the words: 'I send you some cakes for your two little girls. Those directed to yourself are my first efforts. I hope to see you soon. Your old friend, G.M.' I put the box in the garden room for that night. The next morning I sent it downstairs. The youngest of my children was very sick the day after the parcel arrived. In consequence of this and the servant being also ill, I told the cook to destroy the cakes, except one of the two tartlets and said I would ascertain if there was poison in it or not. On the afternoon of the same day I took part of the tartlet to Mr Glaisyer and other portion I gave to Mr Blaker. I ate no portion of the cake myself.

Although she was an intimate friend of Mrs Beard and often visited the doctor's house with her children, she did not know Christiana Edmunds.

Amelia Mills (sometimes called Annie Elizabeth Mills), Mrs Boys's nurse domestic, agreed with the testimony of the last two witnesses but added that:

> ...both Mrs Boys's children tasted one of the currant cakes, but the younger one ate a great deal more than the elder and became very sick. In about five minutes afterwards the eldest child ate a piece of the tartlets but was not ill until after dinner when she became very pale.

Matilda Hope, the cook in Mrs Boys's household, said that her mistress told her to destroy the cakes on 11th August. She put some water over them and threw them into the dust-hole. In the evening she was told to search for the cakes she had thrown away. She found part of one and gave it to Mr Nathaniel Blaker, the surgeon.

Mr Blaker testified that Mrs Boys had sent for him about eleven o'clock on the night of Friday, 11th August. He found the nurse 'constantly vomiting with violent pains in her stomach and otherwise very ill. She complained of a burning in her throat.'

He tended her for more than a week and from her symptoms he believed she was suffering from an irritant poison – arsenic.

Mrs Boys gave him a piece of cake wrapped in paper which he took with him to the hospital for a Mr Smith to analyse, after which it was sent to Inspector Gibbs.

Walter Henry Smith, a dispenser at Sussex County Hospital, testified that he had received the package of cake from Mr Blaker on 12th August. He had tested it for arsenic and in about half an ounce of cake he found 7 and half to 8 grains of sulphide of arsenic.

At this juncture the Court was adjourned until Thursday, 7th September.

The subsequent proceedings were reported in the *London Standard* and many other newspapers:

THE WHOLESALE POISONING AT BRIGHTON

Christiana Edmunds, who was committed for trial on Thursday [7th September] upon the charge of attempted poisoning, was again brought up yesterday [Friday 8th September] at the Brighton Town-hall for further examination upon the charge of having murdered a little boy named Sidney Albert Barker who died shortly after having eaten chocolate creams, purchased in June last at Mr Maynard's shop. The court and its approaches were again thronged during the day.

Mr Merrifield, deputy stipendiary, presided with a full bench of magistrates. Mr Stuckey, the public prosecutor of the borough, conducted the case for the prosecution. Mr Lamb, solicitor, appeared for the prisoner. Mr Penfold watched the case for Mr Maynard, the confectioner, Mr Gell, as representative of a lad named Barker and Chief Inspector White, chief officer, watched the case on behalf of the police.

Mr Samuel William Bradbury, a chemist who no longer lived in Brighton, testified that in July he had a shop in North Road, Brighton and, about 21st July, he received a letter which was in an envelope and brought to the shop by a boy. He opened the note which purported to be from the chemists, Glaisyer and Kemp, asking him to supply three ounces of common white arsenic; this he did, handing over the arsenic in three separate wrappers.

Mr Stuckey then addressed the court for the prosecution:

> About 2 months ago an inquest was held on the body of Sidney Albert Barker who had died suddenly. A post-mortem examination was made by Dr Letheby and it was established that he died of strychnine. At the inquest Christiana Edmunds was examined, as a voluntary witness, and she herself had fallen ill. She said that she felt ill after eating chocolate creams and had sent samples to a Brighton chemist for analysis which were then sent on to Dr Letheby.'

He also said that 'it was known that Christiana Edmunds had developed a passion for Dr Beard and that she might well wish to get rid of her' [the doctor's wife, Emily].

When asked by the solicitor, Mr Lamb, for evidence of this, Mr Stuckey replied that he was merely suggesting a motive for the poisonings. She had sent boys to Mr Maynard's shop to buy chocolate creams and then, after receiving them, told them to return them and get them changed from three penny ones to four penny ones.

Mr Maynard, suspecting nothing, had put the chocolates back on sale to the general public. Mr Stuckey suggested that Miss Edmunds had poisoned these chocolates and the boy Barker had eaten one that had a large amount of poison inside.

He then reminded the court that since the inquest on his son, Mr Barker had received three letters from different parts of Brighton - one on 27th June, another on the 28th June and another on 1st of July. These letters were proved to be in Christiana Edmunds's handwriting by Mr Netherclift, and they were read out loud to a hushed courtroom:

> Sussex-square, June 27th, 1871
>
> Sir – Having seen the result of the investigation of the inquest of Thursday last, I feel great surprise to find that no blame is attached to any one. I have felt great interest in the case and fully sympathise in your sad loss. Great dissatisfaction is felt at the result by most of the inhabitants and we all feel it rests with yourself now to take proceedings against Mr. Maynard. As a parent myself I could not let

the matter rest satisfied, nor would one in a hundred.

I trust you will come forward for your own sake and the public good. You shall have all the assistance possible. I'm sure the young lady will come forward as I know from good authority she was dissatisfied with Mr. Maynard's conduct: of course supposed he would have taken the step she did and have them analysed.

I can only say that Mr. Maynard, after being duly warned that his chocolates were injurious and had made three persons ill, ought to have them analysed or destroyed them. The public mind is not satisfied and feels great blame is attached to him for selling to your family chocolates from the same stock he had been warned against.

He spoke of investigating and what was his investigating – merely looking over and tasting a few chocolates with his shop-women and the young lady was not satisfied with that even and as to writing to his French agent, it appears he never did. I hope no monetary considerations will prevent you taking proceedings. The Brighton inhabitants are all up in arms at the laxity of proceedings and the want of justice and will assist you in every way: and with the facts tried before unbiased and unprejudiced men, I think Mr. Maynard will not escape scot free.

My feeling of disgust is felt by most of the influential and respectable inhabitants of this town – I am, sir, 'AN OLD INHABITANT AND A SEEKER OF JUSTICE.

PS. The town cannot take up the case again: it rests with you and you shall receive all the aid we can offer. The papers are taking this up, both Brighton and London. See the *London Observer*. [99]

The second letter to Mr Barker read as follows:

Vernon Terrace, June 28th, 1871

...all that can be done now is for you to make further investigations and it certainly seems a duty to yourself and the public, who will, I am assured, never let the matter rest.

Why is Mr Maynard being screened and the whole affair glossed over? He was warned of his sweets and yet he deliberately sells some of the very same to your family and you are to lose your child

---

99 *The Times*, 17th January, 1872

through his great negligence. Why didn't he investigate and destroy his sweets at once?

Are people's complaints to be disregarded? ....I say he took no means to ascertain what was wrong and is certainly answerable for selling those sweets after being warned.

Our lawyer (excuse me for saying it) did very little in your behalf. He never taxed Mr Maynard with not taking steps to know what the sweets really contained and for daring to sell them without a proper investigation – never even writing to inquire of the French agent he had them from. Of course you cannot rest supine. No one could sustain the loss you have done and rest satisfied.

There is a report current that you are going to take proceedings against Maynard. We all hope so here. If you do not someone will take the matter up and you may feel certain when the case is tried before able and intelligent men you may get redress for the wrongs you have received. In our local paper of yesterday there is a paragraph saying, 'what a strange verdict' and you cannot, of course, rest satisfied with it. Such a deadly poison as strychnine ought hardly to be in existence. I believe other evidence might be brought forward having heard of several who have been made ill by Maynard's sweets. I have no doubt that you will take further steps. No parent could let the loss of his child be passed over in this cursory way.

The Brighton police earnestly hope you will do something; for who knows where this might end? More of these sweets may be sold by the maker and other lives lost. The greatest sympathy is felt for yourself and your family and in saying what I have I have only expressed the feelings of most of the Brighton inhabitants.

I remain, sir, yours truly, "C.G.B" [100]

Mr Charles David Miller, of 151 King Street, Hammersmith, who worked in his father's coach building firm, said this:

...I was at Brighton with Mr and Mrs Barker and the little boy on the 12th of June. I remember buying the chocolate creams at Mr Maynard's in West-street, on the morning of that day. I bought 1 shilling's worth. I suppose there would be about 3oz. I asked for the best. I gave some of them to the boy when I returned from the shop

100 *The Times*, 17th January, 1872

in the morning. I bought them some time before eight o'clock and it was eight o'clock when I gave him them.

In the afternoon about four o'clock I gave him some more – one cream. He ate it. About 10 minutes afterwards, as he was going downstairs, he commenced crying. I had asked him before if he liked the creams and he said he didn't.

When he began to cry my sister took him up in her arms and asked him what was the matter. He did not reply but became worse – his limbs getting quite stiff. He died in about twenty minutes after he had eaten the chocolate creams. I believe that he was in good health previously.

I ate some of the creams in the morning when I first gave some to him. I was taken ill in about 10 minutes after. First, I felt a coppery taste in my throat and afterwards my eyes became dim. My legs became rigid and on attempting to leave my chair I fell back. This happened twice. I felt as if all my bones were in one - as if they had no joints. I had several attacks during the day. They were something in the nature of spasmodic attacks. I attempted to eat my dinner but could not.

A medical man was called in to see me. I recollect my brother giving me some creams the same evening. I gave them to Inspector Gibbs.'

His brother, Mr Ernest Miller, testified as follows:

I was in Brighton with Mr and Mrs Barker and their little boy on the 12th of June last. I saw my brother give the boy a chocolate cream about four o'clock on the afternoon of that day. The boy became ill shortly after and a doctor was called in. I was in the house when the boy died which was about half an hour after he had eaten the creams. I tasted the creams but spat them out as I didn't like them. They had a coppery taste. The rest of the creams were thrown away. I bought some other chocolate creams at Mr Maynard's that same evening and they were given to Inspector Gibbs.'

Inspector Gibbs confirmed that he had received the chocolates and delivered them to Dr Letheby's house on the 16th June.

There were numerous newspaper accounts of the evidence given by the staff of Mr Maynard's sweetshop who served the boys with chocolates for Christiana Edmunds, transactions that resulted in the poisoned chocolates being returned to the shop and subsequently resold. The recall of events was not always unanimous and details sometimes differed. However, the following account will suffice to set the scene. George Brooks, a little boy, about ten years of age, testified that a lady - he hadn't really seen her face properly as she had her head down – had asked him to go to Mr Maynard's shop and get an ounce of chocolate creams. She gave him sixpence and he paid 3d or 4d for them. He gave the creams and the change to the lady who was waiting for him at the top of Cranbourne Street. She gave him a penny for his trouble.

Twenty-four year old, Kate Page, who worked for Mr Maynard in his confectionary shop in West Street, said she remembered George Brooks and another boy buying chocolate creams early in May that year. She told the court she had asked another assistant, Charles Schooley, to keep an eye on the boys when they came in to buy chocolate creams. One morning one of the boys came back to change the chocolates saying he wanted two ounces of small three penny creams instead of an ounce of large four penny ones. Two or three of the chocolate creams sent back to be changed were broken. She put them into the broken chocolate drawer and put the rest in the display case. The cases were filled up every morning and therefore some of them might remain there for three weeks or a month.

Charles Schooley remembered that, at the end of May, a boy bought some chocolate creams and afterwards came back and changed them. He had seen the boy give the second lot of creams to Christiana Edmunds.

John Henry Parker, who also worked for Mr Maynard, said he saw George Brooks and another boy come into the shop and buy some chocolate creams. He followed the boys as far as Cranbourne Street where he saw George Brooks give the chocolate creams to a lady. He identified the prisoner, Christiana Edmunds, as that lady.

Miss Anne Meadows, now living in Lincolnshire, said she remembered Adam May coming into the shop to buy chocolate creams about the beginning of June and buying sixpenny worth of the best French chocolate creams. He took them away and returned shortly afterwards when he changed them for a sixpenny box of

Cadbury's creams. The returned creams were put back in the case. (It was made of glass and each compartment held about half a pound of creams.) That case was not filled up on Monday 12th June. On the morning of that day she supplied Mr Charles Miller (Sidney Barker's uncle) with chocolate creams which she took from the glass case in which she had previously put the returned creams from Adam May. Mr Miller bought the same kind of creams as Adam May had brought back. She did not remember seeing Christiana Edmunds in the shop at any time.

William Henry Halliwell, a boy of thirteen, living with his parents at their stationer's shop in North Road, said he knew Miss Edmunds as a customer at his father's shop. On one occasion in March, she left a bag of chocolate creams in the shop. She came to the shop again about three or four days later but denied leaving the chocolates. When she returned to the shop a day or two after that she asked him if he'd found the owner of the sweets. When he said he had not she advised him to eat them as she didn't think anyone would now come to claim them. He did eat one or two and soon after was ill for several days. He went on to say that Miss Edmunds continued to call at the shop and again left a bag of chocolate creams. These were the same as the others but crushed and he put them aside until she called again the next day. His mother had asked Miss Edmunds if she had left a bag of chocolates in the shop but she had denied it. The chocolates were put aside and later thrown in the fire.

At this point Mr Lamb, for the defence, objected to a copy of the *Illustrated Police News* being in court and the Magistrate, Mr Merrifield, ordered it to be removed.

After some repeated evidence from the confectioner, Mr Maynard, Mr George Robert Ware, a chocolate manufacturer, testified that he had supplied Mr Maynard with chocolates for many years and had never had any complaints. He conceded that a person could insert poison into the chocolate creams quite easily using a pin and then smoothing over the hole with a finger.

Next to be called was Dr Beard whose previous deposition was read to the court and signed. He conceded that he had received a number of letters from Miss Edmunds, twenty of which he had destroyed. At the beginning of the year he was away from Brighton (as the 1871 Census confirms), but it was only after she had, in his view, attempted to poison his wife with the chocolate cream, that he mentioned the many letters he had received.

When asked, he said he had never answered any of her letters – adding that when he saw her at his house he 'declined to allow the intimacy - or friendship rather - to exist between us'.

Mr Lamb interjected: 'You had better not alter the word but say "intimacy"'. To this, Dr Beard replied: 'Well, whichever you wish.'

Mr Lamb continued: 'Can you give any reason why you did not take means to prevent these letters being sent to you from time to time from the prisoner?'

'No, I cannot,' came the reply.

'You received letters after the 3rd of July?'

'Yes.'

'Who opened the last one?'

'I did.'

'Who was present?'

'No-one.'

The evidence of Emily Beard, who was present and evidently very unwell, was read and signed by her. In it she said that after Miss Edmunds had put the chocolate cream into her mouth there was an unpleasant metallic taste. She immediately left the room and spat it out. For some time afterwards, however, saliva ran down the side of her mouth and that was followed by an attack of diarrhoea.

This evidence concluded the case for the prosecution.

The Court was told by Mr Lamb that the prisoner, Christiana Edmunds, reserved her defence. She was then formally charged with the wilful murder of Sidney Albert Barker and her case was committed for trial at the next Assizes. She was also subsequently committed for trial on the other charges of attempting to poison Emily Beard, Mr Garrett, Mrs Boys and others, including various small boys. Mr Merrifield said that it was understood that the application for bail had been made in each case and been refused.

Christiana's demeanour during her court appearances was seemingly unconcerned, almost casual. According to *The Times*, describing the close of the hearing of 31st August, 'the Town Hall had been surrounded by people anxious to catch a glimpse of the prisoner. She made no sign of fear and was throughout the day apparently the least excited person in the court.'

Trial at The Old Bailey

Understandably, Christiana Edmunds's legal advisors requested that her case should not be heard at Lewes Crown Court, in the County of Sussex, as, on account of the publicity and sensational element surrounding the alleged poisonings, she would not be afforded a fair trial. Virulent local gossip had been embellished by a number of unflattering photographs of Christiana Edmunds which were displayed in shop windows in the town. The same objection had been raised in the case of the Rugeley poisoner, William Palmer, whose trial was diverted to London under the Central Criminal Court Act of 1856. Christiana's case was, therefore, scheduled to be opened on Monday 15th January, 1872, at the Central Criminal Court at the Old Bailey. Whilst awaiting trial Christiana was removed from Lewes Gaol and taken to Newgate Prison which, according to an article in the *Pall Mall Gazette*, she found far from congenial.

Gaol Accommodations of Fastidious Inmates

The objection raised by Miss Christiana Edmunds to share a cell in Newgate occupied by "an educated woman in custody on a charge of bigamy"[101] is utterly incomprehensible. That lady charged with bigamy should object to share a cell of a lady charged with murder would not be surprising but Miss Edmunds surely must see on reflection that she is extremely fortunate in the companion of her captivity.

Both ladies have yet to be found guilty before anyone has a right to cast a stone at them and for the same reason they surely ought not to

---

101 This was probably Eva Maria Barbara Eugenie Jeanette Pierlo, sentenced to three days' imprisonment for bigamy. By 1871, her circumstances had deteriorated although she was described in *The Times* as "ladylike".

cast stones at each other. Miss Edmunds's other complaint – namely, that she may not wear her bonnet and sealskin jacket in chapel – is of a far more serious character.

If Newgate chapel is constructed after the fashion of other chapels and churches that have no connection with the gaol, the draughts of cold air, bringing coughs, colds and rheumatism on their wings and rendering those places of worship often so dangerous to health and life, render a bonnet and sealskin jacket almost indispensable garments for any lady forming a member of the congregation.

At the same time, Mr Jonas, the governor, is much to be pitied. To him, personally, it is probably a matter of indifference what fashions are adopted by those ladies who are visitors at his establishment. He would perhaps not object to *Le Follet* being regularly supplied to every inmate of the gaol: it is therefore unfair on the part of the ladies in Newgate to attack that most kind-hearted and meritorious public officer because he is powerless to act on their judgement entirely in matters of taste.

Reporting on the trial, the *Illustrated Police News* informed its readers that the prisoner in the dock appeared to be:

> ... a young, bright and not uncomely lady. But the prisoner's youthful appearance seemed to heighten the horror of the crime charged against her – the dread of the fate to which she stood exposed. And, in truth, apart from the hypothesis of insanity, it seemed difficult to connect the quiet, lady-like, almost girlish, woman in the dock with a murder, or rather, a series of murders, that made the statement for the prosecution sound more like a tale taken from the annals of the Borgias than a narrative of modern days.
>
> The first impression produced by Miss Edmunds could hardly fail to be favourable from its contrast to the hideous photographs with which the window-gazing public has been made familiar.[102] A slightly-made and pale-faced woman, who gives the idea that ill-health has made her look older than she really is; and yet, even without making any such allowance, you would scarcely set her down as more than thirty.

---

102 As with the case of the murderous maid, Kate Webster, 1879, the images of her produced at the time of her trial were taken from an effigy in Madame Tussaud's Waxwork Museum yet in the flesh she was described as quite good-looking.

> The prisoner was simply dressed, wearing a black velvet mantle with a small fur tippet around the neck; and the only noticeable peculiarity in her appearance was a large coronet of hair surmounting the smooth locks braided in a fashion now long out of date.
>
> Throughout the day she sat with her small, tightly-gloved hands folded across her knees, perfectly calm and self-possessed to all outward semblance; and only for one moment, when an allusion to her family was made by the counsel, did her nerve give way.

A report from the *Reading Mercury*, on Saturday 20th January, 1872, entitled 'The Brighton Poisoning Case', gives a clear account of the opening day of the trial:

> The trial of Christiana Edmunds for several alleged attempts to commit murder by poisoning took place on Monday morning at the Central Criminal Court and the proceedings excited very great public interest. Mr Baron Martin took his seat on the Bench at 10 o'clock and the prisoner was then placed at the bar.

Christiana was allowed to be seated throughout the proceedings and was first arraigned for the wilful murder of Sidney Albert Barker. The presiding judge was Lord Chief Justice Sir Samuel Martin, referred to as Baron Martin. Mr William Ballantine, Serjeant-at-Law, and Mr Straight appeared for the prosecution and Mr John Humffreys Parry, Serjeant-at-Law, Mr Poland and Mr Worsley conducted the defence.

William Ballantine opened for the prosecution in a short address in which he stated briefly the general outline of the case:

> There are four separate indictments against Miss Edmunds – one for the murder of the child Barker and the remaining three for attempts to murder. It is upon the first of these four charges that the prisoner is at present being tried. Yet, though each charge is distinct and separate, all are, according to the theory of Miss Edmunds's guilt, so connected together that their disassociation from one another is difficult.

Indicating the prisoner in the dock he told the court that,

> Miss Edmunds had conceived a violent passion for Dr Beard, a medical man who tended her at Brighton. Whether from jealousy

or from some other motive, she attempted to poison Mrs Beard. In consequence of that lady's illness – arising as her husband believed, by poison administered to her by the prisoner – he broke off his acquaintance with Miss Edmunds.

To divert suspicion from herself the prisoner is charged with introducing poisonous matter into sweetmeats sold by a confectioner at Brighton, Mr Maynard, with causing the distribution of these poisoned sweetmeats to a number of children, thereby bringing about the death of one child and the mortal illness of other persons; and with endeavouring, by a series of frauds, forgeries and pretences, to create a belief that large quantities of poisoned sweetmeats issuing from Mr Maynard's shop were in circulation in Brighton – and that therefore Mrs Beard's illness might be explained without any suspicion falling upon the prisoner herself.

In the course of the trial, continued Serjeant Ballantine, it will be shown that,

> ...the poor little lad, Sidney Barker, died almost immediately after eating some chocolate lozenges [creams] purchased at Mr Maynard's shop by his uncle, Mr Charles Miller, on the 12th of June: that his symptoms pointed to poisoning by strychnine and that an analysis made upon the contents of the stomach proved death to have been caused by strychnine in the lozenges some of which he had eaten.

The boy's father, Mr Albert Barker, and his two brothers-in-law, were called and repeated the evidence they had already given at the inquest into the boy's death and at the subsequent Magistrates' Court in Brighton. Also called were Dr Richard Rugg, the surgeon who had treated the child and Dr Henry Letheby who performed the post-mortem examination of the contents of the stomach. This was followed by testimony from a number of witnesses, reported in numerous newspapers.

One of the first witnesses sworn was the Brighton chemist, Mr Garrett, who said:

> I know the prisoner and for some years she has been in the habit of dealing at my shop. I did not know her name. She came to my shop on the 28th of March and purchased some articles for the toilet and then asked if I would supply her with a little strychnine for the purpose

of destroying cats. I objected strongly to letting her have any at first. She said she was a married woman and had no children and there was no fear of mischief. I ultimately supplied her with 10 grains but I required her to bring a witness. She left the shop and fetched Mrs Stone and I made the entry of the sale and it was signed first by the prisoner and then by Mrs Stone. The prisoner gave the name of Mrs Wood and her address as Hill-side, Kingston, Surrey.

On the 15th of April the prisoner came to me again and said that the poison had not acted and I gave her 10 grains more and she signed my book and said the purpose she wanted the poison was to kill a dog.

On the 8th of June, I received a paper from a little boy, purporting to be signed by Messrs. Glaisyer and Kemp, chemists, asking me to supply them with a quarter of an ounce of strychnine. I wrote a note to Messrs. Glaisyer and Kemp and gave it to the boy and he returned in half an hour with another letter enclosing a half-crown and I enclosed one drachm of strychnine in a bottle and labelled it and sealed it and handed it with the change to the boy.

I remember the inquest being held upon the deceased boy and on the 11th of July I received a letter purporting to come from the borough coroner (Mr Black) asking me to send him my register of poisonous drugs sold by me. I gave the messenger the book and he brought it back to me and a few days afterwards I missed a leaf. It was the leaf immediately preceding the entries relating to the sale to Mrs Wood. I did not see the prisoner again until she was in custody in the police-court.

Called to the witness box, Mrs Caroline Stone told the court:

I formerly carried on the business of dressmaker at Brighton. I was present in the shop when some strychnine was sold by Mr Garrett. The person to whom it was sold, whom I cannot positively identify as the prisoner, came to my shop and purchased a veil and paid for it and left. She returned in five minutes and then said that she wished me to do her a great favour which was to go and sign the book at Mr Garrett's that she might get some poison for stuffing birds. She said that she and her husband were naturalists and lived at Kingston, near Brighton. I went with her and signed the book at Mr Garrett's. I afterwards accompanied her a second time to Mr Garrett's shop and she had a second supply of poison.

When questioned, Mr Thomas Glaisyer had this to say:

> I am one of the firm of Glaisyer and Kemp, chemists. The three documents produced by the last witness are not in my handwriting and I know nothing of the application for his [Garrett's] poison book.

Next called to testify was Mr David Black, who said:

> I am the Borough Coroner for Brighton. The signature to the letter produced by Mr Garrett is not in my handwriting and I know nothing of the application for his poison book.

Eager followers of the case were further regaled with the scene in the court that day though much of the evidence given was, in essence, the same as that given at the Magistrates' hearing in Brighton during the August and September of the previous year. Press reports informed readers that 'several children were placed in the witness box and swore with remarkable directness and coherence to the fact that they had been suddenly ill after eating sweets from Maynard's shop which had in each case reached them through the hands of a lady in the dock.'

First to testify was young Adam May, who was eleven years old, but small for his age:

> I am 11 years old and live with my parents at Brighton. I see the prisoner in the dock and I believe I saw the same lady in Portland-street, Brighton. She asked me if I would go on an errand for her and she told me to go to Mr Maynard's shop and purchase sixpenny worth of large chocolate creams. I purchased the creams for her. The lady was waiting for me at the bottom of Portland-street and I gave her the bag which she undid and looked at the chocolates and said they were not the right sort. She gave me a large piece of chocolate cream. This was after I had been back to the shop and told the young lady that they were not the sort I wanted. I took back a sixpenny box of small chocolates. I gave them to the lady and she said they were the right sort and she gave me a large piece of chocolate cream.
>
> I did not see her again until three months afterwards at the top of King-street. She again asked me if I would go on an errand for her and I asked her if I could go and ask my mother and she said 'yes'. I went and asked her and then went on an errand for the lady. I took a note to Mr Garrett's shop with a note and brought back something

like a book in a brown paper parcel. I took it to the prisoner and I gave it to her and she walked away with it. When I gave the prisoner the parcel she gave me four pence halfpenny. Not long after that I again saw the prisoner in King-street, Brighton, and she asked me if I should like some 'bulls'-eyes'. I said I should and she gave me some.

Next came Miss Anne Meadows, who told the court she was working as an assistant in Mr Maynard's shop in May and June, 1871. She knew Adam May and remembered him coming to the shop for six penny worth of the 'best French chocolate creams' in the beginning of June. She then told the court:

After he had left the shop he returned in ten minutes and brought the creams back and said they were not the sort that was wanted and I returned them to the case whence I had taken them and gave him a sixpenny case of English creams.

I remember a young gentleman named Miller coming to Mr Maynard's about a week after this transaction occurred. The cases were filled up every morning but I know that no creams were added to the partition in which those creams were placed before they were sold to Mr Miller. I believe that I quite emptied the compartment in giving the quarter of a pound to Mr Miller.

Kate Page, one of Mr Maynard's assistants, remembered a boy called George Brooks, who, with another boy, came into the shop on 14th May and she served him with an ounce of large four-penny chocolate creams. He came back soon after and changed them for two ounces of small three penny creams and she noticed that some of the returned creams were broken so she put away in 'the broken drawer'.

Charles Schooley, another of Mr Maynard's employees, said that Kate Page had asked him to keep an eye on boys coming in to buy sweets – possibly there had been some trouble with boys caught shop-lifting - and, when George and the other boy left the shop, he followed them and saw George give the bag to the prisoner, Christiana Edmunds.

George Brooks, who lived in Russell Street, Brighton, corroborated Kate Page's evidence, but added that Miss Edmunds had given him a penny for his trouble.

Next in the witness box was William Guy, who said:

> I am 12 years old and live at Brighton with my parents. In April I met a lady in North-street and she asked me to go to Mr Maynard's for chocolate creams. I was to buy three ounces and she gave me a shilling. I got the chocolates and took them back to the lady and she said I had got the wrong ones. I obtained others at the shop of Mr Maynard and gave them to her, when she went away with them. She told me to say that the chocolates were for Mrs Field. The prisoner is the same lady.'

The much maligned Mr John Goddard Maynard (who told the court that he was going blind), testified that he had been a confectioner in West Street, Brighton, for more than thirty-five years. Mr Cadbury and Mr Ware manufactured the chocolates for him and, ever since they were introduced, he had sold large quantities of them in his Brighton shop. He told the court:

> I cannot say when I first heard complaints about the creams I sold. I think it was about the middle of April. The prisoner was the person who complained that the creams were poisoned and that she intended to have them analysed. I told her I wish she would do so. I never keep strychnine or poison of any kind in my shop. The prisoner introduced herself to me at my private house and said that a lady friend of hers had eaten some chocolates bought at my shop and they had made her ill. In consequence of what she said I had my chocolates tested and they were found to be quite pure.

Mr George Robert Ware testified that he had been a chocolate manufacturer for thirty-three years, had supplied Mr Maynard with French chocolate creams for eighteen or twenty years and had never had a complaint - nor did he ever keep poison of any kind on his premises.

Mr David Black, the Brighton Coroner, was recalled and repeated the evidence Christiana Edmunds had given at the inquest into the death of Sidney Barker. During the enquiry she had told him that she had bought some chocolate creams from Mr Maynard's shop and subsequently suffered violent stomach pains and a burning sensation in the throat. She had gone to complain to Mr Maynard and told him and his wife that she had been made ill. He insisted she try a chocolate cream in the shop and it tasted fine. There was no metallic taste She had taken some of the chocolates she'd bought to a local chemist, Mr Julius Schweitzer, to be analysed and at first he had thought she was 'nervous and fanciful' but he altered his opinion when he tasted one himself and said he would make an analysis and give her the result in writing. This she gave to Dr Richard Rugg, who had attended the sick boy.

The grocer's wife, Mrs Harriet Elizabeth Cole, of 32 Church Street, Brighton, was recalled and told the court:

> The prisoner came to my shop in March last and after she had left I found a packet of chocolate sweets with Mr Maynard's name on it. I and a young lady who was staying with me ate some of the chocolate creams and we were very sick and ill afterwards. The prisoner came to my shop after the month of March a second time and when she had left I found lemon bulls-eyes and some chocolate creams. My daughter put one of the chocolate creams in her mouth and spat it out again directly.

She gave the remainder of the creams to a boy called Henry Walker and Caroline, his mother, testified that she had been very ill after eating one of the chocolates given to her son by Mrs Cole.

Another boy was called to give evidence - Henry Halliwell, aged thirteen, who told the Court that Christiana Edmunds had stopped him in the street and given him a chocolate which had made him ill. Likewise young Benjamin Caulthrup testified that he had been given chocolate by the prisoner which made him sick and giddy.

A ten year old girl, Emily Selina Baker, described by the paper as 'a pretty child', testified that she had met Christiana Edmunds in the street as she came out of school. Christiana asked Emily if she liked sweets. When she said 'yes' she was given a bag containing chocolate creams, lemon drops, acid drops and cough drops. She took them home and her mother picked out five or six chocolates and gave them to her. One of them was very bitter and she spat it out. Within half an hour she felt very sick and giddy and was ill for two days.

The girl's mother, Mrs Harriet Baker, was then called to give evidence and stated that Mr Maynard's name was on the bag of sweets and about eight or nine days later Christiana Edmunds called at her home and asked if there was anyone sick in the house but when Mrs Baker said that her young daughter had been unwell, the prisoner said nothing more and simply walked away.

Miss Charlotte Elizabeth Petitt, the Edmunds' housemaid, confirmed that the prisoner was a single lady living with her mother at 16 Gloucester Place, Brighton, and, when questioned by the defence, she was able to testify that whilst both ladies behaved with decorum, Christiana, in particular, always treated her kindly.

Inspector Gibbs was called and repeated the evidence he had given at the Magistrates' Court hearing, that he had gone to Christiana Edmunds's home on 17th August to arrest her for administering poison to Mrs Emily Beard. She was lying on a sofa looking pale and when the warrant was read to her she protested with the words: 'Me poison Mrs Beard! I have been nearly poisoned myself!'

Dr Letheby confirmed that the symptoms suffered by some of the children who had eaten the chocolate creams could have been produced by the administration of strychnine.

Mr Netherclift reiterated his previous testimony - that the letters supposedly from Messrs Glaisyer & Kemp, Mr David Black, the coroner and the handwritten notes in the six boxes of poisoned sweetmeats were all written by the prisoner, Christiana Edmunds.

At this point the prosecution, Mr Serjeant Ballantine, proposed to call Dr Charles Beard for re-examination but Mr Parry, for the defence, objected. However, the judge conceded that Dr Beard should be called. One can imagine the stir caused by the appearance of the next witness, Mr Charles Beard, M.D. – engendering, no doubt, much nudging and craning of necks as he stepped into the witness box. There were no salacious observations, however, for his testimony was very brief, merely confirming that he was practising as a doctor in Brighton in September, 1870, and that the prisoner had been one of his patients and had frequently visited his house.

The spectators so eagerly gathered in Court that day were further disappointed when the Judge, Baron Martin, suggested that Dr and Mrs Beard should be entirely left out of the case. He said that he had read their depositions and, 'there was a good deal of their evidence he should not admit at all.'

This puzzling statement, on which the Judge chose not to elaborate, ended the case for the prosecution and the hearing was adjourned until the following day, Tuesday, 16th January.

On the second day of the trial the interest in the case was such that several national newspapers reported detailed accounts of the proceedings. Readers were told that, before the Court re-assembled on Tuesday, 16th January, 'the learned judge said that he should like to see one of the chocolate creams and it was handed to him. He was informed they were what were called French chocolates, but they were manufactured by a Mr Ware.'

After his inspection, Christiana Edmunds was again brought into Court from Newgate Prison and once more placed in the dock, charged with the wilful murder of Sidney Albert Barker.

Serjeant Parry, in addressing the jury for the defence, mainly relied on the plea of insanity, regaling the Court with accounts of members of Christiana's family afflicted with insanity.[103]

The *Mercury* drew its readers to a crucial point regarding the charge of the murder of Sidney Barker, made by Serjeant Parry, who

> ...argued that there was no legal proof that the prisoner had caused the death of the child Barker. He could not deny that the prisoner had given chocolate creams containing some noxious ingredients to a number of children but he must deny that the poisoned chocolates taken by the deceased boy were proved to have been passed to him by the prisoner. This fact must be distinctly proved before they could convict the prisoner.

Whilst admitting that it had been established that a bag of chocolates had been bought and then returned to Mr Maynard's

---

103 These details were given in full in subsequent petitions submitted to the Home Office by her mother and a relative by marriage, Mr Sydney Cornish Harrington.

shop, Parry contended that there was no positive proof that the prisoner had put poisoned chocolates in *that* bag - which were later bought by Mr Miller, the deceased boy's uncle - and that only *positive* proof would be needed to justify a conviction on a charge of wilful murder.

The *Mercury* article continued:

> Seldom has there been a more painful scene in court than that caused by the appearance of Mrs Edmunds (the prisoner's mother) in the witness-box. The unhappy lady, who had all the look of extreme old age, was for a long time unable to speak for her sobs. There was something inexpressibly pitiable in the story of her life as she gasped it out in sentences broken with tears.

When her mother was being questioned, Christiana was seen to be weeping bitterly. Between sobs, Mrs Ann Christiana Edmunds told the court that:

> The prisoner is my daughter and her father, now dead, was an architect in Margate. In 1843 my husband became insane and was sent to a private lunatic asylum at Southall where he was confined until August, 1844, when he returned home for consideration of expense. He remained at home until March, 1845, when he had to be sent to the Peckham Lunatic Asylum. He remained there until March, 1847, when he died in the asylum.

She went on to say that Christiana's father was always raving that he had millions of pounds and he attempted to knock down a medical man with a ruler and was so violent he had to be locked in his room. Her mother then testified that after Christiana was told by Dr Beard she must not visit his house or write any more letters she was in a state of great nervous tension, pacing up and down, saying, "Oh, I shall go mad." Her mother had said, 'You are mad already; you, of all people ought to be particular,' alluding to her father, which she had never done before.

Questioned further by Mr Serjeant Ballantine, the old lady told the court:

> In consequence of statements made by Dr Beard, I demanded a retraction from him and threatened to put the matter into the hands

of a lawyer. She was greatly excited by these statements [Dr Beard's insinuations] and I could not restrain her. She said that the Beards had never spoken to her since the matter of the chocolates. She went about the room quite mad. She behaved with kindness to the people in the house. She was beloved by everybody.

Her testimony continued as she listed the mental afflictions of other members of her family:

> I had a son named Arthur Burn Edmunds. He was subject to epileptic fits from a child and was taken to Earlswood Asylum where he remained until 1866 and died there. I had a daughter who is now dead. She attempted, when in a fit, to throw herself from a window.
>
> My father, Mr Burn, was a major in the army. He was quite childish before he died. I had a brother who had a daughter. She was imbecile.

In 1853, she told the court, her daughter, Christiana, suffered an illness and was sent to London:

> On her return she was paralysed and could not walk. She would come from her room at night into mine and say she could not breathe. As a child she walked in her sleep. Recently, and for some time back - ever since she had known Dr Beard - I have noticed a great change in her demeanour.

Asked the age of her daughter, Mrs Edmunds said:

> 'She is now about 43 years of age', adding that it was 'a period of her life the approach of which she had always dreaded.'

'All this was wrung from the wretched mother,' the *Mercury* informed its readers, 'by questions gently and kindly put but in the midst of it all there came in response a wailing cry from the dock: "This is more than I can bear!"'

It seems likely that this anguished cry was indicative of Christiana's extreme distress at hearing her true age so publicly divulged.[104]

To support the defence plea of insanity the expertise of a number of medical men was sought, including Dr John Steward, who produced the medical certificates under which the prisoner's father, William

---

104 In the *Newgate Calendar* her age was given as thirty-four and it was commented that "she had the idiotic vanity to deny her real age".

Edmunds, was first admitted to the Lunatic Asylum at Southall and which stated that he was 'a dangerous lunatic'.

Dr Henry Armstrong, proprietor of the Lunatic Asylum at Peckham, gave evidence of Christiana's father's admission to his institution where he died in March, 1847.

Dr George Grabham, a resident physician at the Earlswood Asylum, produced the certificates relating to the admission of Christiana's brother, Arthur Burn Edmunds, in February, 1860. He certified that he died there in January, 1866.

The doctors were followed into the witness box by the Reverend Thomas Henry Cole, the chaplain at Lewes Gaol, who was of the opinion that Christiana Edmunds was, like her father, of unsound mind.

Cole, who first met Christiana when she was on remand prior to appearing before the Magistrates' Court at Brighton Town Hall, gave the following statement:

> There was a rule of the gaol to notice the condition of the minds of prisoners admitted. Prisoner was under his observation from the 19th August to Christmas Day.' [until she was removed to Newgate to await trial at the Old Bailey]. He noticed a very peculiar formation of the eye and the motion of the eye was also very peculiar. He noticed a vacant expression in them. He had many conversations with her. They were perfectly coherent. They struck him as being extraordinary considering the circumstances under which she was placed. He found unnatural calmness and exceeding levity. He had spoken to her regarding the position in which she stood and she broke out into an extraordinary laugh. He endeavoured to fix her mind on the gravity of the charge but she seemed to have no power to fix her mind. She would sometimes cry and then burst out into a laugh. She never appeared to realise her position. He formed the opinion that she was of unsound mind.[105]

Dr William Wood, a physician at St Luke's Hospital - formerly at The Bethlehem Hospital - said he had seen Christiana Edmunds at Newgate about a fortnight ago in company with other medical men. He was very much struck with her absolute indifference to

---

105 *The Times*, 17th January, 1872.

her position but he failed to impress on her the seriousness of her situation. He believed her quite incapable of understanding her position and incapable of distinguishing right from wrong.

> I asked her if she thought it was wrong to attempt to destroy the life of Mrs Beard because she thought her husband wanted to get rid of her. After a pause she did say she thought it would be wrong.

However, in his opinion her mind was so weak that she was really incapable of judging between right and wrong in the same way as other people would.

She had told him that she would prefer a verdict of guilty rather than one of insanity.[106]

Dr Lockhart Robertson, one of the Visitors of the Court of Chancery, stated that he had great difficulty in forming an opinion about the prisoner; she seemed, he said, 'to be on the borderland between crime and insanity' and although her intellect was quite clear and free from any delusion, he thought that her moral sense was deficient as he had often observed in descendants of the insane. After careful consideration he came to regard her as 'morally insane'.

Alice Over, who had known the prisoner for six years and had lived at her house for two years, described Christiana as 'lady-like, quiet, and kind in every way.' She did notice, however, that about March or April, 1871, she appeared strange, not so quiet and said she thought she was going mad.

The last witness to be called for the defence was Dr Henry Maudsley who had also visited Christiana with Drs Wood and Robertson and agreed with them that her mind was impaired.[107]

Mr Serjeant Parry then summed up his case with a powerful

---

[106] Daniel M'Naghten, was a young artisan who suffered from a persecution complex and was convinced he was being spied upon by the Prime Minister, Sir Robert Peel, who had established the Metropolitan Police force in 1829. In 1843, M'Naghten shot Peel's Private Secretary by mistake; as a result of his trial and the verdict of 'insanity' the M'Naghten Law was introduced to safeguard those who kill whilst suffering from mental illness and unable to distinguish right from wrong.

[107] The pioneering psychiatrist, Dr Henry Maudsley (1835-1918) helped found and fund the building of the world-renowned Maudsley Hospital, in South London.

appeal to the jury to return a verdict of 'not guilty' on the grounds of insanity. Having presented a history of family defects and the evidence of the medical men as to Christiana's unsound mind, he felt sure the jurors would agree that her intellect was severely impaired. He confessed that the 'whole case completely puzzled him. He had never in the course of his long experience, or of his reading, met with a similar case.'

Having listened to Mr Serjeant Parry's appeal, William Ballantine rose to make an equally vigorous reply, pointing out what he considered to be the weak points in the evidence of insanity, emphasising the prisoner's extreme cunning in planning and executing the poisonings for which she was charged, the result of which was the death of Sidney Barker.

In his summing-up the Judge dwelt mainly upon the evidence concerning the commission of the crime and treated the issue of insanity as one of subsidiary importance. He charged the jury,

> ...not to acquit the prisoner on the plea of insanity unless they were convinced that she was incompetent to understand the nature of her offence, when she put into circulation the poisoned sweets which caused the death of the child Barker.
>
> The jury retired to consider their verdict at 10 minutes to four and returned into court an hour afterwards with a verdict of *Guilty*.
>
> The prisoner had been removed from the dock while the jury was deliberating and on their return she was brought in again. She walked to the front of the bar, her bearing at that supreme moment being singularly firm. It was also respectful and becoming. She heard the verdict without apparent distress. In the few words of complaint she addressed to the Judge she spoke with much modesty and propriety and afterwards heard the sentence with fortitude.
>
> Being asked if she had anything to say why the court should not give her judgement to die, the prisoner replied that she wished she had been tried on the other charge which had been brought against her [that of attempting to poison Emily Beard].
>
> As to the improper intimacy which she said existed between herself and Dr Beard she had wished to be examined on that subject.

Judge Baron Martin, who had by this time assumed the black cap, explained to her that it did not rest with him for her to be tried on that charge.

The prisoner said, 'It is owing to my having been a patient of his and the treatment I received in going to him, that I have been brought into this dreadful business. I wish the jury had known the intimacy, his affection for me, and the way I have been treated.'

The Judge replied that he was not at all disinclined to believe her statement. He believed the unhappy circumstances in which she placed herself towards the end of 1870 probably led to the position which she was now in; but the truth of that only confirmed the propriety of the verdict. He was quite satisfied the unhappy circumstances under which she became acquainted with Dr and Mrs Beard led to her poisoning fruit and a variety of other things. But he had but one duty to perform. He concurred with the verdict of the jury. That she had no desire to kill that particular child he could well believe: but she had got into a morbid state of mind in consequence of her relations with Dr and Mrs Beard and that had led to all that had occurred. That he believed to be the truth of the matter; but he wished to keep Dr and Mrs Beard entirely away with the view of giving her the fairest trial in the position in which she stood.

He himself believed she was guilty and that the verdict of the jury was correct in rejecting the defence of insanity. In truth he believed there was no reliable evidence to go before the jury on that point and that they felt it impossible to arrive at any other conclusion.

The real question was, not whether she was a person of weak mind but whether her mind was in a state to distinguish right from wrong. He only said he believed, in his judgement, the verdict was a right one, and right upon both points.

The law imposed upon him the duty to pass upon the sentence of death which he proceeded to do in the prescribed form, directing at the same time that it be carried into effect in the county of Sussex and adding, with much fervency, might the Lord have mercy on her soul.[108]

The following description, which appeared in the *London Globe*, 17th January, 1872, manages to portray the dramatic tension in the

---

108 *Reading Mercury*, 20th January, 1872.

Central Criminal Court that day:

> The scene that was enacted yesterday evening at the Old Bailey, on the occasion of the conviction and sentence of Christiana Edmunds, was one of rare occurrence, and for its romantic ghastliness was almost unexampled, even in the annals of the Newgate Calendar. The old and dingy-looking Court was densely crowded during the reply of Serjeant Ballantine and the summing-up of Baron Martin.
>
> The prisoner sat unmoved and seemingly unconcerned. A female warder of the prison, who sat behind her in the dock exhibited far more emotion, and looked far more wretched. The prisoner wore no bonnet, but her hair was carefully and even coquettishly arranged in heavy folds across her head. She was dressed neatly, with a black velvet cloak and well-fitting gloves of some dark colour.
>
> At 3:40 o'clock the jury retired, and were absent for an hour. The prisoner was removed from the dock, but Baron Martin retained his seat upon the bench, and the crowd of spectators hardly dwindled during the weary hour of waiting for the verdict. There was much talking and even some laughing, a strange reaction from the enforced silence and the stillness of suspense during the previous hours of the day.
>
> The Judge perused the *Times*, the Sheriffs and the chaplain chatted pleasantly, the members of the Bar engaged in learned discussions on the relation of insanity to crime, and in criticisms upon the speeches of counsel and the personal appearance of the beautiful young ladies who sat behind the bar seats; and so the time passed until the return of the jury, when to the buzz of conversation succeeded a solemn stillness, during which the names of the twelve were called over, the prisoner during this process standing at the front of the dock, with the female warder in close attendance, and two uniformed turnkeys taking their places noiselessly behind her.
>
> "You say that she is guilty, gentlemen, and that is the verdict of you all?"
>
> There is a dreadful pause. Men's hearts beat with sympathetic excitement, and women's faces blanch with terror; but the bonnetless woman in the dock neither moves a muscle nor changes colour in the least degree during the dreadful proclamation, "Silence while sentence of death and execution according to law is passed upon the prisoner at the bar."

'Has she anything to say? Yes, she has. She whispers to the female warder, who whispers to the jailer, who says aloud that the prisoner wishes to speak. Amid profound silence her voice is heard, clear, musical and steady, as if the awful moment was one of the most ordinary occasions of her life. She desired, she said, to be tried upon the other charges that had been brought against her, in order that the jury and everyone should know the nature of her intimacy with Dr. Beard, of the treatment she had received, and how she had been "brought into this dreadful business" – those were her words.

When she ceased to speak, the learned Judge proceeded to pass sentence, touchingly and feelingly enough. Baron Martin was much overcome with emotion, and at the dreadful words, "hanged by the neck till your body be dead," he broke down and hid his face, during a pause when a pin might have been heard to drop. Presently he recovered his self-possession, and at the conclusion of the sentence the solemn "Amen" of the Newgate Chaplain sounded like a knell.

Then occurred a scene but seldom witnessed, and the like of which may not often be seen again. In the mercy and justice of the English law a woman condemned to death who is *enceinte,* is respited until after the birth of her child. It is usual, therefore, to interrogate the convict upon the point at the time of sentence, and before the date is fixed for execution. The question was put by the Clerk of Arraigns in the usual way. The prisoner again whispered to the female warder, who again whispered to the jailer, who said aloud, "She says she is, my lord."

There was a profound sensation among the bystanders at the unexpected announcement, which was not diminished when the words, "Let the Sheriff impanel a jury of matrons forthwith," were heard. Such is the law from ancient times and in obedience to the injunction the under-Sheriffs, with swords, cocked hats and frills, sallies into the body of the Court and galleries in quest of matrons.

After about twenty minutes a dozen well-to-do and respectably-dressed women – who could have supposed that a dozen such were to be found in such a place? – were captured and directed to enter the jury-box, into which they marched and took their seats as if it was a matter of everyday occurrence.

Mrs Adelaide Whitty, the forewoman, was sworn separately, and then the rest in a body. It was arranged that they should see the prisoner in the Sheriff's parlour. They retired and the prisoner was removed. Half an hour elapsed, when a messenger came into Court, and an inquiry was made aloud by the Judge whether there was an *accoucheur* in Court. Presently a police surgeon, Mr J. Beresford Ryley from Woolwich, was found, and directed to join the matrons.

Half an hour more of suspense and eager interest. A messenger again comes in and whispers, and the rumour goes about that the doctor requires a stethoscope. There is a touch of comedy even in the midst of the tragic scene, for they say that a policeman has been sent to fetch one, but has brought back a telescope instead. More delay, more suspense. Here they are at last. The prisoner again at the bar, the matrons again in the box. The verdict is spoken by the forewoman in a single word "Not".

The humanity of the rule of law which leaves this delicate matter to the decision of twelve women accidentally present in court during a murder trial – and a jury of matrons must be impanelled *de circumstantibus* – is, notwithstanding the undoubted antiquity of the custom, very questionable, and the result has on more than one occasion proved to be very fallible. The sort of women who care to be present at such sad scenes are not presumably the most intelligent or best educated of the community, and the question which they have to investigate might in modern days of medical science be answered far more satisfactorily by a medical man. Besides, the question itself is somewhat difficult, even for medical men to answer, and one about which there has been much professional disputation in modern times.

Christiana's Fate

After Christiana's conviction there was a concerted effort on the part of her solicitor, Mr Lamb, to collect, compile and submit petitions to the Secretary of State, the Right Honourable Henry Bruce, for a reprieve on the grounds of insanity.

It was announced in the local press that:

> On Monday afternoon an influential meeting of the clergy, magistrates and principal inhabitants of Margate was held to consider submitting a petition for a reprieve on behalf of Christiana Edmunds. Resolutions were adopted in favour of the presentation of a petition [referred to as a 'memorial'], to her Majesty and a committee was appointed to

make the necessary arrangements.

On the 17th of January, the day after he had passed the sentence of death on Christiana Edmunds, Baron Martin wrote to the Home Secretary expressing his doubts about executing a woman of unsound mind. He wrote:

> I desire to call your attention to the case of Christiana Edmunds who has been tried and convicted before me of murder. I do not think it necessary to trouble you with a copy of my notes, the evidence will be found in the Times and other Newspapers of the 16th and 17th instant. In my opinion the verdict was in point of law right. A defence was set up of Insanity which failed in evidence. The matter which I desire to bring under your consideration is whether she is a proper subject for execution.

After outlining the facts of the case, he continued:

> My own impression is that altho' capable of knowing right from wrong she is affected by an hereditary taint of insanity and that the improper attachment she formed for Dr Beard caused or increased a morbid state of mind which led to the poisoning of the chocolate creams and also to an endeavour to cast the blame upon Mr Maynard, the Confectioner from whom they were bought. My belief is that she is insane to a considerable extent. I have spoken to several of the Judges on the subject and find a difference of opinion amongst them. Some appear to think that if she were legally and properly convicted she ought to be executed but the majority are of a contrary opinion. I myself think it would be a public scandal if a person commonly deemed mad or insane should be put to violent death.
>
> What I would suggest is that there should be done what was done by Sir George Grey in Townley's case[109] viz. that her state of mind should be investigated by some competent and indifferent medical men and then it will be for you on their report to decide whether a person in the state of mind in which she is ascertained to be is a proper

---

109 In 1863 George Townley stabbed his fiancé to death when she told him she wished to marry another man. Townley was tried, found guilty and sentenced to death, but was subsequently granted a reprieve on the grounds of insanity when his wealthy family employed lawyers and their own medical witnesses to certify that Townley was in fact insane. The announcement of the respite caused immense public disquiet since it was felt that a well-to-do family had effectively paid to pervert justice.

subject for execution. In my judgement it is a matter of considerable difficulty and entitled to very great and grave consideration.'

The Home Secretary, persuaded by Baron Martin's opinion that Christiana was, in fact, insane, despite the verdict with which he had originally concurred, commissioned the celebrated Dr William Gull[110] and Dr William Orange, Medical Superintendent of Broadmoor Asylum, to examine Christiana and assess her state of mind.

The Home Office report from Drs Gull and Orange, dated 23rd January, 1872, stated that:

> ...the acts referred to and acted by her were the fruit of a weak and disordered intellect with confused and perverted feelings of a most marked insane character. The convict stated she had an easy childhood and womanhood up to the time named without any special crisis to show mental or bodily disorder but there is proof of an indifferent intellectual state prior to the history which has led up to the present state.
>
> We were both impressed with the honest and simple account and demeanour of the convict. We were satisfied that her communications to us were in good faith and truthful so far as her frustrated feelings admitted.
>
> The crime of murder the convict seems incapable of realising as having been committed by her though she fully admits the purchasing and distributing the poisons as set forth in the several counts against her. On the contrary, she even justifies her conduct and in an insane way tries still to give a justification for it. We have no doubt that the convict is insane and that she ought to be treated accordingly.

Dr Ryley, the Metropolitan Police Surgeon who had examined Christiana Edmunds for pregnancy prior to sentence being passed, added his voice to the clamour for a reprieve. He published the

---

110 Sir William Gull was held in high regard by the medical profession as a first rate diagnostician. The previous year Queen Victoria had awarded him a baronetcy for successfully treating the Prince of Wales for typhoid fever. In 1876, he was called to the bedside of Charles Bravo, poisoned with antimony. See *Murder at the Priory: The Mysterious Poisoning of Charles Bravo*. Sir William's fee for his examination of Christiana Edmunds was fifty guineas but it appears that he was still waiting to be paid in June of that year.

following statement in the *British Medical Journal*:

> I was requested by the solicitor for the defence of Miss Christiana Edmunds to visit her in Newgate Prison with the view of certifying, if possible, to her insanity. I was, unfortunately, unable to see her on the occasion of my first visit owing to the absence of the prison surgeon.
>
> I subsequently attended her trial and was asked by the Sheriff to assist the twelve matron ladies impanelled to investigate her assertion of pregnancy...

When it was ascertained that she was not pregnant, Dr Ryley observed that,

> ...it was then, when the last frail straw on which she leant abandoned her to her doom that the full peril of her situation dawned upon her for the first time and the awful aspect of her despair was very terrible to behold. The poor ladies who were her unwilling judges wept around her while she, unhappy creature, looked from one to the other in mute, unspeakable woe.
>
> It would not be becoming in me to publish all she said to us but I may mention that she asked, with a weary agony in her voice, "Oh, how shall I sleep tonight?"
>
> I recommended her to ask the prison surgeon for a chloral hydrate draught and sincerely hoped within myself that she would find in him, not only a healer of the body, but a tender and compassionate physician to her poor, aching mind....
>
> I sincerely hope that something may be done to reverse her sentence. Her heedless aspect throughout all her trial and the false statement of pregnancy bear, in my opinion, in conjunction with the facts proved at her trial, *prima facie* evidence of insanity and when these facts are associated with her family history a strong case, I opine, is made out on which to memorialize the Home Secretary [to reprieve the death sentence].[111]

The Home Office also received a letter from one of Christiana's friends, a Miss Eliza Love Clark, pleading for a merciful reprieve. In

---

111 *British Medical Journal*, Vol. 1, No. 577 (January 20th 1872), p. 80

addition, a similar, heartfelt plea came from some nuns, The Sisters of Mercy.

Also sent was *The Humble Petition of Anne Christiana Edmunds of No. 16 Gloucester Place, Brighton, in the County of Sussex.*

The document listed the many members of the Edmunds family who had been deemed insane and confined to Asylums, details of which had been made known at both the Magistrates' Court and during the trial at the Old Bailey.

These were also listed in more detail in the lengthy petition forwarded to the Secretary of State by Mr Sydney Cornish Harrington, of Datchworth, Hertfordshire, who stated that his sister had married Christiana's elder brother, William Edmunds. William was a very excitable character and threatened to commit suicide if he was prevented from marrying Harrington's sister; consent was only reluctantly given, despite the whole family's misgivings, for fear he would kill himself if thwarted.

Harrington also recollected Christiana's father, William, before he was committed to the Asylum at Peckham, being cared for at home with the help of John and Mary Stroud. The night before he was committed John Stroud was quietly sitting listening to William's 'stories about his immense wealth and the vast number of cities he had built when he suddenly sprang out of bed and grappled with him' until Stroud managed to overpower him. It was only with the help of William's wife, Ann, that they were able to get him back into bed. The next day he was taken to the Asylum in a strait-jacket.

He had been an architect with the Margate Pier Company and one of his colleagues recalled going to his office to find him in his night-gown and with a knife in his hand. This employee also said that William's mother was 'very eccentric' as was his aunt, Mary, who used to write 'offensive and annoying' letters to friends and strangers alike whilst in the throes of a feud with the Boys family in Margate.[112] There was insanity on both sides of Christiana's family

---

112 It is probable that Christiana targeted Mrs Elizabeth Boys under the misapprehension that she was connected to the Boys family that was involved in the Edmunds v Boys feud in Margate many years before.

– her maternal grandfather 'was imbecile and had to be fastened to his chair' and his sister, Rachel, was 'something more than eccentric'.

Christiana's sister, Louisa Agnes, had been a violent hysteric who was only prevented from throwing herself out of a window by the intervention of her mother, Ann, and a servant. Arthur Burn Edmunds, Christiana's younger brother, was an inmate of Earlswood Asylum where he died in 1866.

The petitioner also gave an account of Charles Lambert Evershed, a member of the Royal College of Surgeons, who was acquainted with the Harrington family and had made a professional visit to Christiana in prison. He remarked on the extraordinary dilation of the pupils of her eyes as though 'subject to the action of belladonna'.

He also noticed that, even when she was listening intently to what he was saying and looking directly at him, her eyes appeared to be looking into space. He further observed that whenever he was speaking to her of her ailments she would always break in with "Dr Beard used to do this. Dr Beard used to give me that."

He was moreover 'struck with her remarks to him, a comparative stranger, concerning her relations with Dr Beard telling him much of their familiar intercourse and of the hours she used to spend alone with him in his billiard room and it was only from a feeling of delicacy that he did not mention the subject to her family.'

Mr Harrington went on to inform the Home Secretary that, although his sister had married Christiana's elder brother, William, until Christiana's arrest he knew nothing about the rest of the family. It was when he learned that at the Magistrates' Court it was said that Christiana had no male relatives in England and limited financial means that he went to Brighton to offer assistance to Ann Edmunds by providing support and the money to pay for her daughter's defence.

Since then he'd had several meetings with Christiana both at Lewes Gaol and Newgate Prison but found it difficult to engage her in conversation – she would always bring the subject back to Dr Beard and the only occasion she became upset was when he told her that Dr Beard had shown him her letters; she had then 'burst out in the presence of the Matron of Lewes Gaol with the expression, "Now you have made me wretched indeed!!"'

On Wednesday, 17th January, the day after her conviction and sentence of death, Mr Harrington went to see her in Newgate Prison, in the presence of the Governor and one of the warders, and was shocked, not only at the appearance of her eyes, which were glaring and unnaturally contracted, but her remarks were "I am going to Brighton to see Dr Beard!!" "They have promised to take me to Brighton to see Dr Beard!!" then, in a quiet voice, she said: "The Police have sent a woman to track me and she has been following me all night."

Again she repeated, as if delighted: "I am going to see Dr Beard. I am going to Brighton." She kept repeating this the whole time and Harrington found it disturbing; he held out his hand to her, saying, "Chrissie, won't you shake hands with me?" and she replied, "Oh, yes." He held out his hand but she only touched it and said: "I am going to Brighton to see Dr Beard – they have promised me I shall go to Brighton and see Dr Beard."

Sydney Harrington finished by stating that he had 'seen and conversed with many insane persons in various countries but had never seen one that he more firmly believes to be insane than the prisoner. Your memorialist earnestly prays that you will be pleased to take the above mentioned facts into consideration and to recommend to Her Majesty to commute the capital sentence passed upon the said convict, Christiana Edmunds.'

The *Daily Telegraph*, 22nd January, 1872, wrote at some length about the dilemma faced by the Home Secretary:

> Tomorrow week is the date appointed for the execution of Mr Watson:[113] according to common usage, the sentence of the law will

---

113 Rev. John Selby Watson (1804-1884), scholar and translator: Headmaster of Stockwell Grammar School, 1844 to 1870. Shortly after completing his book, *History of the Papacy to the Reformation*, he killed his wife, Anne, in a fit of rage. He stood trial for murder at the Old Bailey in January, 1872. He pleaded insanity which was dismissed by Mr Justice Byles in his summing up. The Jury found him guilty but with a recommendation for mercy on account of his age and previous good character. As with the Christiana Edmunds case, the Judge changed his

be carried out on Miss Edmunds a few days later: and during the short interval of time between to-day and Tuesday week the Home Secretary will have to arrive at a decision on the fate of both the condemned prisoners. We use the word "both" advisedly because, as everybody feels, there is no legal or logical connection between the offences of the two criminals...

When a prisoner is placed in the dock on a criminal charge, the advantages and disadvantages of good social status are about equally balanced. On the one hand, the educated prisoner has in his favour the antecedent improbability of his having committed a heinous offence, and the strong hope that his case will be ably defended.

On the other hand, if his guilt be once brought home, the moral enormity of his crime is aggravated by the fact of his superior education; and, when convicted, the very circumstances of his position render it more difficult for his judges to incline towards the side of mercy. Again it is obvious from the facts that the Home Secretary will be ill-advised if he should endeavour in either case to evade responsibility by basing the decision simply and solely on the opinion of the presiding Judge. Were that principle once established, the Judge and not the Minister would become the ultimate arbiter in all capital cases; and the one advantage possessed by our present anomalous system lies in the fact that the Home Secretary can take cognisance of various circumstances possessing what we may call extra-judicial character.

Though Watson could plead extreme provocation – his home life was proved to be one of sustained domestic misery... In the case of Miss Edmunds, however, no argument based on provocation that she might have received could be of any possible avail. Even assuming, as a mere matter of hypothesis, that she had endured the cruellest wrongs to which a woman could be subjected at the hands of some third party, these wrongs could not justify the character of the crime she committed, in compassing death by poison of people against whom she had no possible cause of complaint.

If Miss Edmunds is to be reprieved, the one solitary plea available on her behalf is that of insanity. This plea was shown to be absolutely conclusive. The *prima facie* evidence elicited at the trial, to show that she was out

mind and urged the Home Secretary to reprieve Watson. His sentence was changed to penal servitude for life and he died in Parkhurst Prison on 6th July, 1884, aged eighty.

of her mind, was well-nigh overwhelming; but to that evidence, as we understand, considerable additions will be made in the case laid before the Home Secretary, by a mass of testimony which, from our technical rules of evidence, could not be brought forward at the trial.

The correspondence between the unhappy lady and Dr Beard, which, by the ruling of the Court, could not be legally connected with the question whether she did or did not murder Sidney Barker, will, we understand, be brought to the notice of Mr Bruce; and that correspondence – whether interpreted as corroborating her appeal to the object of guilty affection or as proving her to have been labouring under a mere delusion – may obviously have a most important bearing on the issue whether she was insane or not during the period when her schemes for wholesale poisoning were concocted, were devised and executed.

The history, too, of her previous career, and of her family, will be submitted with a detail that is impossible in a Court of Justice. While the forms of our legal procedure exclude substantial portions of the data from the view of the Court, it is obvious that many physiological facts, as well as the nice yet momentous question of moral responsibility, present problems which no ordinary jury is competent to investigate; whereas there would manifestly be no difficulty, on such exceptional occasions, in securing for the ultimate authority the aid of persons fully competent to expound the whole story of the facts. At what decision the Home Secretary, acting as a Judge of Appeal, may ultimately arrive in either case, it is not for us to assume; but we are sure, that, if he should find it consistent with his duty to incline to mercy, he will carry with him the sympathies of the public.

The *Chelmsford Chronicle*, dated Friday, 26th January, 1872, was one of many that announced a reprieve:

REPRIEVE of CHRISTIANA EDMUNDS

In consequence of an opinion expressed by Baron Martin that Christiana Edmunds, recently convicted before him of murder and sentenced to death, should not be executed, and that her state of mind should be investigated by some competent medical men, Mr Bruce appointed Sir.W.W.Gull, M.D., and Dr Orange, superintendent of the Broadmoor Criminal Lunatic Asylum, to make the suggested examination. These gentlemen, having had an interview of four hours' duration with the prisoner, have certified to Mr Bruce that they find her to be of unsound mind. Under these circumstances, and on these grounds, the sentence of death passed upon her will not be carried into effect and measures will shortly to be taken for her removal to Broadmoor Asylum.'

The Times, on Thursday, 25th January, addressed the matter in some detail:

> ...if Christiana Edmunds was not mad and if homicide without direct personal malice is ever to be punished with death, she eminently deserved to suffer the extreme penalty of the law. But such a decision would, we think, in any case have done violence to public feeling. All material doubt, however, must be set at rest by the certificate now given by Sir William Gull and Dr Orange. They have made a careful examination of the convict's present mental condition and they report that, as a matter of fact, she is of unsound mind.
>
> It is impossible, however, to escape the reflection that there is something very anomalous in the means by which this conclusion is arrived at. The certificate of two distinguished physicians is deemed by the Home Secretary of sufficient weight to practically reverse the verdict of a Jury, formally approved in Court by the Judge, on the very point in question.
>
> We make no complaint of this result for, as we have said, we believe substantial justice has been done: but the method is none the less remarkable.
>
> The defence of insanity was raised for Christiana Edmunds in open Court, medical men of high reputation were called to sustain it and it was supported by strong presumptive evidence. The Judge, however, sums up decidedly, and even roughly, in a sense adverse to the plea and directs the Jury that they have simply to consider whether at the time the prisoner committed the crime she knew right from wrong.
>
> The Jury bring in a verdict of *guilty* and the Judge declares his belief that they were "correct in rejecting the defence of insanity".
>
> ...the theory of the trial is that the Law overrules, if necessary, the opinion of physicians. The practice exemplified in the reprieve is that the opinion of two physicians overrules, if necessary, the decision of the Law. The case illustrates, in short, very forcibly the extreme

perplexity of the law on this subject. In the case of Christiana Edmunds they (the Jurors) did their duty following the ruling of the Judge.

There was in her conduct an extraordinary disproportion of means to ends and a prolonged concentration of mind on one extravagant plot which seems more readily explained by insanity that by any other hypothesis….

During nearly a year she was intent upon sustained and circuitous devices for secreting strychnine and fixing a bad reputation upon the sweet meats of a particular shop, running the risk, as she at length saw, of scattering death among innocent children and for no other purpose than that of dispelling a private accusation which had thwarted an unlawful attachment.

If she was in full command of her faculties, she was a monster of wickedness; but if she was the victim of a morbid possession, the persistency, the cunning and the irrational rationality of her conduct would exactly correspond with the usual characteristics of such lunatics.

Anyone who had visited a lunatic asylum will know that the stress laid at the trial on the acuteness of her anonymous letters to the father of the child, Barker, was wholly mistaken. Nothing is more common than for lunatics actually confined in asylums to address the most ingenious and plausible letters to those who are responsible for keeping them in confinement.

The progress of knowledge must to some extent affect rules of law as well as other ancient institutions; and, if such cases as the present clearly show the inconsistency of law and medical science, Juries ought no longer to be exposed to the pain and temptation of pronouncing verdicts correct in law but unjust in fact. Christiana Edmunds is now pronounced *not guilty*. Any Jury who may try a similar charge in the future will be aware of the issue of her case. It will not contribute to the respect felt for justice to compel them to go through the form of giving a solemn verdict which they know will be afterwards reversed.

Christiana's solicitor, Mr Lamb, presented a petition *after* the reprieve was granted, with this accompanying letter:

The enclosed memorial was prepared by me as attorney for Miss

Edmunds. By a cursory glance at the signatures it will be seen that the Prayer of the Petition was supported by the Mayor and many of the Aldermen and Town Councillors of Brighton, by the Committing Magistrates and other Justices of the Peace for Brighton, by Dr and Mrs Beard, Mr Garrett, Mr and Mrs Boys and others to whom the poisoned sweets were sent and generally by many highly intelligent and respectable inhabitants and visitors of Brighton. [114]

Immediately I was informed that Her Majesty had graciously commuted the sentence passed upon my client I closed the memorial but have since considered it desirable that the document should be forwarded to you for the purpose of proving if necessary that the Public were not indifferent to the evidence which was tendered at the Trial in proof of the Prisoner's state of mind during the commission of the acts laid to her charge.

However, some press reports expressed doubts about changing a jury's verdict from Guilty and a sentence of death.[115]

The *Daily Telegraph*, on Friday, 26th January, 1872, printed an article referring to a similar plea of insanity on behalf of a Mr Watson who had been found guilty of murder - this plea, however, had been rejected by Mr Bruce, the Home Secretary, resulting in a sentence of penal servitude for life. The article then turns its attention to the case of Christiana Edmunds:

> Meanwhile, however, great care must be taken not to allow feeling to overpower judgement by giving undue weight to the plea of insanity in cases of murder. A hot temper and extreme provocation are no excuses for the crime, though they may justify a different feeling towards the criminal and even a minor punishment.

---

114 There were well over two hundred signatures in the petition, including ex-Mayors and various clergymen – also, many were residents of Grand Parade including two of Mrs Boys's servants, Amelia Mills and Emma Helsey, who gave evidence for the prosecution, also signed the plea for mercy. Another signature was of Mr Merrifield, the magistrate who presided over the Court hearings in Brighton when Christiana was first charged.

115 The diarist James Henry Mangles recounts the following conversation with Alfred Tennyson on 21st September, 1872: '[Tennyson] produced a photo, asked me what I thought of it. I guessed "George Elliott!!" He was shocked. It turned out to be Miss Edmunds, the Brighton poisoner. It had everything horrible, he said, written on her face. She ought to have been hanged.' (In *Tennyson at Aldworth*, edited Earl A. Knies.)

No doubt the able men who have made insanity their special study increase the difficulty of treating crime by showing that insanity may be hereditary and latent, and may exist with much outward self-control, great intelligence and high cultivation.

In Miss Edmunds's case it is difficult not to believe that there was an hereditary taint about her which takes from her full responsibility for her acts, though where the line of responsibility must be drawn is hard to say...

The *Pall Mall Gazette* also expressed reservations on Wednesday, 24th January, 1872:

...since after the trial of the case she was surrendered to the judge for sentence, and by the judge was sentenced, on the ground that she was sane, we doubt Mr Bruce's right to reprieve her on the ground that she is not sane, unless his own private judgement is strengthened by a more authoritative and independent opinion than that of *The Telegraph*. Most of the arguments advanced by that journal are quite inadmissible.

The "nourishment of morbid attachment, which, whether her passion was encouraged or rejected, was absolutely certain to excite her nerves to the utmost intensity" is scarcely to be adopted as a moral excuse for murder. Or if it be so adopted then the "nourishment of morbid attachment" for other people's property (not uncommon among men generally accounted sane) must be held as depriving highway robbers of conscious guilt.

It is absurd to say, too, that the wretched creature's offences were "purposeless and irrational". They were committed for the very purpose, and for the very reasons, that have led women into more crime, probably, than any others: first, the gratification of an overmastering passion: next, the concealment of guilt.

Crime to divert suspicion of crime is among the commonest of offences. But then, it is said, the crime is so monstrous in its conception and proportions that she must be mad who committed it. There are two answers to this; in the first place, madness is a very unsafe explanation of monstrous crimes... The records of the slave trade abound with instances of monstrous crime; but we do not assign them to insanity though we do agree that they were committed in "absence or deficiency of moral sense".

In the next place, it is not proved that Christiana Edmunds ever contemplated the commission of wholesale murder, which brings the word 'monstrous' into this unhappy discussion. Her moral guilt (though not her legal responsibility) is to be estimated by her design; and who knows that she meant to kill anybody?

Of course we leave Mrs Beard out of the question.

But apart from any murderous intent she may have been betrayed into in that case through nourishing a morbid attachment what proof is there that she meant to kill? Mrs Beard had not been poisoned to death – she had only been made ill; and it would have fully served her rival's purpose if a variety of other people had been made ill about the same time in a similar and unaccountable way.

...but though we can find no positive evidence whatever to show that Christiana Edmunds was insane when she committed a crime that was certainly not without motive and method and probably never had in her mind the proportions it wears for us, there is the fact that she belongs to a very mad family.

And we end as we began by insisting that her own insanity has yet to be shown: that Mr Bruce's opinions or those of the *Daily Telegraph* do not suffice in such a case; and that if Christiana Edmunds is to be reprieved on the score of insanity, some really competent authority should be adduced to show grounds for the assumption that she inherited madness and was probably over-mastered by it. But if she is to be reprieved for the far simpler reason that she is a woman, and not a man, we have nothing to say whatever.

Following the reports of Christiana's protest about not being allowed to wear a bonnet to chapel when she was in Newgate awaiting trial at the Old Bailey, the following article appeared in the *Sheffield Daily Telegraph* on Monday, 29th January, 1872:

PRISON MADE EASY

"Gentlemen" awaiting their trial for murder at New York seem to have uncommonly easy times of it. At all events they suffer from none of the inconvenience of which the Brighton prisoner, Christiana Edmunds, so bitterly complained on her removal from Lewes Gaol to Newgate. The article gives as an example of the more liberal treatment of American prisoners by citing one inmate, a 'Mr Stokes'

– 'his cell has been most handsomely fitted up' with 'a new spring mattress' and the apartment is 'richly carpeted' and hung with fine picture and looks more like a lady's boudoir than a cell.

The article also informs its readers that 'Mr Stokes' spends a leisurely morning, having breakfast and 'perusing the morning papers'. Later in the day he is interviewed and photographed by representatives of newspapers and ends the day with a quiet evening playing cards with other inmates.

Against the act of mercy, the *Brighton Daily News* has not a word to say but it expressed regret 'that conclusive evidence of Miss Edmunds's insanity was not forthcoming at her trial for the delay in making the discovery will certainly bring up a variety of serious matters for speculation in the mind of the public.'

The *Freeman's Journal* for 26th January reported that:

> ...the next criminal, whoever he or she may be, that shall undergo the last penalty of the law, will be unjustly executed, if it be a true maxim that equal justice shall be meted out to all; because Miss Edmunds committed her crime with consummate art, cunning and skill, and after a jury has convicted her and the judge pronounced sentence without holding out hope, she is discovered to be irresponsible for her acts.

On Wednesday, 7th February, the *Derby Mercury* published a letter from 'a medical man' in which he described Christiana as 'that inhuman tigress' who had 'escaped her well-merited doom'. She was, in his opinion, 'a bold, unscrupulous woman, making a deliberate attempt to poison a lady, whose husband she coveted...it is an outrageous scandal upon a noble and enlightened profession to find medical men ready either for the love of infamous notoriety or sordid gain, to falsify their honest convictions by enunciating ridiculous theories, perverting facts, and drawing from them unwarrantable and sophistical [sic] conclusions with the view of misleading and deceiving the lay public.

The *Spectator* offered further criticism of the verdict of insanity in the case of Miss Edmunds:

> Mr Bruce has not only respited the prisoner Christiana Edmunds but

has quashed the decision of the Court which tried her by directing that she be sent to Broadmoor as a criminal lunatic.

The true reason for this interference with justice is – namely, the dislike of the popular journalists to the punishment of death against any persons except Communists; and we have also endeavoured to trace some of the consequences of elevating the children of mad people into an aristocracy privileged to commit crime with impunity.

The official pretexts for the decree are, however, that Baron Martin recommended it – which we do not believe, as the Judge was bitter against the plea set up by the defence; that Sir W Gull thought the convict mad, which may be quite true, and is just as important as anybody else thinking so; and that Dr Orange, superintendent at Broadmoor, thought so, too.

Dr Orange, of course, is a first-class expert but so were the four mad-doctors whose evidence on the trial was rejected. It is, however, useless to criticise the doctors, the real reason for pardon being that a weak man thought the papers would scold him if he hanged a woman of some education and refinement whose father was mad. Had Christiana Edmunds been a servant she would have been hanged without more ado, and we would never have heard a word about her latent 'insanity'.

The article then refers to the case of the Rev. John Selby Watson and ends by saying:

> ...we have a nervous feeling that a very different measure of justice has been dealt out to him and to certain criminals of a lower class, whose reprieve has been steadfastly, we do not say unjustly refused, and we have the greatest possible fear of a suspicion of class-justice gaining ground with the English people.

A letter from William A Guy, M.B., King's College, was published in *The Times* on 26th January, objecting to a statement by Baron Martin that 'a poor person is seldom afflicted with insanity and it is common to raise a defence of that kind when people of means are charged with the commission of crime'.

He goes on to quote from *Criminal Statistics* for the years 1836 to 1867 and points out that 186 homicides during that period were acquitted on the grounds of insanity and another 92 subsequently declared insane. Most of these cases, he argues, were *'men and women of poor or working class'*. He cited a number of well-known cases who had escaped the death penalty on the grounds of insanity before concluding:

> I assert, then, with confidence that it is nothing less than a libel on English justice and fair dealing to insinuate, as many persons of every class among us are doing, that the plea of insanity is to be reckoned among the exclusive luxuries of the rich... I have had to study within the walls of a convict prison every form of insanity, real and feigned: have certified cases as insane about which doubts had been raised before they were sent there; and I have watched more than one case day by day, for weeks together; and I state as the broad result of seven years' experience that the difficulties of coming to a just decision are often so great as to justify to the full all the differences of opinion found to prevail among the learned and experienced physicians who are called to give evidence on this class of cases in our courts of law.
>
> A jury for the fact of killing, a committee of experts, and a written report for the guidance of the Home Secretary – these are the procedures which would secure the result we all aim at, strict justice to rich and poor alike, whether that consists in the more merciful punishment of the gallows, or the more cruel sentence of a living death in a convict prison or lunatic asylum.

The *Tamworth Herald* printed the following article on Saturday, 3rd February 1872:

SIR. W. GULL ON INSANITY

> Referring to the case of Christiana Edmunds in the Presidential address which he delivered at the Clinical Society of London on Friday evening, Sir William Gull said that the study of insanity is part of the study of vital dynamics which is familiar to physicians.
>
> The lawyer and the ordinary observer says "the man is mad" because he has committed an act of overt insanity – a crime, perhaps: but it often happens that in diseases of the brain – in insanity, as in other diseases, the crime is only an indication of the sudden stress which has been laid upon a weak and diseased organ which has long been suffering from latent disease.
>
> When medical men are called upon to state their grounds for believing

that insanity exists in any given case of crime they are commonly expected to produce evidence that the disease had previously manifested itself. It is when the stress is laid upon the weak organ – heart or brain or abdominal organ – that it often supplies for the first time evidence of its insufficiency or of its disease.

This is an everyday experience of physicians in such coarse forms of organic disease as mitral disease of the heart or even some forms of peritonitis. It is the frequent experience of physicians also in cases of insanity. It is sometimes said, when insanity is discovered as the cause of a crime, that it could not have existed because it did not show itself before; it would be more just frequently in such cases to admit that it did exist because it has shown itself. It was sometimes said that an ignorant man was as good a judge of insanity as the most experienced physician, but physicians – at least, life-long students of men – could not admit this.

A rather distressing account, entitled 'The Brighton Poisoning Case' appeared in the *Morning Post* on 5th February 1872:

> The prisoner, Christiana Edmunds, has not yet, it appears, been removed to the Criminal Lunatic Asylum at Broadmoor, but still remains at Lewes Gaol. Since her arrival some rather curious particulars have transpired in regard to her conduct after her conviction. It appears that when she was sent from Newgate [after the trial] in the custody of one of the warders and a matron, she was under the impression that she was going to be taken to Brighton and she remained perfectly quiet until the train turned off the main line at Hayward's Heath to proceed to Lewes, and when she found that this was the case she became very excited and jumped up and exclaimed: "Dr Beard, Dr Beard! He has been the cause of this," and pulled down the window before she could be prevented and attempted to get through it, at the same time exclaiming "that she would throw herself out".
>
> She was, of course, promptly laid hold of and the warder told her that if she conducted herself quietly she would be treated kindly but if she attempted any act of violence he should be compelled to put her under restraint by placing handcuffs on her. This appeared to have some effect; but still during the remainder of the journey she continued to rave about her connection with Dr Beard and expressed her regret that all the facts had not come out at her trial

that she wished to have made public. It seems that after the decision arrived at by the matron jury with regard to the question whether the prisoner was pregnant or not, an intimation was conveyed to her that if she was dissatisfied with that decision, and still persisted in her assertion that she was pregnant, she might, if she pleased, be examined by the surgeon at the gaol at Newgate, if she consented to submit to such an examination and wished it to take place. The prisoner, it appeared, coolly replied: "It is of no use now" and said she would decline to submit to any further examination.

On the 2nd of July, the *Brighton Daily News* announced that,

> ...the prison authorities at Lewes have at last received the Secretary of State's warrant for the removal of Christiana Edmunds to an asylum. The warrant is dated the 27th of June and was received from the Home Office on Saturday, ordering that the prisoner be removed to the Broadmoor Lunatic Asylum, Berks.

Even before Christiana's move to Broadmoor a copious and increasingly exasperated correspondence had begun between Mr Jones, Clerk to the Visiting Justices of Lewes, and the Home Office – the bone of contention being the cost of transporting the prisoner from Lewes Gaol (where she had been housed since her conviction at the Old Bailey) to Broadmoor Asylum. Nor did the matter end there. Although Mrs Edmunds, Christiana's mother, and other members of her family, offered to pay 14 shillings a week towards the cost of her maintenance in Broadmoor, the Home Office insisted that the parish of Brighton should be held responsible.

The *Daily Telegraph,* in May that year, ran an article that highlighted the problem of funding:

> Miss Edmunds, The Murderess – The Mayor of Brighton has uttered an indignant protest at the course taken by the Home Office in the case of Christiana Edmunds. In the first place, the cost of prosecuting this woman for murder was charged upon the town, and secondly, after her conviction, the Government, without communicating with the local authorities, sent down two medical men to inquire whether she was insane and, by their finding, she is to be a life-long charge upon the rate-payers. His Worship characterised the proceedings as one of the grossest pieces of injustice ever perpetrated.

The *Manchester Evening News* joined the debate on Saturday, 7th September, 1872:

CHRISTIANA EDMUNDS

Yesterday the question of an order upon the parish of Brighton for the maintenance of Christiana Edmunds, now an inmate of Broadmoor Lunatic Asylum, was again before the Brighton magistrates. A previous application had been made while the prisoner was confined in Lewes Gaol: but Mr Somers Clarke, solicitor for the parish of Brighton, objected that the prisoner must be removed to Broadmoor before an order could be made. The bench upheld the objection and the prisoner has since been moved by order of the Home Office. Yesterday, therefore, the Town Clerk (Mr David Black), acting on instructions from the Secretary of State, renewed the application. Mr Clarke again took an objection, namely, that the order should be applied against the parish of settlement (Canterbury), not the parish of irremovability (Brighton) and enforced his point by an elaborate argument.

This impasse was not easily resolved and letters continued to fly between the Brighton parochial authority, the redoubtable Mr Jones and the Home Office for several years. Throughout the whole of 1875, numerous letters, increasingly tetchy in tone, were passed between Mr Jones and Dr Orange, Superintendent of Broadmoor, contesting Christiana's maintenance costs and several between the Home Office and Mr Jones referring to an order on the Parish of Brighton to include "all reasonable charges for enquiring into such person's insanity and for conveying her to the Asylum" The costs were listed as: 'Dr Gull's fee £52.10.0. Conveyance of prisoner to Asylum. £3.12.7., together £56.2.7.'

There was even an argument about the cost of Christiana's single rail ticket and the return fares paid by the accompanying warders from Lewes Gaol. Subsequently, the problem landed on the desk of the Under Secretary of State, Mr Liddell, and the correspondence continued with red-tape delaying tactics on both sides. The hard-pressed but stubborn Mr Jones continued to defer responsibility for payment and the correspondence between him and the Home Office and Dr Orange continued throughout the year 1875 and beyond. In March, 1878, according to Home Office files, the matter of Christiana's maintenance at Broadmoor was still in contention - by which time she had been classified as 'A Criminal Pauper Lunatic'.

Christiana, of course, would have been completely unaware of all the bureaucratic wrangling. When she finally arrived at Broadmoor her cheeks were rouged and she was wearing 'a large amount of false hair'. Dr Orange noted that she was 'very vain' though she may have been simply concerned about her appearance and determined to try to maintain her normal standard of dress.

The surgeon at Lewes Gaol who signed her transfer papers seemed unconvinced of her diagnosed insanity though he did classify her as 'delicate of constitution and prone to hysteria'.

It was noted that when her elder brother, William, died whilst she was in Broadmoor she appeared unaffected by the news. Although there was no mention at Christiana's trial of any siblings other than those who had died or were deemed insane, in Mark Stevens's book, *Broadmoor Revealed*,[116] he mentions her elder sister, Mary (married to the Rev. Edward Benjamin Foreman with whom she had four daughters), who helped Christiana by smuggling into the hospital contraband cosmetics, quantities of false hair and items of clothing. This greatly annoyed the Matron in charge of the female wing as she objected to having to waste time repeatedly searching Mary's parcels. Apparently, in 1874, when the Matron found that a cushion sent to Christiana had been stuffed with false hair, she complained to Dr Orange, who, though he couldn't really see this misdemeanour as all that serious, banned the receipt of any more parcels.

In that same year, the authorities at Broadmoor became aware that Christiana was writing to the Rev. Mr Cole, the chaplain at Lewes Gaol with whom she had formed a friendship whilst on remand. The objection was not the correspondence as such but the fact that she was writing to him secretly 'in conformity with her state of mind to prefer mystery and concealment'. The following year her room was searched and 'various concealed items' were found and Dr Orange commented, that 'she deceives for the pure love of deception'.

---

116 In his book *Broadmoor Revealed*, Mark Stevens, senior archivist at the Berkshire Record Office, relates some of the life stories of the more interesting patients, including Christiana Edmunds and the painter, Richard Dadd.

Despite this propensity for subterfuge, Christiana appears to have been 'generally quiet and biddable' and was given access to the Terrace and pleasantly landscaped gardens where trusted patients were allowed to play games of croquet. She was not *that* well-behaved, however, as it was noted in 1876 that 'her delight and amusement seems to be in practising the art of ingeniously tormenting several of the more irritating patients so that she could always complain of their language to her whilst it was difficult to bring any overt act home to herself'.

It was also noted that when her mother visited her she would greet her devoid of make-up in an attempt to look as desolate as possible.

Perhaps for the benefit of the male doctors at Broadmoor, Christiana continued to apply make-up and elaborately style her hair and, in 1877, when she was nearly fifty, it was noted that 'she affects a youthful appearance' and 'her manner and expression evidently lies towards sexual and amatory ideas'. However, for the most part, Christiana showed no obvious signs of insanity; she spent much of her day engaged either in embroidery, painting or etching. These and other occupations, such as playing croquet and dancing, were encouraged by Dr Orange.

In 1880, after eight years at Broadmoor, Christiana wrote the following letter to the Home Office:

> Broadmoor Asylum.
> Oct. 30. 1880.
>
> Sir
>
> I venture to petition for my release from the Broadmoor Asylum I have been eight years in confinement and am very anxious to regain my liberty. I earnestly trust that my conduct has been such as to gain for me the favourable regard of the Superintendent and those over me. I shall feel very grateful if you will kindly consider my petition and grant my release.
>
> I remain Sir Your humble petitioner
> Christianna Edmunds[117]

117 It will be noted that Christiana signed herself *'Christianna'* in this letter. In the Census of 1861 she is listed as *'Christianna'*, which was also her mother's middle name; all contemporary accounts of the case, however, spell her name with just one 'n'.

Christiana's appeal was recorded in this manner:

> Broadmoor Asylum, 30th October, 1880. Christiana Edmunds: Admitted 5th July 1872, from Lewes Gaol. Tried at the Central Criminal Court, 8th January 1872 following the murder of a boy, no relation, by placing poison in sweet meats. Was sentenced to death and afterwards reprieved and declared insane. Is at present tranquil and orderly in her conduct but her mind is unsound. Petitions for her release.

In response, a civil servant, identified only as NM on the docket in which Christiana's letter was retained, contacted Broadmoor on 2nd November, 1880. The asylum staff advised him that she was not fit for release and the following day he recommended that they tell her that the Secretary of State could not comply with her appeal. Godfrey Lushington, at that time the legal Assistant Under-Secretary to the Home Office, endorsed this recommendation on 4th November, 1880, and, on 9th November, a letter was sent to the Superintendent at Broadmoor; it probably contained an official instruction to convey the result of the appeal to Christiana.

The newspaper reporters, who were so prolific with their coverage of the various court proceedings at the time Christiana's crimes became known, soon had more current cases to write about. She did have one champion, however, a gentleman called Herbert M Keene, of Chancery Lane, who wrote the following letter to the *London Evening Standard*:

> TO THE EDITOR OF THE STANDARD
>
> Sir, With the recent discovery that glucose contains poison, perhaps you will afford me space in the columns of *The Standard* to suggest, if not too late, that the evidence on which a criminal verdict was found against Christiana Edmunds should be reviewed. It will be remembered that Christiana Edmunds was found guilty of dropping chocolate creams in the neighbourhood of Brighton which were picked up by children who died.
>
> I understand that the "cream" of this sweetmeat is invariably glucose, and, as it is now known that glucose can contain arsenic, possibly the chocolate creams in question may have been the cause of deaths, but Miss Edmunds may have been innocent of the crimes attributed to

her.[118]

Mr Keene followed this with another letter to the Secretary of State at the Home Office expressing his concern that the glucose manufacturing process might allow 'poisonous matter' into the chocolate. He ended his letter: 'Should you come to the conclusion that a possible mis-carriage of justice has arisen, or if to your mind there should be a "doubt", I conclude my remarks with the full assurance that you will advise Her Most Gracious Majesty the Queen to pardon Miss Edmunds and so restore her to freedom.'

Unfortunately, Mr Keene seemed to have forgotten that it was proved beyond doubt at her trial that Christiana purchased various quantities of poison and no 'innocent' purpose was ever suggested. He wrote to the Home Office again in February, 1901, requesting a reply to his letter but according to a memo 'he appears to be a busybody' and no further action was taken.

There was no mention of Christiana Edmunds in the press as the years passed and, as her family members died, she grew old and alone in Broadmoor. Her mother died in 1893, aged ninety three, and her sister, Mary, in 1898 - and it is not known whether Sydney Cornish Harrington continued to visit her. He may have felt that, after the death of his brother-in-law, William Edmunds, no further contact was strictly necessary.

In 1886, in accordance with the Criminal Lunatics Act of 1884, an annual report was issued in which it stated that Christiana, No.9472, had a good degree of education and was temperate in her habits. The same comments were entered in the year 1904 but her 'bodily health' was described as 'indifferent' and her mental condition 'enfeebled, unfit for discharge'. This assessment was rubber-stamped in 1905 and again in 1906.

According to Mark Stevens in *Broadmoor Revealed*, in 1892, when Dr George Blandford was preparing a new edition of his book,

---

118 Tuesday, 4th December, 1900.

Insanity and Its Treatment, in which he had quoted Dr Orange's original report on Christiana, he contacted Dr Orange's successor, Dr Nicolson, to ask if he had seen any change in her during her time at Broadmoor. 'Dr Nicolson replied that he had seen no change in Edmunds during the fifteen and a half years that he had known her'.

More detailed records show that she suffered a bad bout of influenza in 1900 and the following year her sight was failing; by 1906, she could barely walk. As she lay in the Infirmary shortly before the 1906 Christmas Ball she was heard to ask another patient if her eyebrows looked all right. When assured that they did, she was said to have remarked:

> I think I am improving. I hope I shall be better in a fortnight. If so, I shall astonish them: I shall get up and dance – I was a Venus before and I shall be a Venus again!

Did Christiana make it to the Christmas Ball that year, heavily made-up and with her hair, false or otherwise, elaborately styled? And did she get up and dance to impress the less flamboyant patients and the male members of staff? Christiana Edmunds died nine months later on 19th September, 1907. She was seventy-eight years old and the cause of death was recorded as Senile Debility. Without relatives to request otherwise she was probably buried in the cemetery at Broadmoor.

One of the uncertainties of this unusual case remains - did Dr Beard reciprocate Christiana's infatuation? He did use the word 'intimacy' when questioned in court and then tried to change it to 'friendship', although the term 'intimate' in those days didn't have the same suggestion of a sexual relationship as it does today. Did their 'friendship' begin as a mild flirtation only to spiral out of control and totally consume Christiana during their anatomical drawing sessions in the billiard room, or did she simply misread the doctor's interest in her? Was he, perhaps, flattered by the attention at a time when he was possibly feeling marginalised by his wife, Emily, who, not only had to perform her duties as a doctor's wife, but also to manage a household containing four young children - the youngest was two years old at the time – and five live-in servants. She was described as being *'extremely unwell'* in court and in Christiana's letter to Dr Beard she refers to her as *La Sposa* and describes seeing her in the street looking *'thin and ill'*.

The tone of the letter is over-familiar, inappropriately commenting on the doctor's wife looking rather less than attractive - by implication, as compared to Christiana, fashionably dressed and a lady of leisure, free to flirt and indulge in romantic fantasies.

Was Christiana deluding herself - did she actually imagine she was pregnant by Dr Beard or was this simply used as a futile defence ploy to defer execution? If she knew that it was quite impossible for her to be pregnant - she had been in custody for five months prior to the trial - why did she agree to such a desperate tactic? She must have known that by making such an announcement she was insinuating that her intimacy with the doctor had been physical in the fullest sense. She was also exposing herself to the shame that such an announcement would engender, not only for her and her family, but also for Dr Beard and his wife.

Her emotional prostration when Dr Ryley and the matrons pronounced her 'not pregnant' might indicate that she did, in fact, believe or hope that she was carrying the doctor's child.

At the time of her obsession with Dr Beard, Christiana was forty-three years old and the prospect of marriage and motherhood unlikely. Many doctors at the time prescribed to the popular catch-all view that sexual frustration could lead to a condition later studied by Dr Freud and others - that of 'female hysteria' - which some thought could lead to insanity. As marriage and the bearing of children were considered the prime function of women, elective female celibacy was deemed unnatural, except for women with a religious calling. Yet it seems clear that Christiana's unmarried state was not from choice and her barren spinsterhood must have contrasted cruelly with the doctor's lively household of a wife and a clutch of healthy children. It seems likely that Christiana was, indeed, subject to a condition loosely termed 'female hysteria', the symptoms of which she had suffered from previously and subsequently heightened by her infatuation with Dr Beard. At the time of her poisoning spree she was approaching middle age and the onset of the menopause with its incumbent hormonal imbalance and psychological trauma. This was even suggested by Baron Martin in his letter to the Home Secretary the day after her conviction, rather an unusually sensitive observation for a Victorian High Court judge to make. It was a period in her life that her mother admitted to dreading, partly on these grounds but also, perhaps, because Christiana's father had succumbed to mania at a similar age.

As a reasonably attractive and well-educated woman, Christiana must have had one or two suitors in her younger days; but did they detect something not quite right about her, or did they know of her family history? Her only prospect was to continue living with her elderly and emotionally fragile mother. Though sufficiently well-off not to need employment she was left with little else to do but read, attend to her embroidery, walk the Promenade, make social calls for afternoon tea and regularly attend church.

Clearly, all the doctors who examined Christiana to assess her state of mind conceded that she was insane and therefore she fulfilled the criteria for applying M'Naghten's Law to her case - that she didn't know that what she was doing was wrong and therefore could not be held responsible for her crimes. Yet this was a woman who was in control of her mind and actions well enough to pursue her poisoning campaign in a contrived and coldly calculating way, enjoying the secrecy and deceit and revelling in the knowledge that she was, for quite a while, successfully outwitting the police. It seems unlikely that she ever considered the lives she was endangering and, though tormented by her own emotional pain, she gave no thought to the agonising death suffered by little Sidney Barker when she went about distributing the poisoned sweets.

The cruelty in her nature was further manifest when she chose - if she was telling the truth when she told Mr Garrett she needed the poison for that purpose - to practise her poisoner's craft on stray cats and a much-loved pet dog, thereby condemning them to an excruciatingly painful death.

One of the warders at Lewes Gaol, however, saw no obvious signs of insanity and Dr Nicolson, who succeeded Dr Orange as Superintendent of Broadmoor, said that she *'confessed'* and *'showed remorse'*, which must indicate an understanding of her crimes. It is also revealing that she told Dr Wood at the beginning of her trial that she would prefer to be found guilty than to be classified as insane.

In addition to all the insanity prevalent in the immediate members of the Edmunds family - father, brother, Arthur, sister Louisa Agnes and, though not committed, the elder brother, William, both Christiana's grandfathers were of unsound mind and in consequence her whole life must have been blighted by the knowledge of all the insanity in the family. She may have been continually reminded of it whenever she misbehaved or showed any signs of eccentricity. Indeed, when she was distraught over Dr Beard's rejection her mother chided her for saying that 'she would go mad' and reminded her that she ought to choose her words more carefully on account of her father's insanity.

With so many advances in psychiatry a woman presenting with similar symptoms today would probably be briefly hospitalised, given intensive therapy or full analysis and eventually released into the community on long-term medication and supervision. Had she been acquitted, however, her life would have been intolerable for she would never have escaped all the shame and recrimination. By being sent to Broadmoor she was, in fact, escaping a rather mundane and unfulfilling life as a spinster and an unstable one at that - the subject of endless gossip and innuendo, as her infatuation with Dr Beard would have remained a source of ribaldry and derision.

As for Dr Beard, it was rumoured that he and his family went to live in Scotland after the trial to escape from the scandal surrounding his involvement in the Christiana Edmunds case. This was not so; Dr Beard continued as a medical practitioner in Grand Parade, Brighton, until 1879. For the next three years he was employed as a Medical Inspector for the Local Government Board, based in Lancashire.

He was back in Brighton in 1887, where, once more, he worked as a medical practitioner. From the latter part of 1891 to 1907, the Beard family were living in London's Shepherd's Bush. At this time the household consisted of Dr and Emily Beard, both now seventy-three years old, their son, Arthur, aged thirty-eight, and their daughter, Edith, aged thirty-four. There was no mention of the other three siblings, Hugh, Frank and Emily Elizabeth. By 1911, Charles and Emily Beard, now aged eighty-three, were living at St Matthew's Vicarage, Oakley Square, in North London, where their eldest son, the Reverend Hugh Spencer Beard, was the resident vicar. Emily Beard died in 1912, aged eighty-four, and, before Charles Beard died on 23rd December, 1916, aged eighty-nine, he had been living at the Holloway Sanatorium, referred to as a Lunatic Asylum, in Virginia Water, Surrey.[119]

As for Christiana, life at Broadmoor, at least in the early years, was probably abhorrent to her although she was reported to spend her days doing her embroidery and etching and, as a 'compliant' patient, she would have been allowed to walk freely in the terraced gardens and play croquet with the other patients. This afforded her a safe environment, shielding her from the pressures of life and the ridicule of her former friends and neighbours. One can only speculate whether her quiet and compliant behaviour was a sign of resignation or the result of a medically induced condition. Medicated or not, she obviously enjoyed inventing devious little

---

119 Emily Beard was described as feeble-minded in the few years before her death and it seems evident that Charles Beard was similarly afflicted by the end of his life. But, at least in Dr Beard's case, the label 'Lunatic Asylum' may be misleading. Both parties were long-lived and, not surprisingly, may have developed related mental conditions which would be diagnosed today as Alzheimer's disease or senile dementia.

schemes for hoodwinking the hospital staff – like persuading her sister to smuggle in a regular supply of false hair and make-up - to alleviate the grinding boredom of an institutionalised existence. She was also found to be indulging in a covert correspondence with the Rev. Thomas Cole, the chaplain at Lewes Gaol, perhaps, in her deluded state, seeing him as a substitute for Dr Beard. And what better way to liven things up than by teasing some of the more volatile inmates until they retaliated, thus giving her the chance to affect sanctimonious umbrage and complain to staff about their offensive language?

Planning and carrying out these petty ploys and scams must have kept her amused, helping to relieve the monotony of her life and perhaps deflect a little of the despair and despondency engendered by her terminal incarceration.

Selected Bibliography and Resources

Contemporary Sources

A Genuine and Full Account of the Parricide committed by Mary Blandy (Oxford, 1751), British Library.

A New and Complete Collection of the most remarkable Trials for Adultery, etc (London, 1780).

Authentic particulars of the life of James Greenacre and Sarah Gale: and their extraordinary trial for the wilful murder of Mrs. Hannah Brown (London, c. 1837), Harvard Law School Library.

Awful Confession of Greenacre to the Murder of Hannah Brown (London, c. 1837), State Library of New South Wales.

Capt. Cranstoun's Account of the Poisoning of the Late Mr. Francis Blandy (London, 1752), British Library.

Genuine Letters That Pass'd Between Miss. Blandy and Miss. Jeffries, Before and After Conviction (London, 1752), Harvard Law School Library.

Miss Mary Blandy's Own Account of the Affair between her and Mr Cranstoun (London, 1752), British Library.

The Female Parricide. Being a circumstantial relation of the cruel poisoning of Francis Blandy, gent...by his only daughter, Mary Blandy, etc (London?, 1752), National Library of Scotland.

The Genuine Lives of Capt. Cranstoun and Miss Mary Blandy (London, 1753), British Library.

The Genuine Trial of John Swan, and Elizabeth Jeffreys, spinster, for the murder of her late uncle Mr. Joseph Jeffreys, etc (Dublin, 1752), Huntington Library.

Selected Bibliography

The only true and authentic trial of John Swan and Miss. Elizabeth Jeffreys, etc (London, 1752), Bodleian Library, Oxford.

The Trial of Katharine Nairn and Patrick Ogilvie For the Crimes of Incest and Murder (London, 1765), Harvard Law School Library.

The Tryal of Mary Blandy (London, 1752), British Library.

Secondary Sources

D'Enno, D. *Foul Deeds & Suspicious Deaths Around Brighton* (Wharncliffe Books, 2004, 2008)

Flanders, J. *The Invention of Murder* (HarperPress, 2011)

Gaute, J. H. H. and R. Odell, *Murder 'Whatdunit'* (Harrap, 1982)

Goodman, J. (ed.) *The Christmas Murders* (Penguin, 1989)

Hindley, C. *The History of the Catnach Press* (London, 1886)

Hughes, R. *The Fatal Shore* (Collins Harvill, 1987)

Jackson, S. *Death by Chocolate* (Fonthill Media, 2012)

Knies, E. A. (ed.), *Tennyson at Aldworth* (Ohio Univ. Press, 1984)

Nash, J. R. *Look for the Woman* (Evans and Company, 1981)

Roughead, W. (ed.), *Trial of Katharine Nairn* (William Hodge, 1926)

Roughead, W. (ed.), *Trial of Mary Blandy* (William Hodge, 1914)

Stevens, M. *Broadmoor Revealed* (Pen and Sword, 2013)

Whittington-Egan, R. and M. Whittington-Egan, *The Bedside Book of Murder* (David & Charles, 1988)

Archival Collections

Bodleian Library, Oxford

British Library Newspaper Archive (references for particular contemporary newspapers are included in the text)

Harvard Law School Library

Huntington Library

Selected Bibliography

National Archives. London:

> The Christiana Edmunds case – files HO/45/9297/9472
> The Katharine Nairn case – files SP 54 24
> The Mary Blandy case – files SP 54 41, TS 11 864 2948

National Archives: New South Wales

National Library of Scotland

Newgate Calendar

Index

Adams, Mary, 80
Addington, Dr Anthony: calls on Mrs Blandy, 6; attends Mr Blandy, 15, 25–6; analyses sediment and powder, 17; post-mortem on Mr Blandy, 18; evidence at inquest, 19, 21; evidence at trial, 25–7; warns servants, 70
Addington, Henry, 1st Viscount Sidmouth, 6n
Adolphus, Mr, 168, 180, 183, 184
Agate, Emily, 233, 239
Ambler, Mr, 22
America: easy prison life, 286–7
anatomization: of felons, 40–1, 136, 142, 196n
Andrews, Frances, 176–7, 195
Angel (ale-house), Henley Bridge, 18, 34, 74
Armstrong, Dr Henry, 267
Arnold, Sarah, 83–4
arsenic: accidental poisoning by, 151; in glucose, 295–6; poisoning symptoms, 127, 128; restrictions on sale, 107n, 236n; solubility, 134; tests for, 17n, 224n
Aston, Mr, 22

baby-farmers, 209
Baker, Emily Selina, 262–3
Baker, Mrs Harriet, 263
Baker, Joseph, 87
Bale, Mary Ann, 174n
Balfour, Sheriff James, 130–1
Ballantine, Serjeant William, 256–7, 263, 265, 269
Banks, Mary, 32–3

Barker, Albert: death of son, 223; receives anonymous letters, 225, 247–9; evidence at trial, 257
Barker, Sidney: poisoned, 223, 247, 249–50; inquest, 223–5, 232–3, 247
Barrington, Mr, 22
Bartlett, Adelaide, 106n
Bateman, Mr (of Walthamstow), 96
Bathurst, Henry, 22, 23–4, 34–5
Beard, Dr Charles: career, 221n; relationship with Christiana Edmunds, 221–3, 228, 234–5, 253, 297–8; goes to police, 229; evidence at magistrates' court, 234–5, 252–3; evidence at trial, 263–4; signs petition for mercy, 284; later years and death, 301
Beard, Mrs Emily: domestic duties and ill-health, 298; poisoned, 222, 234; receives poisoned parcel, 228, 233, 239; evidence at magistrates' court, 233–4, 253; signs petition for mercy, 284; later years and death, 301
Beauclerk, Lord George, 111
Bell (public house), Henley, 6, 74
Bertie, Mr, 78
Binfield, Elizabeth ('Betty'): invited to Scotland by Mary Blandy, 12; notices sediment in gruel pan, 13, 28; salvages arsenic from fire, 15; Mary attempts to bribe, 17; evidence at inquest, 19, 21, 32; characterised as hostile witness, 32
Birtwhistle, Dr, 155, 181–2
Black, David, 244, 259, 261–2, 292

Index

Blaker, Dr Nathaniel, 222, 228; evidence at magistrates' court, 243, 245–6

Blanchard, Mrs, 173–4

Blandford, Dr George: *Insanity and Its Treatment*, 296–7

Blandy, Mr (Mary's uncle), 16

Blandy, Mrs Anne (née Stevens; Mary's mother): described, 2; charmed by Cranstoun, 4; falls ill at Turville Court, 5; seeks medical advice in London, 5; borrows money from Cranstoun, 6; final illness and death, 6

Blandy, Francis (Mary's father): described, 2; exaggerates Mary's dowry, 2–3; welcomes Cranstoun into family home, 4; antipathy toward Cranstoun, 5, 7; altercation in the Strand, 5; tea laced with 'love-powder', 7–8; poisoned, 9, 12; learns of Mary's treachery, 14–15, 16; seen by Dr Addington, 15, 25–6; last conversation with Mary, 16–17; death, 17; post-mortem, 18; coroner's inquest, 19, 21; wealth at death, 20; assessment of character, 67–8

BLANDY, MARY: family background, 2; appearance and character, 2; attracts suitors, 2–3; meets Captain Cranstoun, 3; affair with Cranstoun, 4, 5–7; convinced 'love-powders' beneficial, 7–8, 9, 12n; trusting and gullible, 8, 66; accounts of supernatural manifestations, 8, 27, 45, 53, 61; curses father, 21, 30; poisons father, 9, 12–13; exchanges letters with Cranstoun, 9–12, 62n; treachery discovered, 14–15; destroys evidence, 15, 19; warned by Dr Addington, 15; letter to Cranstoun intercepted, 15–16; begs father's forgiveness, 16–17; confined to room, 17–18; flees and apprehended, 18–19, 31, 34; taken to gaol at Oxford Castle, 19–20; fettered, 20, 31, 69; newspaper reports, 21, 34, 36; indicted by Grand Jury, 21; tried for murder (*see* Blandy trial); found guilty and sentenced to death, 39–40; imprisoned at Oxford Castle, 40–1; poem to Cranstoun, 41–2; her account of affair, 42–6, 51–3, 72–3; Cranstoun's account, 66; corresponds with Elizabeth Jeffries, 46–61; final days, 61–3; 'dying declaration', 61–2; execution, 63–5; interment, 64; grave, 65; forfeitures, 39n, 73; assessment, 67–72; continuing fascination of case, 73–4; spectral phenomena associated with, 74

Blandy House, Henley, 2, 74

Blandy trial: held at Oxford Assizes, 21–2; public attendance, 22; bench and legal teams, 22; indictment, 22–3; Mary's appearance and demeanour in court, 23; plea, 23; opening speeches for prosecution, 23–5; evidence for the prosecution, 25–30; Mary's address to jury, 30–2; evidence for the defence, 32–4; motion to call another defence witness refused, 34; closing speech for prosecution, 34–5; judge's summing up, 35–8; verdict, 38–9; sentence, 39–40

Bleakley, Horace, 42

Bodkin, William, 168, 169, 173, 183

Bond, Robert, 154–5

Booth, William, 237–8

Boswell, Alexander, 120n

Boys, Mrs Elizabeth, 228, 245, 277n, 284

Bradbury, Samuel, 229, 242, 246–7

Bravo, Charles, 275n

Brazenor, Robert, 243

Bremner, James, 146

Bridewell Prison and Hospital, Clerkenwell, 81, 159n

Brighton, 220–1, 291–2

Brighton Daily News, 232–3, 287, 291

Brighton Police Court, 230, 231

Bristol Mercury, 242

British Medical Journal, 276

Broadmoor, 291, 292, 293–5, 296–7, 301–2

Brooks, George, 251, 260–1

Index

Brown, Mrs (nurse to Elizabeth Jeffries), 95n, 98–9
Brown, Hannah: appearance, 172, 174; background, 218–19; sober and industrious habits, 171, 172, 219; intended marriage to James Greenacre, 156–7, 170–1, 180; last known movements, 172–3; murdered by Greenacre, 192–3; body parts discovered, 154–5, 156, 169–70; autopsies, 155–6, 181–3; inquest and burial, 155; remains identified, 156, 171; blood-stained shawl recovered, 180; Greenacre's first statement claiming accidental death, 160–1, 175; Greenacre admits killing, 192–4; murder weapons found, 216
Brown, Sergeant Michael Callow, 181
Brownrigg, Elizabeth, 176n
Bruce, Henry, 273, 275, 281–2, 284, 287–8
Bucket's Hill, Epping Forest, 84, 98
Buckle, Mrs, 86, 89
Buckle, Edward, 79–80
Bucks Herald, 196–7, 200
Burn, Major John (Christiana Edmunds' grandfather), 266
Byles, Mr Justice, 279n
Bywaters, Frank, 78n

Calais, 145, 146
Caledonian Mercury, 95n, 96n, 137
Campbell, Lieut. George, 107, 126
Campbell, Sheriff George, 128, 134–5
Campbell, Katharine, 112–14, 119, 122–3, 136
Canterbury Villas, Edgware Road, 154–5
Capel, Miss (Cranstoun's mistress), 8, 66
Carnegie, Dr James, 107, 135; evidence at trial, 126
Carpenter's Buildings (No. 6), Camberwell, 175–7, 197, 199
Casbolt, Frances, 89n
Catnach, James, 204–5
Cato Street Conspiracy (1820), 196n, 205

Caulthrup, Benjamin, 262
Cawley, Thomas, 33
Central Criminal Court *see* Old Bailey
Central Criminal Court Act (1856), 254
Champion (newspaper), 199–200
Chelmsford Chronicle, 281–2
Chelmsford Gaol, 78, 91, 94–5
Clark, Anne: co-habits with Alexander Ogilvie, 105; arrives at Eastmiln, 105; reputation, 105, 114, 120; spies on Patrick and Katharine, 106–7; her suspicions, 108–9; dismissed from Eastmiln, 109; presents herself as prosecution witness, 110; segregation from other witnesses, 110–11, 122–3, 136; admissibility as witness, 114–15; evidence at trial, 115–20; assessment, 150–1
Clark, Eliza Love, 276
Clarke, Richard, 86
Clarke, Somers, 292
Clarkson, Mr, 168, 169, 172
Clerkenwell Prison, 158, 160
Clifton, Mr, 83, 89–90
Clifton, Mrs Anne, 83, 90
Clissold, Thomas, 177
Cole, Harriet Elizabeth, 239–40, 262
Cole, Rev. Thomas Henry, 267, 293, 302
Coleridge, Mr Justice, 168
Coltman, Mr Justice, 168
common purpose (legal doctrine), 78n
Cooper, Gillingham, 39n, 73
Corney, Elizabeth, 172–3
Cornhill Magazine, 73
Cotton, Rev. Horace, 195 & n, 200, 203, 205, 211
Cox, Mr, 78
Cox, Jane, 150
Cranstoun, Lady (*née* Kerr; William's mother), 3n, 7, 9, 10, 45
Cranstoun, Lord (William's brother), 65, 67
CRANSTOUN, CAPTAIN WILLIAM: appearance and character, 1–2, 3; meets Mary Blandy, 3; begins affair

309

Index

with Mary, 4, 5–7; marriage to Anne Murray, 4; financial position, 6–7; puts 'love-powder' in Mr Blandy's tea, 7–8; complains of supernatural manifestations, 8; womanising, 8, 66; leaves Henley for Scotland, 9; exchanges letters with Mary, 9–12; sends powder to Mary, 9–10; warrant for arrest, 20; execrated at Blandy trial, 24–5; escapes to France, 65–6; his account of affair, 66; Mary's account, 42–6, 51–3; illness and death, 66–7; last will and effects, 67; assessment, 68–71
Criminal Lunatics Act (1884), 296
Cullen, Dr (of Edinburgh), 135
Curtis, William, 228, 240

Daily Gazette for Middlesbrough, 230–1
Daily Telegraph, 279–81, 284–5, 291
Dalrymple, Sir David, 114
Davies, William, 88–9
Davis, Evan, 170–1
Davis, Mrs Hannah, 171–2, 180
Davis, Hannah, Jr, 180
Davis, Mary, 18, 34, 37
Dean, Mrs (friend of Blandy family), 19–20
death sentence, 40 & n, 191
Derby Mercury, 20, 21, 70, 72, 77–8, 94–5, 287
Diaper, Elizabeth, 86–8
Diaper, John, 87
Dickson, Patrick, 107, 126–7
Dillon, Susan, 174–5, 176, 195
Dow, Margaret, 137, 147, 149
Dundas, Henry, 114

Eastmiln, Forfar, 104, 119–20, 128, 143, 147–8
Edinburgh Castle, 110–11
Edinburgh Courant, 137
Edinburgh Weekly Journal, 137
Edmonds, Mr, 176, 195
Edmunds, Ann (Christiana's mother): character, 222; evidence at trial, 265–6; petitions for daughter's reprieve, 277; Broadmoor costs, 291; visits Christiana in Broadmoor, 294; death, 296
Edmunds, Arthur Burn (Christiana's brother), 266, 267, 278
EDMUNDS, CHRISTIANA: family history of insanity, 264, 265–7, 277–8, 300; paralysis, 266; relationship with Dr Beard, 221–3, 228, 234–5, 253, 297–8; letters to Dr Beard, 225–7, 234; poisons Emily Beard, 222, 234; contaminates chocolate creams, 247, 250–2, 261; procures strychnine, 235–7, 241; poisoning campaign, 240, 252, 262–3; poisons dog at Gloucester Place, 107n, 242, 243; poisons Sidney Barker, 223, 247, 249–50; evidence at Sidney Barker inquest, 224, 232–3; vendetta against Mr Maynard, 224–5, 232–3, 248–9; letters to Albert Barker, 225, 247–9; as 'Dorothea', 227n; obtains Poison Register, 237, 239; procures arsenic, 237–8, 242, 246–7; stays at Margate, 241; sends out poisoned parcels, 228–9, 233, 238, 239, 240, 244–6; questioned by Inspector Gibbs, 228–9; arrested and charged, 230, 238–9; in Lewes Gaol, 267, 278–9; magistrates' hearing, 230, 231, 233–53; appearance and demeanour in court, 231; additional charges, 242; committed for trial, 253; vilified, 254; transferred to Newgate from Lewes, 254; in Newgate, 254–5, 267–8, 276, 278, 279; waxwork effigy, 255n; trial (*see* Edmunds trial); petitions for reprieve, 273–9, 283–4; examined by Gull and Orange, 275, 281; press debate on reprieve issue, 279–81, 282–3, 284–6, 287–8; sentence commuted, 281–2; moved to Lewes Gaol, 290–1; costs and funding squabble, 291–3; at Broadmoor, 293–5, 296–7, 301–2; smuggles

310

Index

contraband, 293; petitions for release, 294–5; as Venus of Broadmoor, 297; failing health and death, 297; vanity, 266, 293, 294, 297; insanity, 267–9, 275, 276, 278–9, 295; female hysteria, 293, 298–9; menopause, 299; cruelty and heartlessness, 299–300; assessment, 297–300, 301–2

Edmunds, Louisa Agnes (Christiana's sister), 278

Edmunds, Mary (*later* Foreman; Christiana's sister), 293, 296

Edmunds, William (Christiana's brother), 277, 293

Edmunds, William (Christiana's father), 223n, 265, 266–7, 277

Edmunds trial: held at Old Bailey, 254; Christiana's appearance and demeanour in court, 231–2, 255–6, 271; bench and legal teams, 256; opening speech for the prosecution, 256–7; evidence for the prosecution, 257–64; judge inspects chocolate cream, 264; opening speech for the defence, 264–5; insanity defence, 265–9; Christiana breaks down in court, 266; reply by the prosecution, 269; judge's summing up, 269; verdict and sentence, 269–72; pleads pregnancy, 272; examined by jury of matrons, 272–3, 276, 290–1

Ellerthorn, Sarah, 180

Elliot, Sir Gilbert (Lord Justice-Clerk), 111, 139–40

Emmet, Ann, 9, 13, 36, 70

Empire, The (newspaper), 214–16

Epping Forest, 84, 96, 97–8

Evening Telegraph, 73–4

Evershed, Charles Lambert, 278

executions, 205n

Fay, John, 212

Fellows, William, 89n

Feltham, Inspector George, 179–80, 198, 203

Fenning, Eliza, 68n, 195n

Ferguson, Elizabeth, 134

Ferguson, Fergus, 117

Fisher, Richard, 19, 30, 37

Forbes, Dr Thomas, 83, 89

Ford, Mr, 22, 34

Foreman, Rev. Edward Benjamin, 293

Foster, Sir Michael, 78

France: Cranstoun escapes to, 65, 66; Katharine Nairn flees to, 144–5, 146

Frazer, James, 113

Freeman, John, 184

Freeman's Journal, 157, 287

Friend, Adelaide Ann, 241

Froster, William and Anne, 122

Gale, George: parentage, 197, 217; as infant, 157, 160, 175, 177, 178, 204; whereabouts unknown, 212, 216n

GALE, SARAH: background, 217; birth of son George, 197; relationship with Greenacre, 210, 218; birth and disappearance of second child, 159, 197–8, 209; seen at Carpenter's Buildings around time of murder, 175–7; cleans up crime scene, 176, 195; lodges at the Wignells, 178; pawns property belonging to Hannah Brown, 179; arrested and taken into custody, 157, 179–80; appearance at court, 157, 158–9; statement to magistrates, 162; committed for trial, 162; trial (*see* Greenacre trial); Greenacre exonerates, 193–5; in Newgate, 162, 199, 211; letter from Greenacre, 203–4; transportation to New South Wales, 211–12; described in later life, 212; life in Australia, 212–13, 217, 218; reported death in 1858, 213–16

Gall, John, 81, 85

Gallant, Anthony, 84

Gallant, Elizabeth, 86

Garrett, Isaac: sells poison to Christiana Edmunds, 229, 235–7; lends Poison Register, 237; goes to police, 238; poisoned, 228;

311

Index

evidence at magistrates' court, 235–8; evidence at trial, 257–8; signs petition for mercy, 284
Gascoyne, Mr, 78
Gay, Maria, 174
Gay, William (Hannah Brown's brother): identifies remains, 156; evidence at trial, 173–4; applies for reward, 199–200
Gentleman's Magazine, 144–5
Genuine and Impartial Account of the Life of Miss M. Blandy, A (pamphlet), 61–4
George III, King, 139
Gibbs, Detective Inspector William: investigates Brighton poisonings, 225, 229; questions Christiana Edmunds, 228–9; takes evidence for analysis, 224, 243, 250; makes arrest, 230; evidence at magistrates' court, 238–9; evidence at trial, 243, 263
Gilloch, John, 111–12
Girdwood, Dr Gilbert Finley, 155–6, 182–3
Glaisyer, Thomas, 244, 259
Glaisyer and Kemp (Brighton chemists), 236–8
Glass, Catharine, 171
Gloucester Place (No. 16), Brighton, 221, 228–9, 238–9, 241–2
Goodman, Jonathan (ed.): *The Christmas Murders*, 185–6, 210n
Gower, Sir Samuel, 81, 91
Grabham, Dr George, 267
Grafton, Augustus Fitzroy, 3rd Duke of, 139, 141
Grand Parade (No. 64), Brighton, 221
Grassmarket, Edinburgh, 142
Gray, Robert, 113
Green Man (public house), Walthamstow, 81
Green Man and Bell (public house), Whitechapel, 81, 85
GREENACRE, JAMES: background, 163–5; possible involvement in Cato Street plot, 196; 'snake oil salesman', 198–9; relationship with Sarah Gale, 210, 218; suspected of infanticide, 159, 197–8, 209; intended marriage to Hannah Brown, 156–7, 170–1, 180; calls off marriage, 172, 173–4; murders Hannah Brown, 192; dismembers body and conceals remains, 181, 192–3; actions after murder, 177, 178, 193–4; his new invented washing-machine, 167, 206 & n; seeks fourth wife, 206–8; arrested and taken into custody, 157, 179–80; attempts suicide, 157–8, 181; appearance at court, 157, 158–9; statement at preliminary hearing, 160–1; committed for trial, 162; in Newgate, 162; issues press statement, 162–3; writes autobiographical account, 163–6; condemns press coverage of case, 165; financial situation, 165–6; writes to his family, 166–7; trial (*see* Greenacre trial); in Newgate awaiting execution, 191–2, 195–6, 199, 200, 203–5; confession, 192–5; offers body for anatomization, 196; reward issue, 199–200; execution date fixed, 200; complains of misrepresentation, 203; last letters from prison, 200–3, 204; final hours, 203, 204; execution, 204–5; broadsides on, 204–5; buried in prison grounds, 205; notoriety, 208, 210n, 217; assessment, 208–11
Greenacre, W., 166–7
Greenacre trial: public interest and attendance, 167–8; bench and legal teams, 168; arraignment and pleas, 168; opening speech for the prosecution, 168–9; evidence for the prosecution, 169–83; opening speech for the defence, 183–4; evidence for the defence, 184; judge's summing up, 184–5; verdict, 185–6; Greenacre addresses court, 186–7; condemnation and sentence, 187–91
Griffith, Rev. (of Chelmsford Gaol),

96–7
Griffiths, Catherine, 89
Gull, Sir William, 275 & n, 281–2, 292; on insanity, 289–90
Gunnell, Susan: maidservant, 70; humours Mary Blandy over ghosts, 45; life savings, 66; falls ill after drinking Mr Blandy's tea, 9; observes Mary, 12; her suspicions, 13–14; salvages arsenic from fire, 15; evidence at inquest, 19; evidence at trial, 28–30
Guy, William, 261
Guy, William A, 288–9

Halliwell, William Henry, 252, 262
Hareby, Mr (Walworth surgeon), 197
Harman, Robert, 17, 19, 28, 30
Harrington, Sydney Cornish, 264n, 277–9, 296
Harvey, Mr, 78
Hatsell, Mr, 78
Hayes, Mr, 22
Hayes, Catherine, 156n
Hayward, Serjeant, 22, 24–5
Headlands, Henrietta, 175–6
Helsey, Emma, 244–5, 284n
Henry Wellesley (convict ship), 211, 212
Hereford Times, 208
Herne, Edward, 18, 19, 21; evidence at trial, 33
Higgins (or Dickens), Ezekiel, 169
Higgins, Thomas, 177
Hindley, Charles, 93n; *The History of the Catnach Press*, 204–5
Hobler, Mr (solicitor), 203
Hope, Matilda, 245
Humphrey, Dr Frederick, 223
hysteria, 298–9

Illustrated Police News, 252, 255–6
incest, 110n, 152
infanticide, 159, 197–8, 209
insanity defence, 288–9

Jack, Thomas, 134
James, Anne, 32
JEFFRIES, ELIZABETH: birth and early childhood, 75; sexually abused by uncle, 60, 76, 100, 101–2; licentious and wanton ways, 89, 100–1, 102; relations with John Swan, 76, 79; plots murder of uncle, 76–7, 80, 82, 84; intercedes on behalf of Swan and Matthews, 81, 85; actions on night of murder, 79–80, 82, 83–4, 93–4; arrested, 77; committed to Chelmsford Gaol, 78; corresponds with Mary Blandy, 46–61, 75, 94; trial (*see* Jeffries trial); confession, 93–4; removed from prison to private apartment, 94; her coffin, 94–5; execution, 95–9; interred, 98; estate and forfeitures, 39n, 73, 94n; assessment, 99–103
Jeffries, Joseph: adopts and raises Elizabeth, 75, 100; sexual abuse allegations, 60, 76, 100, 101–2; peephole into her bedroom, 83; threatens to disinherit, 100–1; relations with John Swan, 88, 89–90; entertains guests, 83; shot, 77, 79–80, 83–4; examined by doctors, 84; his will, 84; estate and bequests, 99
Jeffries trial: bench and legal teams, 78; charges, 78; Elizabeth's appearance and demeanour in court, 91, 92–3; opening speech for prosecution, 78–9; evidence for the prosecution, 79–81, 82–6; evidence for the defence, 86–91; judge's summing up and verdict, 91
Johnson's Lock, Regent's Canal, 155, 169–70
Jonas, Edmund, 255
Jones, Mr (Lewes justices' clerk), 291, 292
Judgement of Death Act (1823), 40n
jury of matrons, 136–7, 143, 272–3, 276

Keene, Herbert M, 295–6
Kerr, Lady Jane *see* Cranstoun, Lady
Kerr, Lord Mark (William Cranstoun's uncle), 3

Index

Ketch, John 'Jack', 98n
Knight, Margaret, 233, 239
Knowler, Mr, 78
Knowles, Joseph, 179

Lacy, Mr, 78
Ladyard, Nathaniel, 89n
Lamar, John, 111
Lamb, Charles: defends at Edmunds trial, 230, 242, 247, 252, 253; petitions for reprieve, 273, 283–4
Lane, Mr and Mrs (of Henley), 18, 30, 34
Lane, James Hunter, 183
Leeds Times, 242
Legge, Heneage, 22, 35–8, 39–40
Letheby, Dr Henry, 224, 226, 232, 247, 257, 263
Lewes Crown Court, 254
Lewes Gaol, 254, 267, 278–9, 286, 290, 291, 300
Lewis, Dr William, 17, 18, 19, 21; evidence at trial, 26–7
Lindsay, Alexander, 123–4, 131–2
Littleton, Robert: posts mail for Mary Blandy, 10; hears Francis Blandy complain of poisoning, 14–15; intercepts letter, 15–16; evidence at inquest, 19, 21; evidence at trial, 30
Lloyd's Weekly, 214
Lockhart, Alexander, 110, 112–13, 135–6, 151
London Daily News, 231–2
London Globe, 270–3
London Magazine, The, 66–7, 70n
London Standard, 158, 165n, 246, 295
Louth and North Lincolnshire Advertiser, 214
Lushington, Godfrey, 295

Maidment, James, 147
Manchester Evening News, 292
Mangles, James Henry, 284n
Margate, 223n, 241, 273, 277
Married Women's Property Act (1870), 194n
Marsh test, 17n, 224n
Martin, Mrs, 83, 85, 88, 90–1, 96

Martin, Joe, 88, 101
Martin, Sir Samuel, Judge (Baron Martin): appointed Edmunds trial, 256; ruling on Dr and Mrs Beard's testimony, 263–4; pronounces death sentence, 269–72; urges reprieve, 274–5, 281, 299; criticised, 288–9
Marylebone magistrates' court, 157, 158–9, 160
Matthews, Thomas: drawn into murder plot, 76–7; buys pistols, 81; arrested for drunken brawling, 81, 85; arrives at house, 77, 82; loses nerve and flees, 77, 82; apprehended as material witness, 77–8; evidence at trial, 80–1, 82–3; as unreliable witness, 83, 91; characterised as villain, 97; exonerated, 99
Maudsley, Dr Henry, 268
May, Adam, 237, 239–40, 251, 259–60
Maynard, John: confectionery business, 261; sells chocolate creams, 221, 223, 249; sweets contaminated, 247, 250–2, 261; Christiana Edmunds complains to, 232–3, 261; framed, 224–5, 248–9; evidence at Sidney Barker inquest, 233; evidence at magistrates' hearing, 252; evidence at trial, 261
M'Carty, Mr (barrister), 137–8, 140–1, 150
M'Coon, Mr, 96–7
Mead, Jeffery, 85
Meadows, Anne, 251–2, 260
medical testimony: criticised in Edmunds trial, 287
Meik, Dr Peter, 108, 119, 122, 127, 138
menopause, 299
Merrifield, Mr (Brighton magistrate), 230, 242, 252, 253, 284n
Miles, Richard, 19
military uniform: allure of, 69
Millam, James, 118, 119, 122; evidence at trial, 131, 133
Miller, Charles, 223, 249–50, 252, 257
Miller, Ernest, 250, 257

314

Index

Miller, Thomas, 140–1
Mills, Amelia, 245, 284n
Mills, John, 85
Miss Blandy's Walk, 7
Miss Mary Blandy's Own Account of the Affair between her and Mr Cranstoun (pamphlet), 42–6, 72–3
M'Kenzie, James, 131
M'Murdo, Dr, 196
M'Naghten Law, 268n
Monro, Dr Alexander, 136, 142
Montgomery, James, 139
Morgan, Mrs (wise woman), 7, 9
Morning Post, 203, 290–1
Morton, Mr, 22
Mounteney, Mary, 6, 7, 14; evidence at trial, 27–8
Murder Act (1751), 40–1, 196n
Murray, Anne (Mrs Cranstoun), 3, 4, 67

Naires, Mr, 22
NAIRN, KATHARINE: marries Thomas Ogilvie, 104; affair with Patrick Ogilvie, 104–5, 106; witness accounts of her infidelity, 111–12, 113, 115, 120; talk of poisoning husband, 106, 107, 116; receives packet from Andrew Stewart, 107–8, 116–17; poisons husband, 108, 121; and husband's illness, 118, 121–2; arrested on incest and murder charges, 109; declarations before Sheriff of Forfar, 128–9; moved to Tolbooth, 109; questioned by Sheriff of Edinburgh, 130–1; indicted, 110; trial (*see* Nairn trial); found guilty on both counts, 135; examined for pregnancy, 136–7, 143; sentence postponed and returned to Tolbooth, 137; petitions on behalf of unborn child, 143; birth of daughter, 143; escapes from Tolbooth, 143–6; daughter's death, 144n; flight to Calais, 144–5, 146; later life and death, 146–7; assessment, 148–9
Nairn, William (Katharine's uncle), 144, 145–6
Nairn trial: indictments, 110; petition for segregation of Anne Clark, 110–11; record of trial, 111; evidence for the prosecution, 111–32; evidence for the defence, 132–5; closing speeches, 135; verdict, 135; plea in arrest of judgement, 135–6; Katharine pleads pregnancy, 136; Ogilvie sentenced to death, 136; jury of matrons, 136–7; Katharine's sentence postponed, 137; M'Carty's opinion, 137–8; press interest, 138; unsound verdict, 151–2
Nethercliff, Frederick, 225n, 243, 263
New South Wales, Australia, 211–12
Newcastle Courant, 3, 22, 23, 31n, 64–5, 69–70, 73, 213
Newgate Calendar, 1–2, 75, 77, 109, 195n, 217, 218, 266n
Newgate Prison: and Cato Street Conspirators, 196n; Edmunds at, 254–5, 267–8, 276, 278, 279; Gale at, 162, 199, 211; Greenacre at, 162, 191–2, 195–6, 199, 200, 203–5
Nicholas, Edward, 18, 19
Nicolson, Dr David, 297, 300
Noon, Job, 213
Norton, Benjamin, 6, 12, 15, 16, 19, 26; evidence at trial, 27
Nottingham Guardian, 233–4

Ogilvie, Alexander: background, 105; learns of brother's death, 109; stops burial, 122; opposes post-mortem, 109, 127, 138; sells Eastmiln cattle, 119–20, 133; adduces damning letter from Katharine Nairn, 131; petitioned as heir-presumptive, 143; charged with bigamy, 147; voluntary banishment from Scotland, 147; assessment, 149–51; death, 152–3
Ogilvie, Isobel (*née* McKenzie; 'old Mrs Ogilvie'): described, 105; learns of plans to poison Thomas, 108, 117; blames Katharine, 115;

Index

warns Thomas, 117, 118–19; not called as trial witness, 132; as heartless matriarch, 153
Ogilvie, Dr John, 122, 126, 127–8
Ogilvie, Martha, 125–6
OGILVIE, PATRICK: affair with Katharine Nairn, 104–5, 106, 111–12, 113, 115, 120; dismissed from Eastmiln, 106, 120–1; acquires laudanum and arsenic, 106–7; sends packet to Katharine, 107; confronted by Anne Clark, 119; arrested on incest and murder charges, 109; declarations before Sheriff of Forfar, 129–30; moved to Tolbooth, 109; questioned by Sheriff of Edinburgh, 130; indicted, 110; trial (*see* Nairn trial); found guilty on both counts, 135; sentenced to be hanged, 136; cavorts with Margaret Dow while in prison, 137; petitions for reprieve and appeal, 139–40; appeal rejected, 141; 'dying speech', 141; execution and public dissection of body, 142; assessment, 149; tragic family history, 152–3
Ogilvie, Thomas: general state of health, 117, 125–6, 132–3; marries Katharine Nairn, 104; absent for three nights at Dunsinnan, 105, 150; dismisses Patrick from Eastmiln, 106; warned of poison plot, 106–7, 117; quarrels with Katharine, 117; poisoned, 108, 121; illness and death, 108, 118–19, 121–2; cause of death, 127–8, 137–8, 151; burial delayed, 122, 128; post-mortem opposed by family, 109, 127, 138; assessment, 148–9; possible role of Anne Clark in murder, 150–1
Ogilvie, Thomas, Sr, 152
Ogilvie, William, 152
Ogleby, Mr and Mrs, 165n
Old Bailey, 167–8, 200, 254, 256, 271–3, 279n
Only True and Authentic Trial of John Swan and Miss Elizabeth Jeffreys, The (pamphlet), 92–3, 99–101
Orange, Dr William, 275, 281–2, 292, 293, 294
Over, Alice, 268
Oxford, Mrs, 173
Oxford Assizes, 21–2
Oxford Castle Gaol, 19–20, 33, 40–1

Paddington station-house, 157–8
Paddington Workhouse, 171
Page, James, 156, 170
Page, Kate, 251, 260
Pall Mall Gazette, 254–5, 285–6
Palmer, William (the Rugeley poisoner), 254
Parker, John Henry, 251
parricide, 20–1, 40
Parry, Serjeant John Humffreys, 256, 263, 264–5, 268–9
Paterson, John, 134
Payne, Mr, 168, 171, 180
Pegler, Constable Samuel, 155, 169
Penfold, John, 230
Petitt, Charlotte Elizabeth, 241–2, 263
Pharmacy Act (1868), 236n
Pierlo, Eva, 254 & n
pockmarks, 69
Pocock, Mrs (Blandy family friend), 5, 68
Poland, Harry Bodkin, 256
Price, Mr: defends at Greenacre trial, 168, 170, 171, 172, 175, 177, 178; closing speech to jury, 183–4; visits Greenacre in Newgate, 195
Public Advertiser (newspaper), 146

Ralph, Matthias, 155, 169–70
Ramsay, Dr Gilbert, 122, 127, 138
Rattray, Anne, 105
Rattray, David, 111
Rattray, Francis, 148
Rawlinson, Mr (magistrate), 157, 200
Reading Mercury, 256–60, 261, 262, 264, 265–6, 268, 269–70
Regent's Canal, 155, 169–70
Reid, Margaret, 134
Reinsch test, 17n, 224n
rewards, 143, 199–200, 229–30, 242

Index

Reynolds's Newspaper, 2n, 64n, 71, 73
Robb, Captain James, 141, 143, 144
Robertson, Dr Lockhart, 268
Robinson, Mr, 78
Rodgers, Professor Julian, 244
Rogers, Rev. John, 205n
Roughead, William: *Trial of Katharine Nairn,* 105, 110, 111, 137, 142, 145, 146–7, 152–3
Rugg, Dr Richard, 223, 257, 262
Russell, James, 135
Ryley, Dr James Beresford, 273, 275–6

St Alban's Street (No. 1), Kennington Road, 157, 169, 179–80, 199
St James's Workhouse, Paddington, 155
St Mary the Virgin, Henley, 65
St Sepulchre's Church, 205n
Sale of Arsenic Regulation Act (1851), 107n
Sampson, Anne: confined as prosecution witness, 110; pre-trial statement, 115; sleeps in outhouse, 119; collusion with witnesses, 122–3, 136; evidence at trial, 123–4
Schooley, Charles, 251, 260
Schweitzer, Julius, 224, 262
Scots Magazine, 137, 142
Scott, Dr James, 134
Scowley, William, 85
Sheffield Daily Telegraph, 286–7
Sheills, Mary, 136, 145
Shields Daily Gazette, 73
Simmonds, Miss (James Greenacre's third wife), 164–5, 198–9
Sisters of Mercy (convent), 277
Smith, Colin, 107
Smith, Dr Robert, 128
Smith, Thomas, 81–2
Smith, Walter Henry, 246
Smythe, Sir Sydney Stafford, 22
souvenirs and relics: of Greenacre and Hannah Brown, 199
Spalding, George, 122, 131, 132–3, 150
Spectator (magazine), 287–8
Staffordshire Advertiser, 160, 197–9

Staverton, Thomas, 33–4
Stepney Church, 155–6, 181
Stevens, Henry Serjeant (Mary Blandy's uncle), 5
Stevens, Rev. John (Mary Blandy's uncle), 6, 14
Stevens, Mark: *Broadmoor Revealed,* 293, 296–7
Steward, Dr John, 266–7
Stewart, Andrew, 106, 107–8, 116–17, 118, 119, 121; evidence at trial, 124–6
Stewart, Martha, 132
Stockwood, Rev. William, 41, 64
Stoke, Robert, 18–19, 34
Stone, Mrs Caroline, 235–6, 241, 258
Straight, Mr, 256
Stroud, John and Mary, 277
strychnine, 224n, 225, 236n
Stuckey, William, 230, 242, 243, 247
Sturrock, Elizabeth: carries letters for Katharine Nairn, 107, 116, 120–1; sees Katharine mix tea, 108; confined as prosecution witness, 110; pre-trial statement, 115; collusion with witnesses, 122–3, 136; evidence at trial, 120–3
SWAN, JOHN: background, 76; relations with Elizabeth Jeffries, 76, 79; plots murder of Joseph Jeffries, 76–7, 80–1, 82; arrested for drunken brawling, 81, 85; actions on night of murder, 82, 83–4, 93–4; gets drunk after murder, 85; arrested, 77; committed to Chelmsford Gaol, 78; trial (*see* Jeffries trial); enraged at Elizabeth's confessing, 93; execution, 95–9; confesses guilt, 97; strung up on Bucket's Hill, 98
Swaysland, Henry, 242–3
Swinton, Rev. John, 31, 34, 41, 61, 62–3, 64

Tamworth Herald, 289–90
Tatham, George, 228
Taylor, Mr, 180
Tennyson, Alfred, 284n
Terry, Inspector, 238

317

Index

Thatcher, Charles, 175
Thistlewood, Arthur, 196n, 205
Thompson, Edith, 78n
Thornton, Mr (Paddington churchwarden), 156
Thornton, Dr James, 84, 89
Times, The, 192–5, 206, 214, 231, 247–9, 254, 267, 282–3, 288–9
Tindal, Lord Chief Justice, 168, 184–5
Tipping, Mr, 86
Tolbooth prison, Edinburgh, 109, 137, 143–6
Townley case (1863), 274n
transportation: of felons, 191, 211–12
Trial and Execution of Elizabeth Jeffreys, The (pamphlet), 93
Tringham, Constable Thomas, 181
Tryal of Mary Blandy, The (pamphlet), 22, 23–5, 30–2, 35–6, 37–8, 39–40
Turville Court, near Henley, 5
Tussaud, Madame (waxworks), 255n

Ure, John, 128

Walker, Mrs Caroline, 240, 262
Walker, Henry, 240, 262
Wallace, Jean, 133
Walpole, Horace, 39n, 73, 74
Walton, David, 122
Ward, Mr, 169, 177
Warden, Alexander J: *Angus and Forfarshire: The Land and People*, 147–8, 152–3
Ware, George Robert, 252, 261
Warriner, James, 91
Watson, Rev. John Selby, 279n, 284, 288
Webster, Kate, 255n
White, Chief Constable George, 229, 233, 238
White, James, 169
White Lion Inn, Edgware Road, 155
Whitty, Adelaide, 272–3
Wignell, Henry, 178
Wignell, Sarah, 178–9
Wilson, Sir Daniel, 145
wise women (popular healers), 7n
Wood, Dr William, 267–8
Worsley, Mr, 256
Wright, Sir Martin, 78, 91, 98

York Herald, 214, 216–17

www.ingramcontent.com/pod-product-compliance
Lightning Source LLC
Chambersburg PA
CBHW051036160426
43193CB00010B/961